California's Forest Resources, 2001–2005

Five-Year Forest Inventory and Analysis Report

General Technical Report
PNW-GTR-763
November 2008

USDA United States Department of Agriculture

Forest Service

Pacific Northwest Research Station

Technical Editors

Glenn A. Christensen is a forester, **Sally J. Campbell** is a biological scientist, and **Jeremy S. Fried** is a research forester, U.S. Department of Agriculture, Forest Service, Pacific Northwest Research Station, Forestry Sciences Laboratory, 620 SW Main Street, Suite 400, Portland, OR 97205.

Contributing Authors

Dave Azuma is a research forester, **Tara Barrett** is a research forester, **Sally Campbell** is a biological scientist, **Glenn Christensen** is a forester, **Joseph Donnegan** is an ecologist, **Jeremy Fried** is a research forester, **Andrew Gray** is a research forester, **Sarah Jovan** is a post-doctoral scientist, **Olaf Kuegler** is a mathematical statistician, **Karen Waddell** is a forester, and **Dale Weyermann** is a geographic information system (GIS) and remote sensing specialist, U.S. Department of Agriculture, Forest Service, Pacific Northwest Research Station, Forestry Sciences Laboratory, 620 SW Main Street, Suite 400, Portland, OR 97205. **Chuck Keegan** is a research forester and former director and **Todd Morgan** is the director of forest industry research, Bureau of Business and Economic Research, University of Montana, 32 Campus Drive, Missoula, MT 59812.

Cover: Mount San Gorgonio. Photo by Tom Iraci.

Abstract

Christensen, Glenn A.; Campbell, Sally J.; Fried, Jeremy S., tech. eds. 2008.
California's forest resources, 2001–2005: five-year Forest Inventory and Analysis
report. Gen. Tech. Rep. PNW-GTR-763. Portland, OR: U.S. Department of
Agriculture, Forest Service, Pacific Northwest Research Station. 183 p.

This report highlights key findings from the most recent (2001–2005) data collected by the
Forest Inventory and Analysis Program across all forest land in California. We summarize
and interpret basic resource information such as forest area, ownership, volume, biomass,
and carbon stocks; structure and function topics such as biodiversity, forest age, dead
wood, and hardwood forests; disturbance topics such as insects and diseases, fire, invasive
plants, and air pollution; and information about the forest products industry in California,
including data on tree growth and mortality, removals for timber products, and nontimber
forest products. The appendixes describe inventory methods in detail and provide summary
tables of data, with statistical error, about the suite of forest characteristics inventoried.

Keywords: Biomass, carbon, dead wood, diseases, fire, forest land, insects, invasive
plants, inventory, juniper, lichens, nontimber forest products, ozone, timber volume,
timberland, wood products.

Contents

Summary

California's growing population relies on the state's forests to produce a wealth of environmental services, such as dispersed and developed recreation; clean air and water; fish, game, and nongame wildlife habitat; and a rich variety of commodity and specialty forest products. These forests have experienced increasing pressures and stresses brought about by climate change, invasive plants, air pollution, demand for forest products, and rampant exurban development, along with changing disturbance regimes involving fire, insects, and disease. These natural and human dynamics have increased the complexity of decisions about how California's forests are to be managed. The comprehensive, unbiased, statistically grounded information on the status of California's forest resources provided in this report will help managers and policymakers grapple with, and achieve resolution on, those tough decisions. This summary highlights a few key findings.

For a state arguably better known for its cities, beaches, deserts, and farm and ranch lands, California is surprisingly heavily forested. Forests cover about a third of the state's 100 million acres, and most of this forest (19 million acres) is publicly managed. Roughly 2 million acres are reserved in wilderness areas and state and national parks. Despite having generally lower site productivity than most private lands, and owing to sharp differences in management, public forest land accounts for a disproportionately large share of standing wood volume—65 percent of statewide volume for all trees, and 85 percent of statewide volume for the largest trees (those ≥33 inches in diameter). The volume of large trees on the 6 percent of the state's forest classified as reserved is 20 percent of the statewide total. Given the relationship between age and size, it is not surprising that most of the oldest forests (forests where stand age exceeds 200 years) are found on public land.

Forest management, a major determinant of what the forest looks like, how it functions, and what it produces over time, arises from landowner objectives. Thus, tracking ownership patterns and changes in the outlook of broad classes of owners is essential to discerning trends in forest structure and productivity. Responding to shifting priorities of the public they serve, federal forest land managers now emphasize the production of environmental services at least as much as they do wood products. One result of this change has been that most California-grown wood is now produced on private land. Although the area of private forest land in California is substantial—over 13 million acres—only about 5 million acres of it is managed by the forest industry. Roughly 7 percent of this 5 million acres is managed by a comparatively new and rapidly growing owner subclass consisting of timberland investment management organizations (TIMOs) and real estate investment trusts (REITs). These owners may or may not manage primarily for timber production, and evidence suggests that at least some of the forest land they control is ultimately destined for such nonforest uses as residential and tourism development.

Although some harvest occurs on national forests, both anecdotal and inventory evidence suggests that much of it is driven not by timber production goals but by other management objectives, such as reduction of crown fire hazard. Preliminary analysis of harvested inventory trees shows that the average diameter of trees harvested on national forests was about 14 inches, whereas average diameter on privately owned lands was about 20 inches.

Ownership and management differences are also reflected in the current forest structure. Statewide, nearly half of the volume in trees 5 to 9 inches in diameter is found on privately owned forest land; however, only about 15 percent of the volume in the largest trees (≥33 inches in diameter) occurs on these lands. Although the 2005 Resources Planning Act[1] forecasts a decline in per capita lumber consumption in the United States, population growth is expected to generate a 24-percent increase in wood consumption by 2050. Although it is the fourth largest lumber-producing state in the Nation, California is experiencing a decline in timber harvest and wood production because of increasing constraints on timber management on private lands and the precipitous decline in harvest on public forest lands. Capacity for producing wood products of all kinds fell 60 percent from the late 1980s to 2000, and the trend continues unabated—capacity for lumber production fell 15 percent from 2000 to 2005.

However, capacity of wood-using bioenergy facilities increased. Currently California bioenergy facilities have a combined capacity to generate over 470 megawatts of electricity, and further capacity increases are under consideration. Although conditions for the wood products industry appear challenging, California's high-quality timber and very productive forest land, along with the significant regional demand for wood products, will contribute to the continued viability of this industry, which employs over 112,000 Californians. As the demand for forest products increases, the proportion of in-state demand that can be met by California-grown wood will inevitably fall.

Nontimber forest products such as botanical and floral products are available in great abundance, particularly in the moister forests. Swordfern (see "Scientific and Common Plant Names") was the most abundant herb in California's forests, covering 176,000 acres, and greenleaf manzanita, covering 388,000 acres, is the most abundant shrub.

In addition to the influence of forest land ownership and management, disturbance agents—insects, diseases, air pollution, and fire—have long shaped the forested landscape of California and will continue to do so. On over half the forest land area, at least 25 percent of the basal area was observed to have damage caused by biotic or abiotic agents. About 10 percent of sampled sites exhibited a high level of ozone injury and many Sierra Nevada and greater Central Valley forests are exposed to nitrogen pollution, as indicated by lichen community composition. Over 200,000 forested acres have burned per year, on average, between 2001 and 2005. Climate change and increases in population will create greater challenges in managing and mitigating these agents.

Characterizing fire hazard in California forests is a key prerequisite to scoping the magnitude of the fuels management problem and thinking through the fuel treatment options worth pursuing to reduce the frequency of historically uncharacteristic, catastrophic, stand-replacing fire. In modeling crown fire potential under extreme weather, we found that fire would occur as a surface or conditional surface fire in

---

[1] Haynes, R.W.; Adams, D.M.; Alig, R.J.; Ince, P.J ; Mills, J.R.; Zhou, X. 2007. The 2005 RPA timber assessment update. Gen. Tech. Rep. PNW-GTR-699. Portland, OR: U.S. Department of Agriculture, Forest Service, Pacific Northwest Research Station. 212 p.

72 percent of forests, and as a passive crown fire (with individual trees "torching" as fire climbs from the surface fuels up the ladder formed by low-hanging branches) in 20 percent of forests. In only 8 percent of forests would fire occur as an active crown fire; these are the forests where canopy density is sufficient for a fire to move from crown to crown, regardless of the presence or absence of ladder fuels. That such forests are in a slim minority suggests that, although the total area that could benefit from fuel treatment is substantial, in most cases treatment may require only the removal of ladder fuels (typically associated with smaller diameter trees) rather than thinning of the mature trees in the upper canopy.

People affect the forest even when they do not manage it, such as the impact on the forest from people moving into what is called the wildland-urban interface, a rapidly growing and probably irreversible trend. Houses being built in this interface zone account for most of the housing growth in the state over the last 10 years. The presence of more and more homes within and adjacent to the forest exerts pressure on the resource in the form of direct use (e.g., wood-cutting, mushroom collection, running with dogs, and off-highway vehicles), injury of forest vegetation by air pollutants, and the spread of exotic organisms, as well as an implied expectation that forest managers will be tasked with achieving substantial fire hazard reduction on ever-larger areas of forest land.

A. Leto

Yosemite Valley.

Mount Baldy.

Chapter 1: Introduction[1]

This report highlights the status of California's forest resources and demonstrates some ways in which forest inventory data can be used to address contemporary forest issues. The estimates of the amount and characteristics of California's forests provided in this report are the result of observations taken on field plots in the years 2001–2005 by the Forest Inventory and Analysis (FIA) Program of the Pacific Northwest Research Station (PNW).

The FIA Program was created within the U.S. Department of Agriculture, Forest Service in 1928 to conduct unbiased assessments of all the Nation's forested lands for use in economic and forest management planning. The FIA Program was charged with collecting forest data on a series of permanent field plots, compiling and making the data available, and providing research and interpretations from that data. Originally, all plots were assessed within a period of a few years, with periodic reassessments, typically every 10 years in the West. Four FIA units are now responsible for inventories of all forested lands in the continental United States, Alaska, Hawaii, Puerto Rico, and several Pacific island groups.

In 2000, as required by the Agricultural Research Extension and Education Reform Act of 1998 (the Farm Bill), FIA began implementing a new standardized national inventory design and method, in which a portion of all plots in each state are measured each year. Appendix 1 includes an explanation of the differences between the previous and current inventory methods. The effect of the change is that, for the first time in 70 years, all FIA units are using a common plot design, a common set of measurement protocols, and a standard database design for compilation and distribution of data. Under this unified approach, FIA is now poised to provide unbiased estimates of a wide variety of forest conditions over all forested lands in the United States in a consistent and timely manner. The new design will enable FIA units in every state to monitor changes in forest conditions, ownership, management, disturbance regimes, and climate impacts that occur through time.

This report covers all forested lands in California (fig. 1). All estimates are average values for the time between 2001 and 2005. Field crews visited each inventory plot to collect measurements of forest characteristics (fig. 2).

---

[1] Author: Dale Weyermann.

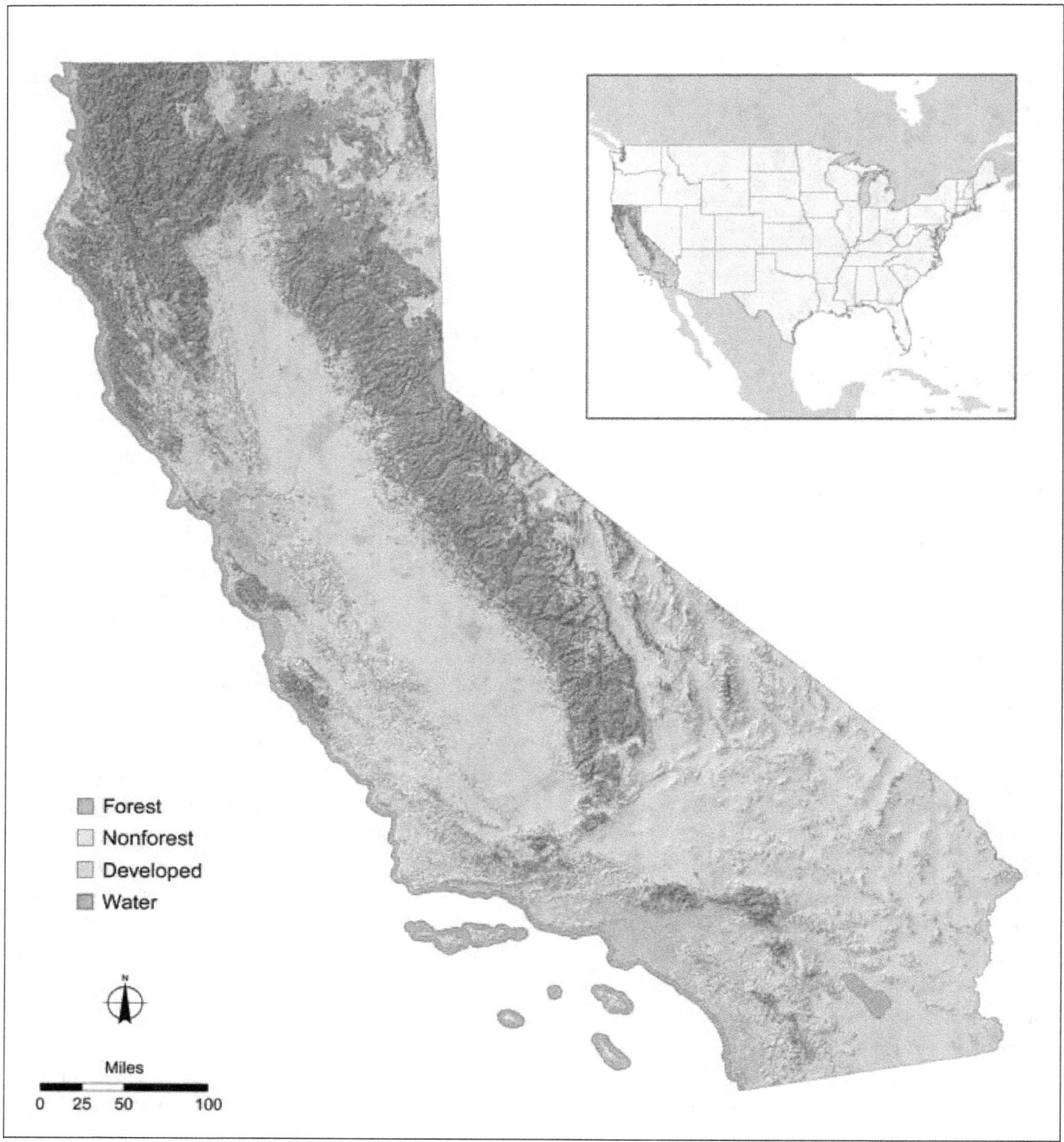

Figure 1—California land cover (forest/nonforest geographic information system (GIS) layer: Blackard et al. 2008; urban/water GIS layer: Homer et al. 2004)

Figure 2—Forest Inventory and Analysis field crews take a wide variety of measurements on each forested plot they visit.

Most measurements use national protocols, but several are specific to forest issues of special interest to California and other west coast states.

Field plots are spaced at approximate 3-mile intervals on a hexagonal grid throughout a variety of forested lands in California (figs. 3 and 4). Plots span both public and privately owned forests, including lands reserved from industrial wood production (e.g., national parks, wilderness areas, and natural areas). The annual inventory involves a cycle of measurements for 10 systematic subsamples, or panels; each panel represents about 10 percent of all plots in California. A panel takes about 1 year to complete (fig. 3) although a few plots are carried over to the next year owing to unanticipated problems with accessing plots (e.g., large

fires, early snowfall). In addition, funding was provided to accelerate the installation of three panels on national forests before they were scheduled. Thus, this California inventory report presents the principal findings from the first five panels (50 percent of the data that will ultimately be collected) outside national forests and eight panels (80 percent of the data) within national forests, all collected in the annual inventory between 2001 and 2005—a total of 3,542 forested plots (fig. 4). Inventory results presented are "expanded" appropriately to account for the sampling intensity, so no additional adjustments by the reader are necessary. Additional information about annual inventories is available in appendix 1 of this report and on the Web (http://fia fs.fed.us/).

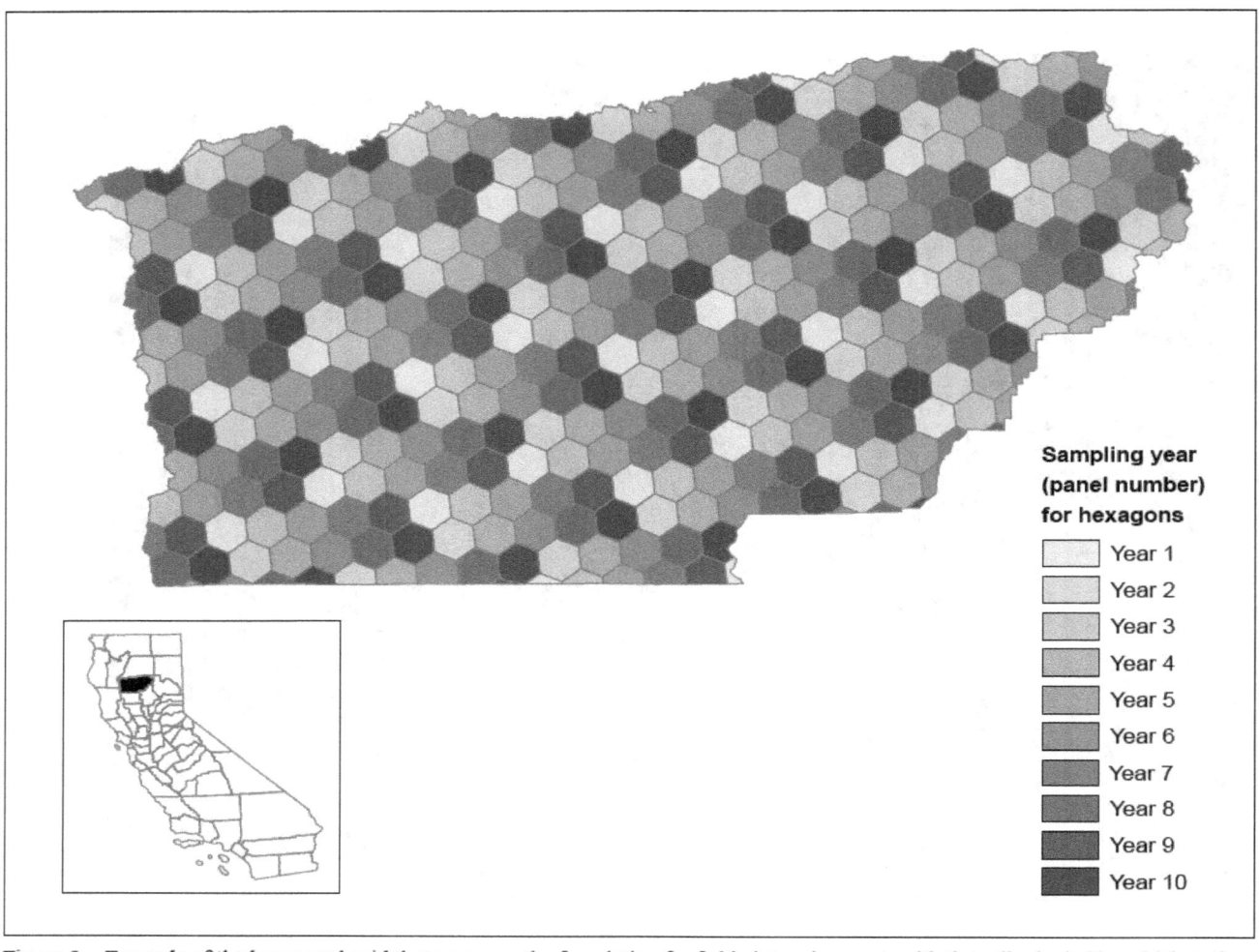

Figure 3—Example of the hexagonal grid that serves as the foundation for field plot assignment, with the cells shaded by which 1 of the 10 annual measurement panels it belongs to, magnified for Tehama County, California. All plots in one panel are sampled in 1 year.

This report presents findings that address many of California's contemporary forest issues and concerns, along with fundamental resource statistics on forest area, volume, and ownership. We also provide policy-relevant findings and statistical summaries related to wildlife habitat, biomass, carbon stocks, and forest disturbance (e.g., urban development, fire, invasive plants, insects, and diseases). Finally, we summarize findings concerning the forest products industry, removals for timber products, and the status of nontimber forest products.

This report consists of 22 issue-focused summaries of current topics in forest health and management. Each summary typically includes background information,

key findings developed from the FIA inventory data, and interpretation. Data are summarized by various geographic and ecological classifications that we felt would be useful to a variety of readers (figs. 5 through 8). Appendix 1 describes the inventory design and methods. Appendix 2 contains extensive tables of measured totals accompanied by estimates of sampling error. These tables aggregate data to a variety of levels including ecological unit (e.g., ecological section or ecosection) (Cleland et al. 1997, 2005; McNab et al. 2005), county, owner group, survey unit, forest type, and tree species, allowing the inventory results to be applied at various scales and used for various analyses. Data are also available for download at http://www.fia.fs fed.us.

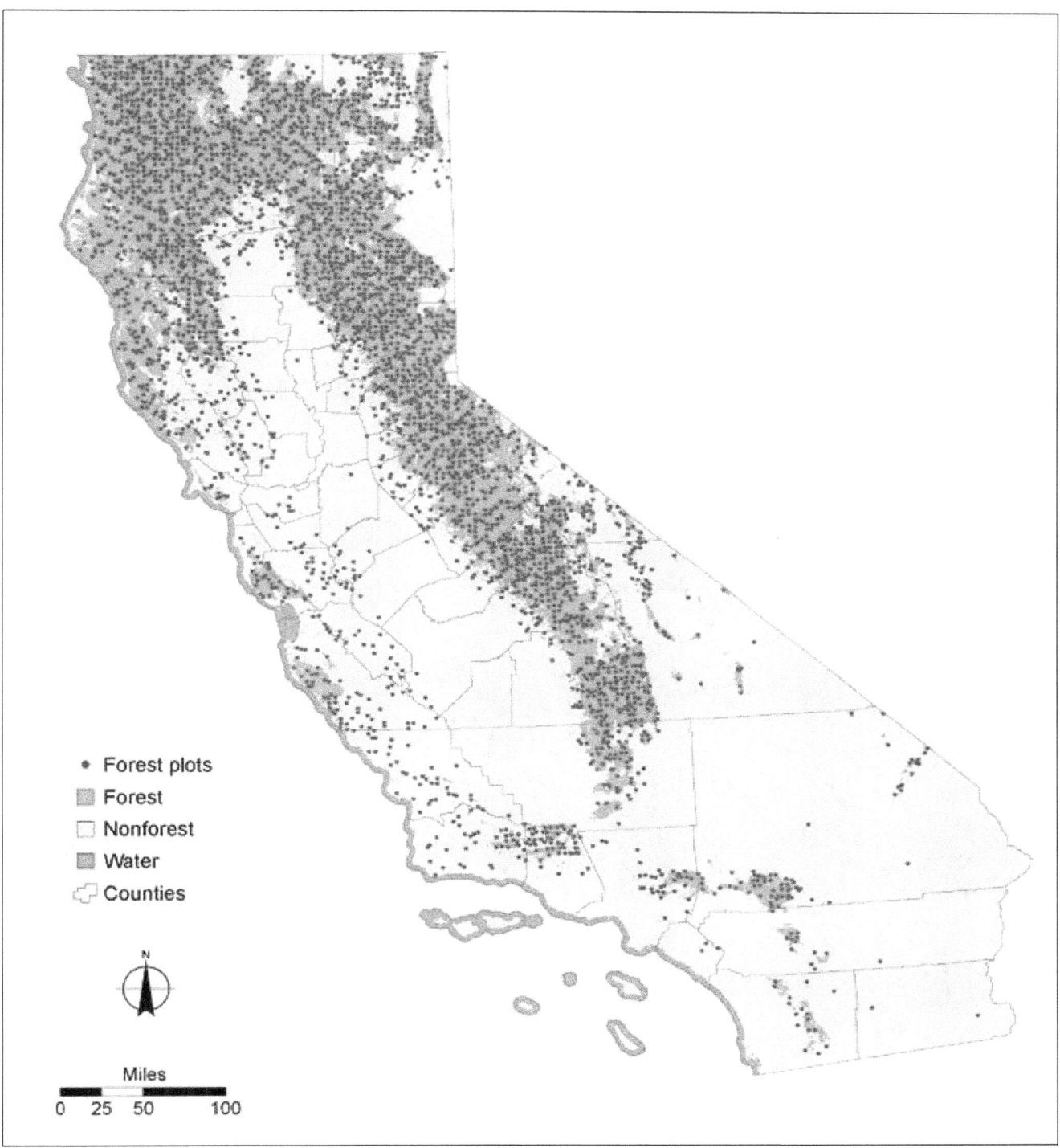

Figure 4—Forested plots measured between 2001 and 2005 provide the data used in this report. Locations are approximate (forest/nonforest geographic information system (GIS) layer: Blackard et al. 2008; urban/water GIS layer: Homer et al. 2004).

Figure 5—California counties (forest/nonforest geographic information system layer: Blackard et al. 2008).

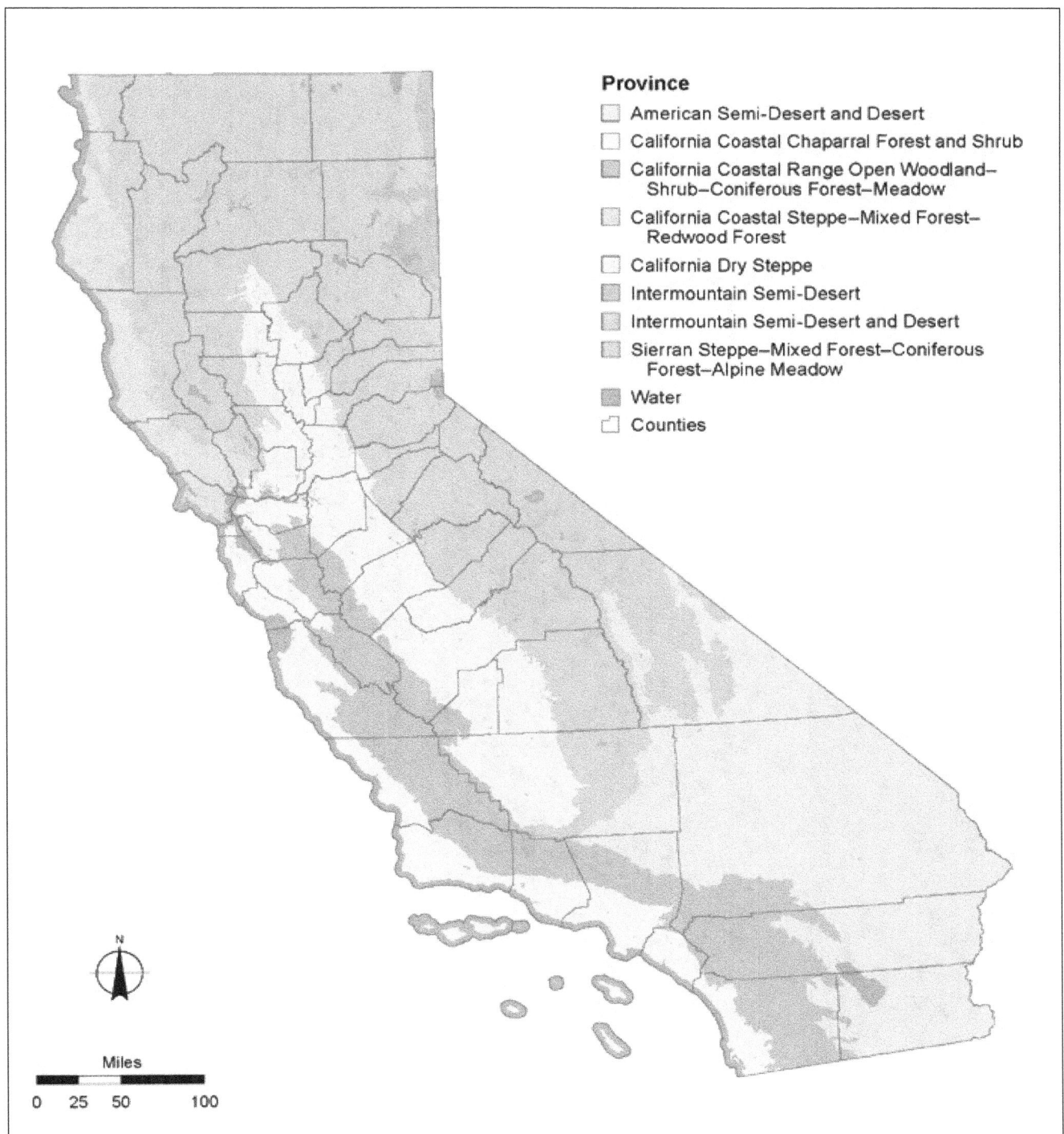

Province

☐ American Semi-Desert and Desert
☐ California Coastal Chaparral Forest and Shrub
☐ California Coastal Range Open Woodland–
  Shrub–Coniferous Forest–Meadow
☐ California Coastal Steppe–Mixed Forest–
  Redwood Forest
☐ California Dry Steppe
☐ Intermountain Semi-Desert
☐ Intermountain Semi-Desert and Desert
☐ Sierran Steppe–Mixed Forest–Coniferous
  Forest–Alpine Meadow
☐ Water
☐ Counties

Miles

0 25 50   100

Figure 6—California ecosections (ecosection geographic information system layer: Cleland et al. 2005).

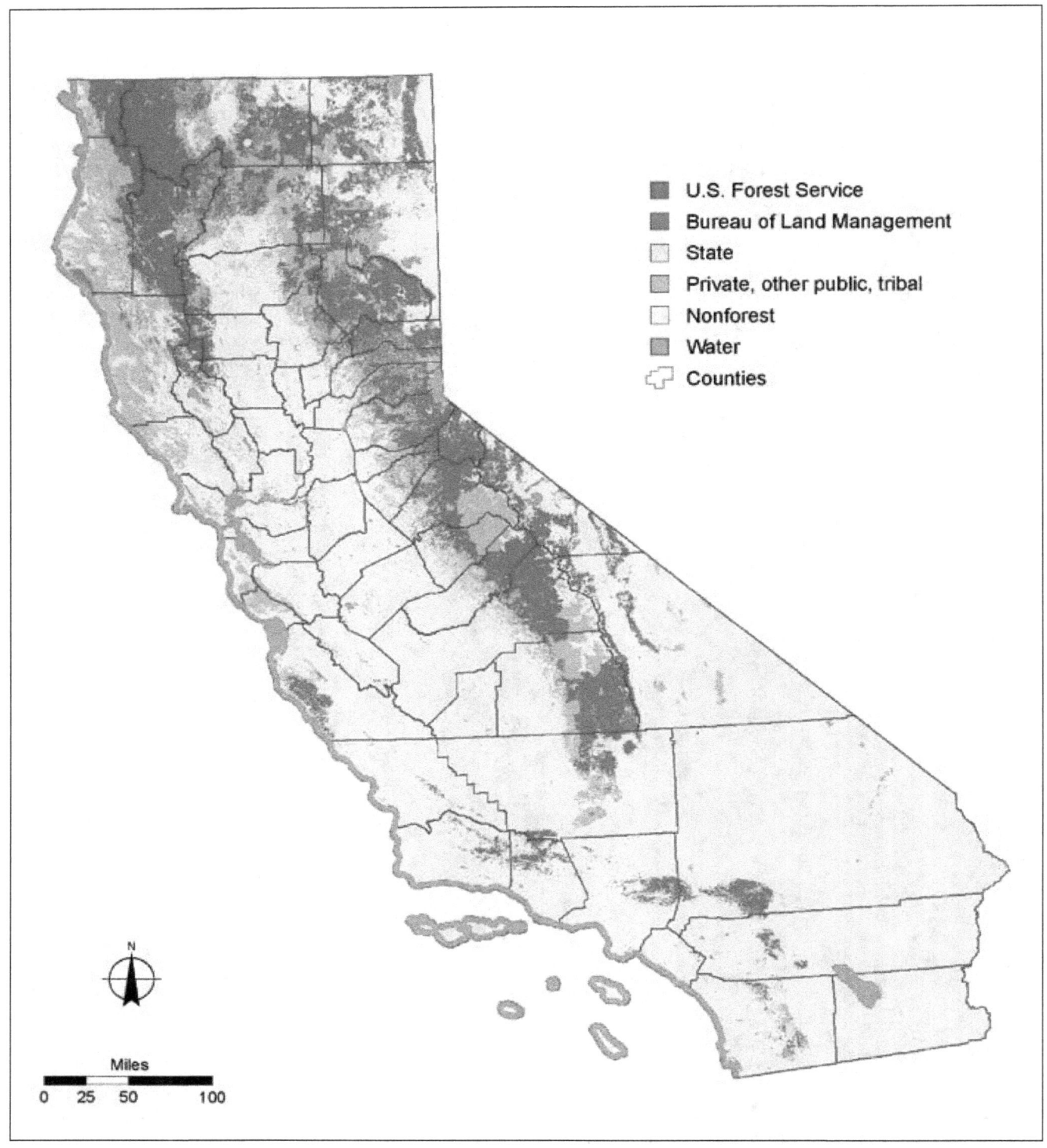

Figure 7—California forest ownership categories (ownership geographic information system layer: California Department of Forestry and Fire Protection 1997).

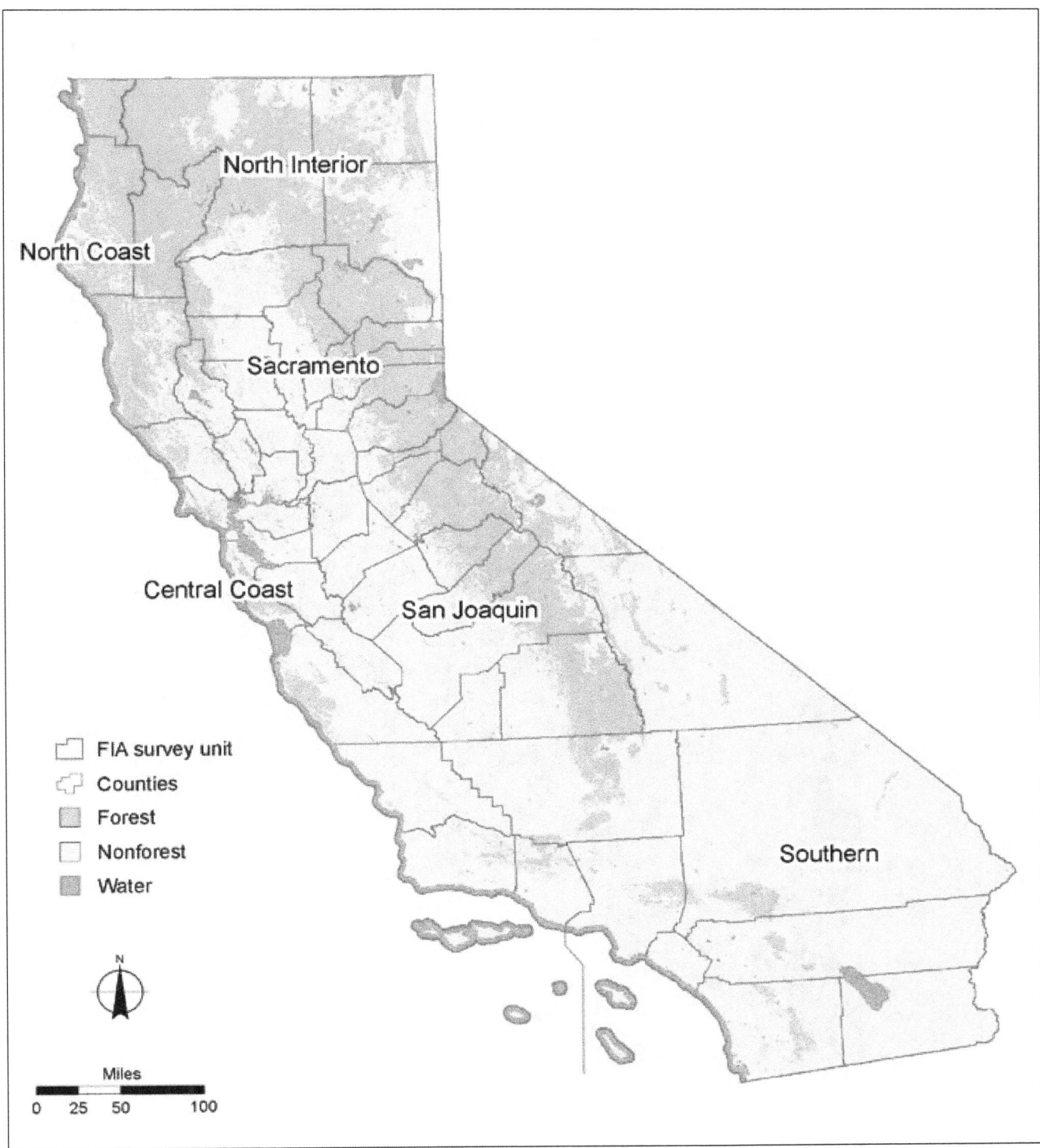

Figure 8—California Forest Inventory and Analysis survey units (county groupings used in this report) (forest/nonforest geographic information system (GIS) layer: Blackard et al. 2008, urban/water GIS layer: Homer et al. 2004).

Western white pine.

Chapter 2: Basic Resource Information

This chapter provides an overview of the distribution, extent, and ownership of California's extensive forests, as well as the amount of wood—volume and biomass— in them. It lays the groundwork for the more specialized analyses and summaries in later chapters. Highlights include a discussion of forest acreage held in public and private hands, characteristics of family-owned forests, and a summary of biomass and carbon stocks in relation to bioenergy and carbon credits.

Forest Area[1]

Background

The distribution of California's forest land can be traced to its climate and geography. The Sierra Nevada's northwest-southeast bulk intercepts much moisture from air masses flowing eastward from the Pacific Ocean (fig. 1). Because of these precipitation patterns, the temperature-moderating effects of elevation, and the state's predominantly Mediterranean climate with its extended summer drought, most of California's forests are found in the mountainous areas, chiefly the Sierra Nevada, Klamath, and Coast Ranges, and in the cool, mesic fog belt along the state's north and central coasts. California's geography creates a diverse assemblage of distinct combinations of climate, elevation, and soil type. Twenty ecosections have been mapped to define and classify this diversity; most of these contain some type of forest.

The composition and distribution of California's forests have been subject to ongoing change throughout millennia owing to factors such as climate, fire, insects, and diseases and in recent years have been joined by another important factor, the pressure of large-scale human development and settlement. California is home to over 30 million people, and with an accelerated rate of housing development in forested areas (Hammer et al. 2007), California is vulnerable to losing forest land through urbanization. The status and trends of forest area are fundamental indicators of forest health at national, state, and local scales and have been consistently assessed by the Pacific Northwest Research Station Forest Inventory and Analysis (FIA) Program for the last several decades.

The FIA assessment consists of both field-crew observations of forest status on the ground and aerial photointerpretation or remote sensing procedures to stratify the sample allowing more estimates of forest attributes (see app. 1 for specific information on sampling methods). International reporting criteria for gauging forest health and sustainability (e.g., Montréal Process criteria and indicators and United Nations Food and Agriculture forest resources assessment) emphasize that the trend in area of forest is one of the first indicators that nations should use in their forest assessments (USDA Forest Service 1997). The FIA Program's tracking of this trend provides statistically unbiased estimates that are not available elsewhere for these international assessments and for national and state assessments such as the Resources Planning Act Assessment (Haynes et al. 2007) and California's quintennial forest assessment (California Department of Forestry and Fire Protection 2003).

Findings

Area by land class—
Approximately one-third of California's 100 million acres meets the criteria for forest land (http://www.dof.ca.gov/html/fs_data/stat-abs/tables/a1.xls) (fig. 9). Forest land is defined as land that is at least 10 percent stocked by forest trees of any size, or land formerly having such tree cover and not currently developed for a nonforest use (see "Glossary" for a detailed definition). The minimum area for classification is 1 acre. The largest proportion of forests in California (about 20 million acres) is classified as nonreserved timberland (fig. 10). Timberland is defined as forest land that is capable of producing in excess of 20 cubic feet of wood per acre per year and where harvest is not legally prohibited. Of all survey units, the North Interior survey unit has the largest share of forest land (35 percent) (fig. 8). By ecological section, the Sierra Nevada has the largest share (30 percent) (fig. 6).

---

[1] Author: Glenn Christensen.

Joel Thompson

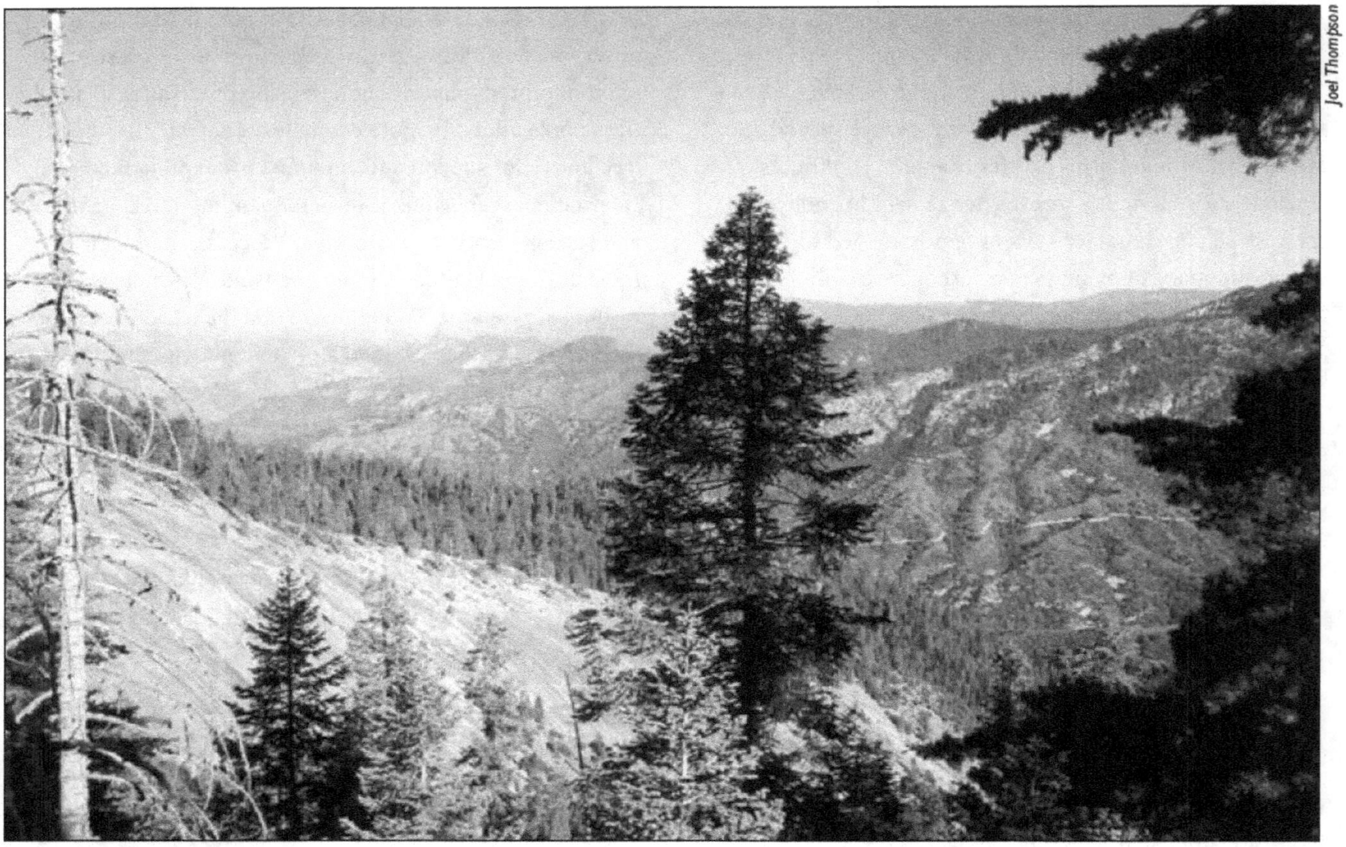

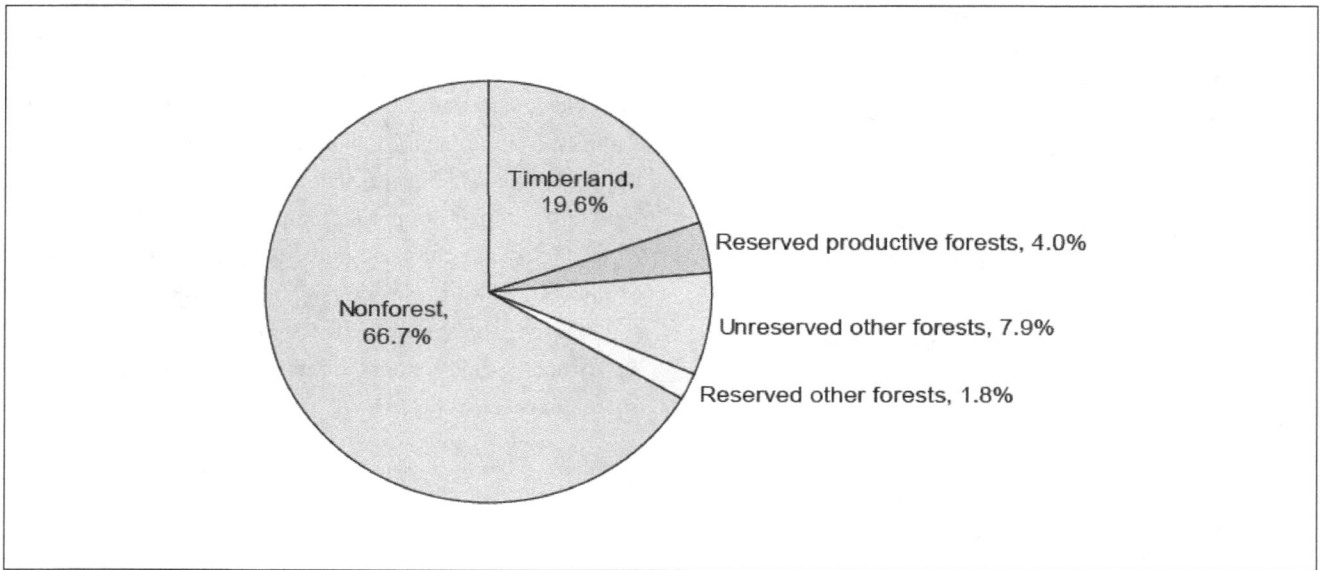

Figure 9—Over 33 million acres in California are forested.

Timberland, 19.6%
Reserved productive forests, 4.0%
Nonforest, 66.7%
Unreserved other forests, 7.9%
Reserved other forests, 1.8%

Figure 10—Percentage of area (acres) by land class category in California, 2001–2005.

Area by forest type group—

The FIA Program classifies forest land based on cover of the predominant live-tree species. More than half (about 57 percent) of California's forests are composed of softwood conifer forest types, totaling 19 million acres. Over 40 percent of acres with these types are classified in the California mixed-conifer group (8 million acres) (fig. 11). A forest type group is a combination of forest types that share closely associated species and similar productivity characteristics. The mixed-conifer group may be composed of several softwood conifer species, including Douglas-fir, sugar pine, ponderosa pine, Jeffrey pine, white fir, red fir, incense-cedar, and other true firs (see "Scientific and Common Plant Names"). Each of four other type groups (ponderosa pine, fir/spruce/mountain hemlock, other western softwoods, and pinyon/juniper) occupies close to 10 percent of the area of softwood forests. The remaining acres are divided between several other type groups, each contributing less than 10 percent of softwood forest area.

Hardwood forest types account for 40 percent (13 million acres) of California's forest land, with the last 2 percent classified as nonstocked—forest land that is less than 10 percent stocked by trees or, in some cases, that has less than 5 percent crown cover. The most common hardwood forest type in California is the western oak group. Oak forests occupy 10 million acres of forest land throughout the state (fig. 12). Although this amounts to only about 28 percent of all forest land, oak forests comprise about 73 percent of all acres classified as hardwood forest type (see the Hardwoods section for more information on oaks).

Area by productivity class—

Nearly 12 percent (4 million acres) of California's forest land is highly productive, defined as having the capacity to grow more than 165 cubic feet of wood per acre per year. About 39 percent of this highly productive land is classified as California mixed-conifer (fig. 13). Mixed-conifer forests also dominate the next highest productivity class (85 to 164 cubic feet per acre per year), accounting for about 34 percent of the forest area in this class. Redwood forests have the highest proportion of their acres (100 percent) in the highest two productivity classes. The western oak forest type group accounts for most of the area—approximately 53 percent—in the lowest productivity class (0 to 9 cubic feet per acre per year).

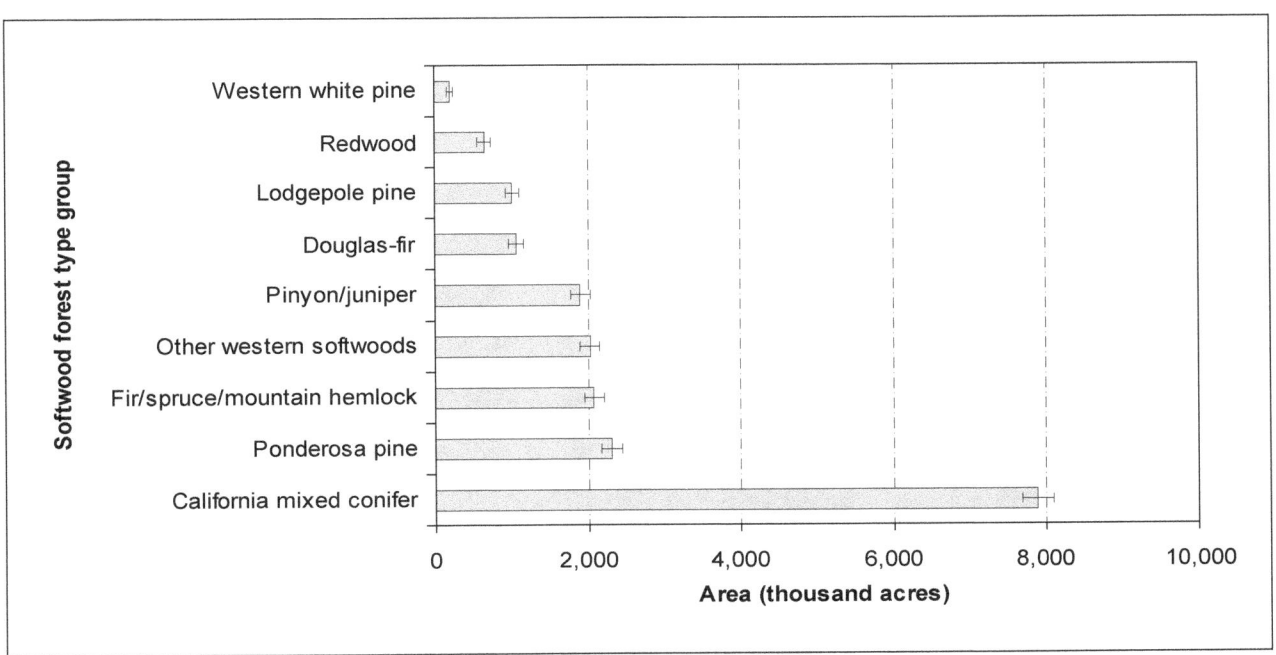

Figure 11—Area of softwood forest type groups on forest land in California, 2001–2005.

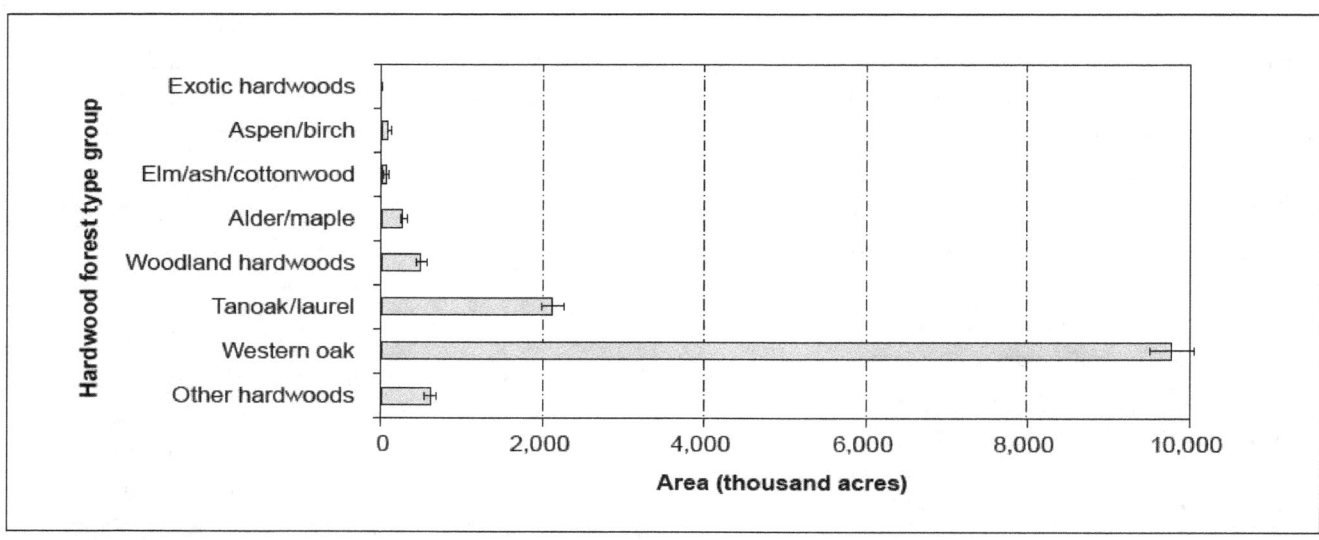

Figure 12—Area of hardwood forest type groups on forest land in California, 2001–2005.

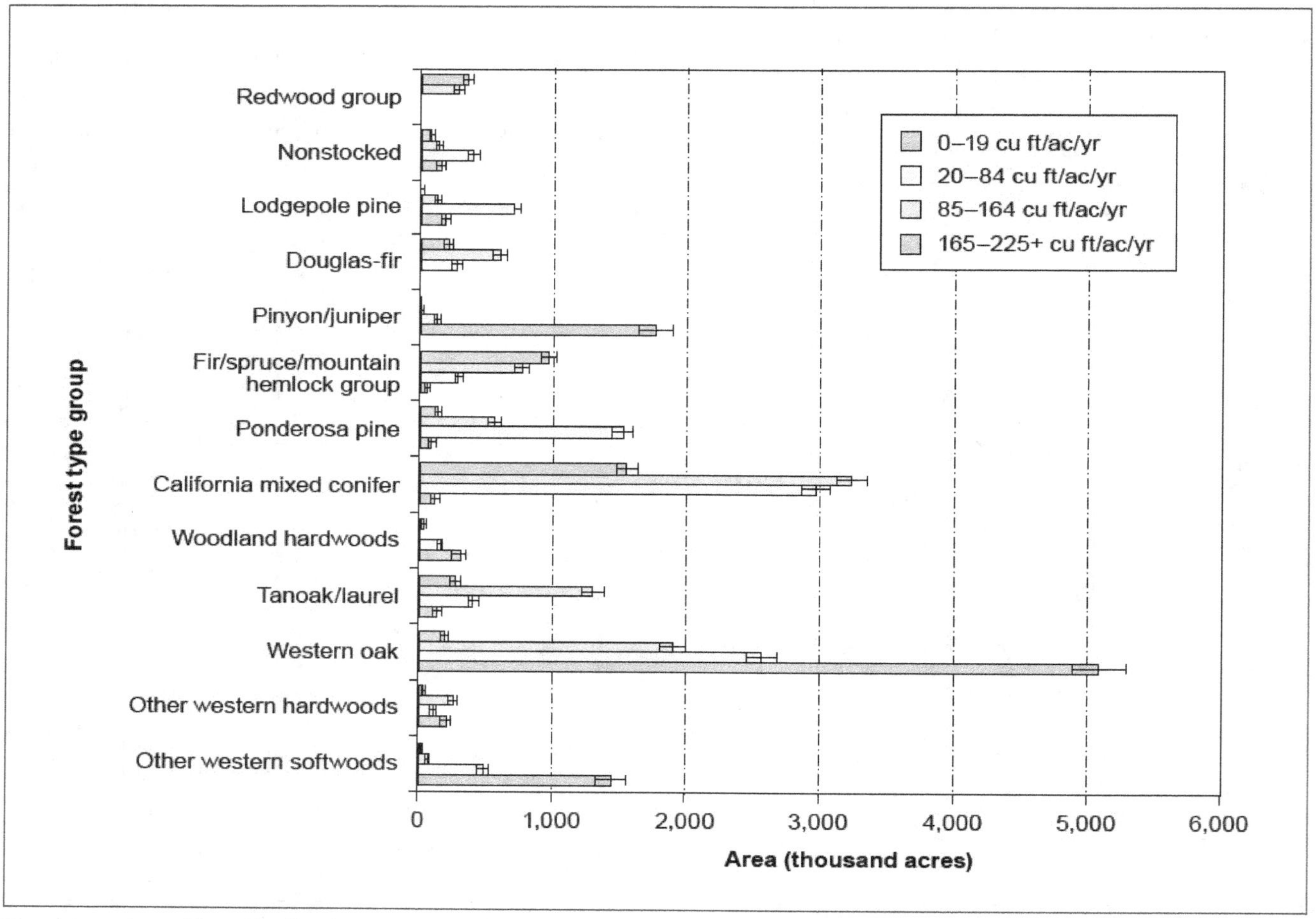

Figure 13—Area of productivity classes by forest type group on forest land in California, 2001–2005.

Interpretation

Overall, statewide acreage of forest land in California has declined from the 1950s to the 1980s but has stabilized more recently (fig. 14). Nearly all the recent decreases have occurred in the oak woodlands; only one plot in forests other than oak woodlands was converted from forest to other uses since the last inventory. We expect change in the extent and distribution of forest land, driven by pressures of development, resource demands, shifts in ownership, changing demographics, and climate change. The impact of these influences on forest area trend across the state will be monitored with repeated FIA measurements.

Forest area tables in appendix 2—

- Table 1—Number of FIA plots measured from 2001 to 2005, by land class, sample status, ownership group, California

- Table 2—Estimated area of forest land, by owner class and forest land status, California, 2001–2005
- Table 3—Estimated area of forest land, by forest type group and productivity class, California, 2001–2005
- Table 4—Estimated area of forest land, by forest type group, ownership, and land status, California, 2001–2005
- Table 5—Estimated area of forest land, by forest type group and stand size class, California, 2001–2005
- Table 6—Estimated area of forest land, by forest type group and stand age class, California, 2001–2005
- Table 7—Estimated area of timberland, by forest type group and stand size class, California, 2001–2005

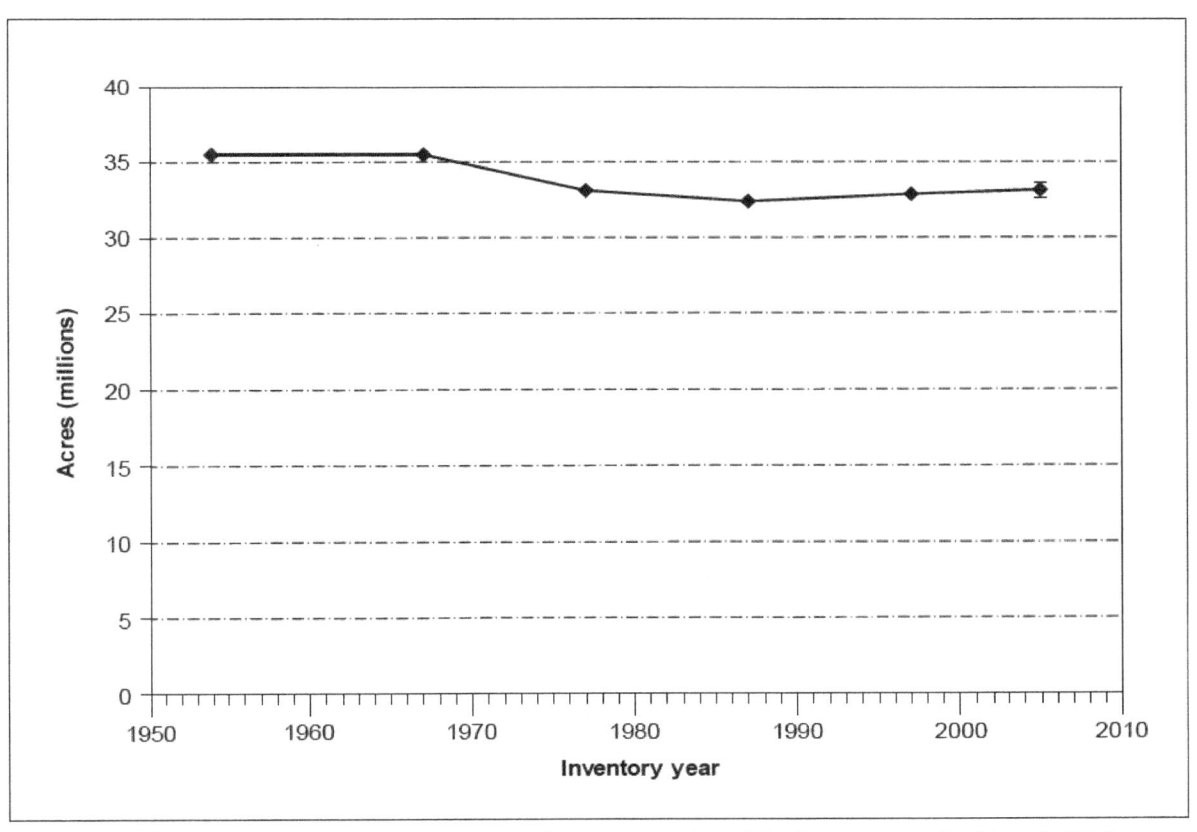

Figure 14—Area of forest land, excluding chaparral, by inventory year in California, 1953–2005 (Smith et al. 2004).

Ownership[2]

Background

Because forest owners differ in their management objectives and intentions, ownership has an important influence on the character of California forests. Federal owners are usually mandated to consider multiple management objectives including, but not limited to, wood production, protection of water resources and wildlife, enhancement of recreation, habitat conservation, and preservation of biological diversity. Although private and corporate owners may also be interested in these ecological and social objectives, they often consider other objectives more important, such as obtaining revenue from the sale of wood products or enhancing the aesthetic and amenity value of their forests. The three classes of ownership discussed here are federal, other public (e.g., state and local government), and private (including corporate and noncorporate private owners) (fig. 15).

Findings

The federal government manages over half of California's 33 million forested acres, most of this within the National Forest System (NFS) (fig. 16). Beginning in the late 1980s, wood production was increasingly deemphasized on federal forests. Production of wood fiber from federal lands decreased from an average of 40 percent of California's total between 1963 and 1987, to 23 percent between 1988 and 2000, to 10 percent between 2001 and 2006 (California State Board of Equalization 2006).

Figure 15—Over one-third of California's 33 million acres of forest land are privately owned.

Federal owners—

About 22 percent of the 15.7 million forested acres of national forest land are congressionally reserved (land where management for the production of wood products is prohibited). On average, older stands with trees in larger size classes tend to be in federal forests rather than in privately owned forests and they occur at higher elevations (fig. 17); the average elevation of federal forests (4,850

---

[2] Author: David Azuma.

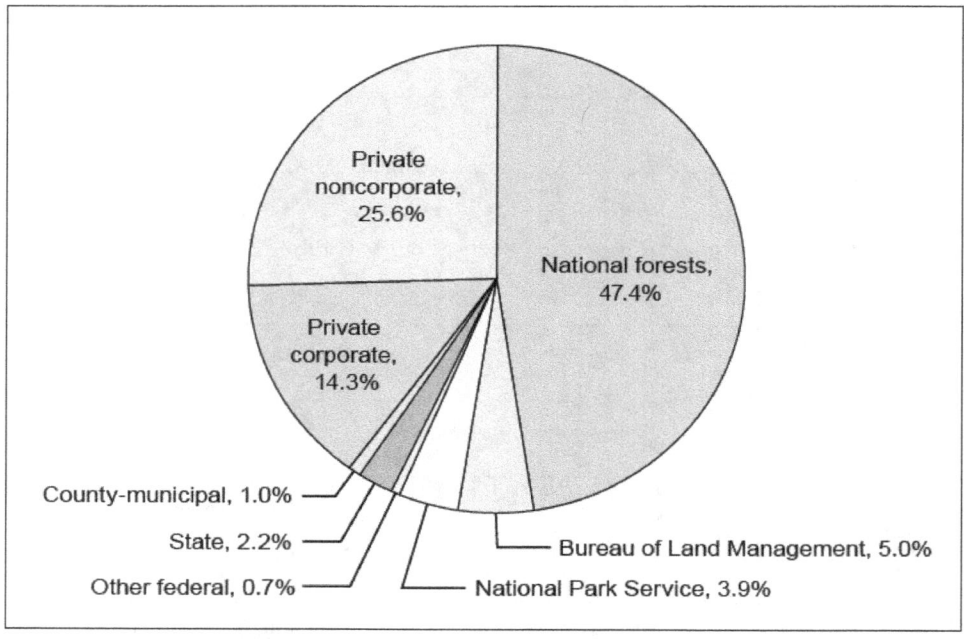

Figure 16—Percentage of forest land by owner group in California, 2001—2005.

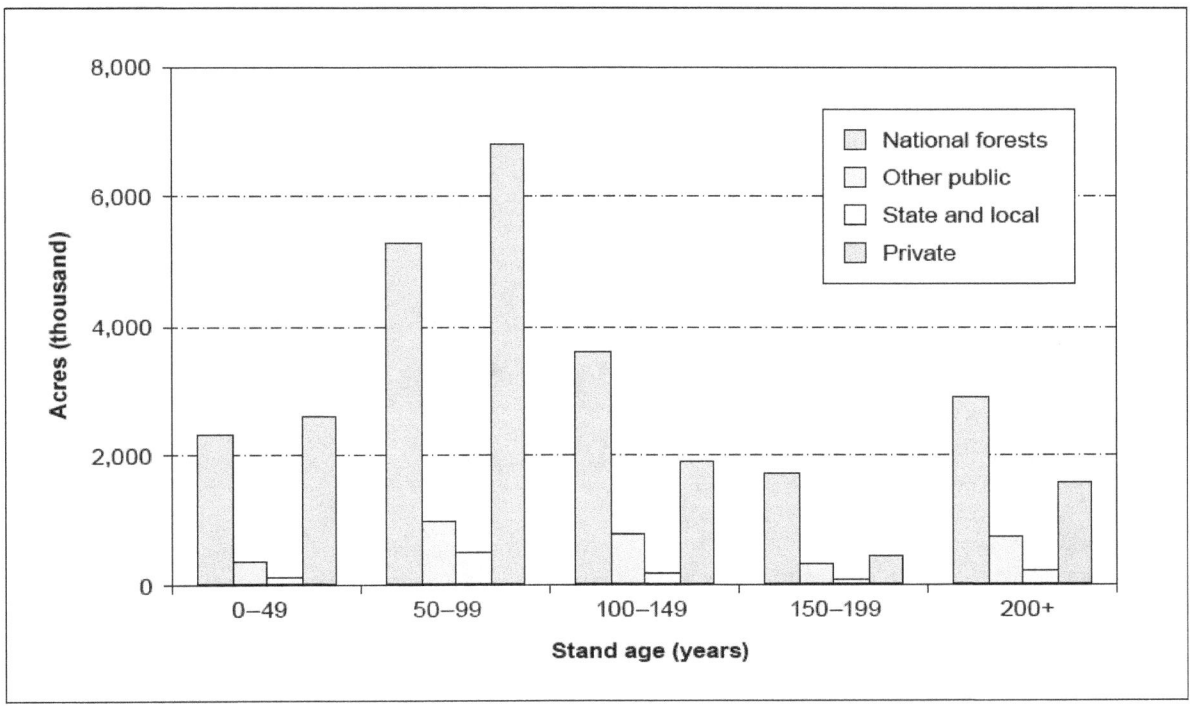

Figure 17—Area of forest land by owner group and stand age class in California, 2001–2005.

feet) is more than double that of private forests (2,344 feet). Although the majority of federal forest land is not reserved in the technical sense, administrative restrictions, as well as practical constraints related to species mix, site productivity, and soil conditions, make many acres unsuitable for wood production. The NFS reports that about 15.4 percent of available forest land is actually harvestable in California, either at full or reduced levels (USDA Forest Service 2007c)

California has about 5.8 million acres of reserved forest land. About 3.5 million of these acres are managed by NFS, mostly in wilderness areas. The remaining acreage is distributed among other public owners, including the Bureau of Land Management (BLM), the National Park Service (NPS), the U.S. Fish and Wildlife Service, and state and county parks. Forests administered by the NPS, such as those in Yosemite, Sequoia/Kings Canyon, Lassen Volcanic, and Redwood national parks, amount to 1.8 million acres. Reserved forest land tends to be in older age classes; more than 67 percent of reserved forests, about 3.9 million acres, are older than 100 years.

Private owners—
Private owners include families, individuals, conservation and natural resource organizations, unincorporated partnerships, associations, clubs, corporations, and Native American tribes. Noncorporate private owners hold about 7.9 million acres of forest land. In contrast to public forest land, private forests, on average, contain younger stands, have more acreage and volume in smaller size classes, and occur on higher-productivity land at lower elevations.

Corporate owners manage about 4.7 million acres of forest land in California. Less than 10 percent of this land is held by timberland investment management organizations (TIMOs) and real estate investment trusts (REITs), which manage around 344,000 acres.[3] These ownership groups are nonindustrial in that their corporate owners generally do not also own or control wood processing facilities. Both REITs

---

[3] Best, Connie. 2007. Personal communication. Pacific Forest Trust. The Presidio. 1001-A O'Reilly Avenue, San Francisco, CA 94129.

Family-Owned Forests: A Survey[4]

The National Woodland Owner Survey, a mail-in, questionnaire-based survey conducted by FIA, provides some insight into private family forest owners and their concerns, current forest management, and future intentions (fig. 18) (Butler et al. 2005, National Woodland Owner Survey 2008). In California, about 99 percent of surveyed family owners have parcels of 500 acres or less making up 58 percent of the area of family-owned forest land (fig. 19). Less than 1 percent of the surveyed owners had written management plans. Timber harvesting has been the recent focus (within the last 5 years) of a fairly large percentage of owners (33 percent), representing a similar percentage of family-owned forest acres (28 percent). The greatest concerns of respondents were issues of passing land on to heirs, fire, trespassing, exotic plants, and property taxes. Future plans for forest land differed: 4 to 7 percent of surveyed owners planned to sell, subdivide, or convert their forests.

Private forest land ownership will certainly change as owners age and pass their land on to heirs who may or may not retain it as forest land. Average parcel size has become smaller over the last 20 years and probably will continue to do so. Land use laws and regulations will influence the rate of conversion of private forest land to other uses.

Figure 18—Small parcel (500 acres or less), family-owned forests make up 58 percent of the acreage in noncorporate private forest land in California.

The ownership survey revealed the following demographics of California family forest landowners:
- 84 percent are older than 55 years.
- 17 percent have earned a bachelor's or graduate degree.
- 94 percent are Caucasian.
- 63 percent are male.
- 45 percent have owned their land for more than 25 years.
- 76 percent use their land as part of their primary residence.
- At least 33 percent have harvested timber, firewood, or nontimber forest products from their land in the 5 years preceding the 2004 survey.

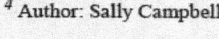

[4] Author: Sally Campbell.

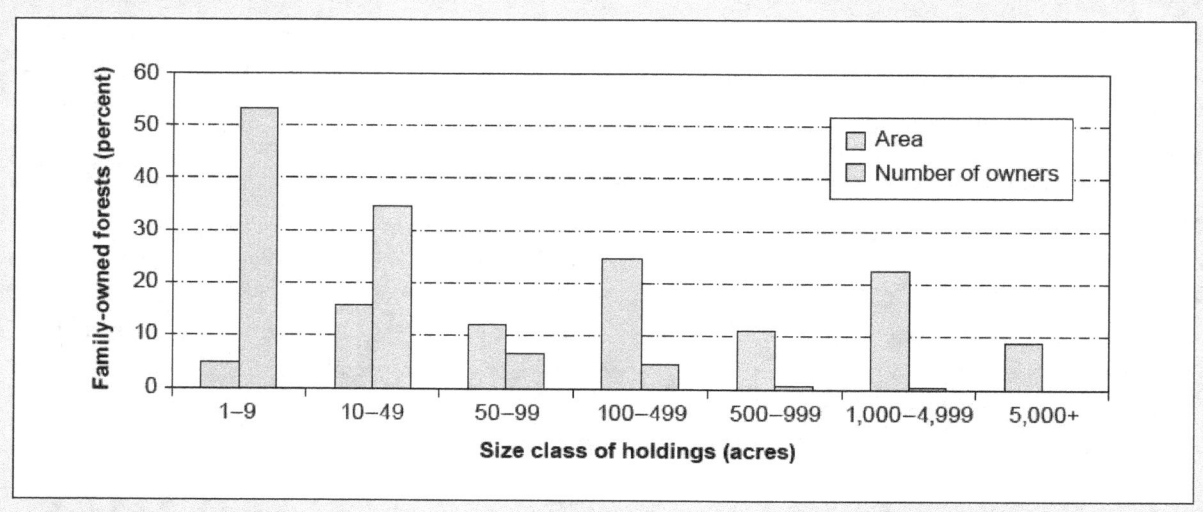

Figure 19—Percentage of area and percentage of number of family-owned forest holdings by size class in California, 2004.

and TIMOs own forest land as an investment category that diversifies their portfolio; as such, forest land must both compete with and complement alternative investment opportunities. The difference between REITs and TIMOs is that REITs directly own forest land, whereas TIMOs manage land that is owned by the investors.

Interpretation

Current ownership of California's forests greatly influences where forest products and other environmental services are available, and in what quantity and quality. From an ownership standpoint, the near future of California's timber products supply looks relatively stable in that the land controlled by large corporate and other private entities does not yet show evidence of imminent, rapid change. Morgan et al. (2004) cover other factors that may influence management and utilization of California's forests. A major concern with diminished wood production on NFS lands is that the burden of meeting the demand for timber products has been shifted onto other public and private lands. An aging ownership base in the noncorporate owner group and the substantial percentage of forested lands now used as primary residences adds uncertainty to the longer term future availability of these lands for timber production. It is unclear what an increased ownership shift from forest products companies to TIMOs and REITs would mean for the management of California's industrial forests. One possible outcome is that more land will be developed for nonforest uses as owners pursue greater financial returns.

Ownership tables in appendix 2—
- Table 2—Estimated area of forest land, by owner class and forest land status, California, 2001–2005
- Table 3—Estimated area of forest land, by forest type group and productivity class, California, 2001–2005
- Table 4—Estimated area of forest land, by forest type group, ownership, and land status, California, 2001–2005

Timber Volume[5]

Background

The current volume of live trees provides the foundation for estimating several fundamental attributes of forest land such as biomass, carbon storage, and capacity to produce wood products. Forest volume can serve as an indicator of forest productivity, structure, and vigor, which together serve as a broad indicator of forest health. Species-specific equations that include tree diameter and height are used to calculate individual tree volumes; these are summed across all trees to provide estimates of conditions at the forest level. The net volume estimates provided in this report for live trees do not include volume for any observed defects, such as rotten and missing sections along the stem.

Findings

California has approximately 95 billion net cubic feet (428 billion Scribner board feet) of wood volume on forest land, with a mean volume of about 2,875 cubic feet (12,879 Scribner board feet) per acre. The greatest proportion is from softwood tree species such as Douglas-fir, true firs, and pines, which collectively make up 81 percent of net live-tree volume on forest land (fig. 20). The remaining 19 percent of live-tree volume is from hardwood species, such as oaks and a mix of many other western hardwood species.

Forest land volume by ownership—
The majority (55 percent) of live-tree cubic-foot volume in California is on forested acres managed by the Forest Service (fig. 21). Most of the rest is on land owned by private noncorporate (18 percent) and corporate (14 percent) owners. State and federal forest land (excluding BLM) tends to have more volume per acre than private land (fig. 22). Average volume on state lands is notably large, reflecting the substantial areas of old-growth redwood forests within state parks and the relatively high levels of inventory on state-owned forest land.

---

[5] Author: Glenn Christensen.

Figure 20—The greatest volume of wood in California is found in the North Interior area (Mount Shasta area shown here).

Forest land volume by survey unit—
Most wood volume is found in the heavily forested northern portions of the state (fig. 23). As shown in the tabulation below, the North Interior survey unit has the highest total wood volume. About three-fifths of the statewide wood volume is divided evenly among three survey units, Sacramento, North Coast, and San Joaquin. The North Coast unit

has the most wood volume per acre. When modeled as an interpolated map, the same trend can be seen in volume per acre—nearly all the wood volume is found in the northern two-thirds of the state.

The following tabulation shows mean and total wood volume of live trees on forest land by survey unit, with sampling error (SE) in parentheses:

Survey unit	Total volume (SE)			Mean volume (SE)	
	Billion cubic feet	*Billion Scribner board feet*	*Percent*	*Cubic feet per acre*	*Scribner board feet per acre*
North Interior	27 (0.8)	126 (4.3)	28	2,746 (74)	12,774 (434)
Sacramento	21 (0.7)	93 (3.7)	22	3,105 (96)	13,920 (555)
North Coast	20 (1.5)	87 (7.7)	22	4,381 (290)	18,578 (1,512)
San Joaquin	20 (0.8)	99 (4.7)	21	2,613 (98)	12,623 (580)
Central Coast	5 (0.7)	18 (3.5)	6	2,094 (222)	7,168 (1,281)
Southern	1 (0.2)	5 (0.9)	1	847 (102)	2,991 (520)
Total	95 (2.0)	428 (10.8)	100	2,875 (59)	12,879 (325)

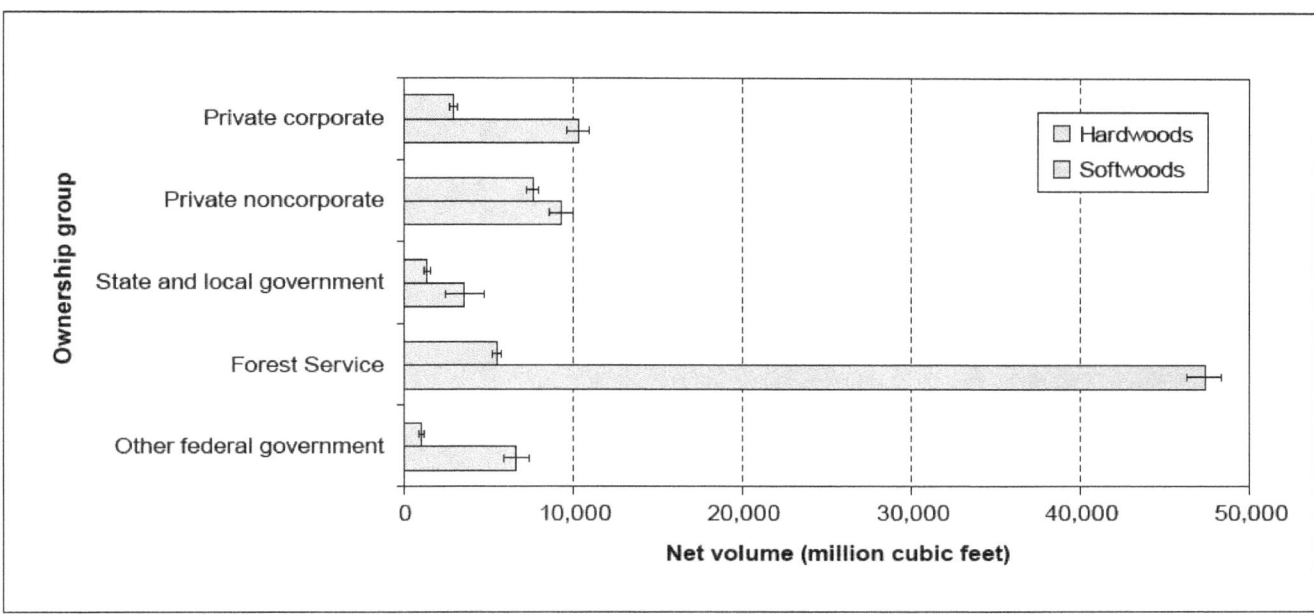

Figure 21—Net volume of all live trees by ownership group on forest land in California, 2001–2005.

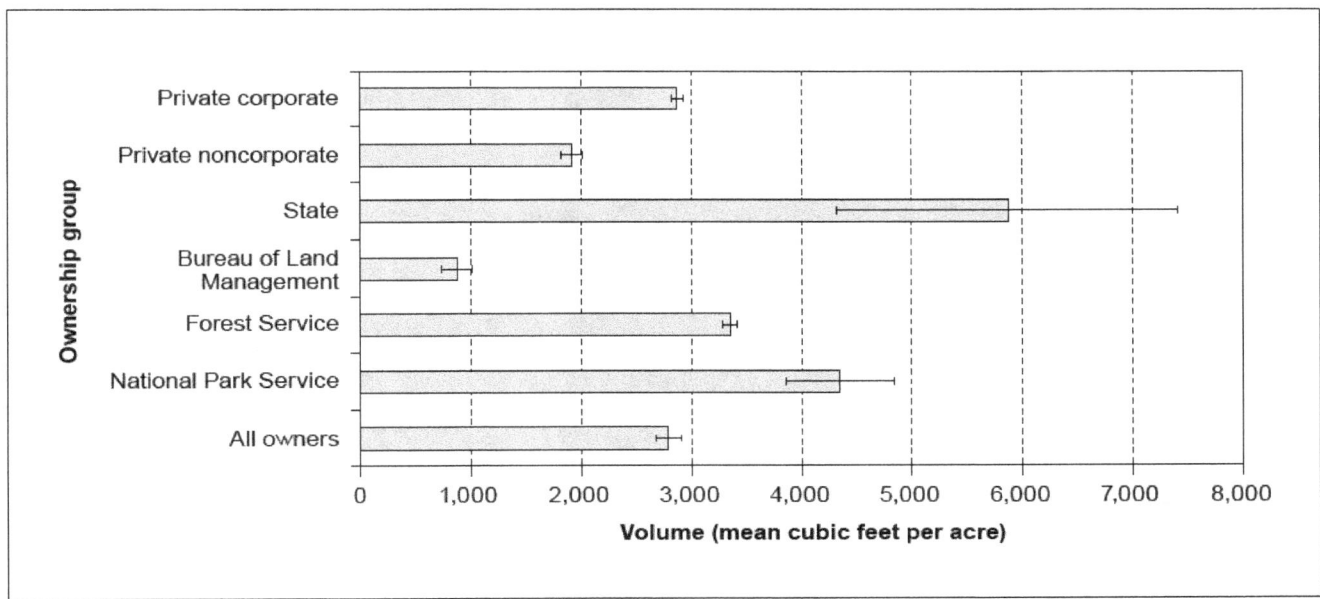

Figure 22—Mean net volume per acre of all live trees by ownership group on forest land in California, 2001–2005.

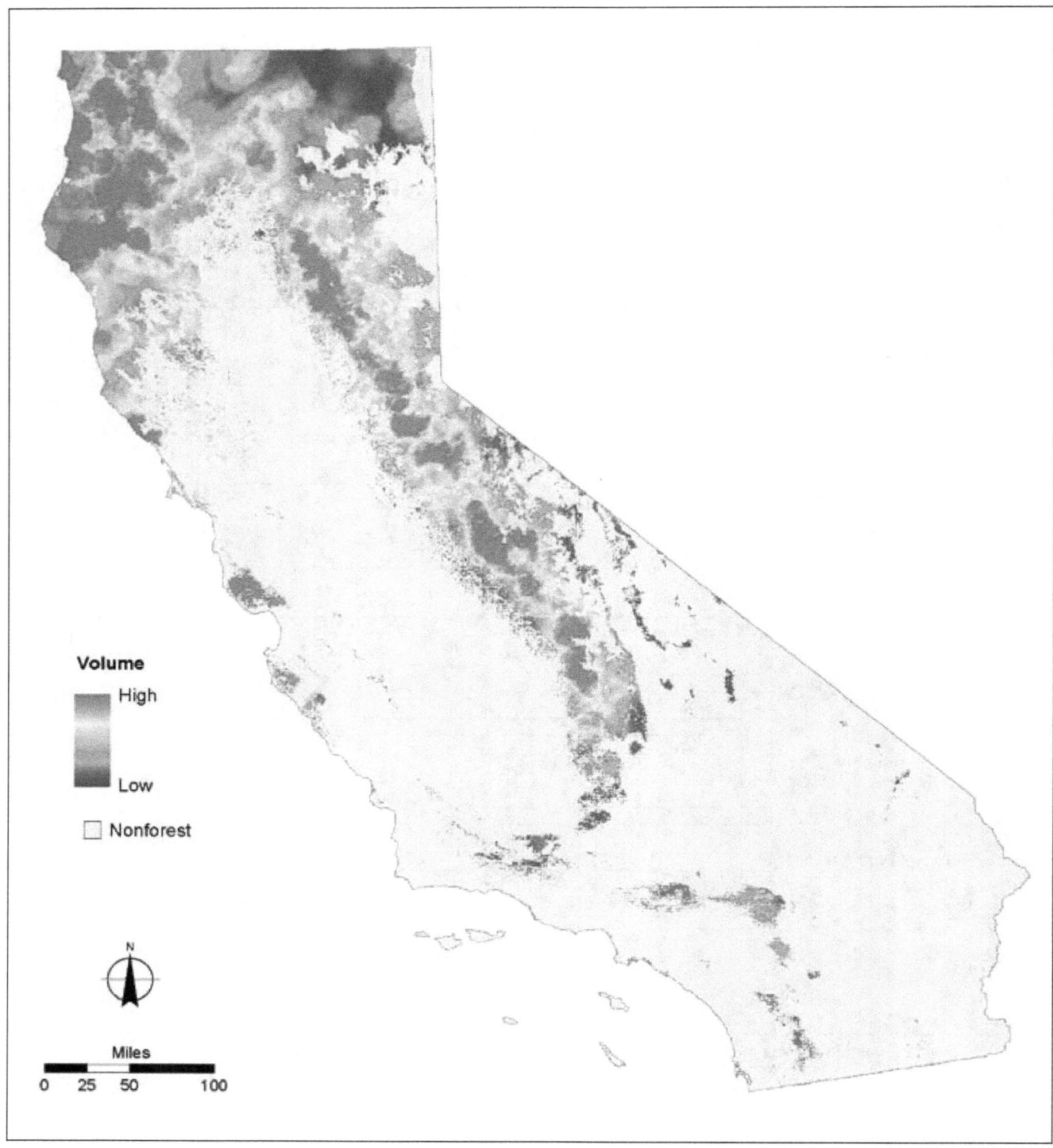

Figure 23—Estimated live tree volume (net cubic feet per acre) in California, 2001–2005. Estimates are kriged predictions of likely volume per acre on forest land, based on mean net cubic foot volume per plot (forest/nonforest geographic information system (GIS) layer: Blackard et al. 2008).

Forest land volume by diameter class—
Approximately 43 percent of live-tree volume for both softwood and hardwood trees is in trees 5 to 20.9 inches d.b h. (fig. 24). An estimated 23 percent of all live-tree volume is in the largest diameter class (trees 37 inches d.b h. and larger), nearly all of which are softwood trees. As presented in the previous section on ownership, a greater proportion of acres in the oldest age classes are in federal ownership (fig. 17). The same is true for volume; federal ownership contains higher wood volume than private ownership (fig. 25). Forty-four percent of the wood volume in trees of the smallest diameter class (5.0 to 8.9 inches d.b.h.) is in forests managed by the Forest Service, whereas 20 percent is in forests managed by private corporate owners. In contrast, 65 percent of the wood volume in trees in the largest diameter class (≥33.0 inches d.b h.) is in forests managed by the Forest Service, and only 6 percent is in corporate forests.

Forest land volume by species group—
Over half (approximately 57 percent) of live-tree volume on California's forest land is in trees of three species groups: Douglas-fir, true fir, and ponderosa-Jeffrey pine. Douglas-

fir accounts for most of the total volume; about 22 percent of all live-tree volume in the state is contained in trees of this species (fig. 26). The true fir species group accounts for slightly less (21 percent), and the ponderosa and Jeffrey pine species group accounts for 14 percent. Of the hardwood species, the oak species group accounts for the most volume; wood volume contained in oak trees makes up 11 percent of total cubic-foot wood volume and 59 percent of cubic-foot hardwood volume statewide.

Volume of sawtimber-sized trees on timberland[6]—
Douglas-fir accounts for 31 percent of the sawtimber volume, true firs 22 percent, and ponderosa and Jeffrey pines 18 percent (fig. 27). This is the volume of wood that is potentially available for manufacturing wood-based products. Among the hardwoods, oaks contribute the most to sawtimber volume, making up about 2 percent of the total.

---

[6] Sawtimber volume is defined as the boles of trees of commercial species that are large enough to produce utilizable logs (9.0 inches d.b.h. minimum for softwoods, 11.0 inches d.b.h. minimum for hardwoods), from a 1-foot stump to a minimum top diameter (7.0 inches outside bark diameter for softwoods, 9.0 inches outside bark diameter for hardwoods).

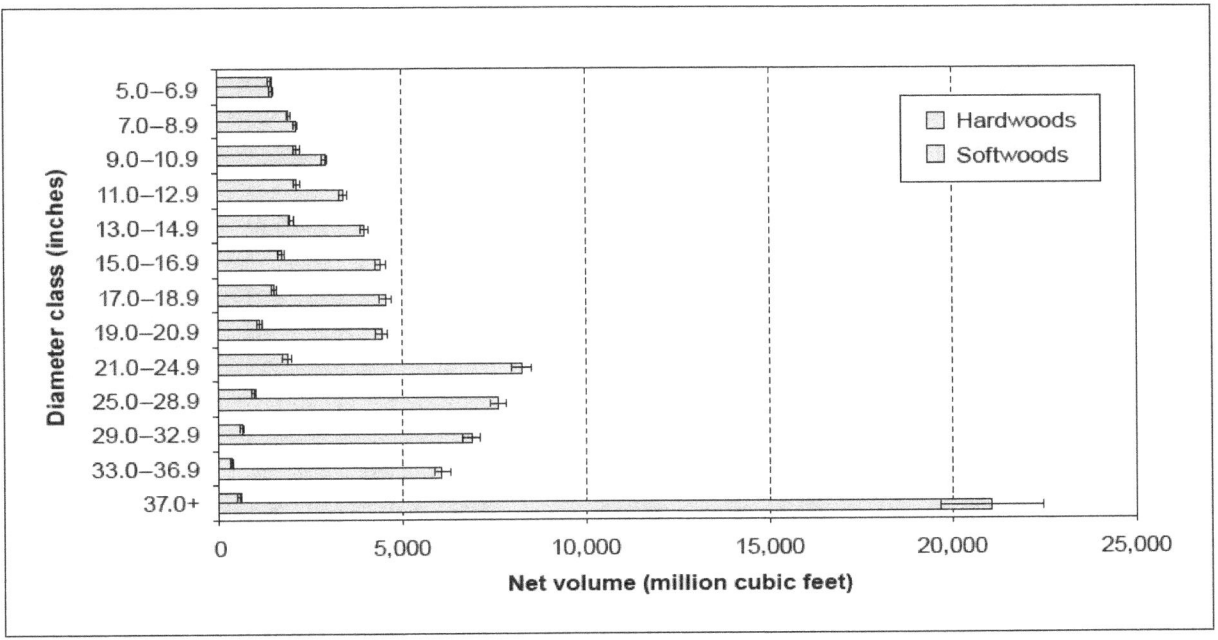

Figure 24—Net volume of all live trees by diameter class on forest land in California, 2001–2005.

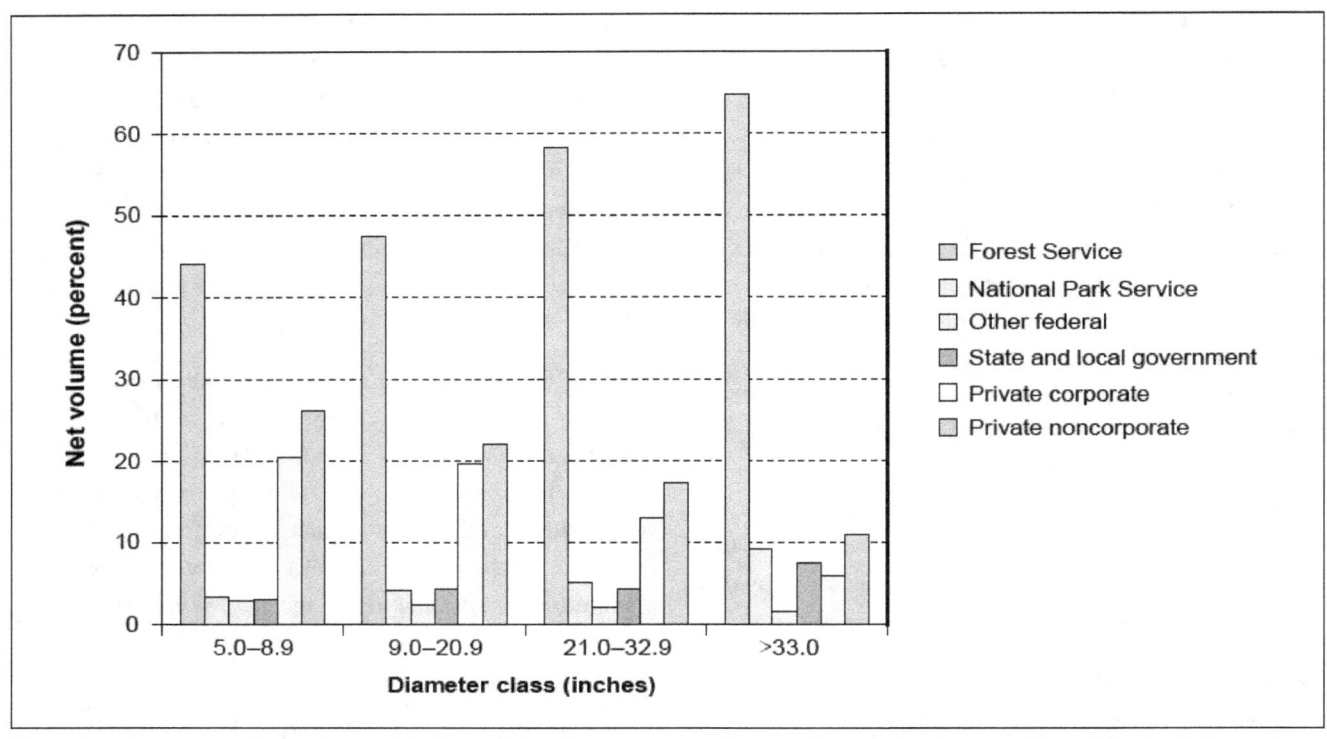

Figure 25—Percentage of net volume of all live trees by diameter class and ownership group on forest land in California, 2001–2005.

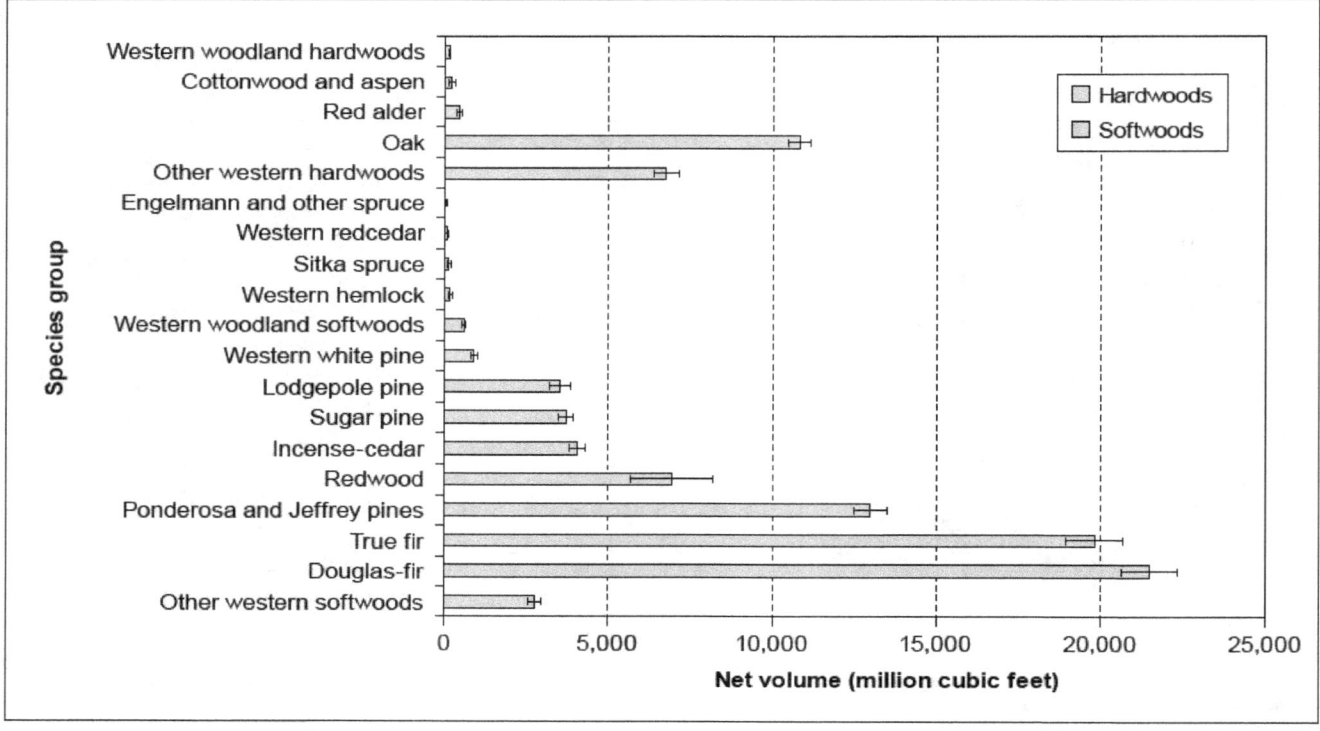

Figure 26—Total net volume of all live trees by species group on forest land in California, 2001–2005.

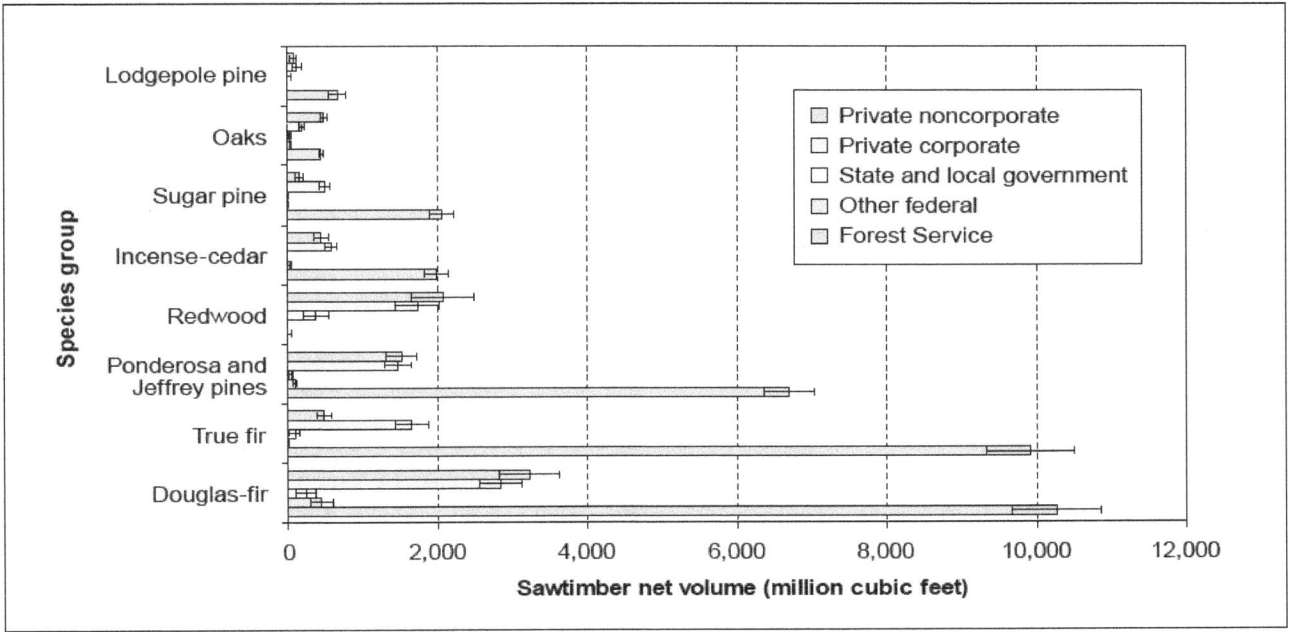

Figure 27—Net volume of sawtimber-sized trees by ownership group on timberland in California, 2001–2005. Excludes the miscellaneous mixed softwood and hardwood species groups and species groups that contribute less than 1 percent of total sawtimber volume.

Interpretation

Statewide estimates of timberland volume over the past 50 years show a recent return to levels seen in the 1950s after declines in the 1970s and 1980s (fig. 28). However, interpreting the difference between current and previous estimates is problematic because of differences between inventory methods (see periodic versus annual inventories in app. 1). Aggregation of wood volume into the six survey units traditionally used by FIA for California forest inventories reveals no major departures from the past. Most of the volume is found in forests in the North Interior, Sacramento, North Coast, and San Joaquin survey units, mainly because the climate in these areas is better able to support forest growth. Southern California forests support lower densities of trees on average. Overall, species contributing the majority of forest land volume (Douglas-fir, true firs, ponderosa and Jeffrey pines, and redwood) also are the most important commercial species. Continued consistent use of the current FIA inventory method will enable the monitoring of trends in volume and other resource attributes over time. The first statewide remeasurement of annual inventory plots is scheduled to begin in 2011.

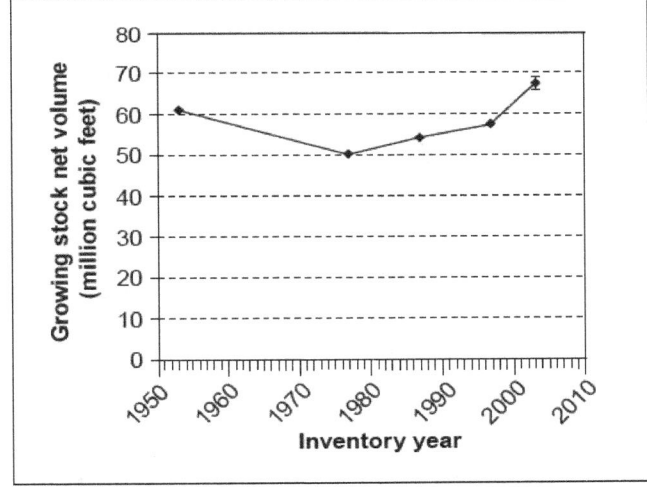

Figure 28—Net volume of growing stock on timberland by inventory year in California, 1953–2005 (Smith et al. 2004). Note: The 2001–2005 timberland volume estimate is based on the annual inventory design and protocols; the previous volume estimates are based on periodic inventories with different designs and protocols. Key differences between current and previous estimates, apart from real change, are due in large part to (1) application of plot stockability factors and stockable proportions to different sets of plots in the periodic and annual inventories (Because stockability defines productivity class, it thus influences the classification of a plot as timberland or not.) and (2) changes in definitions and protocols arising from national standardization of the inventory for qualification as tree, forest land, reserved land, and timberland.

25

Timber volume tables in appendix 2—

- Table 8—Estimated number of live trees on forest land, by species group and diameter class, California, 2001–2005
- Table 9—Estimated number of growing-stock trees on timberland, by species group and diameter class, California, 2001–2005
- Table 10—Estimated net volume of all live trees, by owner class and forest land status, California, 2001–2005
- Table 11—Estimated net volume of all live trees on forest land, by forest type group and stand size class, California, 2001–2005
- Table 12—Estimated net volume of all live trees on forest land, by species group and ownership group, California, 2001–2005
- Table 13—Estimated net volume of all live trees on forest land, by species group and diameter class, California, 2001–2005
- Table 14—Estimated net volume of growing-stock trees on timberland, by species group and diameter class, California, 2001–2005
- Table 15—Estimated net volume of growing-stock trees on timberland, by species group and ownership group, California, 2001–2005
- Table 16—Estimated net volume (International ¼ inch rule) of sawtimber trees on timberland, by species group and diameter class, California, 2001–2005
- Table 17—Estimated net volume (Scribner rule) of sawtimber trees on timberland, by species group and diameter class, California, 2001–2005
- Table 18—Estimated net volume (cubic feet) of sawtimber trees on timberland, by species group and ownership group, California, 2001–2005

Biomass and Carbon[7]

Background

Forest biomass and carbon accumulate in live trees, snags, and down wood in a mosaic of patterns across California (fig. 29). During forest succession, plant biomass builds up at different rates, sequestering carbon from atmospheric gases (carbon dioxide) and soil nutrients into woody tree components over time (Perry 1994). Biomass estimates from comprehensive forest inventories are essential for quantifying the amount and distribution of carbon stocks, evaluating forests as a source of sustainable fuel (biomass for energy production), and conducting research on net primary productivity (Houghton 2005, Jenkins et al. 2001, Whittaker and Likens 1975). Information about biomass and carbon accumulation in forests can help in evaluations of forest sustainability under criterion 5, defined in the Montreal Process (USDA Forest Service 1997), which calls for biomass and carbon estimates to be used as indicators to assess the role of forests in global carbon cycles.

In this section we focus on the aboveground live-tree components of forest biomass. We also make brief comparisons with dead wood biomass, which is addressed more fully in the section on dead wood. Cubic-foot volume and specific gravity constants for each species were used to compute the dry weight of the tree stem in bone-dry (oven-dry) tons (1 ton = 2,000 pounds). Stem biomass was combined with branch biomass (estimated with published equations) to compute the total aboveground dry weight of the tree (from ground to tip). Carbon mass was estimated by applying conversion factors to biomass estimates.

---

[7] Author: Karen Waddell.

Karen Waddell

Figure 29—Biomass and carbon accumulate in live and dead trees of many sizes and ages in western forests.

Findings[8]

Over 2 billion tons of biomass and 1 billion tons of carbon have accumulated in live trees (≥1 inch diameter at breast height [d.b h.]), primarily on unreserved forest land. The majority of this biomass (51 percent) was found on Forest Service land (fig. 30), where almost 24 percent of that was located on reserved forest land. Live trees on timberland contain about 1.5 billion tons of biomass and 786 million tons of carbon. Softwood forest types have double the amount of biomass and carbon of hardwood types, with biomass estimates ranging from a low of 4 million tons in the western hemlock/Sitka spruce type to a high of 724 million

tons in the mixed-conifer type (fig. 31). The predominant hardwood types for biomass accumulation are the western oak group and the tanoak/laurel group, with 414 and 231 million tons of biomass, respectively.

Statewide, trees of softwood species have about 2.5 times the amount of live-tree biomass of hardwood species. Softwood biomass is heavily concentrated in trees larger than 21 inches d.b.h. (fig. 32) of which the most is in the Douglas-fir and true fir species groups. In contrast, hardwood species tend to follow a bell-shaped distribution curve, with a peak biomass in trees of the 9- to 12-inch class.

---

[8] In this section, all references to weight are in bone-dry tons.

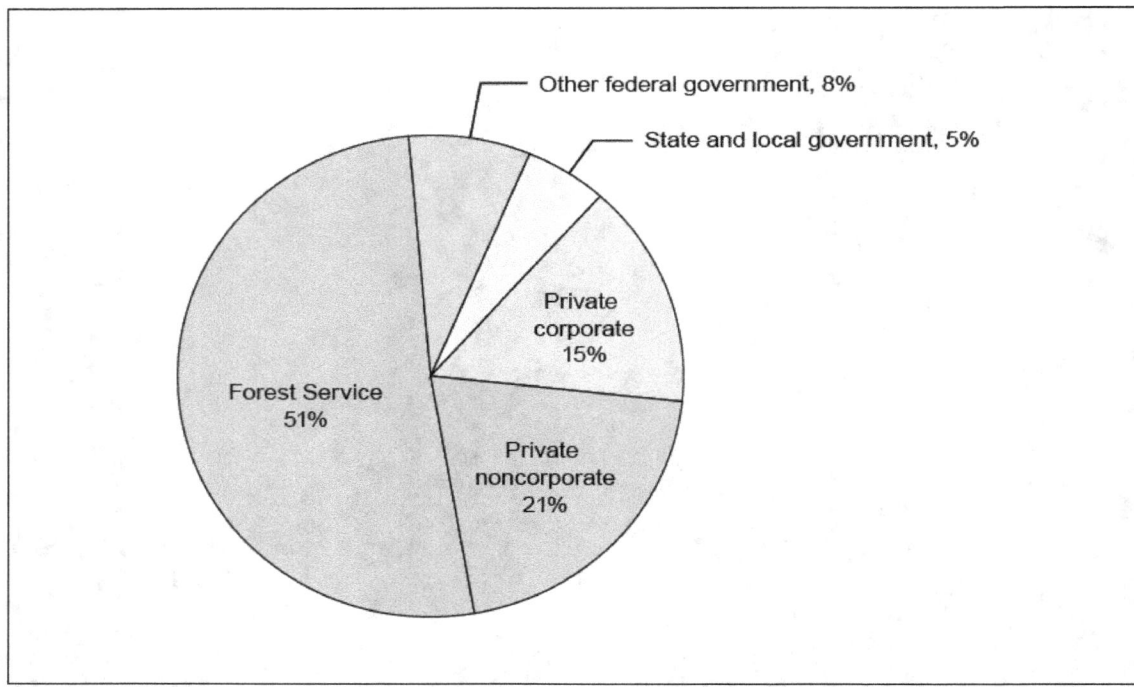

Figure 30—Percentage of aboveground live tree biomass by owner group on forest land in California, 2001–2005.

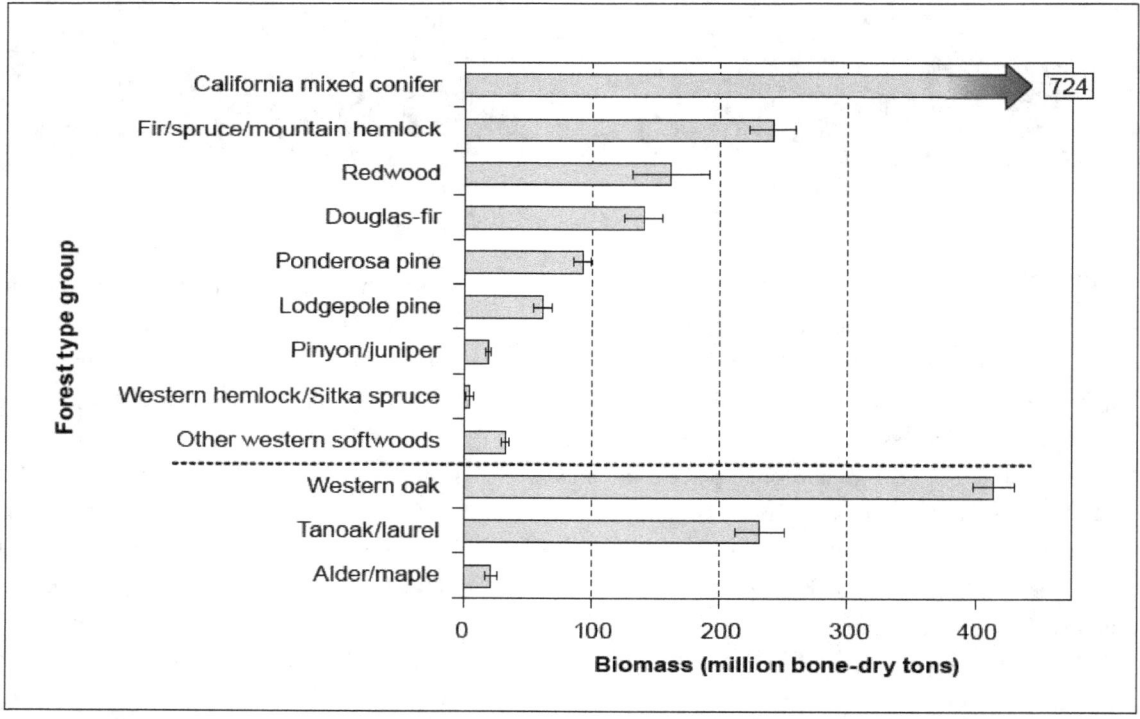

Figure 31—Aboveground live tree biomass by forest type group on forest land in California, 2001–2005.

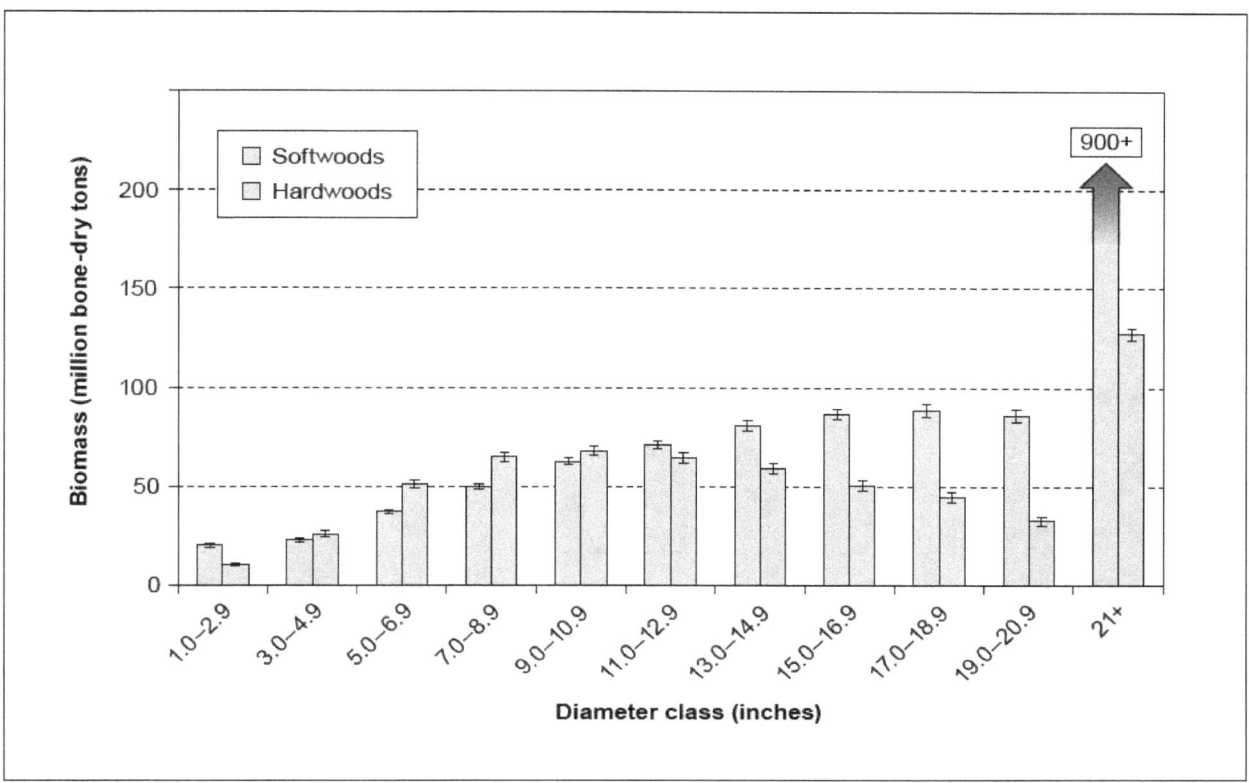

Figure 32—Aboveground live tree biomass by diameter class on forest land in California, 2001–2005.

Dead wood makes up a sizable fraction of wood biomass. Of the 2.6 billion tons of wood biomass in California, snags (≥5 inches d.b h.) contribute 188 million tons, coarse woody material (CWM; wood ≥3 inches in diameter at the large end) contributes 226 million tons, and fine woody material (FWM; wood <3 inches diameter at the point of intersection with the sample transect) contributes 123 million tons to the forest biomass in the state.

About half of biomass is stored carbon, with about 1 billion tons stored in live trees, 97 million tons stored in snags, and 179 million tons stored in down wood (CWM and FWM combined). A closer look at the carbon allocation among live and dead materials within major forest types is shown in figure 33. Most of the carbon is stored in softwood types, with 83 percent in live trees, 9 percent in CWM, and only 8 percent in snags. The bulk of the carbon was found in forests classified as a mixed-conifer forest type, primarily in live Douglas-fir, white fir, and ponderosa pine trees.

On average, we estimated that the total biomass of live trees, snags, and CWM was about 78 tons per acre across the state, which represents a carbon mass of about 40 tons per acre. The redwood forest type group had a mean carbon mass of over 152 tons per acre (fig. 34), with 85 percent of that attributable to live trees. The combined hardwood types had less than half that, with the greatest accumulations of carbon found in the tanoak/laurel (64 tons per acre) and the alder/maple (54 tons per acre) type groups.

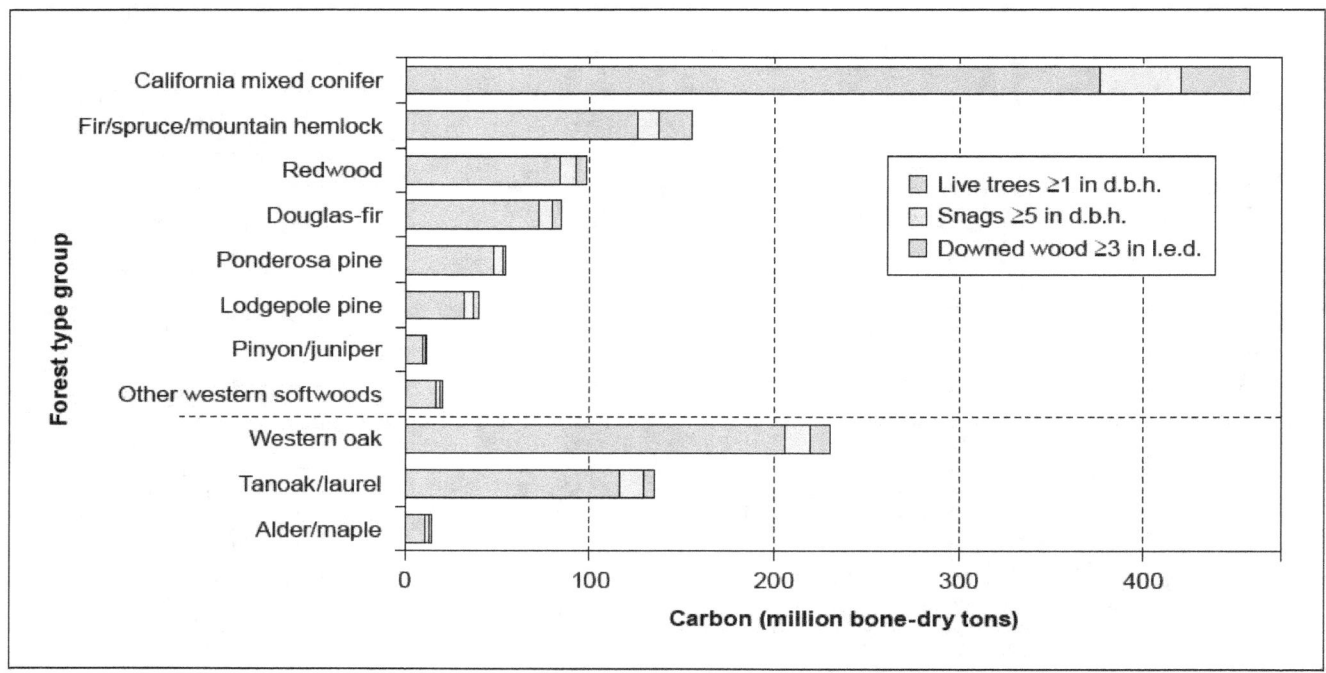

Figure 33—Carbon mass of live trees, snags, and down wood (coarse woody material) by forest type group on forest land in California, 2001–2005; d.b h. = diameter at breast height; l.e.d. = large end diameter.

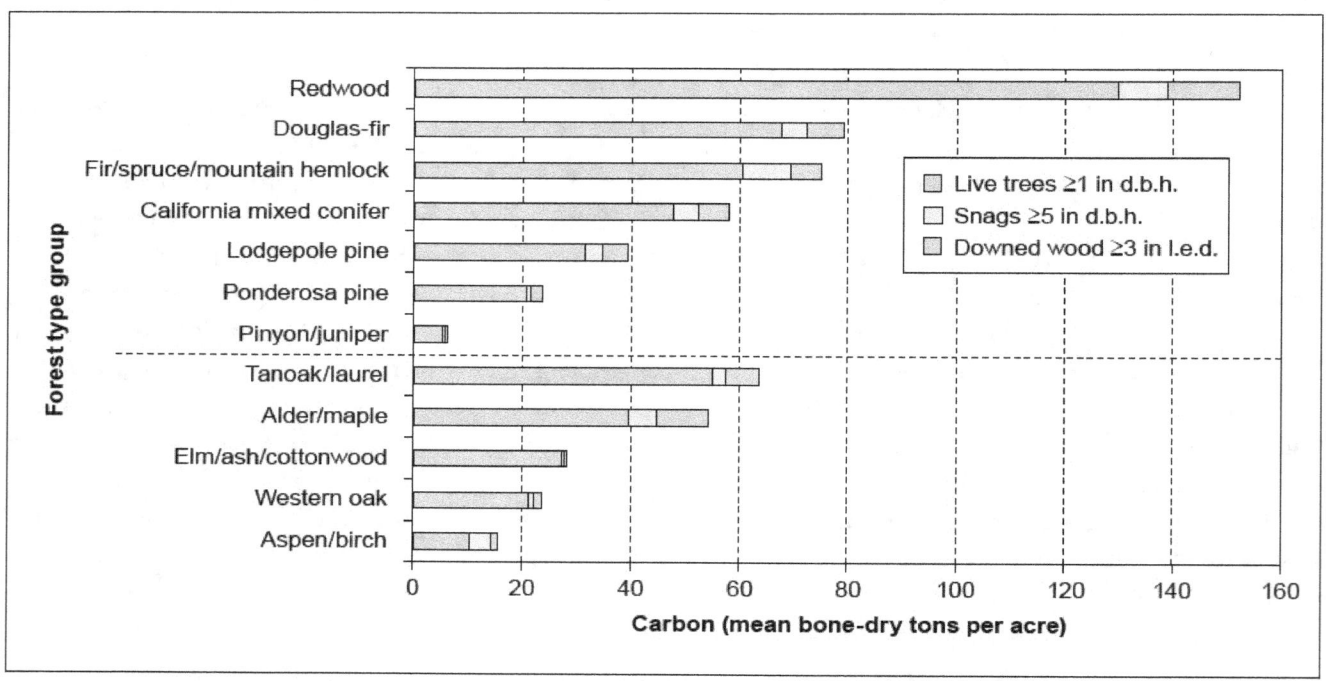

Figure 34—Mean carbon mass of live trees, snags, and down wood (coarse woody material) by forest type group on forest land in California, 2001–2005; d.b.h. = diameter at breast height; l.e.d. = large end diameter.

Interpretation

Substantial quantities of forest biomass and carbon have accumulated in California forests. The current rising interest in biomass as an alternative source of energy will accelerate the need to understand how much source material is available and where it is located. The FIA inventory shows that there is almost four times as much live-tree biomass as dead-wood biomass. This is important, because the preferred source of material for energy production comes from components of the live-tree resource, such as wood residues from harvest operations and sawmills, stems and branches from forest thinning projects, and material from biomass plantations.

For example, in northern California, a small energy company operates a wood-fired power plant that uses local mill wastes, chips, and unmerchantable whole logs (culls up to 6 feet in diameter) to generate over 375 million kWh of electricity per year. As of 2000 there were 25 wood-using biomass energy facilities throughout California (Morgan et al. 2004). As a market in carbon credits develops, actively growing forests have promise for offsetting carbon production from urban and industrial sources. For such a system to function effectively, the various carbon pools will need to be monitored carefully and adjustments made when necessary—for example, planting trees or improving forest health if and when live-tree carbon stocks are lost to insects, fire, harvest, or some other disturbance. When trees are harvested for solid wood products, monitoring techniques must recognize this shift in carbon storage and account for the carbon sequestered indefinitely within buildings, furniture, and other structural materials. Over time, the desired outcome is that California's forests function as a net sink of stored carbon.

Biomass and carbon tables in appendix 2—

- Table 19—Estimated aboveground biomass of all live trees, by owner class and forest land status, California, 2001–2005
- Table 20—Estimated aboveground biomass of all live trees on forest land, by diameter class and species group, California, 2001–2005
- Table 21—Estimated biomass of live trees on forest land by softwood species group, for merchantable tree boles, tops, limbs, stumps, and small trees, California, 2001–2005
- Table 22—Estimated mass of carbon of all live trees, by owner class and forest land status, California, 2001–2005
- Table 23—Estimated biomass and carbon mass of live trees, snags, and down wood on forest land, by forest type group, California, 2001–2005
- Table 24—Estimated average biomass and carbon mass of live trees, snags, and down wood on forest land, by forest type group, California, 2001–2005

Karen Baas

Patrick's Point State Park.

Chapter 3: Forest Structure and Function

The diverse topics presented in this chapter share a common objective: to characterize the structure and function of California's forests. From an ecological perspective, these forests are vital to a wide variety of plant and animal species. We rely on data collected in the Pacific Northwest Research Station Forest Inventory and Analysis (FIA) inventory to describe characteristics of special habitat types such as old-growth and hardwood forests and the status of forest components such as understory vegetation, hardwoods, dead wood, tree crowns, and soils.

Older Forests[1]

Background

Older forests that are in later stages of successional development are an important part of the forest land matrix. They contribute special habitat, aesthetics, resources, and ecological services not provided by younger forests (Franklin et al. 1981). Older forests are not simply forests where little or no disturbance has occurred for long periods; disturbance is the norm in all forests and has helped shape old forests by creating openings and patches of older survivors.

The term "old" is relative; it depends on whose definition is used, the type of forest, and the regional climate. Older forests are not easily defined, because definitions rely on many complex, interacting variables. For example, the old-growth definitions assembled by Beardsley and Warbington (1996) for northwestern California national forests use site productivity, stand age, density, and diameter of live, standing dead, and down trees as criteria. The minimum stand age they used to classify forests as old growth ranged from 125 to 300 years.

By the age of 175 to 250 years, Pacific Coast forests typically attain the structure, species composition, and various functional attributes of older forests (Franklin et al. 1981, Old-Growth Definition Task Group 1986). More complex definitions for old-growth forests often cite a minimum age of 200 years, depending on productivity class and forest type (Bolsinger and Waddell 1993, Franklin et al. 1981, Old-Growth Definition Task Group 1986).

For our analysis, we have simplified the definition for older forests. Our summary uses stand age as the basis for estimates of area and age distribution. We estimate acreage by forest type for stand ages in two categories, ≥160 years old and ≥200 years old. The FIA field crews estimate stand age from the average age of predominant overstory trees, determined by counting the tree rings from small samples of wood (cores) extracted with an increment borer (fig. 35). It is not possible to determine the age of some trees because of internal rot, or because the sheer size of the tree limits the length of core that can be extracted. In addition, some species (e.g., many hardwoods) are not cored because of the risk that the core wound will make them susceptible to pathogens.

Joseph Donnegan

Figure 35—Increment cores are extracted from trees to determine the age of dominant trees in each forested stand that is sampled by Forest Inventory and Analysis.

---

[1] Author: Joseph Donnegan.

Findings

We estimate that approximately 13 percent (4.1 million acres) of the forest area in California has stands in excess of 160 years. About 7.5 percent (2.3 million acres) has stands in excess of 200 years. The vast majority of older forest is found on publicly owned land in national forests and national parks (see "Ownership" section for more details). The California Department of Forestry and Fire Protection recently estimated that approximately 14 percent of California's conifer forests are in old-growth condition; their hybrid assessment relied on FIA data in combination with remote-sensing imagery (California Department of Forestry and Fire Protection 2003).

Among forests with stand ages greater than 160 years, the California mixed-conifer type occupies the greatest area, accounting for 5.5 percent of total forest area (fig. 36). The remaining combined forest types with stand ages older than 160 years make up about 7.5 percent of total forest area. Although the total acreage of the foxtail/bristlecone pine and the bigcone Douglas-fir types is relatively small (75,279 and 7,245 acres, respectively) 100 percent of those types in our sample occurred in stands older than 160 years (fig. 37).

Within older California mixed-conifer stands, there is great diversity in structural characteristics, with tree diameters covering a broad range of classes (fig. 38). Although seedlings and saplings are the most abundant size class, many trees are greater than 40 inches in diameter.

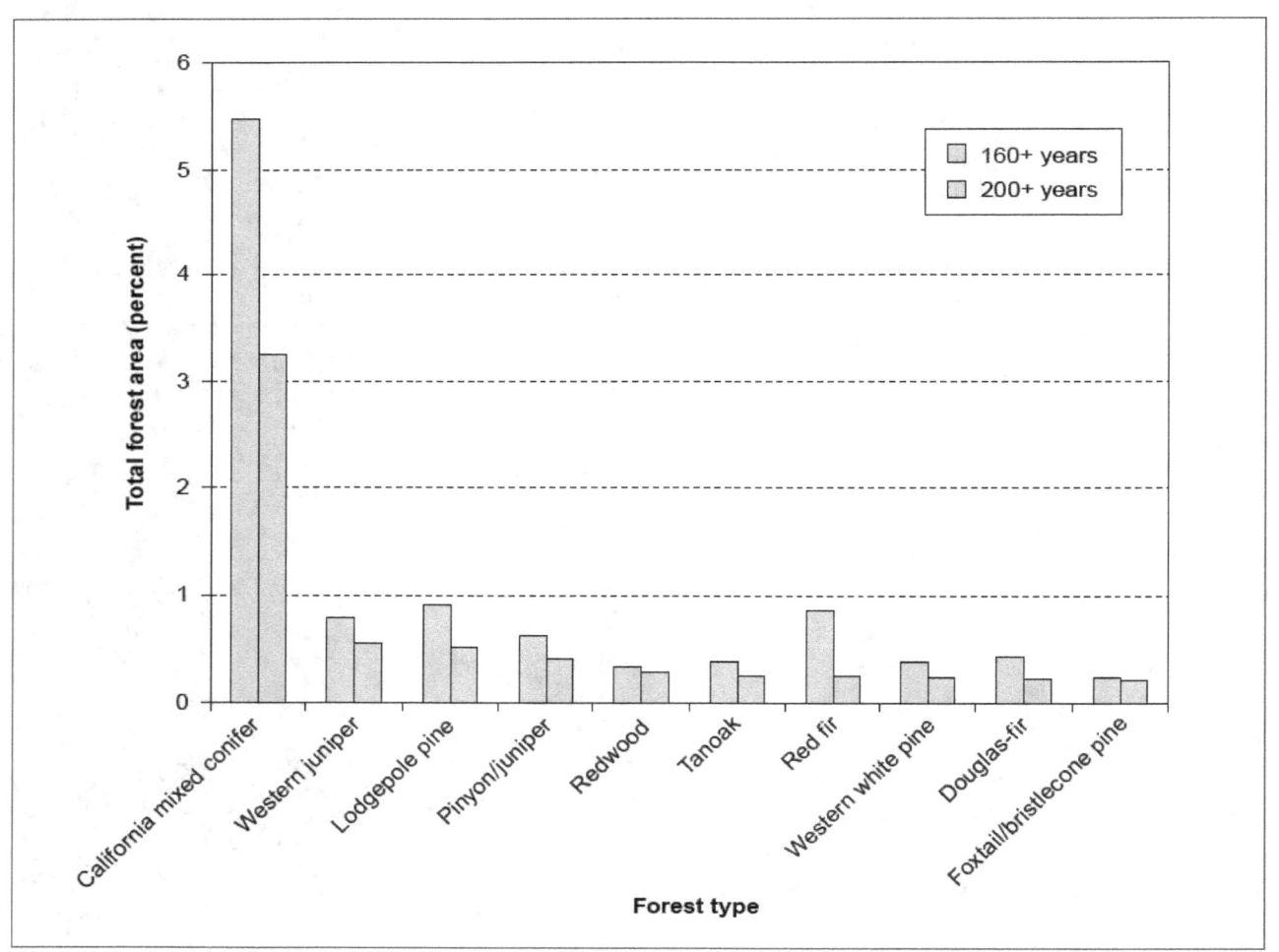

Figure 36—Percentage of total forest area by forest type for stands 160+ and 200+ years old in California, 2001–2005.

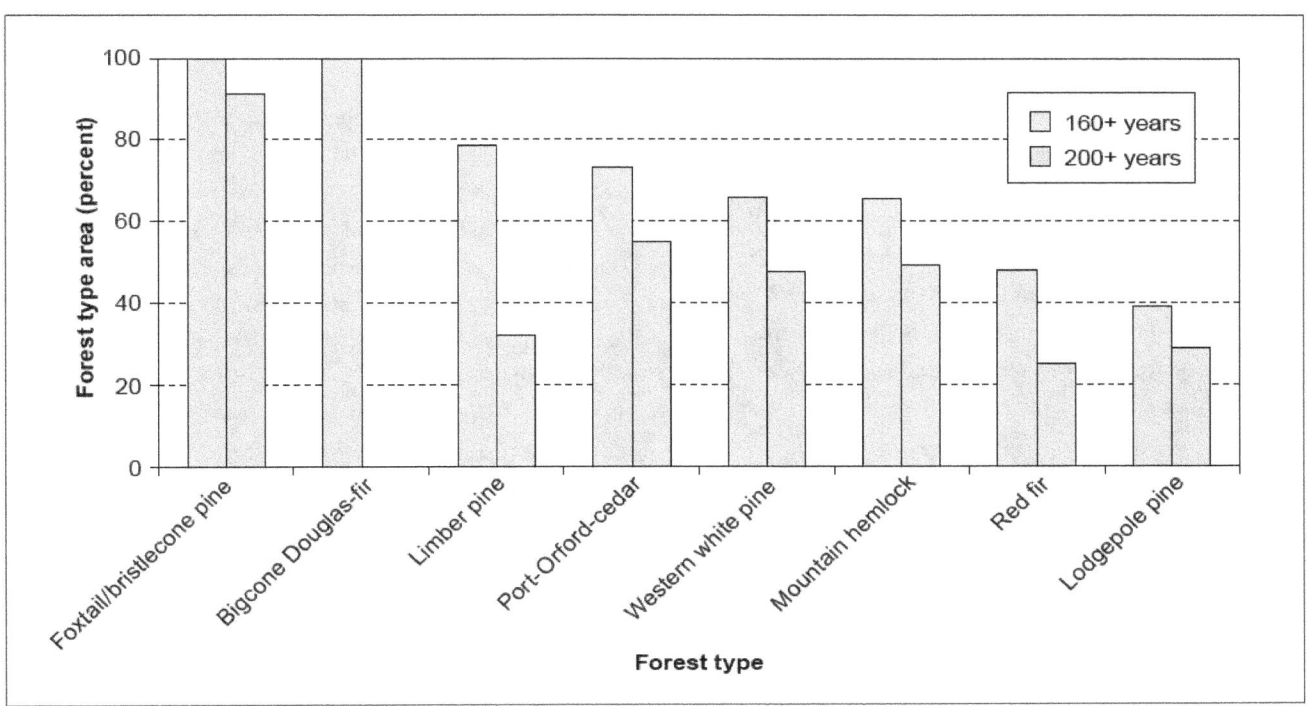

Figure 37—Percentage of softwood forest types in older forest in California, 2001–2005. Note that some forest types (e.g., redwood) do not have high percentages of their total area in older forest conditions and thus are not shown in this figure.

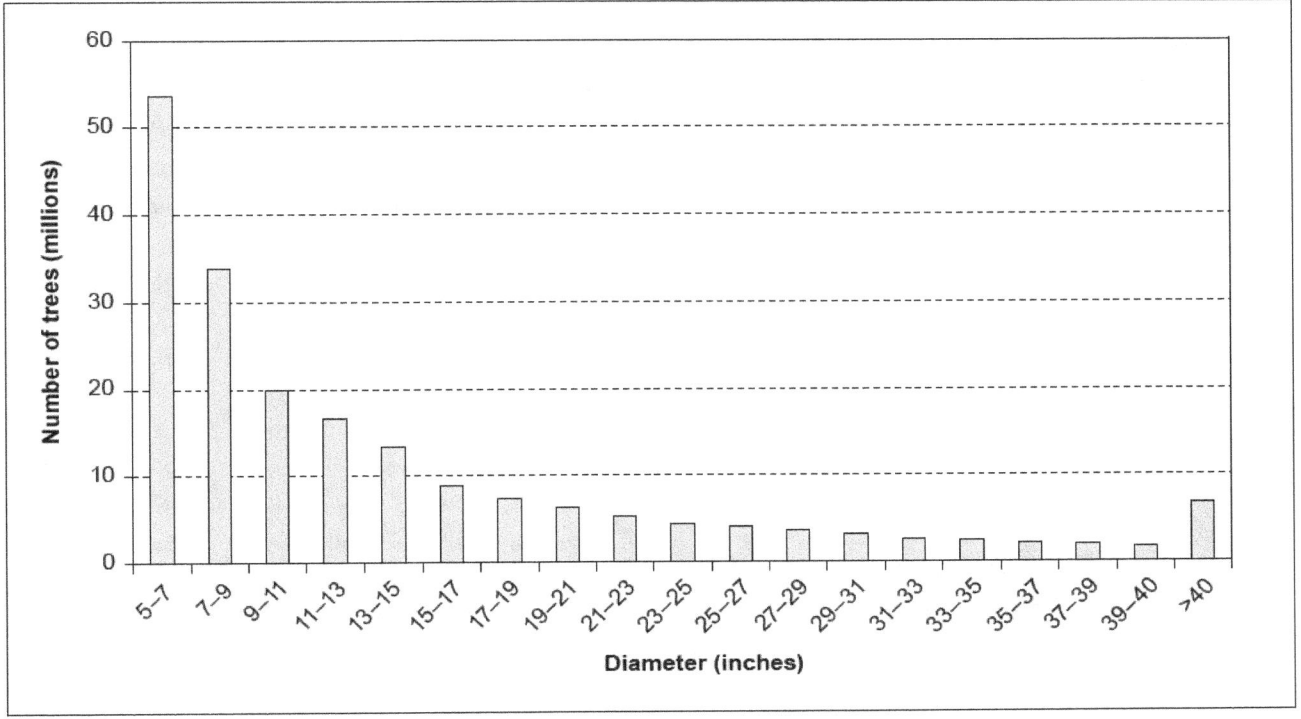

Figure 38—Number of trees by diameter class in older (>160 years old) California mixed-conifer forests on forest land in California, 2001–2005.

Recent work has helped spatially refine estimates for old growth in northwestern California national forests (Beardsley and Warbington 1996) and the Sierra Nevada (Beardsley et al. 1999). For the Klamath, Mendocino, Shasta-Trinity, and Six Rivers national forests, Beardsley and Warbington estimated that approximately 390,000 acres were covered by "pristine" old growth. Using the 2001–2005 FIA data and our simplified definition of older forest, we estimated that approximately 381,000 acres within these national forests have stand ages in excess of 160 years.

Interpretation

Prior to the widespread logging of old forests (before the mid-1800s), these forests had been changing through time from disturbances such as fire and insect outbreaks of varying severity, recurrence intervals, and disturbance synchrony across the landscape (Winter et al. 2002). The amount of old-growth forest that existed at the time of Euro-American settlement is unknown. The 1932 Copeland Report (USDA Forest Service 1932) estimated the area of California old-growth forest to be about 12.7 million acres. Data compiled from older state resource reports (1933–45) estimated the old-growth area in California at approximately 9.5 million acres (Bolsinger and Waddell 1993). Our preliminary results suggest old-growth acreage is less than half the 1933–45 estimate. Additional data will add to the precision of our initial findings.

Dead Wood[2]

Background

Dead wood contributes to the structural complexity and biological diversity of forests throughout California (fig. 39). In this report, we define dead wood as snags (standing dead trees) and down wood (dead woody material on the forest floor) of various dimensions and stages of decay. The presence of dead wood in a forest is known to improve wildlife habitat, enhance soil fertility through nutrient cycling and moisture retention, add to fuel loads, provide substrates for fungi and invertebrates, and serve as a defining element in old-growth forests (Harmon et al. 1986, Laudenslayer et al. 2002, Rose et al. 2001). Because of this, the dead wood resource is often analyzed from a variety of perspectives— too much can be viewed as a fire hazard, whereas too little can be viewed as impairing habitat quality. The amount of dead wood in a forest differs with geographic location, habitat type, successional stage, species composition, and management activities (Harmon et al. 1986, Ohmann and Waddell 2002). Information on the amount of biomass and carbon stored in dead wood can help in evaluations of forest sustainability under criterion 5, defined in the Montreal Process (USDA Forest Service 1997), which recommends that biomass and carbon estimates be used to assess the forest contribution to global carbon cycles. In this report, we analyze data on snags and down wood collected by FIA crews on over 3,500 field plots in the state, and describe the resource in broad terms at the statewide level.

Dead trees with a diameter at breast height (d.b.h.) greater than 5 inches and leaning less than 45 degrees were tallied as snags and measured using the same protocol as live trees. Down wood was sampled along linear transects on each plot under protocols that differed by diameter size class. Information was collected on fine woody material (FWM; pieces of wood <3 inches in diameter at the point of intersection with the sample transect) and coarse woody material (CWM; branches and logs ≥3 inches in diameter at the point of intersection with the sample transect and at least 3 feet long). Dead trees leaning more than 45 degrees

---

[2] Author: Karen Waddell.

Figure 39—Snags (top) provide structural diversity in forest stands. Down wood (bottom) improves habitat and slope stability in many forests across the state.

were tallied as down wood. Estimates of density, volume, biomass, and carbon were developed from these data.

Findings[3]

Dead wood occurs in every forest type that was sampled in California. We estimated 537 million tons of biomass, almost two-thirds of which occurs as down wood (CWM and FWM). At 36 billion cubic feet, volume of snags and

CWM is almost a third of live-tree volume. About 97 million tons of carbon is sequestered in snags, whereas 178 million tons is stored in down wood (CWM = 117; FWM = 62). Statewide, we estimated there are about 5 billion down logs and 430 million snags. The North Coast survey unit had the highest mean density and biomass of dead wood per acre, but the North Interior had the largest diameter snags and logs. The redwood and alder/maple forest types had the heaviest accumulation of biomass on a per-acre basis.

Assessment of dead wood attributes is often more meaningful when comparing average per-acre estimates. Statewide, biomass of down wood (also known as fuel loading) averaged 10.5 tons per acre, varying by forest type and diameter class (fig. 40). The down wood component of the total fuel load (amount of potentially combustible material found in an area) by survey unit is shown below, displayed within the standard fuel hour-classes:

Survey unit	1-hour class	10-hour class	100-hour class	1,000-hour class	Total
		Mean tons/acre			
North Coast	0.3	1.3	4.0	12.2	17.8
North Interior	0.2	1.1	2.7	6.9	10.9
Sacramento	0.2	0.8	2.6	6.4	10.0
Central Coast	0.2	0.9	2.5	2.9	6.5
Southern	0.1	0.6	1.9	5.3	7.9
Total	0.2	0.9	2.6	6.8	10.5

The range in classes from 1 to 1000 hours corresponds to the diameter of down wood pieces as follows: 1-hour (0.1 to 0.24 inches), 10-hour (0.25 to 0.99 inches), 100-hour (1.0 to 2.9 inches), and 1,000-hour (≥3 inches). Each class refers to how fast dead woody material will burn relative to its moisture content. The heaviest fuel loads are in the North Coast and North Interior survey units, with a mean of 17.8 and 10.9 tons per acre, respectively. Flash fuels (1-hour class) have similar loads across survey units, wheras the larger fuels (1,000-hour class) are more variable.

The dimensions of down logs and snags are important when evaluating ecological characteristics of the forest. Of the heavy accumulation of biomass in the redwood and

---

[3] In this report, all references to weight are in bone-dry tons.

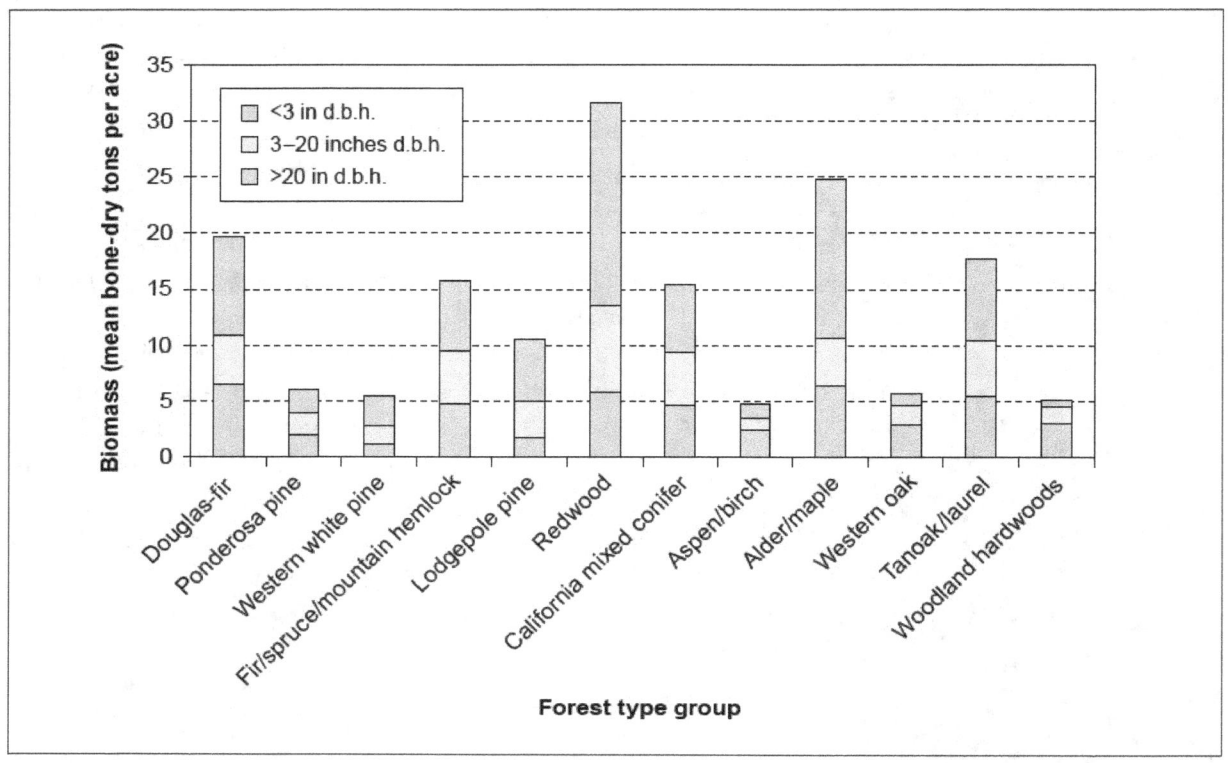

Figure 40—Mean biomass of down wood by forest type and diameter class on forest land in California, 2001–2005.

alder/maple forest types, over 50 percent was contained in large-diameter logs (≥20 inches). Although large logs contain the greatest mean volume and biomass per acre statewide, they are significantly fewer in number than small logs (3 to 19 inches in diameter). We estimated an average of 7 large logs per acre and 144 small logs per acre.

Snags had a mean biomass of 6 tons per acre and a mean density of 13 snags per acre across the state. Almost 88 percent of the snag density was in snags <20 inches d.b.h., with just 0.2 snags per acre in the very large class (>40 inches d.b h.). Softwood forest types had the most biomass and the largest proportion of large-diameter (>20 inches d.b.h.) snags (fig. 41).

Although the total amount of dead wood present in a forest fluctuates over time, the mean density of large-diameter (≥ 20 inches) snags and down logs generally increases with stand age (fig. 42), as shown below:

Stand age in years	Snags		Down wood	
	Diameter classes			
	5 to 19 in	≥ 20 in	3 to 19 in	≥ 20 in
	Mean trees/acre		Mean logs/acre	
1 to 50	10.4	0.9	155.0	8.0
51 to 100	11.5	1.2	148.1	5.1
101 to 150	13.4	2.4	164.7	8.0
151 to 200	13	3.6	170.6	11.6
201 to 250	6.5	3.4	121.0	9.7
251 to 300	7.4	2.9	152.8	11.4
300 plus	10.7	4.4	119.8	11.8
Total	11.4	1.7	143.0	6.4

Large snags ranged from a mean of 0.9 per acre in young stands to 4.4 per acre in stands older than 300 years. In contrast, young stands appear to start out with a higher level of large down wood, most likely remnants from a stand-initiating event such as a fire or harvest. Density of down wood differed by age class, rising and falling slightly over time and reaching a high of 11.8 logs per acre in very old stands.

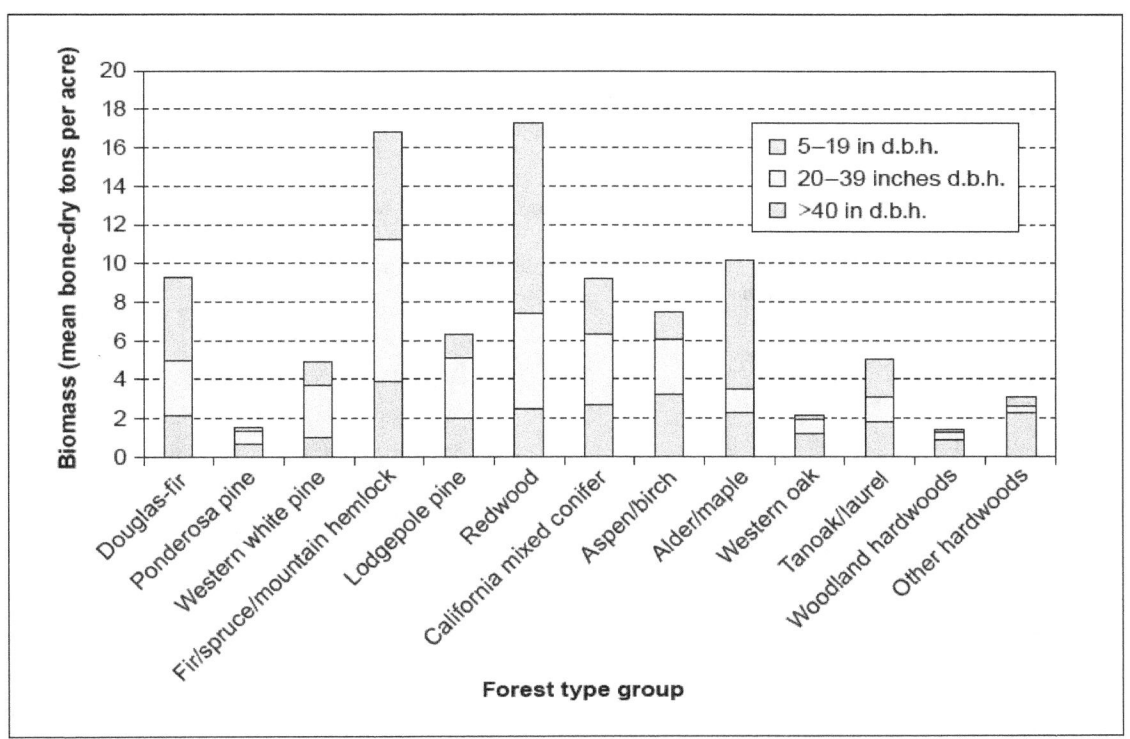

Figure 41—Mean biomass of snags by forest type and diameter class on forest land in California, 2001–2005.

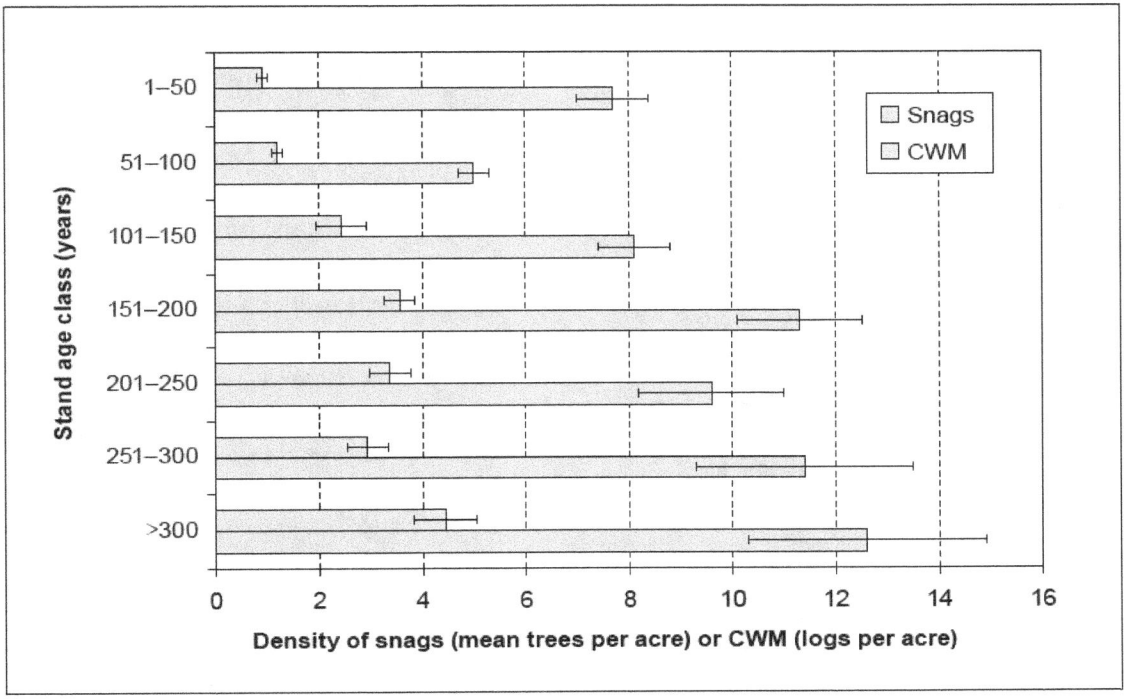

Figure 42—Mean density of down wood and snags by stand age class for large-diameter (> 20 inches) logs or snags on forest land in California, 2001–2005; CWM = coarse woody material.

Interpretation

Dead wood accumulates in different patterns across the wide variety of forest types in California. Many factors influence the size, abundance, and decay stage of dead wood, creating a mosaic of habitats and a range of potential fire behaviors across the landscape. The heavy fuel load observed in the North Coast survey unit is likely due to the greater live-tree biomass and volume accumulations that occur because of the mild, wet climate. Also, trees tend to be larger there, contributing more branches and logs to the fuel structure. Although the North Coast has higher fuel loads than all other survey units, it may not pose a higher fire risk because precipitation and fog are more common in these counties. However, land managers may find it prudent to monitor both of the northern survey units to evaluate these areas as possible sites for fuel reduction.

In general, wildlife species that use dead wood for nesting, roosting, and foraging prefer larger diameter down logs and snags. We tallied dead wood in various size classes throughout California and the estimated density of large snags may not be sufficient for some wildlife species. For example, every survey unit averaged fewer than two large snags ≥20 inches d.b.h. per acre, while smaller snags averaged 6 to 14 per acre in the same areas. Wildlife species favoring even larger snags (≥40 inches d.b h.) would find only 0.1 to 0.5 per acre in this size class across the state, indicating that large dead wood appears to be uncommon in California habitats. This may signal the need for a more indepth analysis of these important habitat elements, in terms of size class distributions needed by individual wildlife species in different areas of the state. Various types of disturbance can radically change the habitat quality of a forest by shifting the balance of live and dead trees or FWM and CWM. Biologists and land managers may find it advisable to monitor these changes to determine whether the density and size distribution of dead wood are adequate for the wildlife species being managed.

Understanding the amount of biomass and carbon stored in dead wood will also allow us to address criterion 5 described in the Montreal Process, regarding global carbon cycles. The FIA databases contain a substantial amount of information about dead wood, including estimates of density, biomass, volume, and carbon for all dead wood components. These data could be used for a more comprehensive analysis of this resource.

Dead wood tables in appendix 2—

- Table 25—Estimated average biomass, volume, and density of down wood on forest land, by forest type group and diameter class, California, 2001–2005
- Table 26—Estimated biomass and carbon mass of down wood on forest land, by forest type group and owner group, California, 2001–2005
- Table 27—Estimated average biomass, volume, and density of snags on forest land, by forest type group and diameter class, California, 2001–2005
- Table 28—Estimated biomass and carbon mass of snags on forest land, by forest type group and owner group, California, 2001–2005

Hardwoods[4]

Background

Forests of hardwood types make up an estimated 40 percent of forest land in California, and hardwood trees compose an estimated 27 percent of total tree biomass. Most of the hardwood forest in California is oak woodland with widely spaced oaks and a shrub or grass understory. Oaks have been used by native people in California for thousands of years, providing food from acorns and material for baskets, medicines, and dye, as well as sustaining a variety of game animals. Today California residents highly value oak woodlands for their aesthetic beauty, watershed protection, wildlife habitat, grazing opportunities, and a diverse array of forest products. California oaks include a number of endemic species, such as blue oak (see "Scientific and Common Plant Names"), valley oak, and Engelmann oak, and serve to enrich the biodiversity of California wildlands.

---

[4] Author: Tara Barrett.

Findings

Forest conversion and oak mortality—

Oak woodlands occur primarily in the foothills, with changes in forest type occurring over a gradient from dry low-elevation sites to higher, more productive areas bordering timberlands (fig. 43). Because of proximity to areas with grazing operations and ongoing development, most conversion of forest land in California occurs in oak woodlands rather than timberlands. Between 1945 and 1975, clearing of oak woodland for rangeland averaged about 32,000 acres per year (Bolsinger 1988). The rate of clearing for rangeland has dropped substantially, but conversion of oak woodland to housing, roads, and other developed uses has since increased. Between 1991–94 and 2001–05, about 2 percent (confidence interval: 0.7 to 4.8 percent) of revisited FIA oak woodland plots were converted to developed land, amounting to approximately 18,000 acres per year. This estimate is derived from 238 plots, of which 4 were converted to urban conditions and 1 to a vineyard. Estimates do not include conversion of oak savanna (wildland with scattered oak trees and less than 10 percent canopy cover) or the fragmentation of oak woodlands by development.

Another factor in sustainability of oak woodlands is harvesting for firewood or other purposes. Only a small proportion of oaks that are harvested in California are used for timber products (Waddell and Barrett 2005). As shown in the tabulation below, 25 percent of oak forest in California shows evidence of past cutting of trees, such as the presence of old stumps. California black oak forest has the most frequent evidence of such cutting.

By contrast, presence of stumps was recorded in 50 percent of conifer forest in California. The most recent assessment of change in California oak woodlands (1981–84 to 1991–94) found that growth exceeded mortality for most oak species, perhaps owing in part to active fire suppression throughout the range of California oaks.

Oak regeneration—

Oaks generally occur in the more xeric (dry) forest lands in the state, and so tree density is low for many oak types. Statewide, more than half the area of valley oak and blue oak forest has a density of less than 50 trees per acre, as compared to about one-third of interior live oak and coast live oak forests, and one-fourth of California black oak and California white oak forests (fig. 44). For more than a century, observers have noticed sparse regeneration in many oak forest types (fig. 45), contributing to the perception that recruitment is insufficient for sustainable populations of several oak species, including blue oaks and valley oaks.

Since the 1970s, dozens of papers have been published about seedling establishment and the survival of oaks in California. We know that, in general, oak regeneration is negatively affected by plant competition, herbivory, grazing, and drought. Oak regeneration appears to be good in some areas and poor in others (Tyler et al. 2006), but we do not have a clear picture of sustainability statewide. Projecting future trends is complicated by limited information on growth and mortality of seedlings and saplings as well as uncertainty about future climate.

Forest type	Total forest area		Forest area with stumps		
	Area	SE	Area	SE	Portion of total forest area
	Acres		*Acres*		*Percent*
Blue oak/gray pine	2,939	163	608	80	21
California black oak	1,513	120	652	82	43
California white oak (valley oak)	278	54	79	29	28
Canyon live oak	2,450	148	599	78	24
Coast live oak	971	91	140	37	14
Interior live oak	1,004	103	186	46	19
Oregon white oak	613	77	132	38	22
Total	9,768	301	2,398	154	25

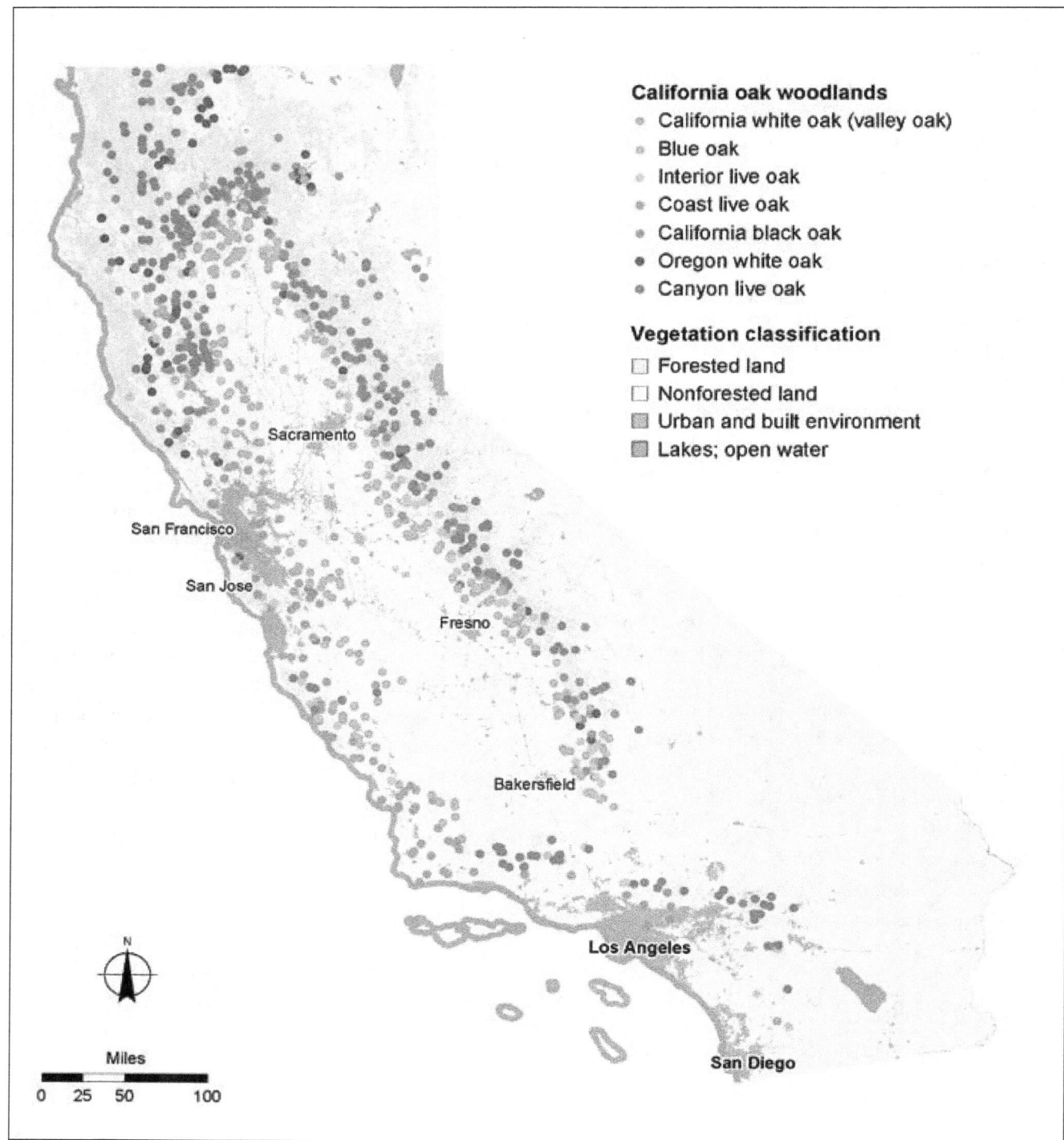

California oak woodlands
- California white oak (valley oak)
- Blue oak
- Interior live oak
- Coast live oak
- California black oak
- Oregon white oak
- Canyon live oak

Vegetation classification
- ☐ Forested land
- ☐ Nonforested land
- ▨ Urban and built environment
- ▨ Lakes; open water

Figure 43—Oak forest types on Forest Inventory and Analysis plots in California, 2001–2005 (forest/nonforest Geographic Information System (GIS) layer: Blackard et al. 2008, urban/water GIS layer: Homer et al. 2004).

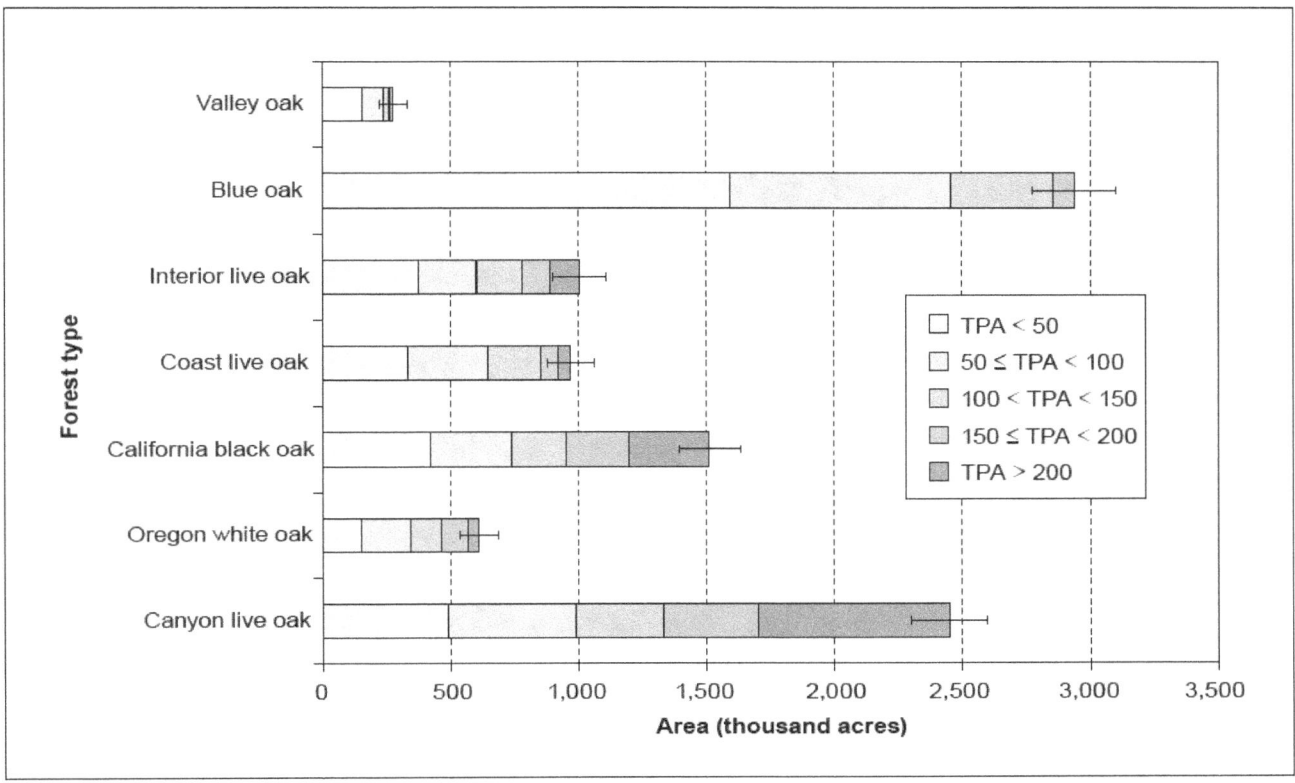

Figure 44—Area of oak forest types by density class on forest land in California, 2001–2005; TPA = trees per acre.

Figure 45—Many oak woodlands in California have few seedlings or saplings present.

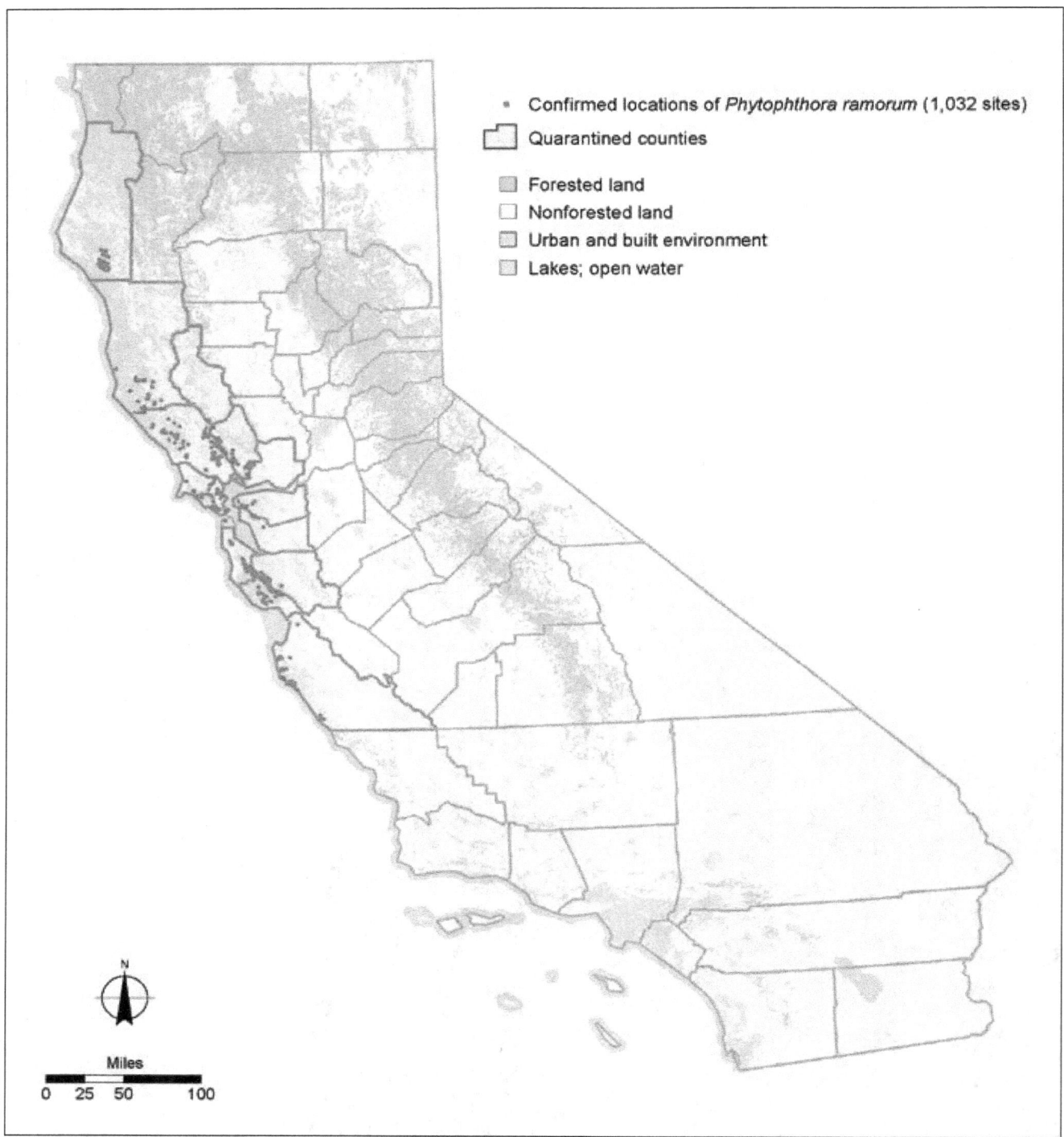

Figure 46—Confirmed locations of *Phytophthora ramorum* (California Oak Mortality Task Force 2006) and quarantined counties in California (APHIS 2007; forest/nonforest geographic information system (GIS) layer: Blackard et al. 2008; urban/water GIS layer: Homer et al. 2004).

Sudden Oak Death[5]

Sudden oak death, a disease caused by the fungus *Phytophthora ramorum*, was first noticed in tanoaks in California in 1995. Most of the major tree species in coastal California are hosts for the disease, including Douglas-fir, coast redwood, coast live oak, canyon live oak, tanoak, California black oak, California bay laurel, bigleaf maple, Pacific madrone, and California buckeye. The pathogen has a large number of additional host species, including ornamentals such as rhododendron and camellia. The disease is having a substantial economic impact on the nursery industry of California.

As of February 2007, Marin, Santa Cruz, Sonoma, Napa, San Mateo, Monterey, Santa Clara, Mendocino, Solano, Alameda, Contra Costa, Humboldt, Lake, and San Francisco Counties were quarantined for the disease (fig. 46). The FIA inventories of unreserved land in these counties show a substantial increase from the 1970s to the 1990s in host species. The increase in numbers and biomass was particularly notable in tanoak, which, along with California bay laurel, has been linked to presence and spread of the disease.

Sudden oak death increases mortality of coast live oak, tanoak, and California black oak, all three of which are important components of coastal California ecosystems. Estimates from the 2001-05 inventory show 499,000 acres of coast live oak forest in the quarantined counties, constituting 22 percent of the region's oak forest. There are an estimated 836 million tanoak trees (excluding seedlings), making tanoak the most numerous species in the quarantined area. California black oak trees, an important source of acorns for wildlife, are less common, with an estimated 54 million trees and 332,000 acres in the California black oak forest type. In

the quarantined area, 78 percent of forest classified as coast live oak, tanoak, and California black oak forest is privately owned, and 7 percent is in reserved land such as state and national parks.

A 2001–05 special study of FIA plots with tanoak or bay laurel provided a rough estimate of more than 150,000 acres where the disease was present. The 2006 air survey by the Forest Health Survey program detected more than 21,000 acres of hardwood mortality in the affected counties; the current prognosis is that disease presence and tree mortality will continue to increase slowly. Control efforts are primarily aimed at preventing the spread of the disease to other parts of California and to other states and countries (fig. 47).

Figure 47—Currently, response to sudden oak death focuses on preventing spread of the disease to new areas. As a reminder for recreationists, signs like this can be found at trailheads throughout quarantined areas in coastal California.

---

[5] Author: Tara Barrett.

Interpretation

Conversion of oak woodland has a social impact disproportionate to the area on which it occurs because conversion usually happens in the high-visibility places where people live, work, and play. Since passage of the Oak Woodland Conservation Act in 2004, California counties have been required to include the conversion of oak woodlands in the environmental impact process specified by the California Environmental Quality Act. Consequently, there has been increased interest in oak conservation and mitigation strategies.

Tables with oak data in appendix 2—

- Table 4—Estimated area of forest land, by forest type group, ownership, and land status, California, 2001–2005
- Table 8—Estimated number of live trees on forest land, by species group and diameter class, California, 2001–2005
- Table 20—Estimated aboveground biomass of all live trees by diameter class and species group, California, 2001–2005

Tree Crowns, Soil, and Understory Vegetation[6]

Background

This chapter highlights three important FIA forest health indicators, tree crowns (the upper part of a tree including branches and leaves), soil, and understory vegetation. These are important structural components in all forest ecosystems. Each indicator can be applied to address a variety of monitoring questions. For example, the amount and vertical layering of different plant life forms (e.g., trees, shrubs, forbs, and grasses) are key determinants of wildlife habitat, fire behavior, erosion potential, and plant competition (MacArthur and MacArthur 1961, National Research Council 2000). Tree crown density, transparency, and dieback are indicators of tree vigor, impacts from disease or other stressors, and potential for mortality

(Randolph 2006). Soil structure and nutrient status contribute to the diversity and vigor of vegetation across California. Because soil development is a slow process (Jenny 1941), protection from erosion, compaction, and nutrient loss is crucial to sustaining forest products and ecosystem services.

The FIA crews visually estimated crown density, foliage transparency, and dieback on phase 3 plots across California. Crown density is the percentage of area within the outline of a full crown that contains branches, foliage, and reproductive structures when viewed from the side. Transparency is the percentage of the live foliated portion of the tree's crown through which skylight is visible. Crown dieback is the percentage of the foliated portion of a crown consisting of recent branch and twig mortality in the upper and outer portions of the crown (Randolph 2006).

Soils were also sampled on phase 3 plots for both physical and chemical properties (O'Neill et al. 2005). Crews recorded forest floor thickness, soil texture, and visual indicators of erosion and soil compaction (e.g., trails and ruts). Soil samples were analyzed for moisture content, percentage of coarse fragments, bulk density, carbon (C) and nitrogen (N) content, pH, and the amounts of extractable phosphorus (P), sulfur (S), manganese, iron, nickel, copper, zinc, cadmium, and lead, as well as the exchangeable levels of sodium, potassium, magnesium, calcium, and aluminum.

Crews sampled understory vegetation on each phase 2 FIA subplot on forest land. Total cover was estimated for the following four vegetation life forms: tree seedlings and saplings (<5 inches d.b h.), shrubs, forbs, and graminoids. Total cover of all four life forms was estimated, and also total cover of bare mineral soil.

A major benefit of the crowns, soils, and understory vegetation indicators will lie in tracking deviations from baseline conditions, meaning that the full functionality of these indicators cannot be fully realized with these first 5 years of data. Thus, the current status of each indicator is summarized only briefly below, to establish baselines for California's forests and to inform readers about the development of FIA forest health indicators.

---

[6] Authors: Glenn Christensen, Joseph Donnegan, and Andrew Gray.

Findings

Crown density ranged from 27 to 48 percent among species groups, with a mean of 38 percent. Mean foliage transparency was 20 percent and was greater for hardwoods than for softwoods (fig. 48). Recent crown dieback was detected for only 2.8 percent of the trees examined. Only four species groups had more than 5 percent of all trees with more than minimal (>10 percent) observed crown dieback: the western woodland softwood (14 percent, mostly pinyon pine), western woodland hardwood (14 percent, mostly mountain mahogany), cottonwood and aspen (10 percent), and oak (7 percent) groups.

Carbon and N in the top 7.9 inches of soil were positively correlated ($r^2 > 0.73$). Their abundance varied greatly across the state and was not significantly related to

elevation, latitude, or soil moisture (figs. 49 and 50). On the 31 plots where soils have been remeasured to date, organic C in the forest floor layer had slightly decreased between 2000 and 2005 (6.71 percent; t = 3.1, p < 0.05). Visual signs of soil compaction were evident on 36 percent of the plots in a variety of forests across California (fig. 51). The mean compacted proportion was 6 percent of plot area. Bulk density was not significantly related to the compaction on plots (logistic regression and chi-square test: p > 0.12), possibly owing to fine-scale heterogeneity and because bulk density is sampled off the plot (to minimize disturbance to the sampled area), whereas evidence of compacted trails, ruts, and compacted areas is visually assessed on the plot. Bare-soil cover was greatest in the drier areas east of mountain ranges, particularly the south-central portion of California.

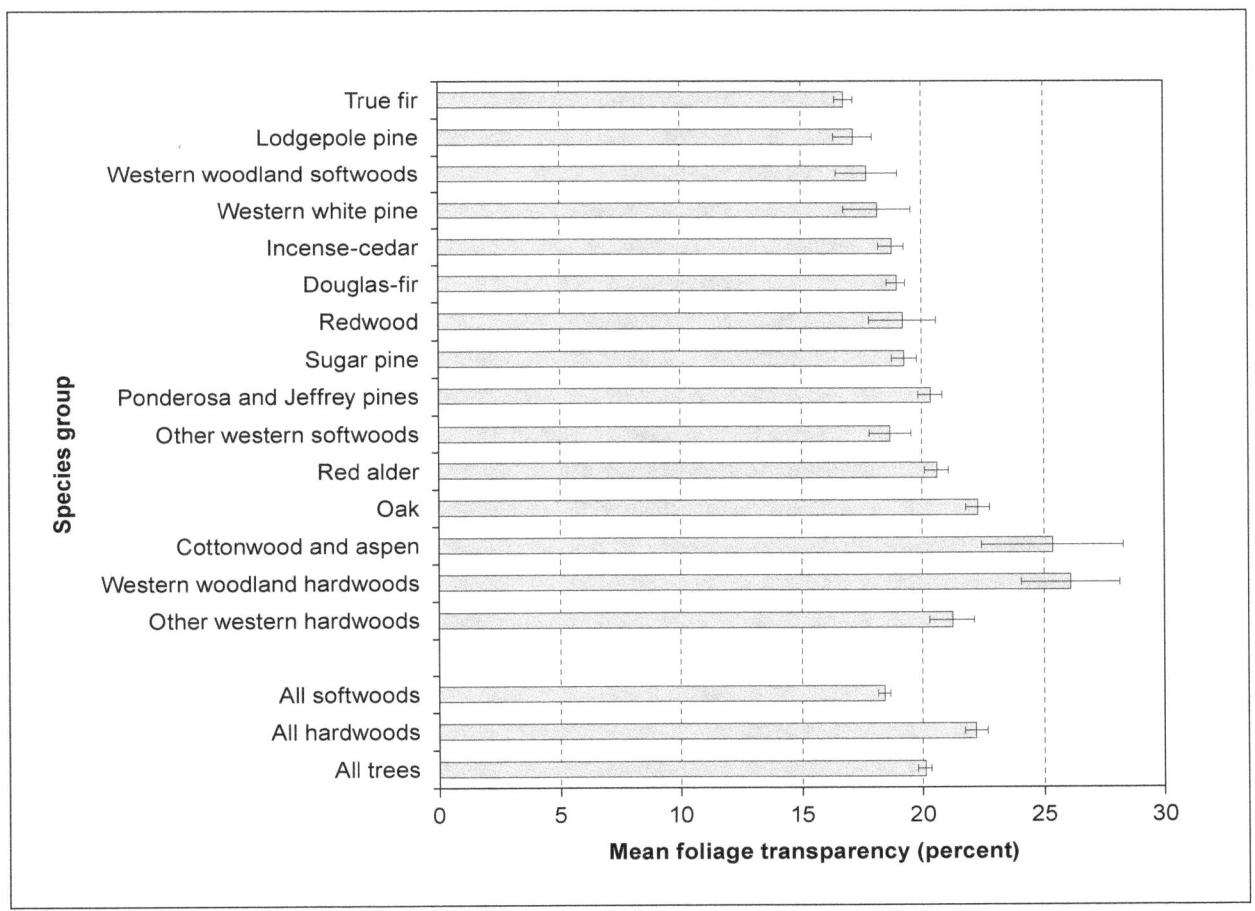

Figure 48—Mean foliage transparency by species group on forest land in California, 2001–2005.

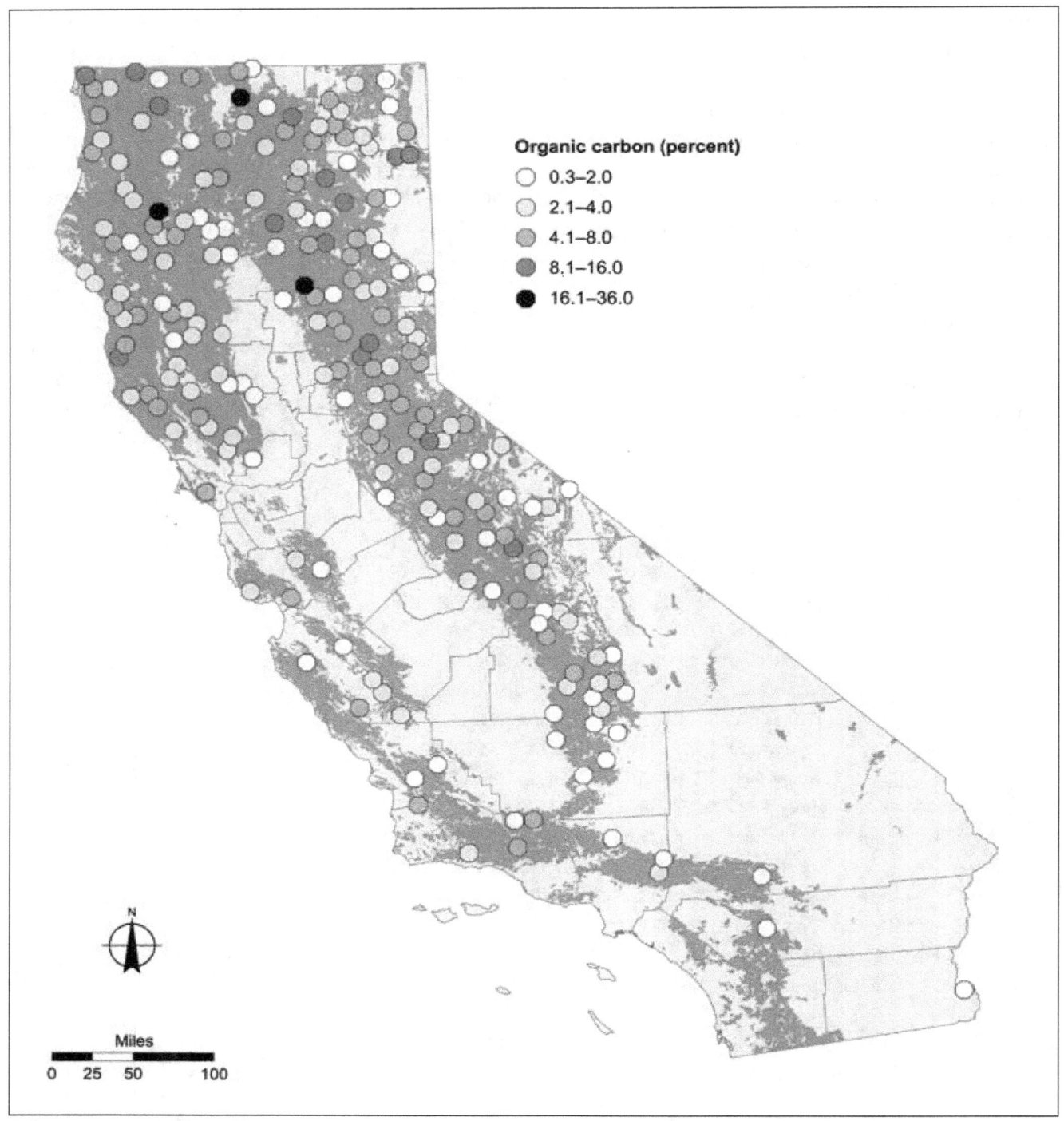

Figure 49—Soil carbon distribution on forest land in California, 2001–2005 (forest/nonforest geographic information system layer: Blackard et al. 2008).

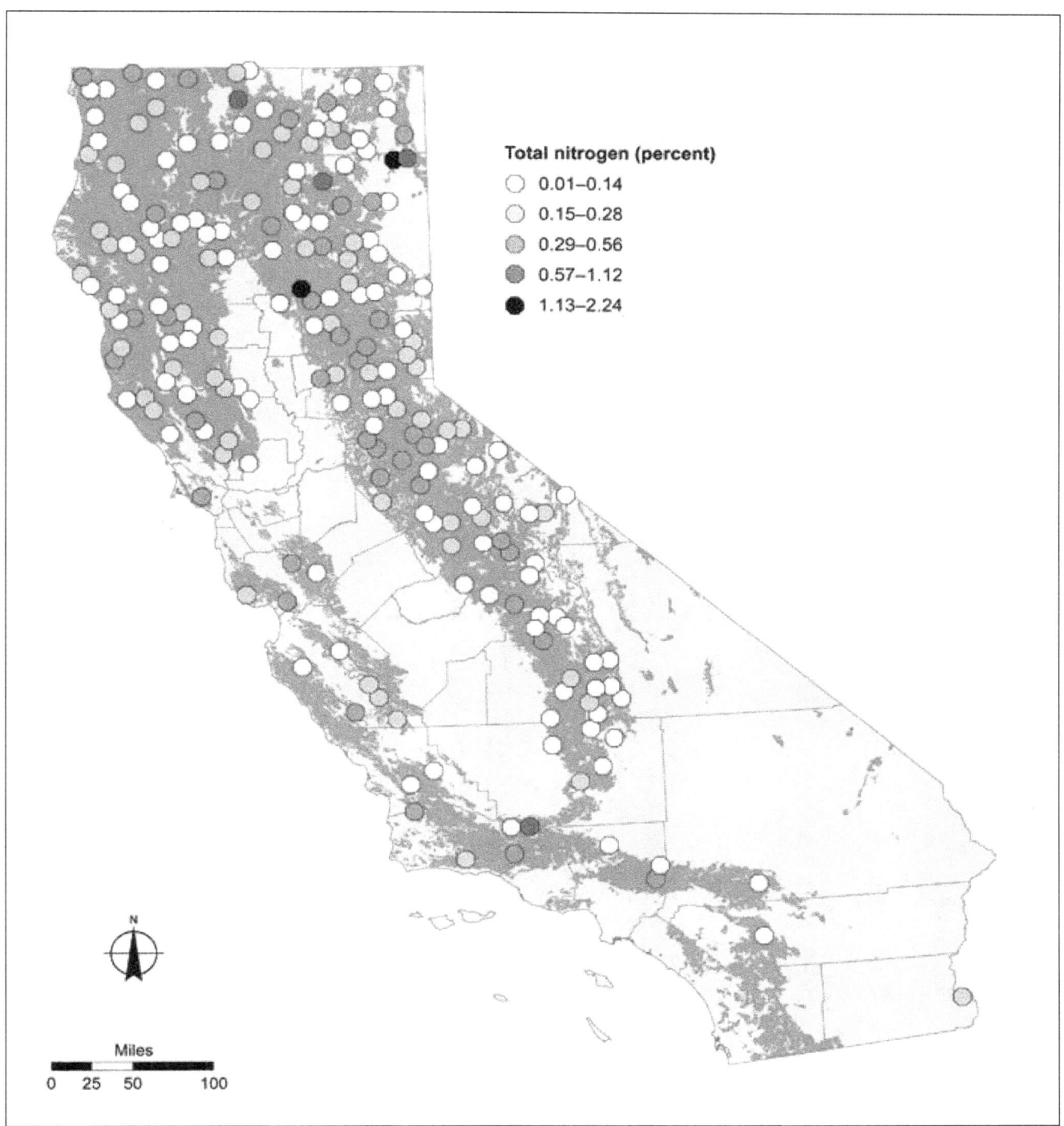

Figure 50—Soil nitrogen distribution on forest land in California, 2001–2005 (forest/nonforest geographic information system layer: Blackard et al. 2008).

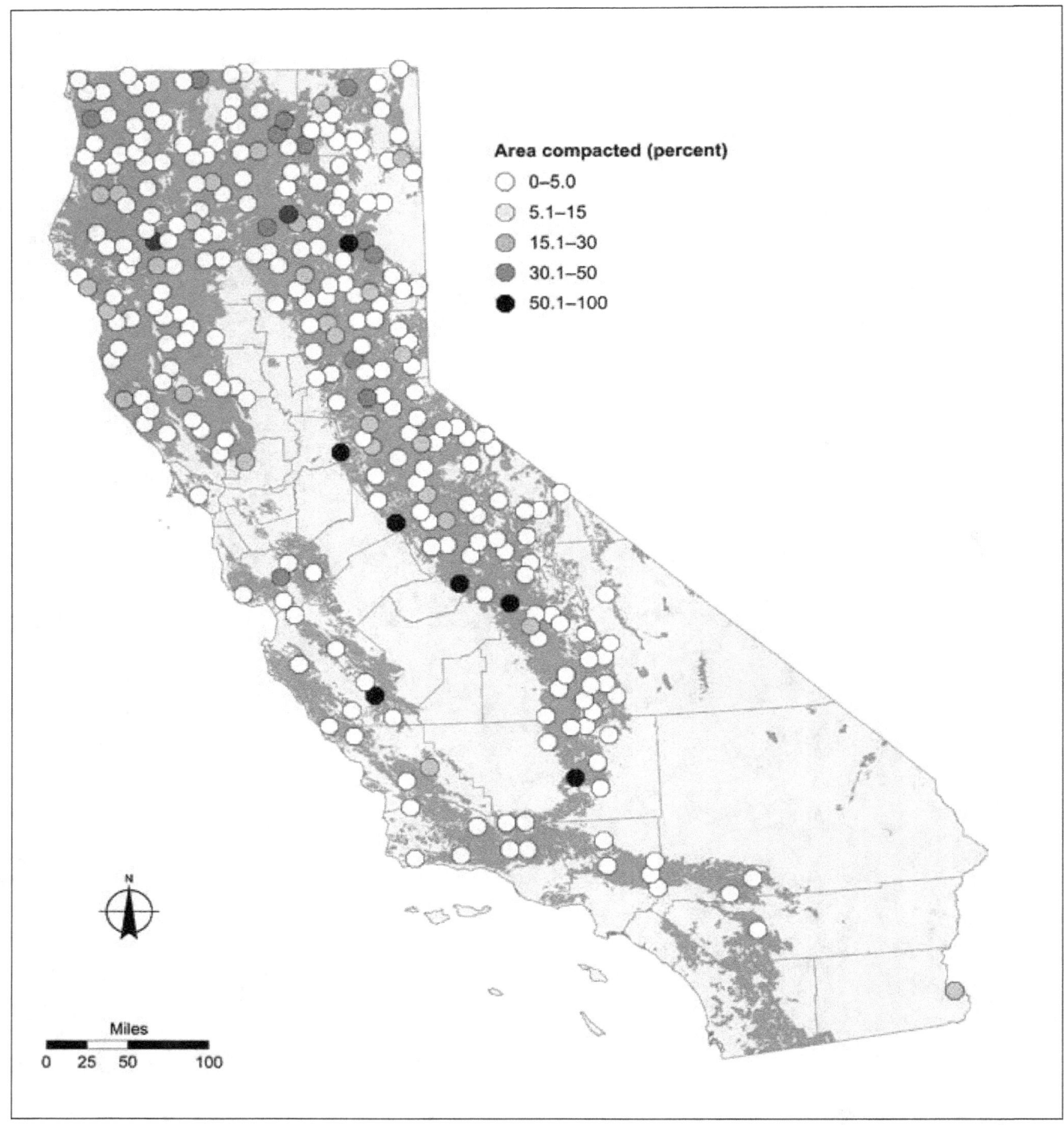

Figure 51—Evidence of soil compaction on forest land in California, 2001–2005 (forest/nonforest geographic information system layer: Blackard et al. 2008).

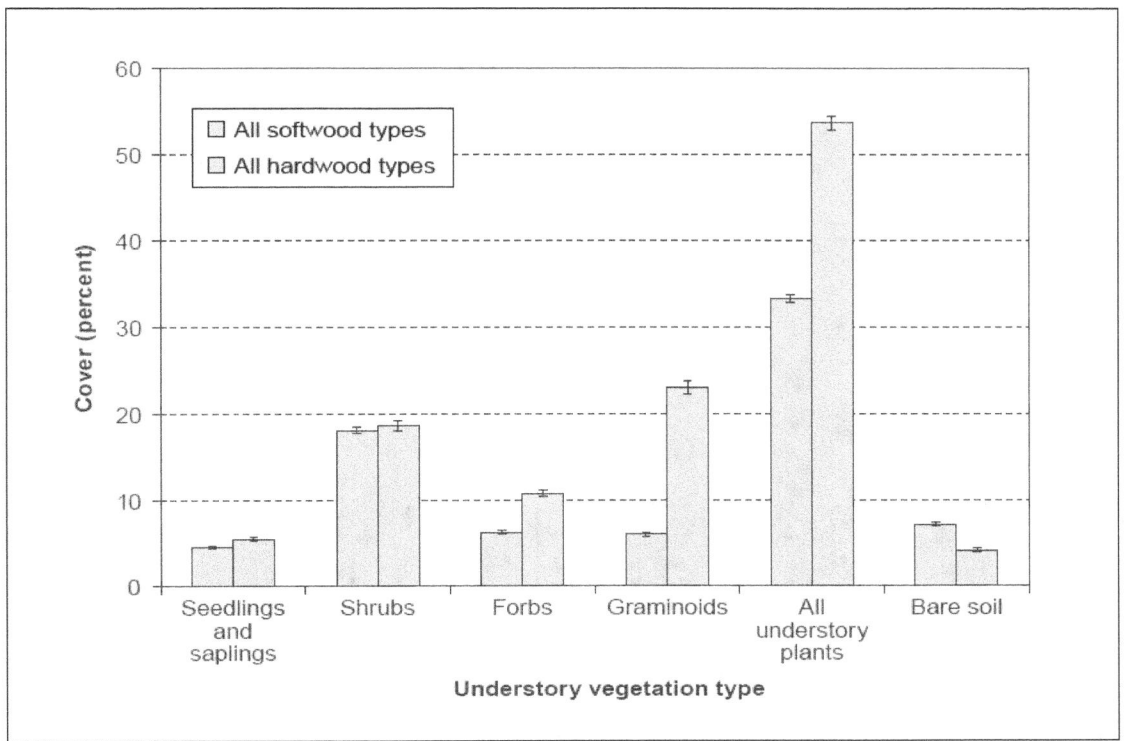

Figure 52—Cover of vegetation life forms and bare soil by softwood and hardwood forests on forest land in California, 2001–2005.

Cover of understory vegetation in California was greater in hardwood than in conifer forests (fig. 52). Within each type, shrub cover was highest in the higher moisture forest type groups (cottonwood/ash and hemlock), while graminoid cover was highest in the drier types (oak and the "other western softwoods" group). Forb cover was greatest in the hemlock and alder/maple groups (fig. 53). Understory cover was greater in stands 0 to 40 years old than in older stands (primarily due to differences in shrub cover), but cover differed little with stand age for stands over 40 years old (fig. 54).

On national forest land, the chaparral vegetation type covered 2 million acres in California's Southern and Central Coast survey units. Chamise was the most common type of chaparral, followed by the mixed and montane type (definitions follow Fried et al. 2004). These estimates differ from the estimates in Fried et al. 2004, which used an early 1990s chaparral inventory, probably because a greater range of shrub vegetation types were included in the analysis presented here and because the classification into chaparral types is highly sensitive to slight changes in abundance of a few species.

Figure 53—Dense understory cover of forbs and shrubs in a hemlock forest.

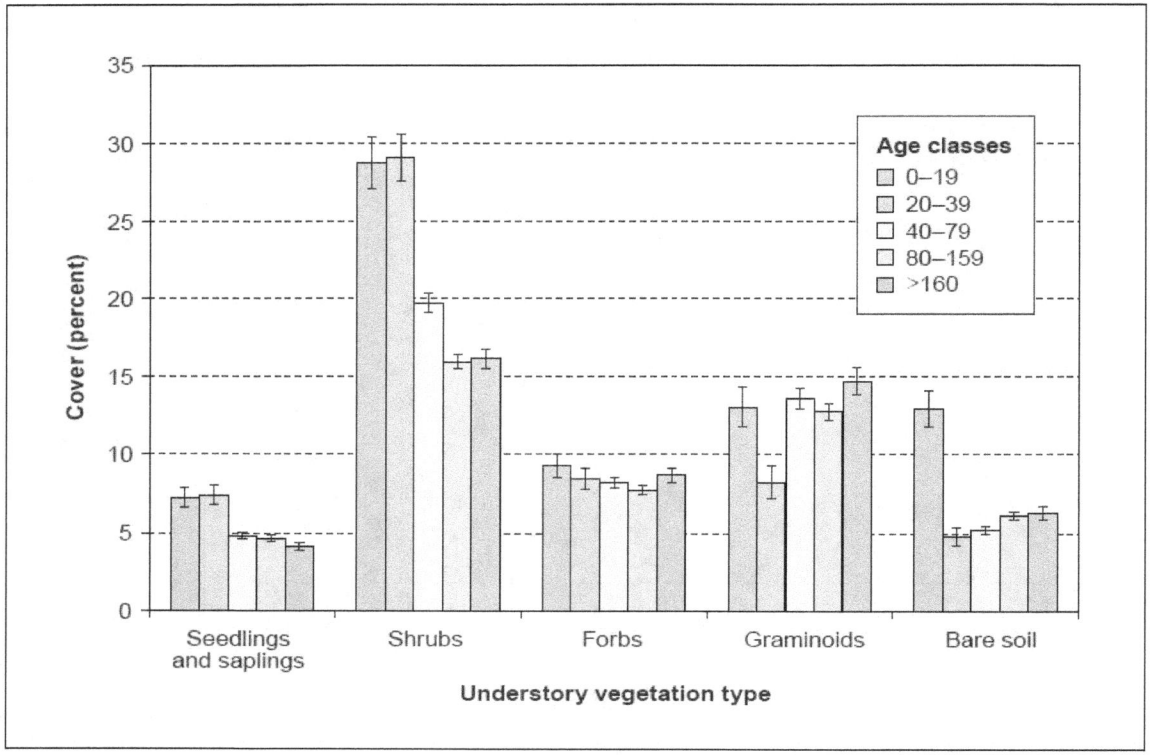

Figure 54—Cover of vegetation life forms and bare soil by forest age class on forest land in California, 2001–2005.

Area of chaparral by type on national forests in southern California is shown in the following tabulation:

Chaparral type	Area	SE
	Acres	
Chamise	821,400	68,000
Coastal transition	249,400	40,900
Mixed and montane	524,600	58,000
Mountain mahogany	136,800	30,900
Scrub oak	275,000	43,900
Total	2,007,100	77,200

Interpretation

Initial results suggest that crown decline is not widespread in California. Most dieback was found in dry forest types in the southeastern part of the state. Future remeasurements will provide more precise estimates of changes in crown health over time. The abundances of C and N were correlated but highly variable across the forests of California.

Soils high in organic C are generally associated with higher levels of microbial activity and key nutrients, including N, S, and P (Mengel et al. 2001). Soils in wet, cool environments tend to be high in organic C, although this pattern was not clear in the data collected to date. Soil compaction was widely dispersed in California's forests. Compaction, which can be caused by heavy machinery, repeated use of vehicles, and trampling by humans or livestock, can inhibit plant growth by decreasing soil pore space and can lead to increased erosion during high-precipitation events.

The amount and composition of understory vegetation differed greatly among the forest types and forest age classes of California. Although all life forms were represented in all forest types to some extent, their abundance appeared to differ according to forest type. Shrubs and graminoids appeared to be particularly sensitive to the overstory tree type (softwood or hardwood) as well as the moisture availability within different forest type groups. Although vegetation abundance differed with age class, the conventional wisdom that dense young forests have very low cover of understory plants does not appear to be prevalent across California.

Tree crowns, soils, and understory vegetation tables in appendix 2—

- Table 29—Mean cover of understory vegetation on forest land, by forest type group and life form, California, 2001–2005
- Table 30—Mean cover of understory vegetation on forest land, by forest type class, age class, and life-form, California, 2001–2005
- Table 31—Estimated mean crown density and other statistics for live trees on forest land, by species group, California, 2001–2005
- Table 32—Estimated mean foliage transparency and other statistics for live trees on forest land, by species group, California, 2001–2005
- Table 33—Estimated mean crown dieback and other statistics for all live trees on forest land, by species group, California, 2001–2005
- Table 34—Properties of the forest floor layer on forest land, by forest type, California, 2001, 2003–2005
- Table 35—Properties of the mineral soil layer on forest land, by depth of layer and forest type, California, 2001, 2003–2005
- Table 36—Chemical properties of mineral soil layers on forest land, by depth and forest type, California, 2001, 2003–2005
- Table 37—Chemical properties (trace elements) of forest floor and mineral soils on forest land, by forest type, California, 2001, 2003–2005
- Table 38—Compaction, bare soil, and slope properties of forest land, by forest type, California, 2001, 2003–2005

Jon Williams

Castle Dome and Mount Shasta.

Tom Iraci

Redwoods.

Tom Iraci

Mount San Gorgonio.

Chapter 4: Disturbance and Stressors

Major disturbance agents and stressors such as insects, diseases, invasive species, air pollution, and fire are among the most powerful agents shaping the structure, species composition, and ecological function of forests. We explore the influence of these agents through analysis of both plot data and predictive models.

Insects, Diseases, and Other Damaging Agents[1]

Background

Insects, diseases, and other damaging agents can have both detrimental and beneficial effects on forest ecosystems (fig. 55). The frequency and severity of damage to trees by biotic agents, such as insects and diseases, and abiotic agents, such as fire and weather, are influenced by a number of factors, ranging from forest structure and composition to management policies and activities. Effects include defoliation, decay, reduced growth, increased susceptibility to other stressors, and mortality. These impacts can affect ecosystem structure, composition, and function. Introduced insects and diseases such as white pine blister rust

(*Cronartium ribicola*) or sudden oak death (*Phytophthora ramorum*) can often have more rapid and intense impacts on ecosystems than native organisms.

The Pacific Northwest Research Station Forest Inventory and Analysis (FIA) Program collects data on damaging agents for each measured live tree and also maps root disease when present. These systematically collected FIA data complement localized ground surveys and the annual aerial survey conducted by the USDA Forest Service forest health protection (FHP) program, which maps occurrence of defoliation and mortality observed from the air. The FIA plot-based sampling protocol allows estimation of acres, trees per acre, basal area, and volumes affected by each agent to be summarized across forest types or large geographic areas. Information is most reliable for damage agents that are common and broadly distributed and least reliable for unevenly distributed, less common agents such as newly established nonnative organisms.

Findings

About 18 percent of live trees greater than 1 inch in diameter showed signs or symptoms of insects or diseases; damage by animals, weather, or fire; or physical defects

---

[1] Authors: Sally Campbell and Dave Azuma.

Figure 55—Fruiting body of stem decay fungus, *Laetiporus sulphureus.*

such as a dead or missing top or stem crack, check, fork, or crook. By comparison, in the Oregon inventory, 27 percent of trees were recorded as damaged. Of the two most common conifer species in California, 11 percent of Douglas-fir (see "Scientific and Common Plant Names") and 20 percent of white fir trees were damaged. Of the two most common hardwoods, 18 percent of canyon live oak and 10 percent

of tanoak trees were damaged. More than 18 million acres had over 25 percent of the basal area affected by one or more damaging agents (figs. 56 and 57). The volume of live trees greater than 5 inches in diameter with one or more damaging agents was almost 34 billion cubic feet—34 percent of total volume (figs. 56 and 57). The overall level of damage was somewhat higher in the San Joaquin, Central

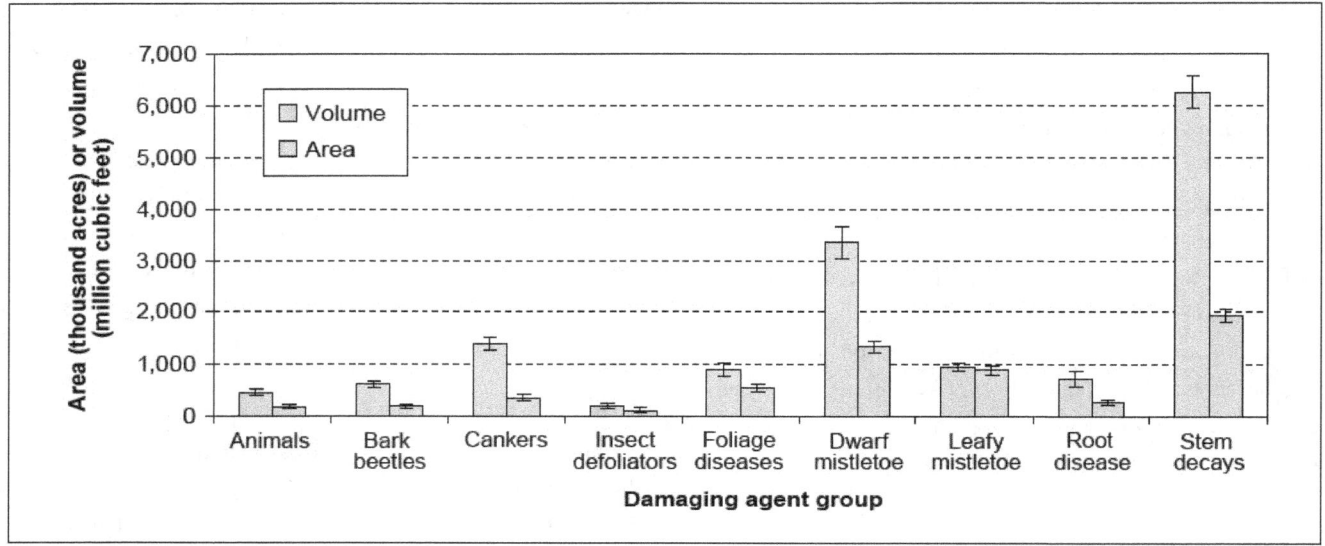

Figure 56—Area and volume of live trees affected by one or more biotic agents on forest land in California, 2001–2005; volume is gross volume of live trees ≥ 5 inches diameter at breast height.; acres are those with ≥ 25 percent of the basal area with damage.

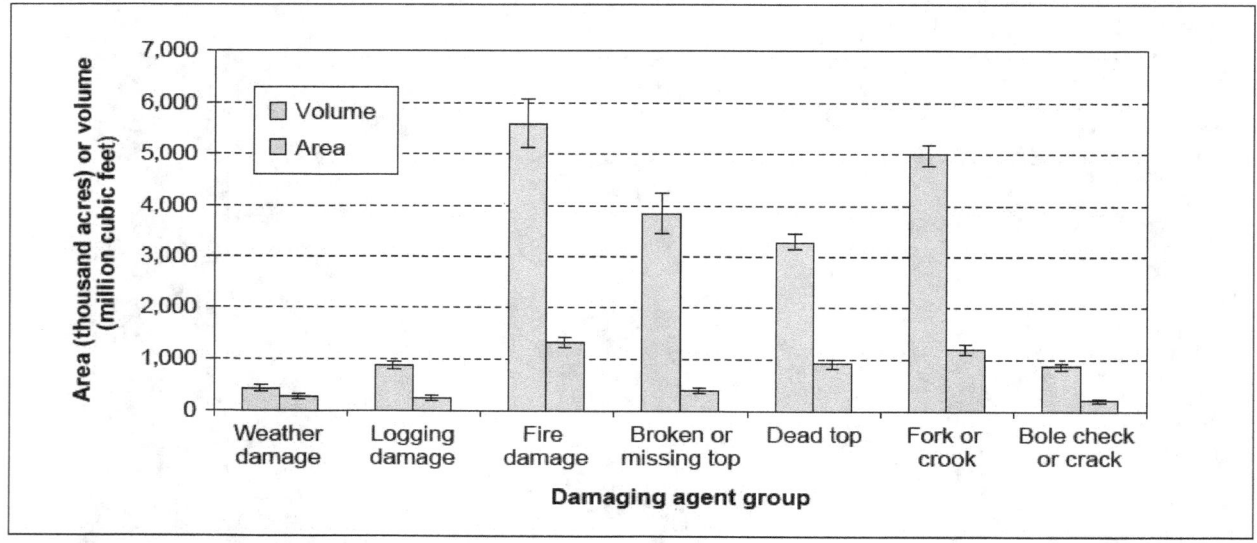

Figure 57—Area and volume of live trees affected by one or more abiotic agents on forest land in California, 2001–2005; volume is gross volume of live trees ≥ 5 inches diameter at breast height; acres are those with ≥ 25 percent of the basal area with damage.

Coast, and Southern survey units than in the others. The most prevalent types of damage, in terms of numbers of trees affected, were physical defects and damage caused by abiotic agents (fig. 57). Of the biotic agents, stem decays and dwarf mistletoes affected the highest volume and the most acres in California (figs. 56 and 58).

Interpretation

Some of the most common biotic (living) agents—stem decays and dwarf mistletoes—are generally more prevalent in unmanaged or older stands. If the current management trends on federal forests continue, we would expect to see increases in these agents on national forests and other federal lands; conversely, we would expect decreases or continued lower levels on private and nonfederal forests, where stands are younger and more intensively managed. The incidence and impact of many insects and diseases are closely tied to past forest management practices that have influenced forest structure and composition.

Some of the greatest threats to California's forests are from native organisms such as bark beetles, whose populations and impacts are increased by drought, high stand densities, and climate change. Recent bark beetle epidemics in southern California and British Columbia, Canada, are attributed to a number of these factors (British Columbia Ministry of Forests 2006, Pedersen 2003, USDA Forest Service 2005, Walker et al. 2006). Introduced insects and diseases also pose significant threats. The impact of an "old" introduced disease—white pine blister rust—on California's five-needle pines is well documented (Kliejunas and Adams 2003), whereas assessments of impacts from newer diseases such as sudden oak death are still underway (California Oak Mortality Task Force 2007). Introduced insects and diseases not yet discovered may also present large risks (Pimentel et al. 2005).

Although FIA under-records bark beetles, insect defoliators, and foliage diseases owing to a number of factors,[2] results of widespread bark beetle epidemics should be observable in future FIA tree mortality data. Annual aerial surveys can also provide excellent, timely information on insect- and disease-caused defoliation. Tracking the incidence of damaging agents over time will become particularly important as changes in climate and in human activities affect the structure and composition of California's forests.

Damaging agent tables in Appendix 2—
- Table 39—Estimated number of live trees with damage on forest land, by species and type of damage, California, 2001–2005
- Table 40—Estimated area of forest land with more than 25 percent of basal area damaged, by forest type and type of damage, California, 2001–2005
- Table 41—Estimated gross volume of live trees with damage on forest land, by species and type of damage, California, 2001–2005
- Table 42—Estimated number of live trees with damage, acres of forest land with greater than 25 percent of the basal area damaged, and gross volume of live trees with damage, by survey unit and ownership group, California, 2001–2005

---

[2] Bark beetles, insect defoliators, and foliage pathogens are likely under-recorded because FIA has difficulty in detecting symptoms of bark beetle attack on live trees prior to mortality, spatially and temporally heterogeneous defoliation events do not necessarily coincide with FIA plot visits, and some damage occurs on upper portions of trees in dense stands, making it hard to detect.

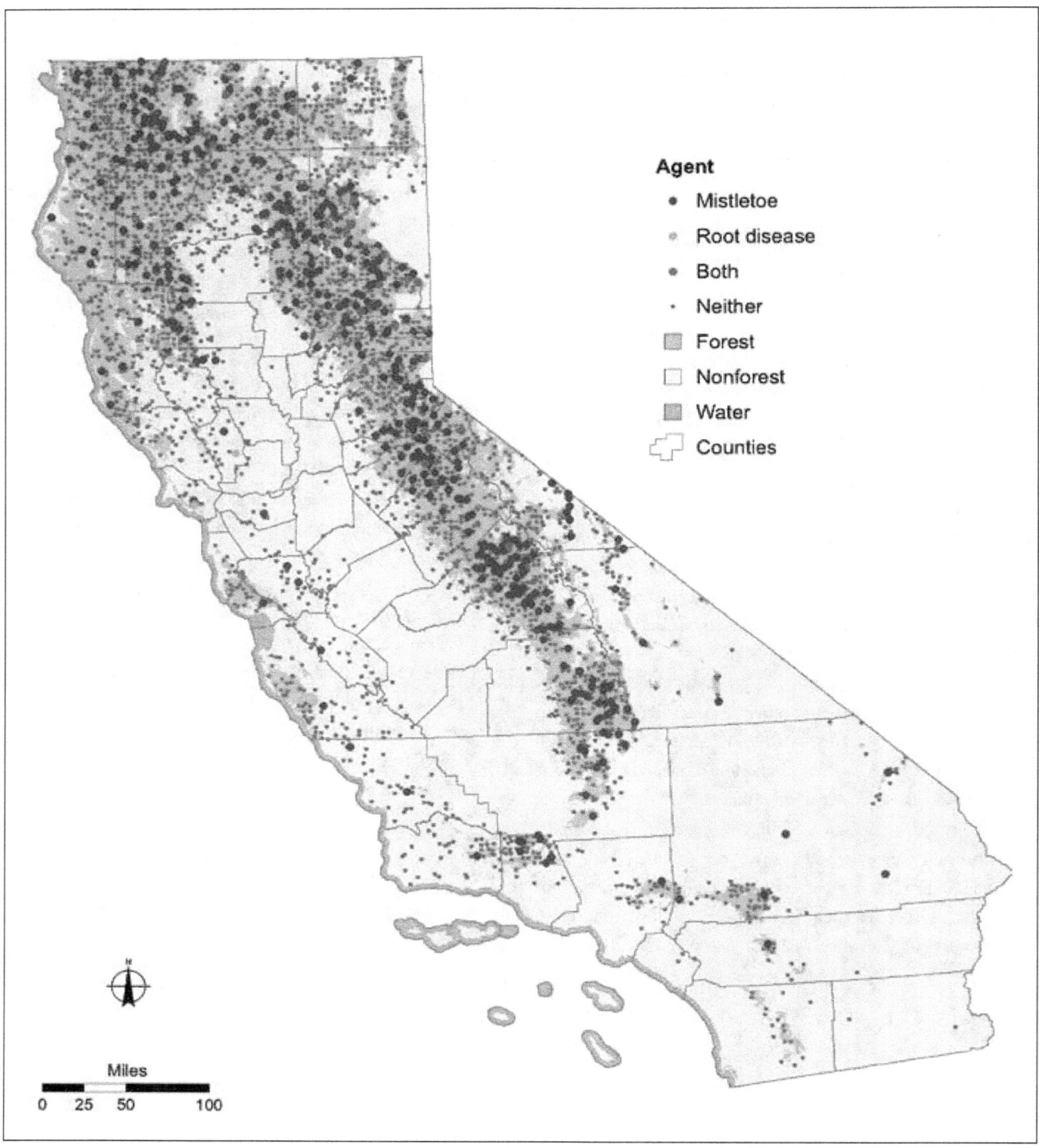

Figure 58—Root disease and dwarf mistletoe incidence on visited Forest Inventory and Analysis plots in California, 2001–2005 (forest/nonforest geographic information system layer: Blackard et al. 2008).

Insect-Related Conifer Mortality in Southern California[3]

Between 1998 and 2003, the mountainous areas of southern California (all or parts of the San Bernadino, San Jacinto, Palomar, and Cuyamaca/Laguna ranges) experienced below average precipitation and an extensive outbreak of insect activity that affected conifer stands in this region (fig. 59). The trees in these forests were already under stress from anthropogenic atmospheric agents (ozone, nitrogen oxides, etc.), and the additional stress of extended drought probably exacerbated the insect outbreak, consisting primarily of bark and engraver beetles. The outbreak manifested itself differently in different geographic regions—in the San Jacinto and San Bernadino ranges, the true fir forests were affected the most; in San Diego County, the pine types were most affected.

An estimated 3.5 million trees were killed. The overall mortality rate for conifers over this 5-year period was 13 percent, and the mortality rate for gray pine, bigcone Douglas-fir, and ponderosa pine exceeded 50 percent. Given the steady increase in residential development in the southern California mountain areas during the 20th century, elevated tree mortality poses increased safety risks to the region's inhabitants. The risk of dead trees falling on nearby homes, roads, and power lines was sufficiently alarming to motivate formation of three multiagency task forces: Mountain Area Safety Taskforce (MAST) in both San Bernardino and Riverside Counties, and Forest Area Safety Taskforce (FAST) in San Diego County, to facilitate rapid removal of dead trees. This response demonstrates the importance of preventive interaction among communities that have become, for practical purposes, cities, located in and near forests with dying trees.

The following tabulation shows the number of conifer trees greater than 5 inches diameter at breast height (d.b h.) that died between 1998 and 2003 on forest land in the counties of San Bernardino, Riverside, San Diego, and Los Angeles, by species (Walker et al. 2006):

Figure 59—Conifer mortality in southern California.

Jeff Mai

[3] Author: David Azuma.

Species	Live and dead	Dead	Dead
	Number of trees		*Percent*
Bigcone Douglas-fir	90,797	49,243	54
Coulter pine	840,473	375,546	45
Gray pine	4,167	4,167	100
Incense-cedar	1,920,557	2,835	0
Jeffrey pine	6,059,420	654,034	11
Limber pine	38,846	1,994	5
Lodgepole pine	702,573	11,139	2
Ponderosa pine	447,086	256,959	55
Singleleaf pinyon pine	6,811,831	495,879	7
Sugar pine	1,045,522	215,200	21
Western juniper	1,214,356	9,363	1
White fir	8,444,104	1,440,597	17
Total	27,619,532	3,506,955	13

Invasive Plants[4]

Background

Invasions of nonnative plants into new areas are having a large impact on the composition and function of natural and managed ecosystems. Invasive plants can directly affect the composition and function of ecosystems. They may also have a large economic impact, either by changing or degrading land use, or through the costs of eradication efforts, which cost the U.S. economy over $35 billion per year (Pimentel et al. 2005).

Nonnative plant invasions competitively exclude desired species, alter disturbance regimes, and are a primary cause of extinction of native species (D'Antonio and Vitousek 1992, Mooney and Hobbs 2000, Vitousek et al. 1996). Despite the importance of invasive plants, most emphasis is given to their local eradication, and so there is little comprehensive information about the extent and impact of nonnative invasions. There is little quantitative information about the magnitude of the problem, which plants are having the most impact, and where these plants are found.

The following summary relies on estimates of the most abundant species found on phase 2 plots. Crews estimated cover of the three plant species with the highest cover in each of three life forms—shrub, forb, and graminoid—as well as of any other species with ≥3 percent cover. Because phase 2 field seasons include several months when many species are not in bloom, and because plant identification skills differ, species were selected for analysis that were readily identifiable by most crews. Because the definition of "invasive" can be quite subjective, all readily identifiable species that were listed as nonnative to the United States

(USDA Natural Resources Conservation Service 2000) were selected for analysis. The proportion of plot area covered by each species was multiplied by the number of acres each plot represented in the inventory to estimate area covered.

Findings

The most common invasive plant found on phase 2 plots in California was cheatgrass, which covered 144,000 acres of forest land (fig. 60). Several other nonnative grasses were recorded frequently, including bristly dogstail grass (see "Scientific and Common Plant Names"), soft brome, and medusahead. Yellow star-thistle was the most abundant nonnative forb, covering 32,000 acres of forest land, and Himalayan blackberry was the most abundant nonnative shrub, covering 34,000 acres. The ecosections with the highest proportion of area covered by the selected nonnative species were in the foothills and interior Coast Ranges around the Great Valley (fig. 61).

Leslie J. Mehrhoff, University of Connecticut, Buwood. org

Figure 60—Cheatgrass is the most common invasive plant in forests of California.

---

[4] Author: Andrew Gray.

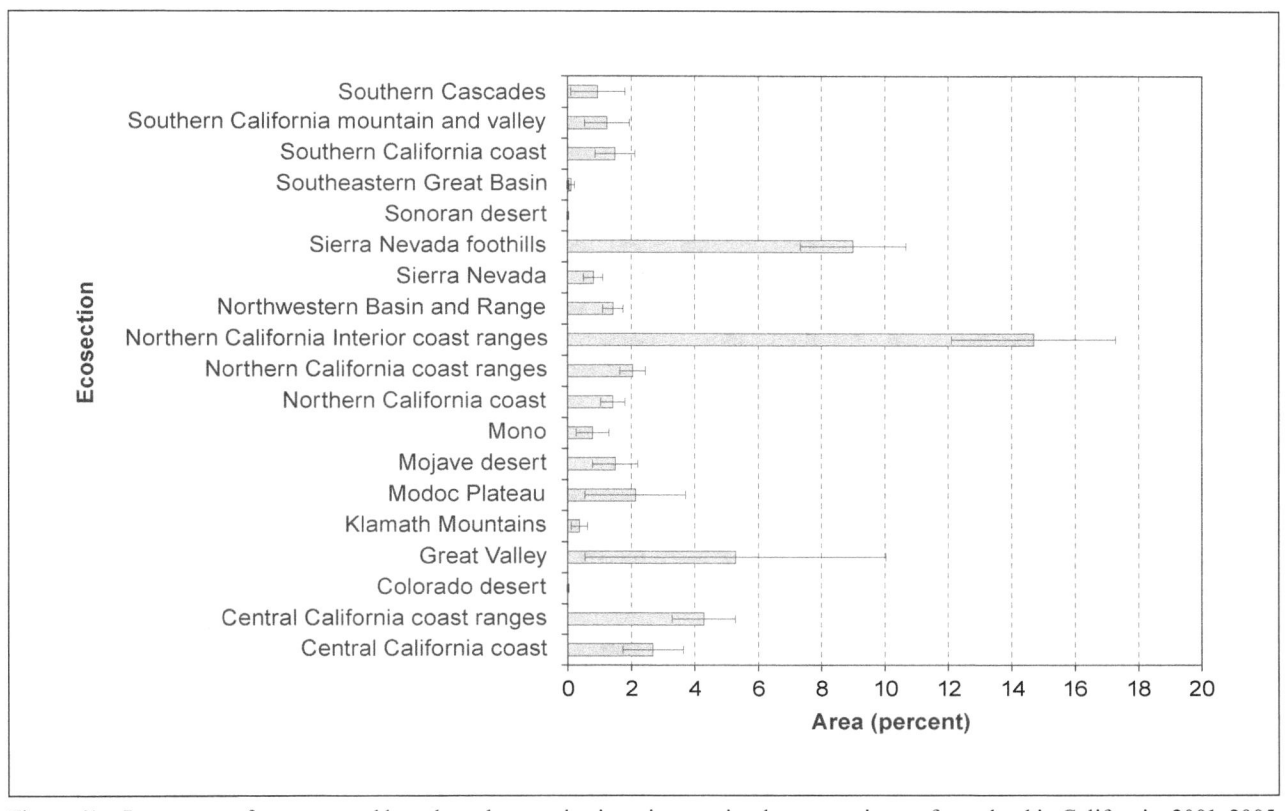

Figure 61—Percentage of area covered by selected nonnative invasive species, by ecosection on forest land in California, 2001–2005.

Interpretation

Nonnative invasive plant species appear to be well established in California's forested lands, with several species covering 50,000 acres or more. Current trends suggest that their importance will increase; for example, knotweed and false brome have high potential to expand their range in California (California Invasive Plant Council 2005). Many of the currently problematic invasive species are grasses or composites associated with relatively dry, open forest habitats.

This combination of sites and species makes the inventory of invasives challenging. The species can be difficult to identify with certainty, and their growing season (when they are most identifiable) is short. The FIA phase 3 vegetation indicator, based on sampling by botanists during the growing season, has yet to be implemented in California. If it were implemented, it could provide comprehensive information on species composition that could inform national indicators on the impacts of invasive plants (Gray and Azuma 2005, Heinz Center 2002). However, the Phase 3 plot density is too low to assess the distribution of most individual species. The FIA phase 2 sample does provide that comprehensive information for readily identifiable species, and potentially for other species if dedicated identification training were to be provided.

Invasive plants table in appendix 2—

- Table 43—Estimated area of forest land covered by selected nonnative vascular plant species, by life form and species, California, 2001–2005

Air Quality[5]

Background

Air quality is an ongoing concern for forest health in California, where population growth is expected to cause increased pollutant emissions from automobiles, industry, and agriculture. The effects of air pollution on vegetation and lichens are variable; common manifestations are visible injury to foliage; reduced growth; increased susceptibility to other stressors such as insects, disease, or drought; and premature mortality (Takemoto et al. 2001). As pollution-sensitive individuals are damaged or killed, ecosystem productivity, structure, and function are affected. Such changes can, for instance, adversely affect wildlife dependent on these species for food or habitat.

The FIA Program monitors injury to plants sensitive to ozone (O_3) and epiphytic (tree-dwelling) lichen communities to evaluate forest air quality. These bioindicators are a valuable supplement to preexisting air quality networks, which measure pollutants at a limited number of forested sites.

Ozone Injury Background

Ozone is highly phytotoxic and is considered a top ecological threat in California (U.S. Environmental Protection Agency 2006) (figs. 62 and 63). For the FIA O_3 indicator, foliar injury was scored on three or more O_3-susceptible plant species at each of 65 ozone plots (biosites). Injury data were combined into a biosite index that indicates local potential or risk for O_3 damage (Coulston et al. 2003). With geospatial interpolation[6] of biosite indices averaged over 6 years, we can predict relative risk to susceptible vegetation across a broader geographic area and identify O_3 problem areas where adverse effects to forest health are more likely. The FIA biosite network is the only statewide O_3 detection program that uses bioindicators to monitor O_3 impacts to forest vegetation.

---

[5] Authors: Sally Campbell and Sarah Jovan.

[6] Interpolation of gridded maps of the biosite index for each year 2000-2005 was done with gradient inverse distance weighting (GIDS). The GIDS technique combines multiple linear regression with inverse distance weighting interpolation, and, like other recently developed interpolation techniques, incorporates elevation as a covariate.

Dan Duriscoe

Figure 62—Ozone injury on blue elderberry causing interveinal necrosis.

Ozone Injury Findings

Ozone injury was consistently detected at many California biosites between 2000 and 2005, indicating site conditions conducive to plant susceptibility and tropospheric O_3 high enough to visibly damage sensitive plant species (fig. 64). Symptoms were detected on five species: ponderosa pine, Jeffrey pine, blue elderberry, mugwort, and skunkbush. Most biosites (83 percent) had a low biosite index, indicating a low risk of injury. About 10 percent had a high biosite index and thus a high risk of injury (fig. 65). More than 267,000 acres, representing 596 million cubic feet of wood volume, are at moderate to high risk, as estimated from the intersection of modeled biosite indices with FIA plot data (Campbell et al. 2007).

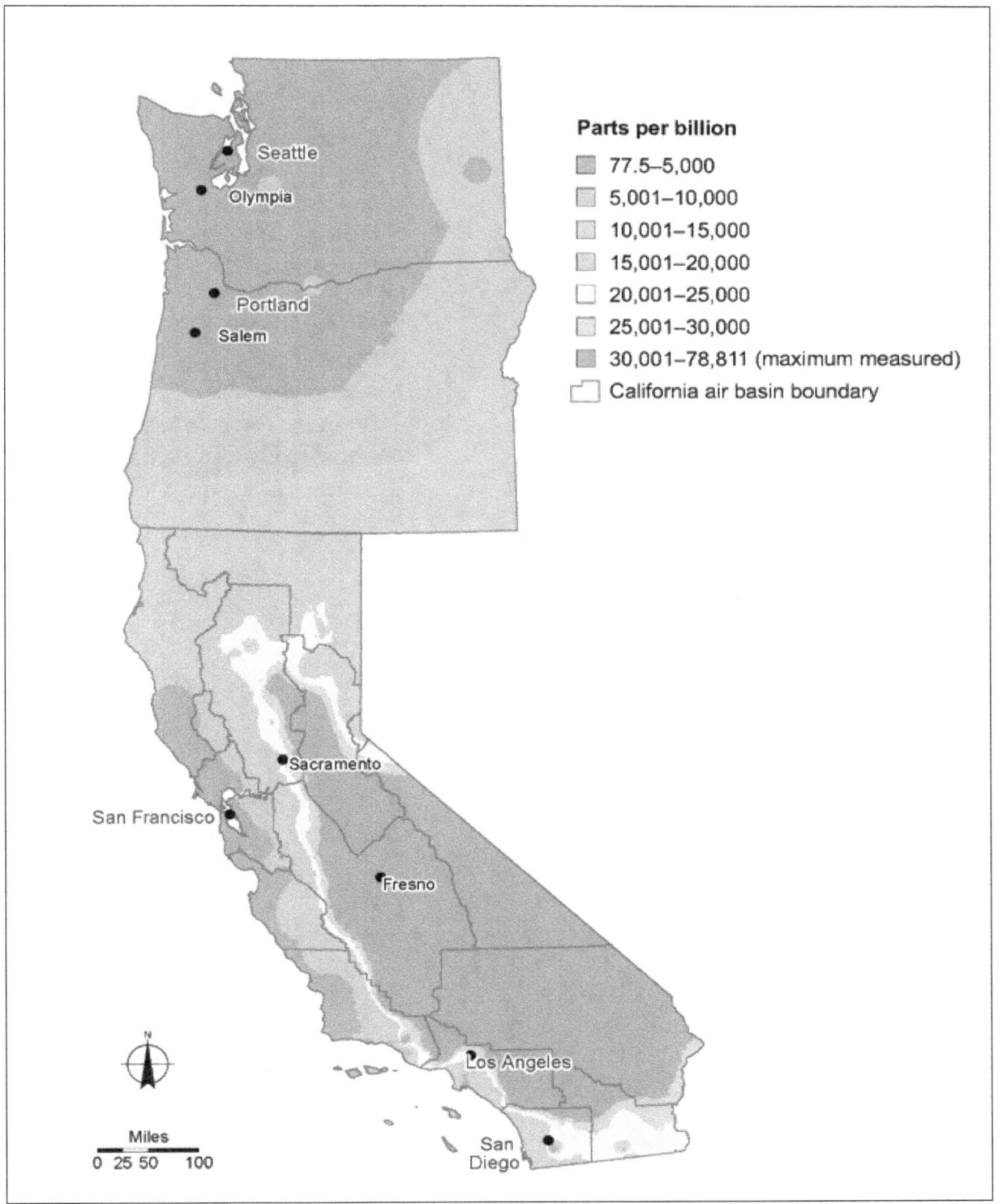

Figure 63—Average ozone exposure in Washington, Oregon, and California, based on cumulative hourly ozone concentrations exceeding 60 parts per billion (SUM60) June 1 to August 31, 8am to 8pm, 2001 to 2005 (SUM60 ozone data: U.S. Environmental Protection Agency 2006).

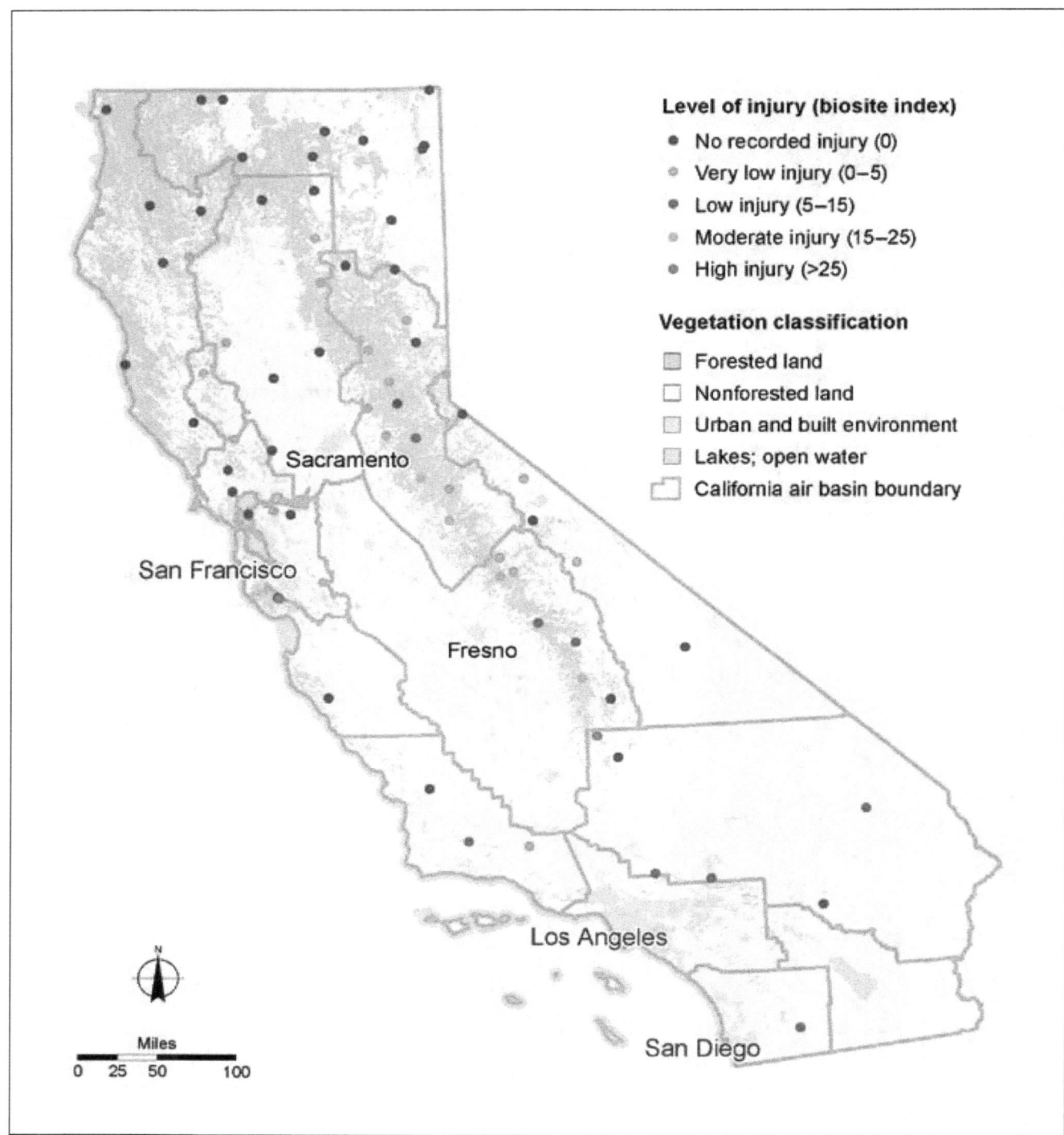

Level of injury (biosite index)

• No recorded injury (0)
◦ Very low injury (0–5)
• Low injury (5–15)
▫ Moderate injury (15–25)
• High injury (>25)

Vegetation classification

▢ Forested land
☐ Nonforested land
▨ Urban and built environment
▨ Lakes; open water
⌐ California air basin boundary

Sacramento

San Francisco

Fresno

Los Angeles

San Diego

N

Miles
0 25 50   100

Figure 64—Forest Inventory and Analysis ozone biosites and average level of injury (average biosite index) in California, 2000–2005 (forest/nonforest geographic information system (GIS) layer: Blackard et al. 2008, water/urban GIS layer: Homer et al. 2004).

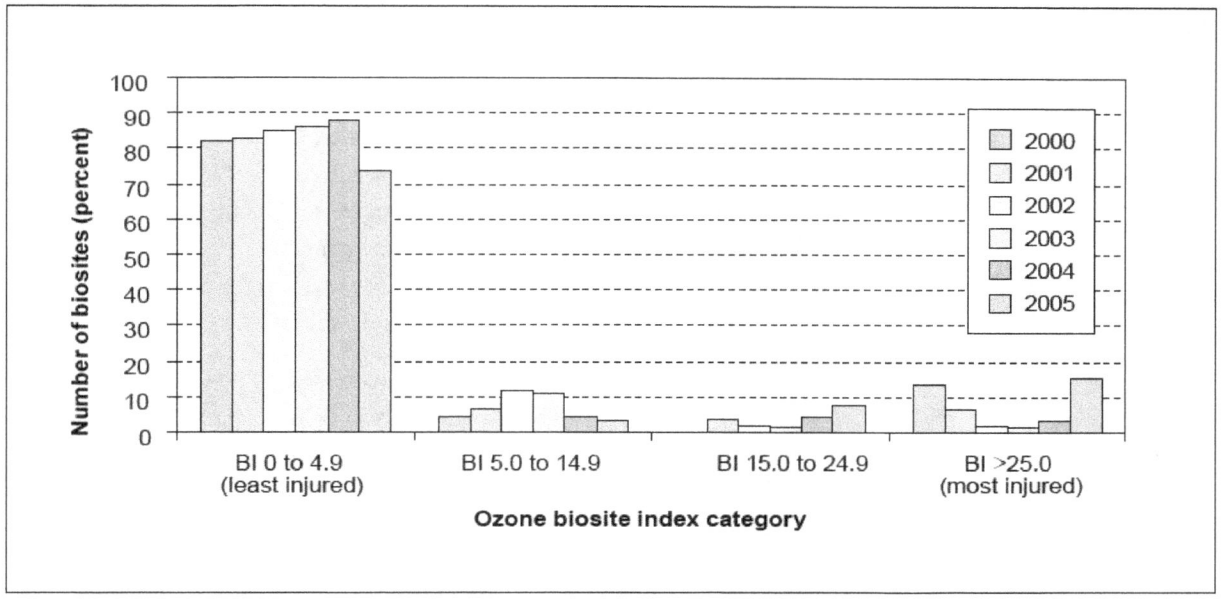

Figure 65—Percentage of ozone biosites by biosite index (BI) class in California, 2000–2005.

Ozone Injury Interpretation

The spatial distribution of FIA biosites with injured bioindicator plants is generally consistent with ambient O_3 monitoring data; regions of high O_3 exposure (fig. 63) tend to coincide with detection of foliar injury. However, there are some discrepancies between average exposure levels and detected injury, presumably because the ambient O_3 is higher than normal in some years and because of natural variability in environmental conditions conducive to O_3 uptake and injury. Ozone concentrations consistently exceed state and national standards in many of California's air basins (Cox et al. 2006) and, as demonstrated by our results, O_3 is injuring forest species in a number of locations in California. Efforts to abate vehicular and industrial emissions have been successful in reducing O_3 from past levels, but continued efforts will be needed as emissions increase with increasing population (Carroll et al. 2003). Annual reassessment of bioindicators on the FIA biosite network will allow statewide tracking of temporal and geographic fluctuations in O_3 injury.

Lichen Community Background

Lichens add considerably to forest biodiversity in California. They contribute to nutrient cycling and provide wildlife with forage and nesting materials. Lichen communities are excellent air quality bioindicators because some species are highly sensitive to pollutants such as acid rain, sulfur dioxide, and nitrogen (N) (fig. 66). For the FIA lichen community indicator, field crews survey epiphytic (tree-dwelling) lichens at 0.94-acre plots and estimate their diversity and abundance. With the help of multivariate models, FIA lichen data are used to score air quality at each plot and evaluate risks to forest health. Two of four models needed for California are complete, covering the greater Central Valley (Jovan and McCune 2005) and the greater Sierra Nevada regions (Jovan and McCune 2006). The models may also be used for mapping and tracking climate change with FIA lichen data (Jovan, in press).

Tim Wheeler

Figure 66—*Physcia adscendens* (gray) and *Xanthoria* spp. (orange) are indicator species of nitrogen, known as nitrophytes.

Lichen Community Findings

Results from 5 years of surveys (1998–2001, 2003) provide strong evidence that many greater Central Valley forests are exposed to N pollution (fig. 67). Plots receiving the worst air quality scores were dominated (up to 100 percent) by nitrophytic lichens, which are weedy species characteristic of high N environments (fig. 66). The worst sites, as might be expected, tended to be forests downwind of large urban areas and intensive agriculture.

Evidence of N pollution was also detected in some Sierra Nevada forests. Surveys of lichen communities indicated that a major N hotspot lies downwind of the San Joaquin Valley, covering forests of the southern Sierra Nevada Range, and stretching northward to include Yosemite National Park (fig. 68). Air quality studies confirm high N deposition to parts of this region (Fenn et al. 2003). Farther north, estimates of high N impact were more widely dispersed across the landscape.

Lichen Community Interpretation

Nitrogen is a key element for all life, but too much of it can be ecologically detrimental. Excessive N alters lichen, plant, and fungal communities, acidifies soil, causes faster accumulation of forest fuels, and increases emissions of greenhouse gases from the soil (Fenn et al. 2003). Remeasurement of lichen communities in 2009 will allow FIA to track changes in N as well as the proliferation of other pollutants that affect lichens.

Air quality tables in appendix 2—
- Table 44—Summary of lichen community indicator species richness on forest land, by location, California, 1998–2001, 2003
- Table 45—Summary of air quality on forest land in the Greater Central Valley as indicated by the Lichen Community Indicator, California, 1998–2001, 2003
- Table 46—Summary of air quality on forest land in the Greater Sierra Nevada as indicated by the Lichen Community Indicator, California, 1998–2001, 2003
- Table 47—Summary of climate on forest land as indicated by the Lichen Community Indicator, derived from the temperature gradient of Jovan and McCune's (2004) model, California, 1998–2001, 2003
- Table 48—Summary of climate on forest land as indicated by the Lichen Community Indicator, derived from the moisture gradient of Jovan and McCune's (2004) model, California, 1998–2001, 2003
- Table 49—Ozone injury summary information from ozone biomonitoring plots, by year, California, 2000–2005

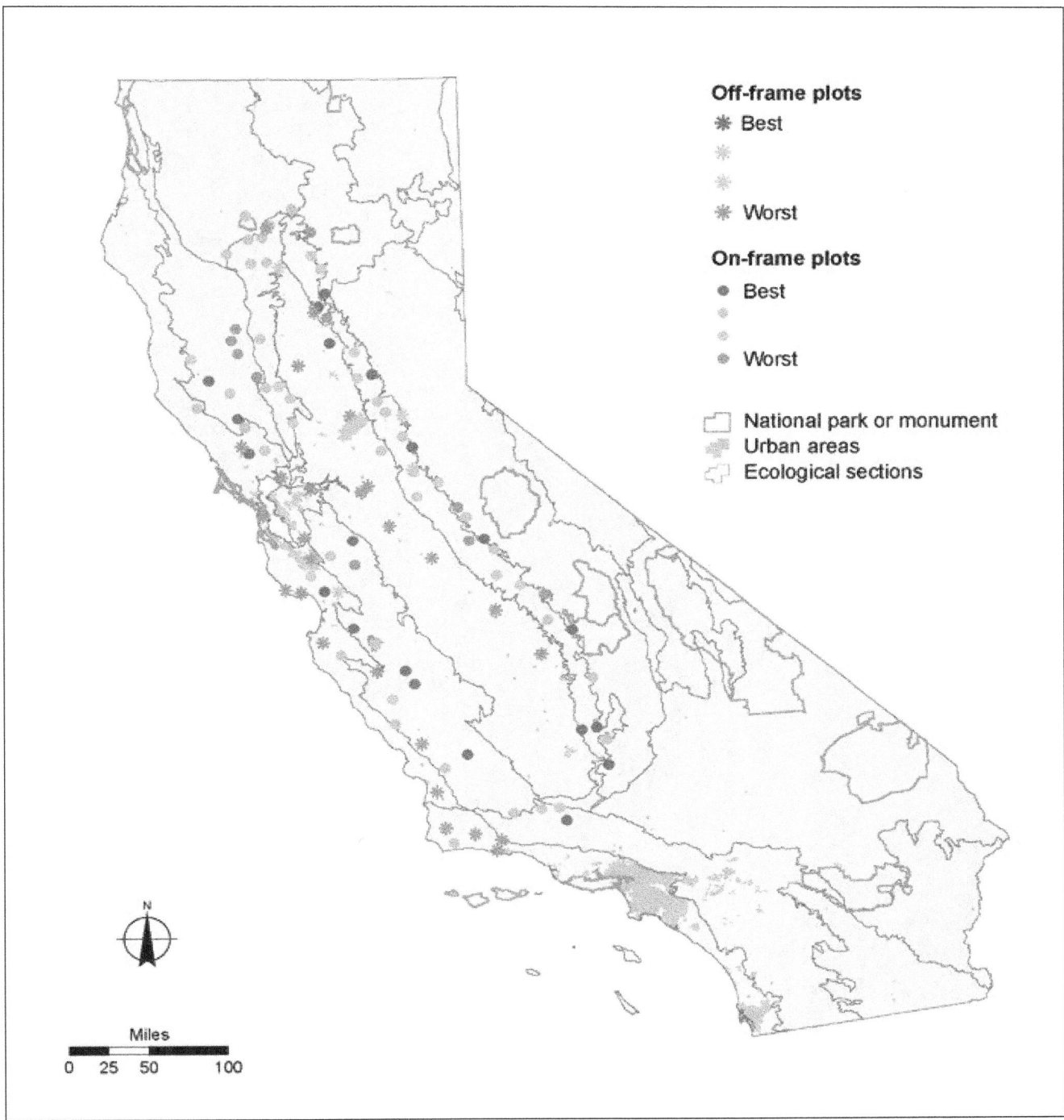

Figure 67—Air quality scores on forest, urban, and agricultural plots in the greater Central Valley, California, 1998–2001, 2003 (Jovan and McCune 2005; ecosection geographic information system (GIS) layer: Cleland et al. 2005; urban GIS layer: U.S. Geological Survey 2001).

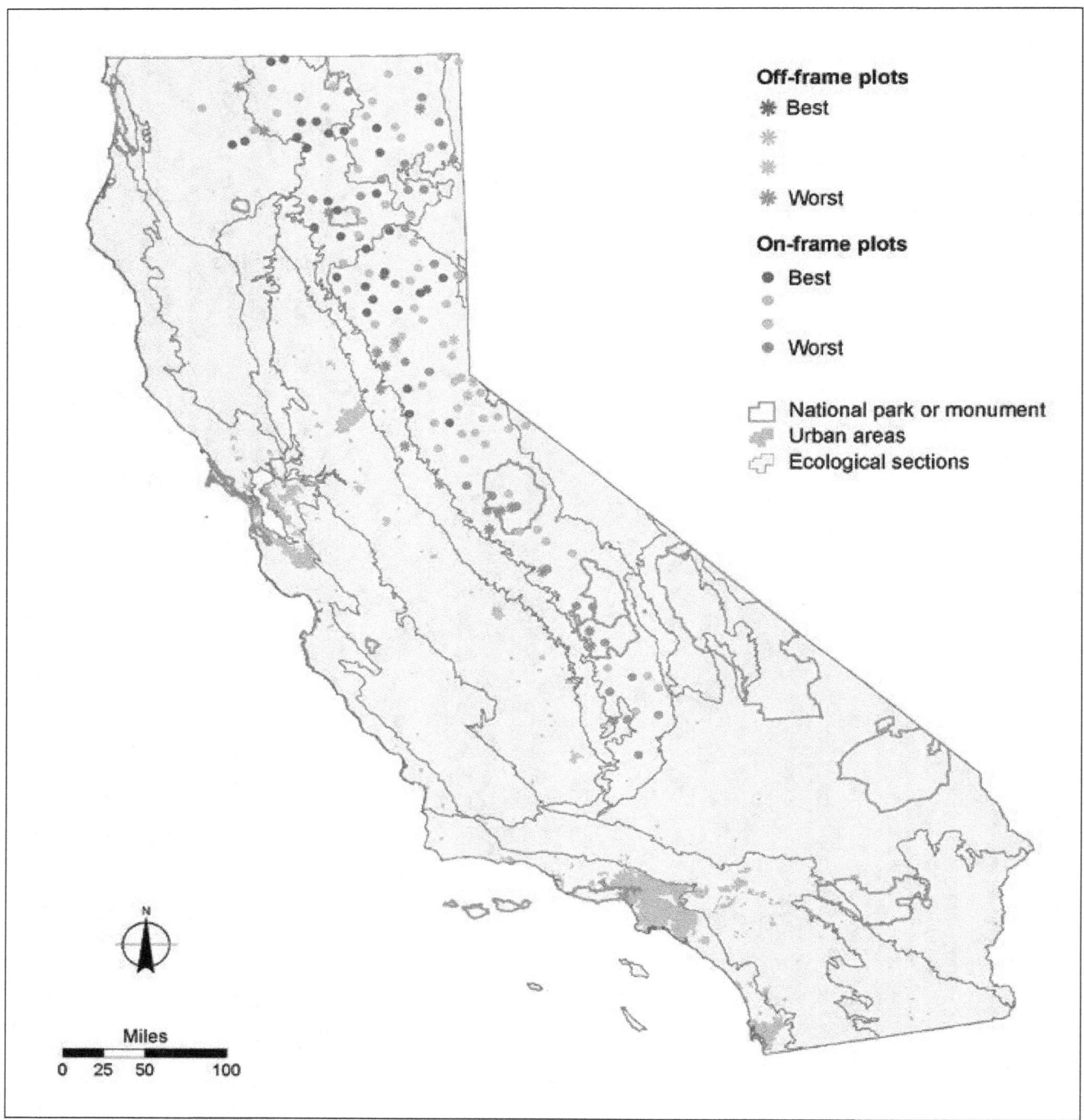

Figure 68—Air quality scores on forest, urban, and agricultural plots in the greater Sierra Nevada, California, 1998–2001, 2003 (Jovan and McCune 2006; ecosection geographic information system (GIS) layer: Cleland et al. 2005; urban GIS layer: U.S. Geological Survey 2001).

Fire Incidence[7]

Background

Nearly all forest types in California have the potential to experience crown or surface fire, although fire incidence differs considerably by region and forest type (fig. 69). State and federal agencies estimate the sizes of all wildland fires and some prescribed fires, map the perimeters of larger fires, and calculate statistics on fire incidence for the lands over which they have fire-protection responsibility. Agencies' fire incidence reports seldom specify the vegetation type that was burned, and in addition, different agencies use different reporting thresholds. Therefore, reliable and con-

sistent estimates of annual burned area of forest across all ownership classes are lacking. The FIA field crews record evidence of surface and crown fire that occurred since the previous plot visit (usually 5 to 10 years), making it possible to estimate both the average forest area and percentage burned per year.

Findings

Over the decade 1995–2004, an estimated 213,000 acres of forest per year burned statewide (range 106,000 to 345,000). Year-to-year variability was considerable, and no statistically unambiguous trends in area burned were observed (fig. 70). The average annual forested area that burned was

---

[7] Authors: Jeremy Fried and Glenn Christensen.

Figure 69—Evidence of fire recorded by field crews can be the result of prescribed burns, as shown here, or naturally caused fires.

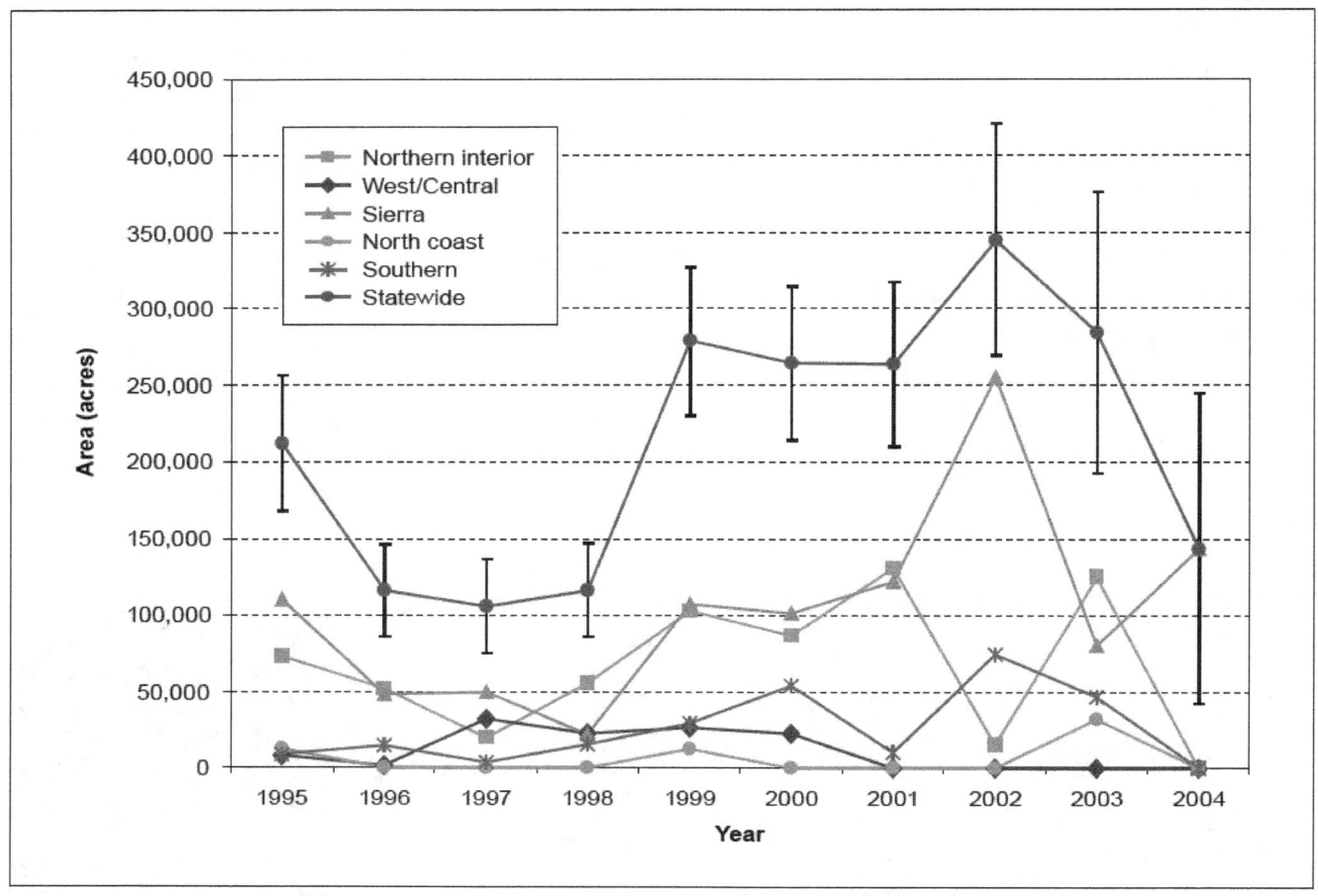

Figure 70—Area of forest burned by ecosection group on forest land in California, 1995–2004.

0.67 percent of the total forested area statewide; the percentage of total burned area ranged from 0.33 percent in 1997 to 1.08 percent in 2002. There was much regional variability as well; the annual 10-year average percentage of burned forest land ranged from 0.24 percent in the North Coast ecosection to 1.11 percent in the Southern ecosection, as shown in this tabulation:[8]

Ecosection	Forest burned, 1995–2004	SE
	Mean percent	*Percent*
Northern Interior	0.50	0.07
North Coast	0.24	0.15
Sierra	0.90	0.12
West/Central	0.57	0.15
Southern	1.11	0.26
Total	0.67	0.06

These estimates compare favorably with data derived from fire perimeter maps maintained by the California Department of Forestry and Fire Protection (CDF) for fires larger than 300 acres, and by the USDA Forest Service Pacific Southwest Region for fires larger than 10 acres.

---

[8] Ecosection groupings (see fig. 6 in chapter 1): Northern Interior—Klamath Mountains, Northwestern Basin and Range, Northern California Coast Ranges, Northern California Interior Coast Range, Southern Cascades, and Modoc Plateau; West/Central—Central California Coast Ranges, Central California Coast, and Great Valley; Sierra—Sierra Nevada Mountains and Sierra Nevada Foothills; North Coast—Northern California Coast, Southern California—Mono, Colorado Desert, Sonoran Desert, Mojave Desert, Southern California Coast, and Southeastern Great Basin.

Those data suggest an average annual burned area (wildfire and prescribed fire combined), across all vegetation types, of 505,000 acres statewide (range 184,000 to 978,000). The CDF statistics show that only 20 percent of the burned area between 1996 and 2005 on nonfederal lands was forest or CDF-defined woodland. Given that federal lands have a much higher proportion of forest land than of other vegetation types, the ratio of burned area observed by FIA to burns mapped by CDF and the Forest Service (213:505 = 0.42) is entirely plausible. Because FIA does not collect a complete ground-based sample of nonforest lands, it is not possible to estimate the area burned in nonforest vegetation types.

Caveats

Because fire is a relatively rare event, the number of plots where recent fire is observed is small—in fact, for some years in some regions, observations from inventory plots suggest no fire whatsoever. Not surprisingly, then, standard errors on estimates of area burned are large. Generating estimates for smaller subsets of the forest land base (e.g., ownership classes or particular forest types) is impractical because of the small sample, because of inconsistent differentiation of fire type (e.g., surface or crown fire) and origin (e.g., prescribed or wildfire), and because field crews do not usually have the training to assess a severity level. For these reasons, for this analysis, all burned acres are pooled. However, we have no reason to believe our estimates are any less accurate than those based on

geographic information system (GIS) databases. Many fire incident reports in these databases have no information on size of the fire. The databases also show large discrepancies between reported sizes and the GIS-calculated burned area. Moreover, the minimum size for inclusion of a fire differs from one database to another. These common problems may contribute to under- or overestimations of the actual burned area.

Interpretation

The year-to-year variability is too large to assess whether there is an increasing trend in area burned in California's forests over the past 10 years. Increased media attention to wildfires and ever-more-earnest discussion among land managers, however, suggests the necessity to more actively manage wildland fuels and generates the impression that area burned is increasing.

We lack landscape-scale historical or paleoecological data to compare with today's average annual rate of 0.67 percent of forest land burned, and so we cannot determine whether this rate represents a departure from historical rates. It is also likely that the distribution of acres burned among severity classes and forest types is changing with climatic fluctuations, but the inventory is not designed to efficiently detect such changes.

Fire incidence table in appendix 2—
- Table 50—Total acres of forest land with a forest fire incident, by year and ecosection group, California, 1995–2004

FIA BioSum[9]

Background

Mechanical treatments to reduce fuel loadings in forests have the potential to produce large quantities of non-merchantable wood. Conventional wisdom suggests that effective treatment requires that large numbers of small stems be removed at considerable cost, and that this harvested material has little or no value.

One widely considered approach to this problem is to develop forest bioenergy production facilities that simultaneously generate renewable energy and increase employment opportunities in rural areas, while achieving economies of scale in harvesting and processing operations (fig. 71). Scientists at PNW-FIA developed an analytical system, FIA BioSum (Forest Inventory and Analysis Biomass Summarization), to guide investors seeking to exploit such opportunities and land managers seeking to attract investment. This system can evaluate a multitude of fuel-treatment prescriptions; assess their economic feasibility in terms of harvest yields and costs, haul costs, and product values; and offer a model-based characterization of the achieved reduction in fire hazard.

Approach

The FIA BioSum integrates data and simulation programs, using linked spatial and relational databases, into a geographically explicit analytic framework for summarizing potential biomass production from fuel treatments (Daugherty and Fried 2007, Fried 2003, Fried et al. 2005, Fried and Christensen 2004). The system relies on publicly available data e.g., inventory plots and GIS layers representing roads, existing wood processing facilities, and land ownership) and off-the-shelf computer simulators. The simulators apply stand prescriptions, assess fire hazard, and evaluate fuel-treatment costs via joint optimization of treatments and processing facility siting. The system requires numerous analytic assumptions, for example, to identify which acres are eligible for

---

[9] Authors: Jeremy Fried and Glenn Christensen.

Figure 71—Mechanical fuel treatment typically involves the removal of numerous small trees that have little or no value as sources of wood products; much of this material is chipped and used as feedstock for biomass-fired power plants.

treatment, what constitutes effective treatment, which logging system to use, appropriate choices of unit haul costs and product prices, and fuel-treatment prescription options. These inputs to the simulation system are best developed in consultation with local experts in fire, fuels, silviculture, and harvest operations.

Findings

The FIA BioSum was applied to a 28-million-acre, mostly forested landscape spanning four ecosections in central and southern Oregon and northern California (fig. 72). As shown below, when the model is set to maximize net revenue, this area can produce $5.9 to $8.9 billion through the treatment of 2.8 to 8.1 million acres, depending on how the problem is constrained. About 61 million to 124 million green tons of woody biomass would be recovered for power generation, sufficient to operate a network of bioenergy plants with a combined capacity of 496 to 1009 megawatts (MW) over a 10-year period. In these scenarios, estimated production potential for merchantable wood products ranges from 8.3 to 12.4 billion cubic feet, most of which would be derived from the harvest of trees larger than 12 inches d.b h (modeling determined that treatments in which removals are

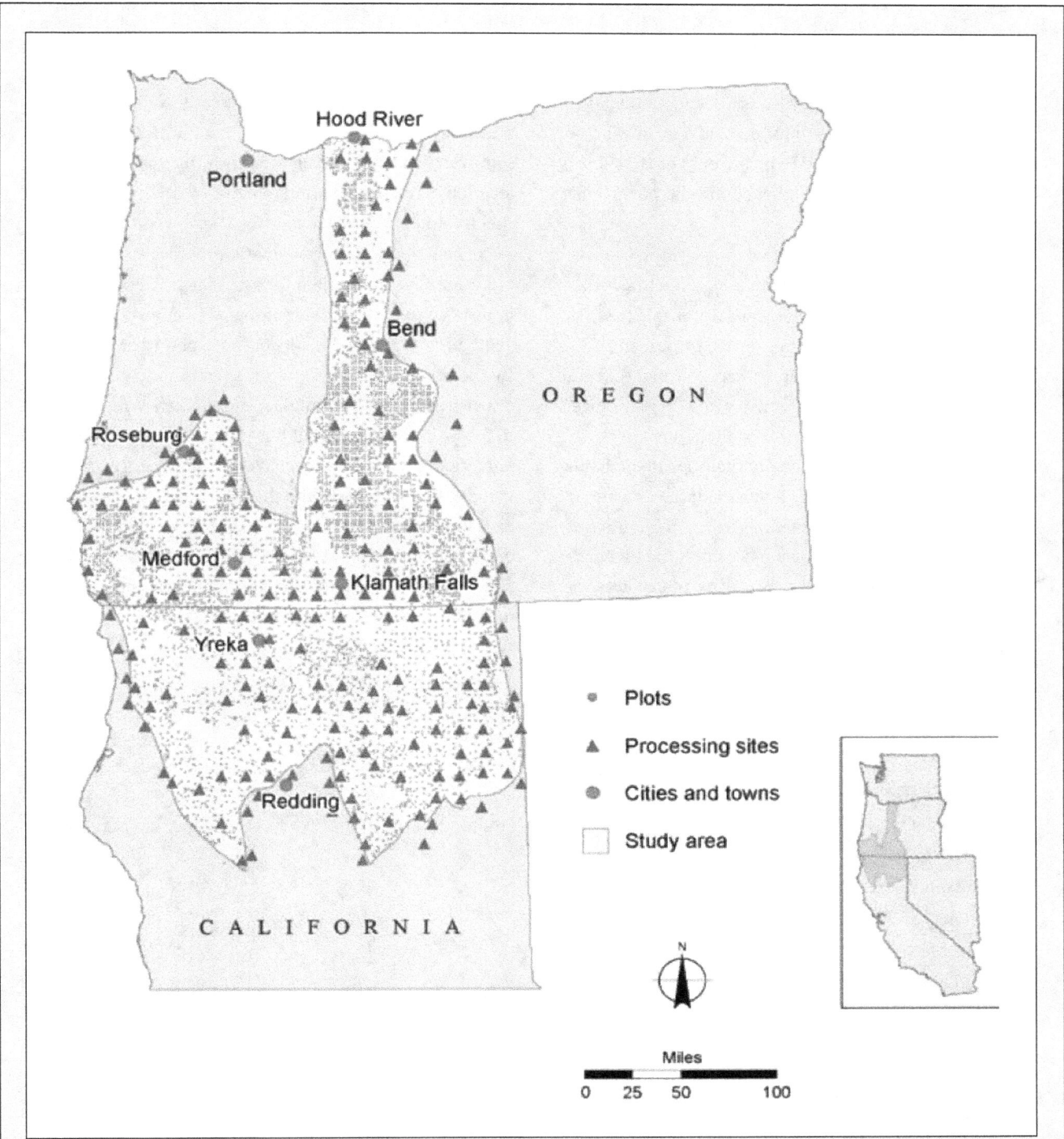

Figure 72—Oregon/California BioSum study area showing locations of inventory plots, sites evaluated as potential power generating facilities, and major cities.

restricted to trees smaller than 10 inches are completely ineffective in reducing crown fire hazard). As shown in the tabulation below, model results depend on the level of treatment effectiveness required, and also on whether all eligible acres are treated (which would entail subsidy on some acres) or only those that contribute positive net revenue to the enterprise.

We evaluated a range of power-generating capacities and conversion efficiencies to assess the tradeoffs of building lower versus higher capacity plants (e.g., increased hauling costs for transporting wood chips longer distances to reach a higher capacity plant). Results suggest that unless small-capacity (<15 MW) facilities achieve efficiencies that are at least 90 percent of what can be achieved by large-capacity facilities, they do not represent a viable alternative given the large amount of biomass removed. The locations selected by the optimization model as the best places to build bioenergy facilities were comparatively insensitive to capacity constraints. Locations that were selected when minimum electrical generation capacity was set high were a subset of those selected when the minimum capacity constraint was set low, lending support to the idea that some places in the forested landscape are inherently well-suited for bioenergy facilities under a variety of potential wood supply and energy pricing scenarios, by virtue of their location on the transportation network relative to where fuel treatments would occur (fig. 73).

The FIA BioSum framework provides a statistically representative foundation for assessing the opportunities to use "waste" from fuel treatments to expand bioenergy generation capacity. Results of these optimizations should not be the only basis for a decision to develop a fuel-treatment program. Decisionmakers will need to factor in the nonmarket benefits and costs of hazard reduction, other resource goals of landowners and land management agencies, and the reluctance of investors to commit capital without a reasonable expectation of sufficient fuel supply. Nevertheless, FIA BioSum provides a starting point for land management agencies to address the fuel supply issue, and serves as a tool for further analysis.

	Scenario			
	1	2	3	4
Constraint on acres treated[a]	Any	All	Any	All
Constraint on effectiveness[b]	Moderate/high	Moderate/high	High	High
Net revenue ($billion)	8.94	6.65	7.15	5.88
Merchantable net revenue ($billion)[c]	7.71	4.74	6.24	4.61
Biomass net revenue ($billion)[c]	1.23	1.92	0.91	1.27
Merchantable volume (billion ft^3)[c]	10.93	12.41	8.35	9.22
Delivered biomass (million green tons)	81.21	123.87	60.92	84.40
Area treated (million acres)	4.49	8.12	2.84	4.05
Highly effective area treated (million acres)	2.53	3.21	2.84	4.05
Number of facilities	31	47	23	30
Bioenergy capacity (megawatts)	661	1009	496	688

[a] "Any" allows the model to select optimal number of acres to treat; "all" requires treatment of all acres that meet effectiveness constraint.
[b] Moderate effectiveness requires a modeled improvement in resistance to active crown fire; high effectiveness requires modeled improvement in resistance to both active and passive crown fire. These criteria limit the number of acres considered in analysis; with the "high" constraint, only high-effectiveness acres are considered for treatment.
[c] Onsite treatment costs are only deducted from merchantable gross revenue. Biomass net revenue equals delivered value net of haul costs.

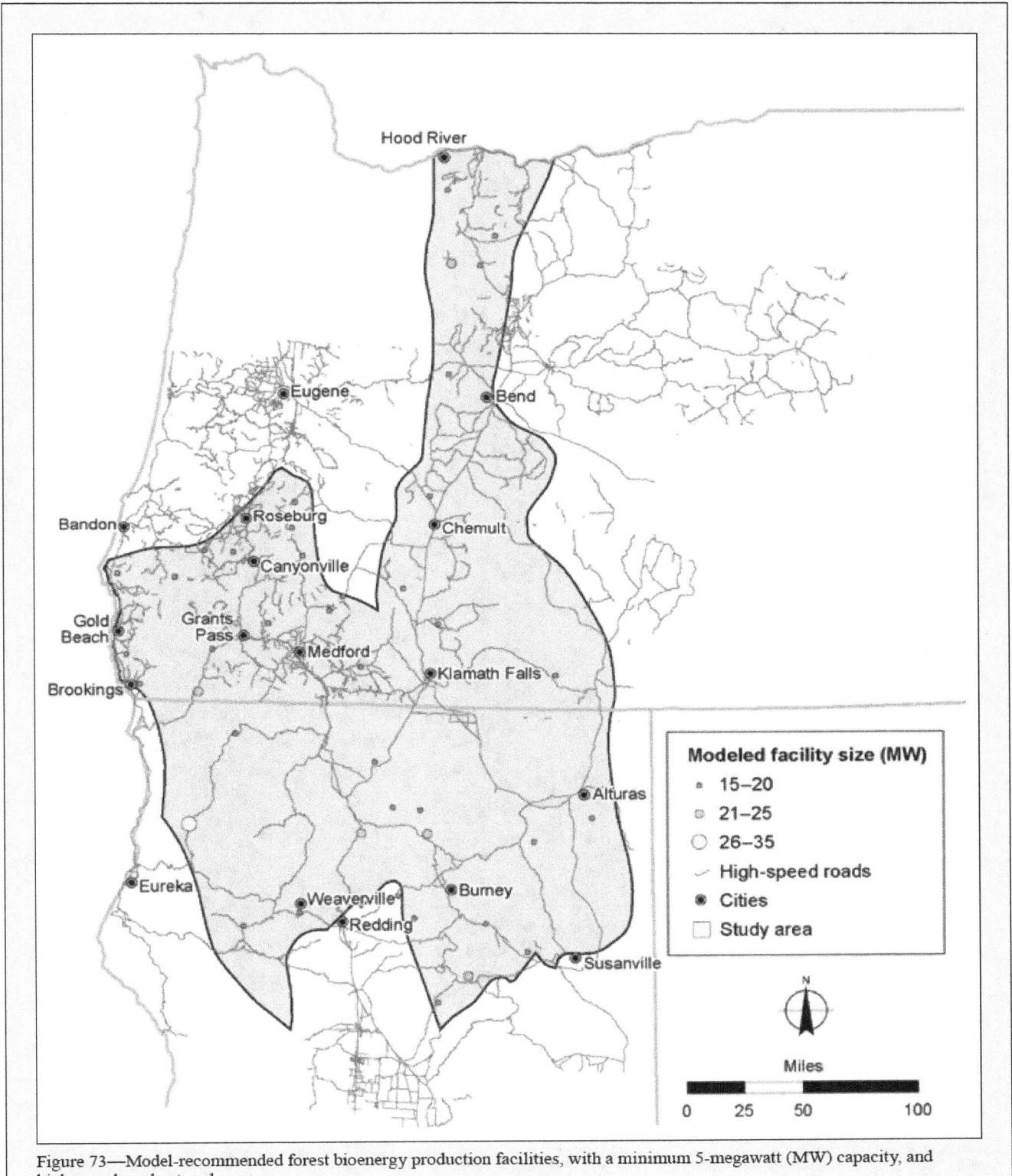

Figure 73—Model-recommended forest bioenergy production facilities, with a minimum 5-megawatt (MW) capacity, and high-speed road network.

Wildland-Urban Interface[10]

Background

Urban and suburban development in or near forests and shrublands is commonly referred to as the wildland-urban interface (WUI) (fig. 74). Housing development in the WUI causes habitat loss and fragmentation (Theobald et al. 1997), threatens wildlife populations (Soulé 1991), and decreases biodiversity (McKinney 2002).

Figure 74—Urban and suburban development in or near forests and shrublands is commonly referred to as the wildland-urban interface. Photo by USDA Forest Service.

Development within the WUI is also a growing concern nationally because of the increasing number of homes destroyed by wildland fire in these areas (National Interagency Fire Center 2007). Protecting homes during WUI fires is extremely challenging (Cohen 2000, Winter and Fried 2001). Human-caused fire ignitions, which tend to be concentrated in WUI areas (Cardille et al. 2001), were responsible for 43 percent of the record-setting 13,113 square miles of forest that burned in the United States during the 2000 fire season (National Interagency Fire Center 2007). In 2003 and 2007, over 4,200 and 3,027 homes, respectively, were destroyed by wildland fires, nearly all of them in southern California during October fires.

We estimated the area of WUI using definitions derived from the Federal Register and the California Fire Alliance (2001),[11] along with census data and land cover maps from the National Land Cover Database (Radeloff et al. 2005). In this analysis, we defined the vegetation cover component to include shrubs and grasses as well as forests (Hammer et al. 2007). Two types of WUI are recognized: interface, in which communities directly abut wildland areas but there is a clear demarcation between development and wildland; and intermix, in which homes and other buildings are surrounded and overtopped by vegetation and resemble islands scattered in a sea of wildland fuel. Using housing density data collected by the census in 1990 and 2000, we estimated changes in WUI area by WUI type and number of homes within this zone.

Findings

The area of WUI and the number of homes within it grew substantially over the 1990s. Intermix communities grew more in area, while interface communities saw the

WUI type	Area			Homes		
	1990	2000	Percentage of change	1990	2000	Percentage of change
	Thousand acres		*Percent*	*Thousands*		*Percent*
Interface	1,789	1,804	0.9	3,164	3,480	10
Intermix	4,678	5,225	11.7	1,306	1,634	25.1
Total WUI	6,467	7,029	8.7	4,469	5,114	14.4

[10] Author: Jeremy Fried. This highlight is adapted from work published as Hammer, R.B.; Radeloff, V.C.; Fried, J.S.; Stewart, S.I. 2007. Wildland-urban interface growth during the 1990s in California, Oregon, and Washington. International Journal of Wildland Fire. 16: 255–265.

[11] Wildland–urban interface is defined as the area where houses meet or intermingle with undeveloped wildland vegetation, and more precisely as areas with a housing density greater than 1 house per 40 acres and dominated by wildland vegetation (USDA and USDI 2001), or situated within 1.5 miles of an area covered in wildland vegetation (California Fire Alliance 2001).

greatest housing increase (see tabulation below). As of 2000, the 5.2 million acres of intermix WUI accounted for 74 percent of WUI area but for only 32 percent of WUI homes. However, the area of intermix WUI grew nearly 12 percent between 1990 and 2000, accounting for most of the overall growth in WUI acres (nearly 97 percent). Growth in intermix WUI areas also accounted for the greatest percentage increase in number of homes: 25.1 percent, a figure far in excess of the 9.2 percent growth in housing across all California.

As illustrated by the comparison of WUI residential growth in two ecosections in the tabulation below, the dynamics of growth in the WUI differ considerably within the state. The number of WUI homes built in the 1990s is much greater in southern California, although WUI homes constitute only 61 percent of the total housing increase there. Housing growth is distributed almost evenly between intermix and interface areas. By comparison, the Sierra foothills region is heavily forested and a hotspot of urban immigration. Virtually all new homes there were built in the WUI, with well over 75 percent located in intermix areas—the WUI type that has expanded the most in area over the decade.

WUI can be found in virtually every California county; however, some of the biggest concentrations of forested WUI are in the foothills of the central Sierra, around the margins of the San Francisco Bay area, and in the mountains of southern California (fig. 75). These areas have considerable acres of wildland intermix, a sub-WUI class in which the average housing density of fewer than 1 house per 40 acres is considered insufficient to meet the requirements for the definition of WUI. These wildland intermix areas have strong potential to become WUI in the near future, unless political or market forces intervene to slow the trend.

Interpretation

Although it may seem small relative to California's total land area (100 million acres), the 7 million acres of WUI calculated in this analysis is considerable relative to the total forest land area of 33 million acres. A substantial fraction of WUI consists of grass and shrub-covered lands, particularly in southern California, and thus does not contribute to the FIA estimate of forest land. Nonetheless, these results are strong evidence that a great deal of forest land has already been affected by development.

Continued WUI growth at rates seen in the 1990s are likely to place extraordinary pressure on California's forest resources. Effects will be especially pronounced in forested regions with rapidly expanding WUI, such as the Sierra Nevada foothills (23 percent) and Sierra Nevada mountains (12 percent). In these regions nearly all new homes are added to intermix areas, where the pressures on forest land in terms of resource use, introduction of exotic invasives, and imperatives to reduce fire hazard are likely to be extraordinary. Without land use controls, strict zoning, or powerful financial counterincentives, increasing rates of conversion of forest land to developed uses are likely to greatly alter the productivity, health, and ecosystem integrity of California's forests.

	1990	2000	Change	Percentage of change
	Thousands of homes			*Percent*
Southern California Coast Ecosection:				
Interface WUI	812	891	79	9.7
Intermix WUI	298	369	71	24.0
Not WUI	2,983	3,078	95	3.1
Percentage in WUI	27	29	61	
Sierra Nevada Foothills Ecosection:				
Interface WUI	56	64	8	14.1
Intermix WUI	119	152	32	26.9
Not WUI	22	22	0	0
Percentage in WUI	89	91	100	

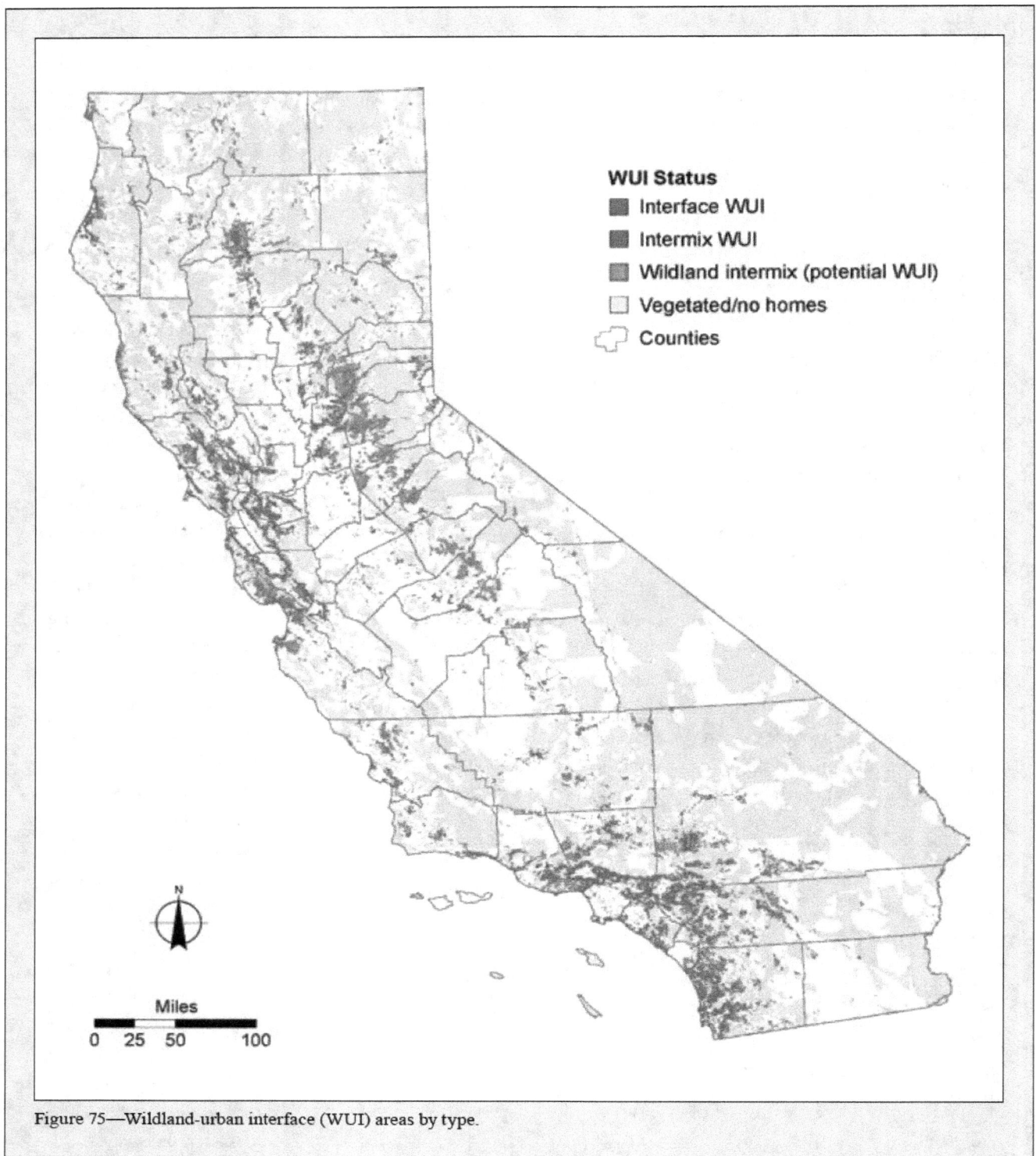

WUI Status
- ◼ Interface WUI
- ◼ Intermix WUI
- ◼ Wildland intermix (potential WUI)
- ☐ Vegetated/no homes
- ⬡ Counties

Miles
0   25   50   100

Figure 75—Wildland-urban interface (WUI) areas by type.

Figure 76—Stands within the McNally Fire in California experienced a variety of fire regimes including mixed-severity with both surface and crown fire (left) and severe crown fire with 100-percent tree mortality (right).

Crown Fire Hazard[12]

Background

Reduction of fire hazard has emerged as a priority issue in California, where fuel treatments are proposed on an unprecedented scale. Characterization of fire hazard often focuses on crown fire potential—the tendency of a forest stand to experience crown rather than surface (ground) fire—because crown fires are typically stand-replacing events (fig. 76). Before an effective fuel treatment program can be developed, it is essential to know initial hazard levels and identify where hazard reduction is most technically, economically, and socially feasible (see, e.g., Barbour et al. 2008; Vogt et al. 2005). The FIA inventory provides an unprecedented opportunity to assess the extent of crown fire hazard across all land ownerships, ecosection groups, and forest types. Examining these statistics on a proportional basis, by forest type and geographic distribution, provides key insights into factors associated with high crown fire hazard.

All plots with forested conditions[13] were simulated with the Forest Vegetation Simulator (FVS) and its Fire and Fuels Extension (FFE) (Reinhardt and Crookston 2003) to calculate indices of crown fire potential and fire type under severe fire weather. Each inventory plot was assigned to the appropriate FVS variant by GIS overlay with the FVS variant layer (USDA Forest Service 2007a), and default values were used for all fuel parameters other than those derived from the tree-level data collected by FIA.[14] Fire type under severe weather was modeled by FFE as one of four classes (see tabulation below), and results were analyzed and mapped.[15]

---

[12] Authors: Jeremy Fried and Glenn Christensen.

[13] The FVS-FFE was applied to all conditions classified as forested on the ground. Despite this classification, some plots contained few or no trees, and therefore stand attributes the model uses to estimate crown fire potential (e.g., canopy bulk density, height to canopy base) could not be calculated reliably. The FFE assumes that sparsely forested conditions have a surface fire regime, which may or may not be true depending on stand structure in the remainder of the area (outside the plot footprint).

[14] Surface fuels were determined via lookup tables based on stand structure (wildlife habitat relationship class in the Western Sierra Nevada) and forest type. For the severe fire weather scenario, FFE default parameters were used such that 20-foot windspeed was set at 20 miles per hour, temperature at 70 degrees F; 1-, 10-, 100-, and 1,000-hour fuel moisture at 4, 4, 5, and 10 percent, respectively; duff-fuel moisture at 15 percent; and live-fuel moisture at 70 percent.

[15] To enable better visualization of the geographic distribution of fire regimes, local kriging interpolation was performed on the ordinal variable, fire type, as if it were a ratio (continuous) variable. This produced a surface of crown fire potential from the plot data, with values ranging from 1 (surface fire) to 4 (active crown fire).

Fire type	Fire characteristics
Surface	Crowns do not burn; only surface fuels on the forest floor burn.
Conditional surface	Existing crown fire will continue as a crown fire, but if canopy gaps interrupt crown fire spread, it will convert to a surface fire and not reinitiate as a crown fire.
Passive	Some crowns will burn as individual trees or groups of trees "torch," with fire climbing from the surface via "ladders" of dead branches and lesser vegetation.
Active	Fire moves through the tree crowns and reinitiates as a crown fire in the event that canopy gaps interrupt its progress.

Findings

Patterns for the crown fire potential indices and fire type were similar, so for simplicity, only the fire type results are reported here. Statewide, under extreme fire weather conditions, fire would likely occur as surface fire on 72 percent of the forest. Active crown fire would be expected on only 7 percent of the forest, and passive crown fire on 20 percent. There is substantial regional variation—for example, only 3 percent of forests in the West/Central and North Coast ecosection groups would have active crown fires under severe weather conditions, whereas 8 to 9 percent of forests in the rest of the state would have active crown fire (fig. 77). It is difficult to predict how these differences in potential hazard translate to events on the ground because incidence of severe weather also differs among these regions.

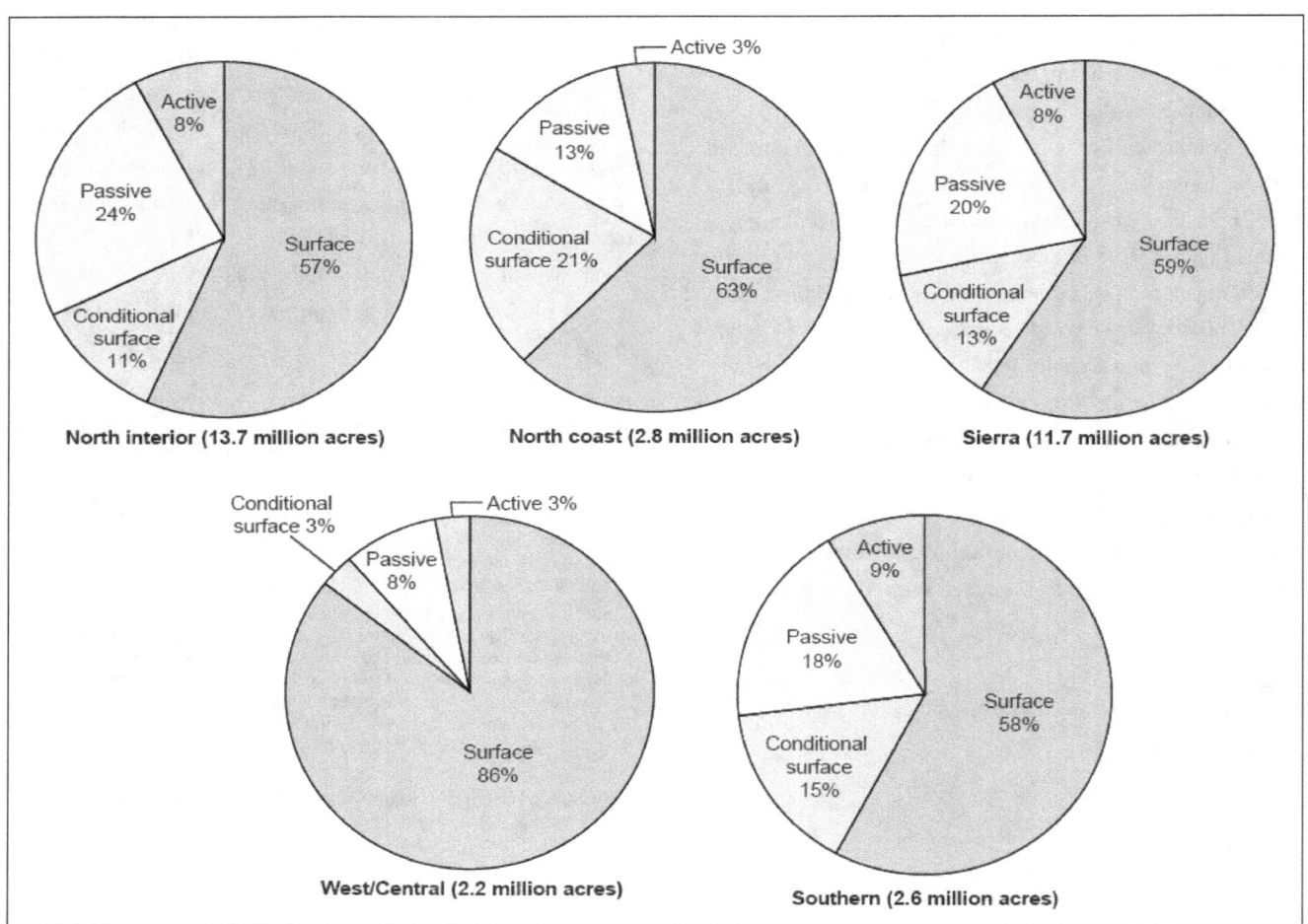

Figure 77—Percentage of forest land in each modeled fire type category by ecosection group in California, 2001–2005.

Incidence of crown fire also appears to differ by forest type. Simulation showed that among the four most prevalent coniferous forest type groups, fir/spruce/hemlock has the highest incidence of active crown fire, and ponderosa pine and Douglas-fir have the lowest (fig. 78), probably because fir/spruce/hemlock forests have denser canopies and are more likely to contain ladder fuels. However, passive crown fire is quite common in ponderosa pine and, to a lesser extent, the mixed-conifer forest type. Fire regime also differs by ownership group (fig. 79), with state lands predicted to have the highest percentage of forests in surface or conditional surface fire regimes (82 percent) and national forest predicted to have the lowest (67 percent). These differences could be due to differences in management, but may also be traceable to differences in age class structure, forest type, and stand history.

Remarkably distinct patterns can be observed in the geographic distribution of likely fire type. Most notable are the concentration of elevated crown fire potential in the northern Sierra and Northern Interior regions and the virtual absence of passive and active crown and conditional-surface fire regimes in the oak forests and woodlands typical of the lower-elevation forests of the state (fig. 80).

Interpretation

These data paint a different picture of fire hazard and fuel treatment opportunity than do maps of fire regime condition class (Schmidt et al. 2002; see the maps at www fs fed. us/fire/fuelman/curcond2000/maps.html). These maps depict most of the area in at least some ecosection groups (notably Northern Interior) as having significantly departed from historical fire regimes, and, by implication, being in urgent need of intervention to reduce fire hazard. Even under the extreme fire weather assumed for this analysis, less than half of the forested lands are predicted to develop crown fires, and an even smaller fraction (<10 percent) can be expected to develop active crown fire. Although crown-fire potential models such as FFE have yet to be rigorously validated against behavior of actual fires, many fire managers regard them as suitable for "ballpark" predictions of what is likely to occur.

These results have implications both for the scope of fuel treatment programs and for the challenges that firefighters will face. In the context of firefighting, building a fire line that disrupts the continuity of surface fuels can be effective in stopping fire spread in areas prone to surface fires. In areas where crown fire, if it occurs, is likely to be

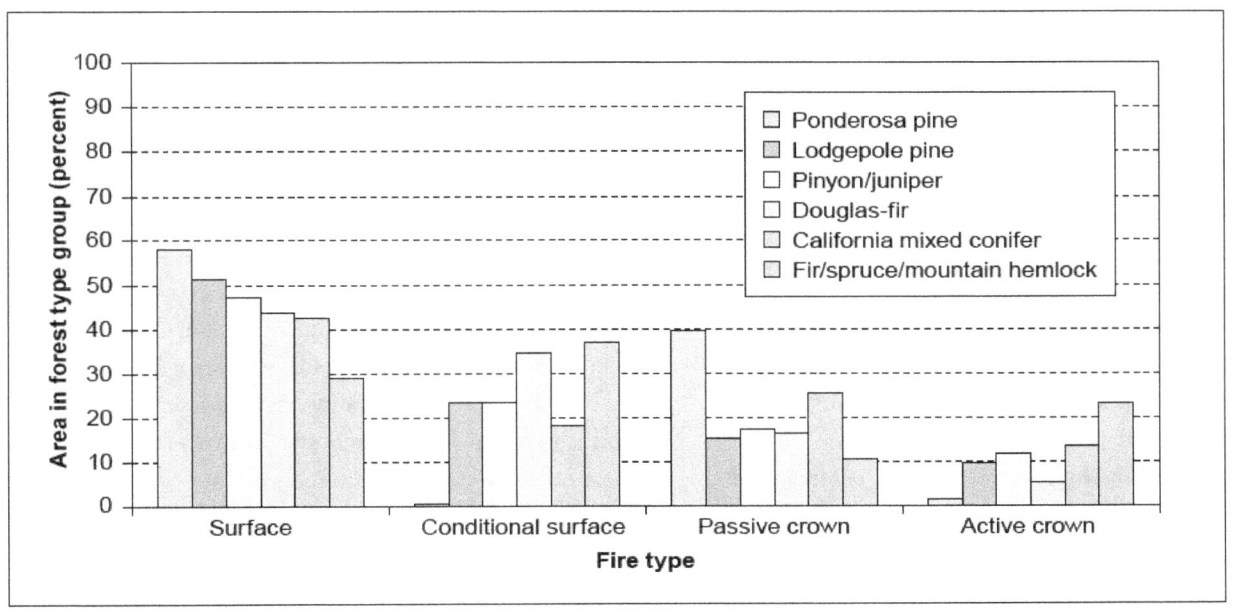

Figure 78—Percentage of forest land in each of the six most prevalent coniferous forest type groups in each modeled fire type class in California, 2001–2005.

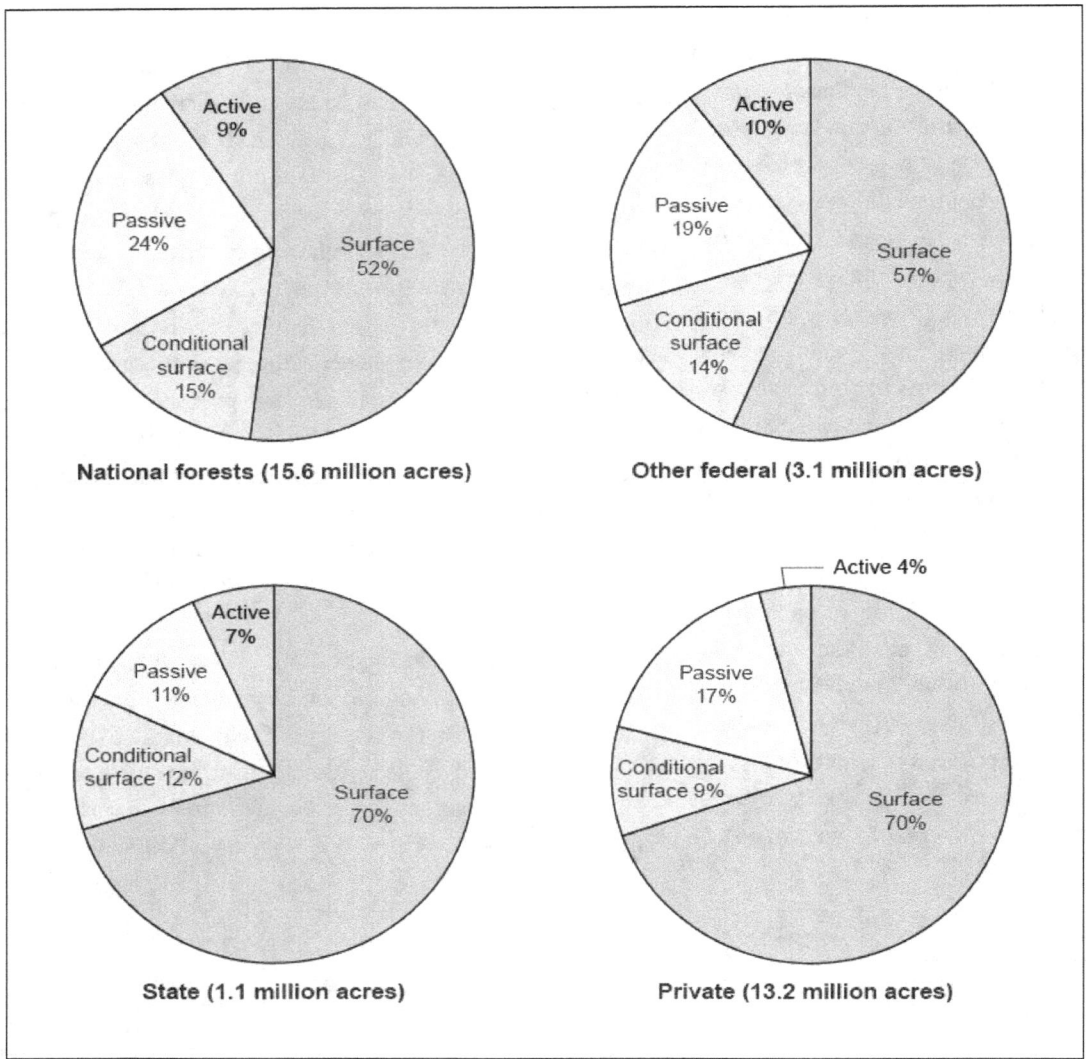

Figure 79—Percentage of forest land in each modeled fire type category by ownership group in California, 2001–2005.

passive, trees will torch individually, and most may die. On those more limited areas where active crown fire is likely to occur, a far more labor- and time-intensive job of line-building to remove standing trees would be required for fire containment efforts to be successful.

From the standpoint of implementing fuel treatments, these results suggest that, if the objective is to reduce crown fire hazard, only a fraction of the forested landscape is likely to benefit from fuel treatment. Spatial analyses of fuel treatments have demonstrated that treating a small percentage of the landscape can reduce landscape-scale fire hazard significantly and sometimes cost-effectively (Finney 2001). These results suggest that the fuels management challenge may be more tractable than has been assumed.

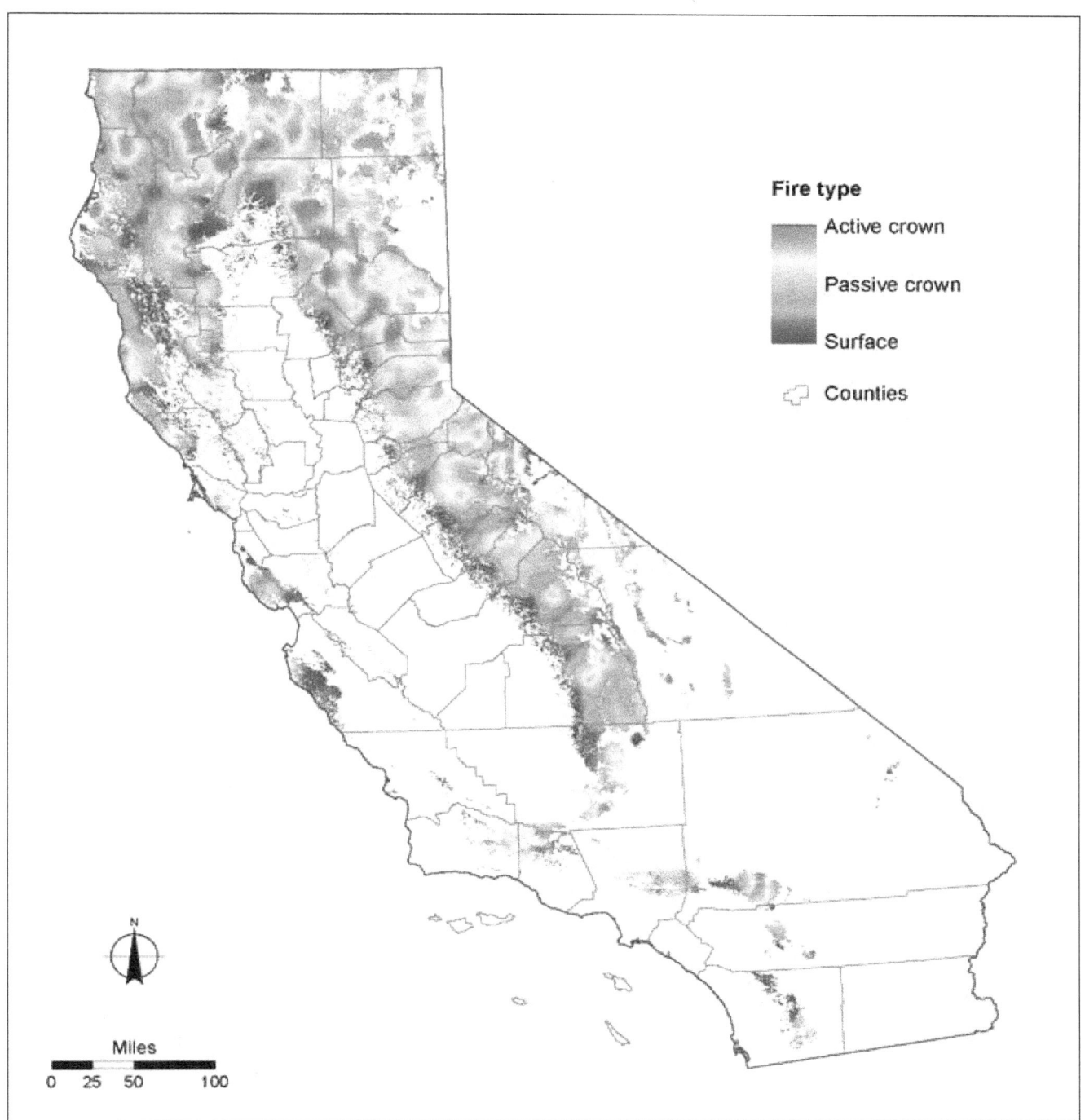

Fire type

Active crown

Passive crown

Surface

Counties

N

Miles
0 25 50   100

Figure 80—Predicted likely fire type in forested areas using kriging as a modeling method (forest/nonforest geographic information system layer: Blackard et al. 2008).

Bristlecone pine.

Chapter 5: Products

California's forests are an essential source of raw materials for goods and services used every day by the state's 36 million residents. The forest products industry makes important contributions to California's economy and environment by supplying wood products, employment and income, tax revenue, and a number of other amenities and services benefiting the people of California. This chapter examines the productive capacity of California's forests and its contribution to the state's economy and environment.

California's Primary Forest Products Industry[1]

Background

California's forest products industry utilizes timber harvested from California and from other states in the Western United States (fig. 81). The industry provides

social and economic benefits by supplying society with wood products, such as lumber and biomass energy, and also through employment and income associated with land management, timber harvesting, and wood products manufacturing. The availability of forests for future harvests and the remaining capacity of the primary forest products industry to utilize timber are important issues facing Californians today.

In cooperation with the Pacific Northwest Research Station Forest Inventory and Analysis (FIA) Program, the Bureau of Business and Economic Research at the University of Montana conducts a periodic census of California's primary forest products industry (i.e., timber processors and users of mill residue). This census is the source of information presented below. It provides detail on timber harvest and flow, as well as comprehensive information about the state's timber processing sectors, product volumes, sales values, and mill residue (Morgan et al. 2004).

[1] Authors: Todd A. Morgan and Charles E. Keegan, Bureau of Business and Economic Research, University of Montana.

Figure 81—Timber from California forests, as well as other states, supplies the forest products industry in California.

Findings

During 2000, 93 primary forest products facilities operated in 28 of California's 58 counties. These facilities included 47 sawmills, 2 veneer plants, 5 medium density fiberboard (MDF) and particleboard plants, 25 bioenergy facilities, and 14 other facilities, including plants for manufacturing pulp and paper, bark products, shakes, shingles, posts, poles, and pilings (fig. 82).

Sales from California's primary forest products industry were about $2.3 billion in 2000. California was its own largest market for wood and paper products, accounting for $1.4 billion (62 percent) of sales in 2000. Nearly all of the energy and electricity produced by the bioenergy sector was used in-state. The majority (63 percent) of lumber produced in California was sold in California, whereas about one-half (47 percent) of product sales from the residue-utilizing sector were in-state. Other primary wood products were sold in higher proportions out-of-state, with California retaining less than 1 percent. The majority (97 percent) of these products were sold in other Pacific Coast States.

Product	2000 product sales value
	Thousands of U.S. dollars
Lumber, timbers, and associated products	$1,492,190
Residue-utilizing sector[a]	$463,990
Energy and electric	$260,235
Other primary wood products[b]	$77,044

[a] Residue-utilizing sector includes pulp, paper, board, and decorative bark manufacturers.
[b] Other primary wood products include veneer, shakes, shingles, posts, poles, and pilings.

Based on sales value and volume of timber processed, sawmills were the largest component of California's forest products industry during 2000, producing 3.1 billion board feet of lumber and achieving sales close to $1.5 billion. The volume-weighted statewide average overrun in 2000 was 1.53 board feet of lumber produced per board foot (Scribner) of timber processed. California sawmills generated more than 3.4 million dry tons of mill residue during 2000, and nearly all of this residue was utilized. Other facilities produced 184,000 dry tons of residues during 2000.

Sawmills and veneer plants together used about 2,217 miiliion board feet (MMBF, Scribner) of timber, 97 percent of the timber received by California timber processors during 2000. The bioenergy sector used almost 55 MMBF of timber. California's total capacity to process timber in 2000 was nearly 2.7 billion board feet (Scribner), of which 83 percent was utilized to process nearly 2.3 billion board feet of timber. California was a net importer of timber, using 151 MMBF (Scribner) of out-of-state timber, while slightly less than 120 MMBF of California timber was shipped to other states for processing.

Consuming almost half (1.7 million dry tons) of the wood residue generated by California's primary wood products industry during 2000, the bioenergy sector is quite important to the industry. The bioenergy sector is composed of cogeneration facilities at sawmills as well as stand-alone facilities using mixtures of urban, agricultural, and mill wastes, timber, and even geothermal energy to generate electricity. The total energy-producing capacity of the wood-using bioenergy facilities exceeded 470 megawatts. During 2000, these facilities generated and sold over 3.1 million megawatt-hours of power.

Approximately 112,700 workers, earning $4.5 billion annually, were directly employed in California's primary and secondary wood and paper products industry during 2000. About 25,000 of these workers were employed in the primary sectors (i.e., harvesting and processing of timber or private land management), earning approximately $900 million in labor income. The secondary component of the industry employed 87,700 workers, who earned approximately $3.6 billion. The secondary industry includes firms that further process outputs from the primary industry; for example, window frame and door manufacturers, truss and remanufacturing facilities, and furniture and packaging makers.

Interpretation

California remains one of the top four softwood lumber-producing states, but faces increasing regulation of timber harvesting practices along with declining harvest levels (see "Removals" section). Improved milling technology has increased product recovery (i.e., overrun) while allowing

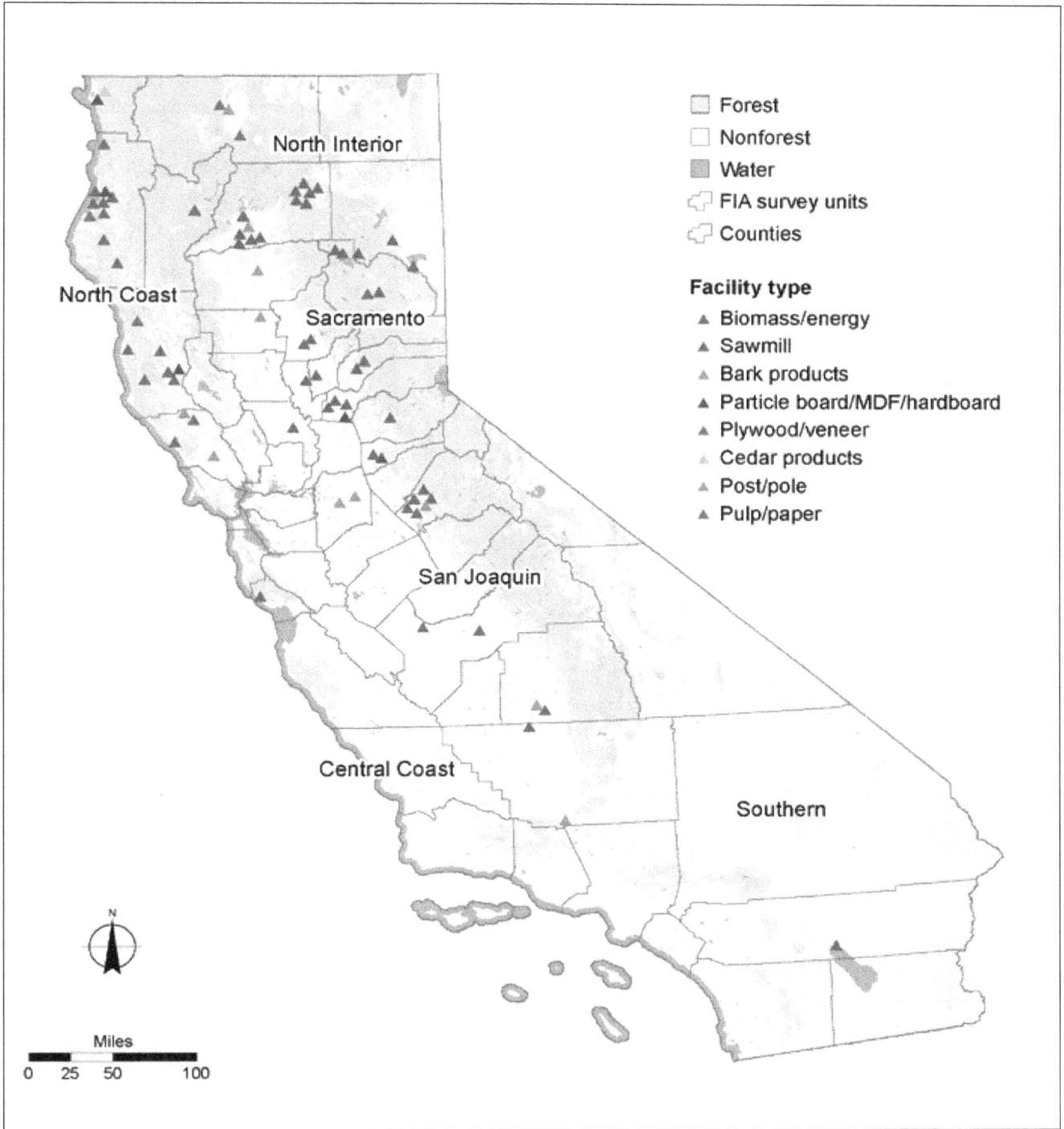

Figure 82—Active California primary forest products facilities by county and resource area, 2000. (forest/nonforest geographic information system (GIS) layer: Blackard et al. 2008; water GIS layer: Homer et al. 2004).

increased utilization of smaller diameter trees. The bioenergy sector's demand for mill residue has likewise contributed to increased utilization of wood fiber. However, the capacity of California's forest products industry to process timber declined nearly 60 percent from the late 1980s to 2000, and dropped further as additional facilities closed between 2000 and 2005. Lumber production declined 15 percent from 2000 to 2005 (Western Wood Products Association 2006). However, quality timber, good growing sites, and high regional demand for wood products may allow California's forest products industry to prosper in a highly regulated operating environment.

Growth, Removals, and Mortality[2]

Background

Increases or decreases in timber volume can be explained by examining growth, removals, and mortality of trees. Comparing removals and mortality to growth addresses one aspect of forest sustainability; when removals and mortality exceed growth, total tree volume will decline. In localized areas, removing trees to reduce risk from fire or insect outbreaks can cause removals to exceed growth, but may benefit the health of the stand. Conversely, widespread mortality from some agent of disturbance such as bark beetles may offset growth gains and thus slow stand development (fig. 83).

Because the current FIA inventory differed from past inventories in how the different parts of the forest land base were measured (i.e., forest land, timberland, and inclusion or exclusion of reserved land), and because the inventories used different definitions of forest attributes (e.g., growing stock), it is not possible to simply compare prior published results with current results to estimate change in the net volume of trees. To minimize the definition-based effects, we estimated net change based on revisited plots and assessed them under our current algorithms and definitions. We estimated current annual gross growth from increment cores taken from a subset of softwood trees on the revisited plots. The difference between net change and current annual gross growth is our estimate for removal and mortality.

Findings

As shown in the tabulation below, growth of softwood trees on timberland exceeds removals and mortality in California, on both National Forest System (NFS) and noncorporate private lands. On corporate private, state, and local government lands, removals and mortality estimates exceed growth estimates. However, because the sampling error associated with all these estimates is large, none of the differences are statistically significant.

Owner group	Annualized net change	
	Total	SE
	Thousand cubic feet	
NFS	117,042	168,537
State and local	-5,458	23,093
Corporate private	-5,929	65,842
Noncorporate private	84,140	67,023
Total	189,794	194,246

On average in California, NFS timberlands are the least productive (as measured by gross growth) compared with corporate lands and noncorporate private. State and local governments control very little of California's timberland area (1.3 percent), so the growth estimate for this ownership group is very imprecise. Softwood gross growth is shown in the following tabulation:

Owner group	Total	SE
	Cubic feet per acre per year	
NFS	85.13	4.35
State and local	261.86	89.93
Corporate private	104.84	12.44
Noncorporate private	109.29	28.39
Total	94.78	5.59

Caveats

The design and definitions used in past inventories are significantly different from those used in our current inventory (see app. 2). The design has changed from a variable-radius to a fixed-radius plot design and from five to four subplots with only the center location of one subplot being the same. As a result, only a small fraction of trees were remeasured

---

[2] Author: Olaf Kuegler.

Karen Waddell

Figure 83—Growth of trees is offset by harvesting and mortality. The mortality shown here was likely caused by bark beetles and/or drought.

in the current annual inventory. Although it is still valid to estimate overall net change based on these different designs, there are some inherent problems. For this chapter we have tried to minimize procedural differences between inventories by comparing only subplots from the two inventories that have the same center location and by applying the same definitions and algorithms to both data sets (i.e., for growing stock, timberland, reserved land, forest type, tree volume). However, a small bias introduced by measurement or model error that may exist in one inventory and not in the other will exaggerate the estimate of net change.[3]

We estimated gross growth by taking tree cores from a subset of trees in our current inventory. Although the field crew was instructed to core one live tree for each condition, representing each species and crown class, that was not always possible. This introduces a small bias with an unknown direction into our gross growth estimate.[4] Furthermore, increment cores were not cross-dated, and standardized ring-width indices were not developed.

---

[3] Because overall softwood trees on timberland grow about 3 percent per year, a total volume bias of only 1 percent per year amounts to about a 30 percent difference in gross growth.

[4] The estimated bias for total volume for California, using the trees selected for gross growth estimate, is 7.1 percent, with a standard error of 2.2 percent. In contrast, the estimated bias for total volume, using the first tree per species, crown class, and condition is 2.3 percent, with a standard error of 2.2.

Removals and mortality are estimated as the difference between gross growth and net change. Even if these estimates are unbiased, they are still subject to sampling error. Thus, the estimate for removals and mortality can be negative. Although such an estimate is still unbiased, it is of course logically untenable. Furthermore, any bias in the gross growth or the net change estimates is also present in removals and mortality estimates.

Past inventories were conducted between 1991 and 1999, whereas the current inventory covers 2001 though 2005. As a result, the remeasurement period differs between 2 and 14 years.

Finally, the sampling errors for most of our estimates are very large compared to the estimates. The reader should be careful to take into account the sampling error when interpreting the estimates.

In 2005, PNW-FIA began collecting information that can be used for growth, mortality, and harvest. The data include remeasurement of previous trees assessed in two of the five periodic subplots and recording of natural mortality and harvest on all five prior subplots. These new data will allow better estimates of change for the next report

Growth, removals, and mortality table in appendix 2—

- Table 51—Estimated gross growth, net change, removals, and mortality of growing stock for soft-wood species on timberland, by species group and owner, California, 2001–2005

Removals for Timber Products[5]

Background

Volume removed from forest inventory during timber harvesting is known as removals (fig. 84). Removals are an important indicator of timber harvest sustainability. Removals that exceed growth could indicate overharvesting and decreasing forest inventory, whereas growth that greatly

---

[5] Authors: Todd Morgan and Charles Keegan, Bureau of Business and Economic Research, University of Montana.

Figure 84—Logging in California forests.

exceeds removals could signal the need for vegetation management to regulate density and species mix, inhibit insect and disease outbreaks, or reduce wildfire hazard.

Removals can come from two sources: the growing-stock portion of live trees (live trees of commercial species meeting specified standards of quality or vigor), or dead trees and other non-growing-stock sources. The two general types of removals are timber products harvested for processing by mills and logging residue (i.e., volume cut or killed but not used). Removals, as reported here, are based on a 2000 census of California's primary forest products industry (Morgan et al. 2004) and a 2004 study of logging utilization in California (Morgan and Spoelma, in press).

Findings

California's 2000 timber harvest for industrial wood products was 2.25 billion board feet (Scribner), and dead trees accounted for 106.4 million board feet (5 percent). The 2000 harvest was about 67 percent of the average annual harvest for the previous 20 years, and only 51 percent of the 50-year average (fig. 85). California's 2004 and 2005 timber harvests were slightly higher than those of the previous 3 years, but lower than in 2000.

Removals for timber products totaled 627.8 million cubic feet (MMCF) during 2000. Growing stock accounted for 444.5 MMCF (71 percent) of removals for products, with the remainder coming from other sources including

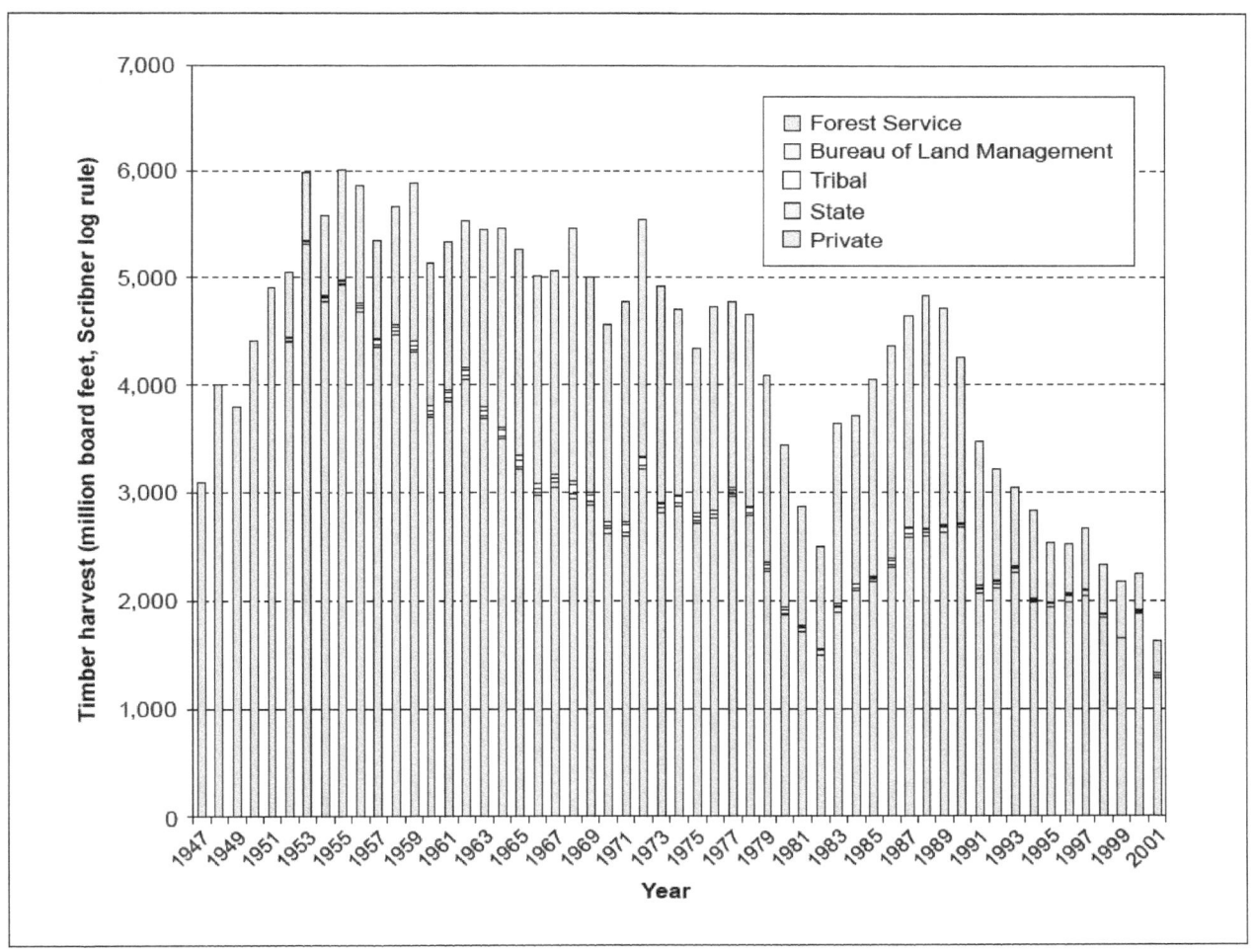

Figure 85—Timber harvest by ownership in California, 1947–2001 (Bolsinger 1980, California State Board of Equalization 2006, Warren 1985-2000).

dead trees. Saw logs were the leading product harvested, accounting for 62 percent of removals for products. Fuelwood, including industrial fuel and residential firewood, accounted for 33 percent, while veneer logs accounted for just 5 percent of removals for products. Softwoods dominated California's harvest, accounting for nearly 99 percent of removals for timber products. The largest volumes of hardwoods were used for fuelwood and pulpwood.

Total removals from California's forests during 2000 were 771.7 MMCF. This included 627.8 MMCF used for timber products and 143.8 MMCF of logging residue left in the forest as slash. Growing-stock removals were 469.2 MMCF. Nearly 95 percent (444.5 MMCF) of growing-stock removals went to produce products, and 5 percent (24.8 MMCF) was not used. Saw logs were the largest component (78 percent) of growing-stock removals, followed by industrial fuelwood (10 percent), and veneer logs (6 percent).

Private corporate timberlands provided 50 percent (232 MMCF) of growing-stock removals, whereas other private and tribal lands supplied 34 percent (160 MMCF). National forests supplied 15 percent of the volume removed from growing stock. Other public landowners, including the Bureau of Land Management and the state of California, provided slightly more than 1 percent.

Douglas-fir was the leading species harvested, accounting for almost 27 percent (125 MMCF) of growing-stock removals (fig. 86). True firs, ponderosa pine, and redwood represented about 21, 18, and 16 percent of growing stock removals, respectively. Sugar pine, cedars, hemlock, lodgepole pine, other pines, and spruces together accounted for 17 percent of growing-stock removals. Hardwoods, including red alder, accounted for less than 1 percent (3 MMCF). Douglas-fir was the leading species harvested for saw logs, and true firs led the veneer log and fuelwood harvest.

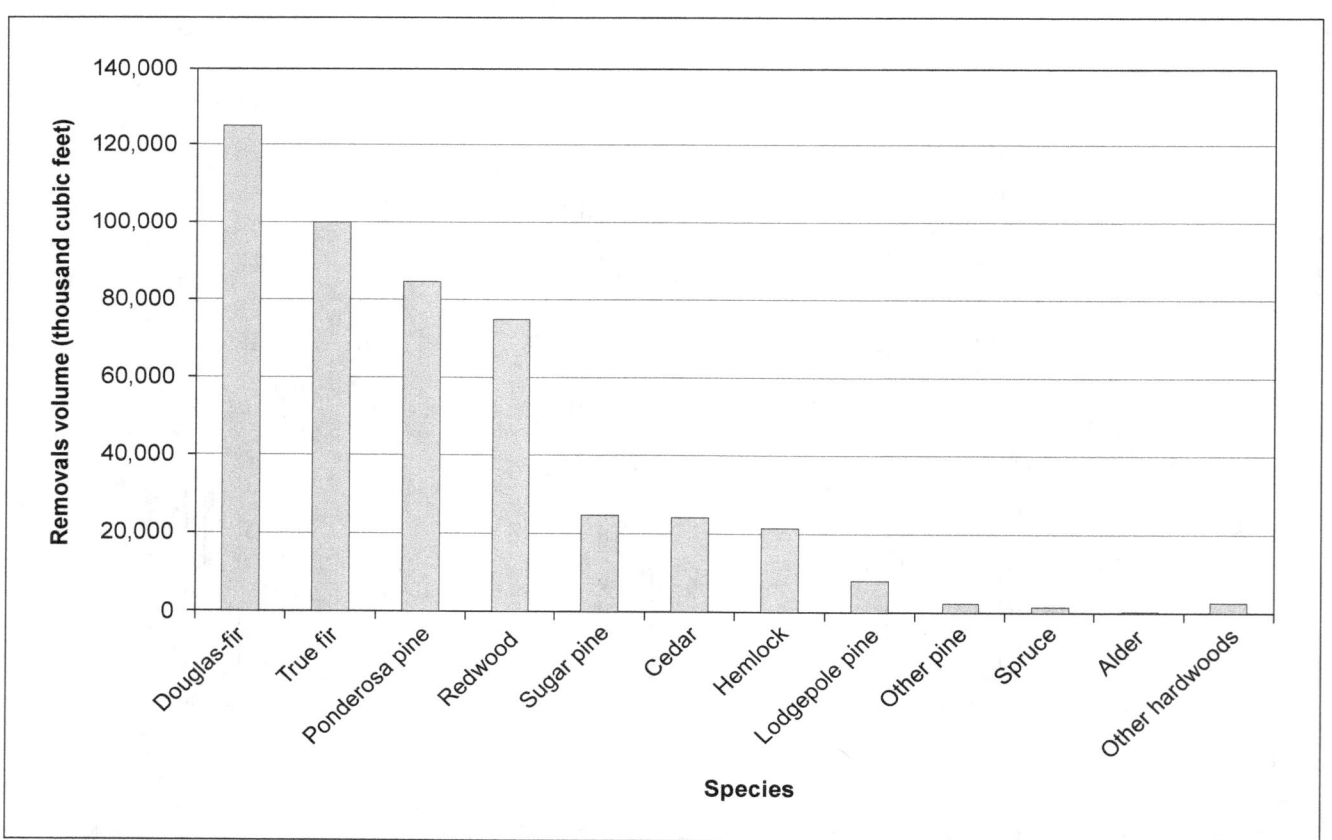

Figure 86—Volume of growing stock removals by tree species in California, 2000. (Morgan et al. 2004).

Interpretation

Sustainability of California's forests depends on sustainable harvest levels and a forest products industry capable of using wood removed from inventory. Statewide, forest growth substantially exceeded harvest. Decreases in California's timber harvest have largely been the result of harvest reductions from national forests. These harvests declined 86 percent between 1988 and 2001, although volume harvested from private lands decreased 43 percent over the same period. These declines in in-state timber harvest volumes have made California's citizens and forest products industry increasingly reliant on out-of-state timber; the volume of imported timber increased 995 percent between 1988 and 2000. Continuing declines in California's timber harvest will impact both the industry and the ability to conduct vegetation management as timber processors and forest operators go out of business.

Removals for timber products tables in appendix 2—

- Table 52—Total roundwood output by product, species group, and source of material, California, 2000
- Table 53—Volume of timber removals by type of removal, source of material, and species group, California, 2000

Nontimber Forest Products[6]

Background

Nontimber forest products (NTFP) are species harvested from forests for reasons other than production of timber commodities (e.g., lumber and plywood). Vascular plants, lichens, and fungi are the primary organisms included in NTFPs (Jones 1999), and are collected for subsistence, recreation, education, and commercial enterprise (Vance et al. 2001). The NTFPs are fundamental to many botanical, floral, and woodcraft industries and are important to medicinal and natural-food industries.

Although harvest of NTFPs is prevalent in Pacific coast forests, relatively little is known about their overall abundance or how they are affected by different land management practices. It is also unclear whether current

levels of harvesting are sustainable or whether they are harming the resources (Everett 1997). Because FIA crews record the cover of the most abundant, readily identifiable vascular plant species found on each phase 2 plot, the inventory can provide useful baseline information on the status and trends of many NTFP species (Vance et al. 2002). Crews also collect samples of epiphytic lichens found on phase 3 plots, allowing the assessment of selected lichen NTFPs.

Lists of vascular plant NTFPs were compiled from the literature (Everett 1997, Jones 1999, Vance et al. 2001) and compared with species recorded on FIA plots. Species that were considered readily identifiable by most crews (i.e., common shrubs or common and distinctive herbs) were included in the analyses, as well as seedlings and saplings of selected tree species (under the assumption that most boughs are harvested from small trees). Cover of each species was averaged across all sampled subplots, and the area covered on each plot extrapolated to all forest land with standard inventory statistics.

Findings

The herb species with the greatest cover was swordfern, which covers 176,000 acres; brackenfern was the next most widespread herb, covering 142,000 acres. The shrubs with the greatest cover were greenleaf manzanita (388,000 acres) (fig. 87), California huckleberry (265,000 acres), and

Figure 87—Greenleaf manzanita is the nontimber forest product that covered the greatest area on forest lands in California, 2001–2005.

[6] Authors: Andrew Gray and Sarah Jovan.

whiteleaf manzanita (227,000 acres). The cover of NTFP tree seedlings and saplings was generally low except for Douglas-fir, which covered 128,000 acres. Plant NTFPs were most prevalent in moist ecosections; the Northern California Coast section (fig. 88) had the greatest percentage of area covered by NTFP plants. Lichen NTFPs were common, with wolf lichen recorded on 54 percent of the forested plots.

Interpretation

California's forests appear to have abundant resources of NTFP vascular plant species, including those used for floral, medicinal, and woodcraft businesses (e.g., swordfern, St. John's wort, and greenleaf manzanita, respectively) and those important for subsistence and recreation (e.g., Oregon grape and California huckleberry). The proportion of plants of a species that produce the desired quality of greens or fruits is unknown, so the utilizable resource may be somewhat less than that suggested by estimates of the covered area. These figures will provide an important baseline for changes over time and could be used for more detailed analyses by ownership or geographical unit.

Nontimber forest products tables in appendix 2—
- Table 54—Estimated area of forest land covered by vascular plant nontimber forest products, by plant group and species, California, 2001–2005
- Table 55—Percentage of forested plots with selected lichen nontimber forest products present, by species, California, 2001–2005

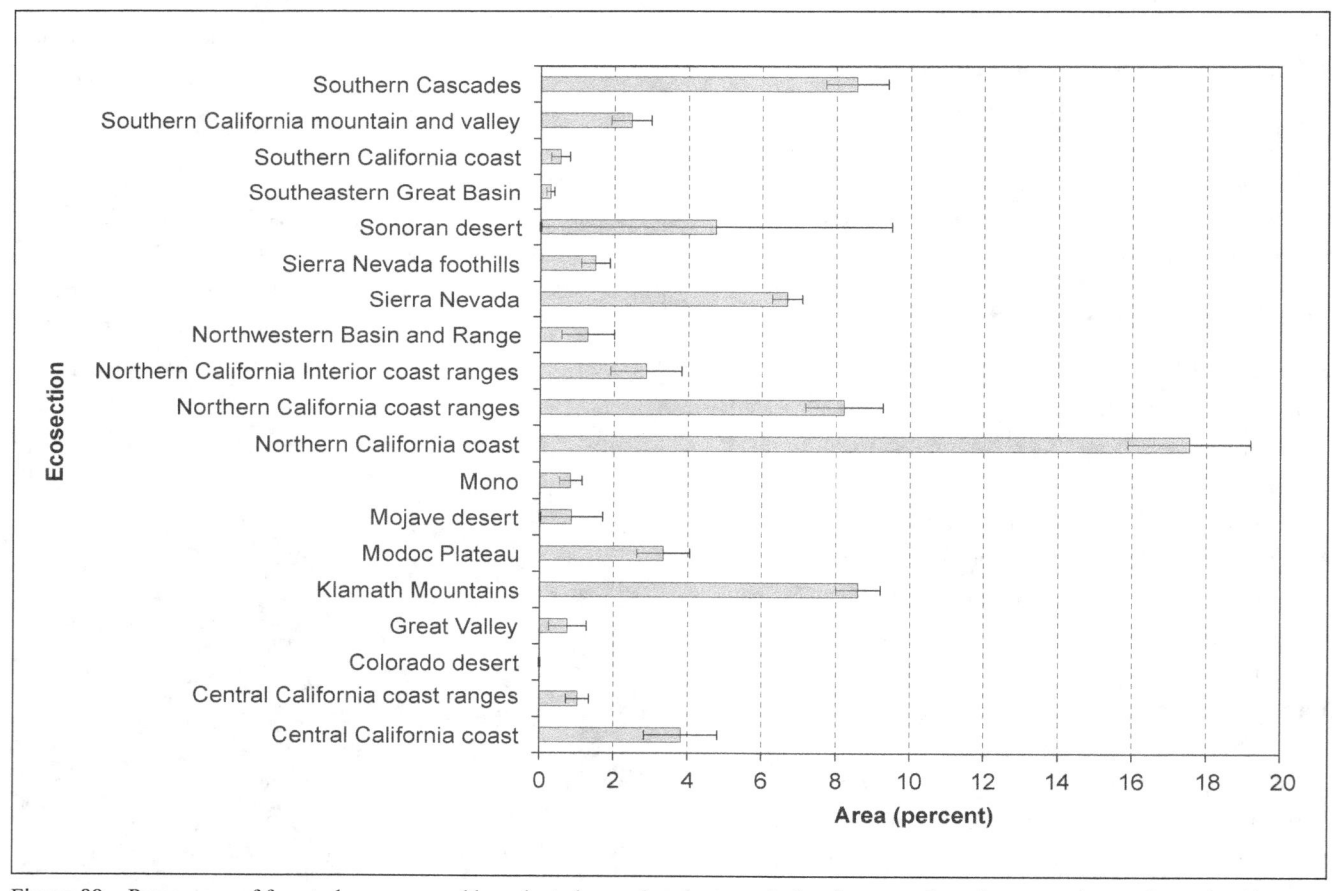

Figure 88—Percentage of forested area covered by selected vascular plant nontimber forest products by ecosection on forest land in California, 2001–2005.

Conclusions

This report has presented an overview of California's forest resources, highlighting information that is new as well as confirming previously known information. We expect some readers will be eager to see more indepth research and analysis on selected topics to fully understand current status, change, and relationships in California's forests. Some possible areas of future work include, but are not limited to, more comprehensive reporting and analysis of forest fuels, carbon dynamics, forest productivity, and forest health issues such as the extent of sudden oak death.

We expect that our own PNW-FIA research staff as well as researchers and analysts from other programs and institutions will investigate many of the questions that can be addressed with the annual inventory data, especially once a full cycle of data has been collected.

The annual FIA inventory, as currently designed, will continue into the future provided funding and support for it are maintained. As directed by the 1998 Farm Bill (Section 253[c] of the Agricultural Research, Extension, and Education Reform Act of 1998), findings from the inventory will be published every 5 years. For California, the next report is scheduled for 2012, after a full cycle of data collection has been completed on all FIA plots.

Glossary

abiotic—Pertaining to nonliving factors such as temperature, moisture, and wind (Goheen and Willhite 2006).

aerial photography—Imagery acquired from an aerial platform (typically aircraft or helicopter) by means of a specialized large-format camera with well-defined optical characteristics. The geometry of the aircraft orientation at the time of image acquisition is also recorded. The resultant photograph will be of known scale, positional accuracy, and precision. Aerial photography for natural resource use is usually either natural color or color-infrared, and is film based or acquired using digital electronic sensors.

air quality index—Value or set of values derived from a multivariate model that examines the composition of lichen communities at each plot to provide a relative estimate of air quality.

aspect—Compass direction that a slope faces.

basal area—The cross-sectional area of a tree trunk.

biodiversity—Variety and variability among living organisms and the ecological complexes in which they occur. Diversity can be defined as the number of different items and their relative frequencies. http://www.epa.gov/OCEPAterms/bterms.html. (21 March 2008).

bioenergy—Renewable energy made available from materials derived from biological sources. http://en.wikipedia.org/wiki/Bioenergy. (21 March 2008).

biomass—The aboveground weight of wood and bark in live trees 1.0 inches diameter at breast height (d.b h.) and larger from the ground to the tip of the tree, excluding all foliage. The weight of wood and bark in lateral limbs, secondary limbs, and twigs under 0.5 inch in diameter at the point of occurrence on sapling-size trees is included in the measure, but on poletimber- and sawtimber-sized trees this material is excluded. Biomass is typically expressed as green or ovendry weight in tons (USDA Forest Service 2006).

biosite index, ozone—A value calculated from the amount and severity of ozone injury at a site (biosite) that reflects local air quality and plant response and therefore potential risk of ozone impact in the area represented by that biosite (Campbell et al. 2007).

biotic—Pertaining to living organisms and their ecological and physiological relations (Helms 1998).

board foot—A volume measure of lumber 1 foot wide, 1 foot long, and 1 inch thick equal to 144 cubic inches. http://www.ccffa-oswa.org/B html. (21 March 2008).

bole—Trunk or main stem of a tree (USDA Forest Service 2006).

bulk density—Mass of soil per unit volume. A measure of the ratio of pore space to solid materials in a given soil, expressed in units of grams per cubic centimeter of ovendry soil (USDA Forest Service 2006).

carbon mass—The estimated weight of carbon stored within wood tissues. On average, carbon mass values are about half of biomass values for trees, and are summarized as thousand tons or mean tons per acre.

carbon sequestration—Incorporation of carbon dioxide into permanent plant tissues (Helms 1998).

chapparal—A shrubland or heathland plant community found primarily in California, USA, that is shaped by a Mediterranean climate (mild, wet winters and hot dry summers) and wildfire. A typical chaparral plant community consists of densely-growing evergreen scrub oaks and other drought-resistant shrubs. It often grows so densely that it is impenetrable by large animals and humans. http://en.wikipedia.org/wiki/Chaparral. (21 March 2008).

coarse woody material (CWM)—Down dead tree and shrub boles, large limbs, and other woody pieces that are severed from their original source of growth. CWM also includes dead trees that are leaning >45 degrees from vertical and are still supported by roots, as well as those severed from roots or uprooted (USDA Forest Service 2006).

cogeneration facilities—One or more parallel generation units producing both electrical energy and steam or another form of useful energy for industrial, commercial, heating, or cooling purposes. http://www.srpnet.com/about/econ/terms.aspx. (21 March 2008).

compaction (soil)—Process by which soil grains are rearranged so as to come into closer contact with one another, resulting in a decrease in void space and an increase in soil bulk density (Helms 1998).

corporate land—An ownership class of private lands owned by a company, corporation, legal partnership, investment firm, bank, timberland investment management organization (TIMO), or real estate investment trust (REIT).

crook—Abrupt bend in a tree or log (Helms 1998).

crown fire—Fire that spreads across the tops of trees or shrubs more or less independently of a surface fire. Crown fires are sometimes classed as running (independent or active) or dependent (passive) to distinguish the degree of independence from the surface fire (Helms 1998).

crown—The part of a tree or woody plant bearing live branches or foliage (Helms 1998).

current gross annual growth—The total growth of a given stand of trees, within a defined area, over the period of 1 year.

cyanolichen—Lichen species containing cyanobacteria, which fixes atmospheric nitrogen into a form that plants can use.

damage—Damage to trees caused by biotic agents such as insects, diseases, and animals or abiotic agents such as weather, fire, or mechanical equipment.

defoliation—Premature removal of foliage (Goheen and Willhite 2006).

diameter at breast height (d.b h.)—Diameter of a tree stem, located at 4.5 feet above the ground (breast height) on the uphill side of a tree. The point of diameter measurement may vary on abnormally formed trees (USDA Forest Service 2006).

dieback—Progressive dying from the extremity of any part of the plant. Dieback may or may not result in death of the entire plant (Helms 1998).

disturbance—Any relatively discrete event in time that disrupts ecosystem, community, or population structure and changes resources, substrate availability, or the physical environment (Helms 1998).

down woody material (DWM)—Dead material on the ground in various stages of decay, including coarse and fine woody material. Previously named down woody debris (DWD). The DWM indicator for Forest Inventory and Analysis (FIA) includes measurements of depth of duff layer, litter layer, and overall fuelbed; fuel loading on the microplot; and residue piles (USDA Forest Service 2006).

ecological region—A top-level scale in a hierarchical classification of ecological units subdivided on the basis of global, continental, and regional climatic regimes and broad physiography. Ecological regions (ecoregions) are further subdivided into domains, divisions, and provinces. The next level down in the hierarchy, subregion, is divided into ecological sections (ecosections) and subsections (Cleland et al. 1997).

ecosections—A level in a hierarchical classification of ecological units for a geographic area delineated on the basis of similar climate, geomorphic processes, stratigraphy, geologic origin, topography, and drainage systems (Cleland et al. 1997).

ecosystem—A spatially explicit, relatively homogeneous unit of the Earth that includes all interacting organisms and components of the abiotic environment within its boundaries. An ecosystem can be of any size: a log, a pond, a field, a forest, or the Earth's biosphere (Helms 1998).

elevation—Height above a fixed reference point, often the mean sea level. http://en.wikipedia.org/wiki/Elevation. (21 March 2008).

endemic—1. Indigenous to or characteristic of a particular restricted geographical area. Antonym: exotic. 2. Referring to a disease constantly infecting a few plants throughout an area. 3. A population of potentially injurious plants, animals, or viruses that are at low levels (see Epidemic) (Helms 1998).

epidemic—1. Entomology: pertaining to populations of plants, animals, and viruses that build up, often rapidly, to unusually and generally injuriously high level. Synonym: outbreak. Many insect and other animal populations cycle periodically or irregularly between endemic and epidemic levels. 2. Pathology: a disease sporadically infecting a large number of hosts in an area and causing considerable loss (Helms 1998).

epiphytic—Describing a plant growing on but not nourished by another plant. (Helms 1998)

erosion—The wearing away of the land surface by running water, wind, ice, or other geological agents (USDA Forest Service 2006).

federal land—An ownership class of public lands owned by the U.S. government (USDA Forest Service 2006).

fine woody material (FWM)—Down dead branches, twigs, and small tree or shrub boles <3 inches in diameter not attached to a living or standing dead source (USDA Forest Service 2006).

fire regime—The characteristic frequency, extent, intensity, severity, and seasonality of fires within an ecosystem (Helms 1998).

fixed-radius plot—A circular sampled area with a specified radius in which all trees of a given size, shrubs, as well as other items, are tallied (USDA Forest Service 2006).

forb—A broad-leaved herbaceous plant, as distinguished from grasses, shrubs, and trees (USDA Forest Service 2006).

forest industry land—An ownership class of private lands owned by a company or an individual(s) operating a primary wood-processing plant (USDA Forest Service 2006).

forest land—Land that is at least 10 percent stocked by forest trees of any size, or land formerly having such tree cover, and not currently developed for a nonforest use. The minimum area for classification as forest land is 1 acre. Roadside, streamside, and shelterbelt strips of timber must be at least 120 feet wide to qualify as forest land (USDA Forest Service 2006).

forest type—A classification of forest land based upon and named for the tree species that forms the plurality of live-tree stocking (USDA Forest Service 2006).

fork—The place on a tree where the stem separates into two pieces; usually considered a defect.

fuel treatment—Any manipulation or removal of wildland fuels to reduce the likelihood or ignition or to lessen potential fire damage and resistance to control; e.g., lopping, chipping, crushing, piling, and burning. Synonym: fuel modification, hazard reduction (Helms 1998).

fuelwood—Wood salvaged from mill waste, cull logs, branches, etc., and used to fuel fires in a boiler or furnace. http://nfdp.ccfm.org/compendium/products/terminology_e.php. (21 March 2008).

fungus—Member of a group of saprophytic and parasitic organisms that lack chlorophyll, have cell walls made of chitin, and reproduce by spores; includes molds, rusts, mildews, smuts, mushrooms. Fungi absorb nutrients from the organic matter in which they live. Not classified as plants; instead fungi are placed in the Kingdom: Fungi (Goheen and Willhite 2006).

geospatial—The combination of spatial software and analytical methods with terrestrial or geographic data sets. Often used in conjunction with geographic information systems and geomatics. http://en.wikipedia.org/wiki/Geospatial. (21 March 2008).

geothermal energy—The word "geothermal" is derived from words literally meaning "Earth" plus "heat." To produce electric power from geothermal resources, underground reservoirs of steam or hot water are tapped by wells and the steam rotates turbines that generate electricity. http://www.ngdc.noaa.gov/seg/hazard/stratoguide/glossary.html. (21 March 2008).

graminoid—Grasses (family Gramineae or Poaceae) and grasslike plants such as sedges (family Cyperaceae) and rushes (family Juncaceae). http://www.biology-online.org/dictionary/Graminoid. (21 March 2008).

grassland—Land on which the vegetation is dominated by grasses, grasslike plants, or forbs (Helms 1998).

greenhouse gas—A gas, such as carbon dioxide or methane, which contributes to potential climate change. http://www.epa.gov/OCEPAterms/gterms html. (21 March 2008).

growing stock—All live trees 5 inches d.b.h or larger that are considered merchantable in terms of saw-log length and grade; excludes rough and rotten cull trees (USDA Forest Service 2006).

hardwood—Tree species belonging to the botanical subdivision Angiospermae, class Dicotyledonous, usually broad-leaved and deciduous (USDA Forest Service 2006).

herbivory—The consumption of herbaceous vegetation by organisms ranging from insects to large mammals such as deer, elk, or cattle. http://www.biology-online.org/dictionary/Herbivory. (21 March 2008).

increment borer—An auger-like instrument with a hollow bit and an extractor, used to extract thin radial cylinders of wood (increment cores) from trees having annual growth rings, to determine increment or age (Helms 1998).

interpolation—A method of reallocating attribute data from one spatial representation to another. Kriging is a more complex example that allocates data from sample points to a surface. http://hds.essex.ac.uk/g2gp/gis/sect101.asp. (21 March 2008).

invasive plant—A plant that has spread or is likely to spread into native flora or managed plant systems, develop a self-sustaining population, and become dominant or disruptive. Invasive plants may be either native or nonnative. http://www.invasivespeciesinfo.gov/docs/council/isacdef.pdf. (21 March 2008).

ladder fuel—Combustible material that provides vertical continuity between vegetation strata and allows fire to climb into the crowns of trees or shrubs with relative ease. Ladder fuels help initiate and ensure the continuation of a crown fire (Helms 1998).

late-successional reserves (LSRs)—Federally managed forests held in reserve for wildlife habitat and thus set aside from most commercial logging. The LSRs may contain old clearcuts as well as old-growth forests. Logging may be allowed in an LSR if it will accelerate development of old-growth characteristics. http://www.umpqua-watersheds.org/glossary/gloss_l html. (21 March 2008).

lichen—An organism consisting of a fungus and an alga or cyanobacterium living in symbiotic association. Lichens look like masses of small, leafy, tufted or crust-like plants (USDA Forest Service 2006).

live trees—All living trees, including all size classes, all tree classes, and both commercial and noncommercial species for tree species listed in the FIA field manual (USDA Forest Service 2006).

mean annual increment (MAI) at culmination—A measure of the productivity of forest land expressed as the average increase in cubic foot volume per acre per year. For a given species and site index, the mean is based on the age at which the MAI culminates for fully stocked natural stands. The MAI is based on the site index of the plot (Azuma et al. 2004).

mesic—Describes sites or habitats characterized by intermediate moisture conditions; i.e., neither decidedly wet nor dry (Helms 1998).

microclimate—The climate of a small area, such as that under a plant or other cover, differing in extremes of temperature and moisture from the larger climate outside (Helms 1998).

MMBF—A million board feet of wood in logs or lumber (Helms 1998).

model—1. An abstract representation of objects and events from the real world for the purpose of simulating a process, predicting an outcome, or characterizing a phenomenon. 2. Geogrpahic information system (GIS) data representative of reality (e.g., spatial data models), including the arc-node, georelational model, rasters or grids, polygon, and triangular irregular networks (Helms 1998).

Montréal Process—In September 1993, the Conference on Security and Cooperation in Europe (CSCE) sponsored an international seminar in Montréal, Canada, on the sustainable development of boreal and temperate forests, with a focus on developing criteria and indicators for the assessment of these forests. After the seminar, Canada drew together countries from North and South America, Asia, and the Pacific Rim to develop criteria and indicators for nontropical forests and, in June 1994, the initiative now known as the Montréal Process began. The European countries elected to work as a region in the Pan-European Forest Process in the followup to the Ministerial Conferences on the Protection of Forests in Europe. http://www.mpci.org/rep-pub/1999/broch_e.html#2. (21 March 2008).

mortality—The death of trees from natural causes, or subsequent to incidents such as storms, wildfire, or insect and disease epidemics (Helms 1998).

multivariate analysis—Branch of statistics concerned with analyzing multiple measurements that have been made on one or several individuals (Helms 1998).

municipal land—Land owned by municipalities or land leased by them for more than 50 years (USDA Forest Service 2006).

mycorrhiza—The usually symbiotic association between higher plant roots (host) and the mycelia of specific fungi. Mycorrhizae aid plants in the uptake of water and certain nutrients and may offer protection against other soil-borne organisms (Helms 1998).

national forest lands—Federal lands that have been designated by Executive order or statute as national forest or purchase units and other lands under the administration of the U.S. Department of Agriculture, Forest Service, including experimental areas and Bankhead-Jones Title III lands (Azuma et al. 2004).

Native American lands—Tribal lands, and allotted lands held in trust by the federal government. Native American lands are grouped with farmer and miscellaneous private lands as other private lands (Azuma et al. 2004).

native species—Plant species that were native to an American region prior to Euro-American settlement. For vascular plants, they are the species that are not present on the USDA NRCS (2000) list of nonnative species (see Nonnative species) (USDA Natural Resources Conservation Service 2000).

nitrophyte—One of a group of lichen species that grow in nitrogen-rich habitats.

nitrogen oxides (NO_x)—Gases consisting of one molecule of nitrogen and varying numbers of oxygen molecules, produced in the emissions of vehicle exhausts and from power stations. Atmospheric NO_x contributes to formation of photochemical ozone (smog), which can impair visibility and harm human health. http://www.climatechange.ca.gov/glossary/letter_n html. (21 March 2008).

noncorporate forest land—Private forest land owned by nongovernmental conservation or natural resource organizations; unincorporated partnerships, associations, or clubs; individuals or families; or Native Americans.

nonnative species—Plant species that were introduced to America subsequent to Euro-American settlement. Nonnative vascular plants are present on the USDA NRCS (2000) list of nonnative species (USDA Natural Resources Conservation Service 2000).

nonstocked areas—Timberland less than 10 percent stocked with live trees. Recent clearcuts scheduled for planting are classified as nonstocked area (Azuma et al. 2004).

nontimber forest products (NTFP)—Species harvested from forests for reasons other than production of timber commodities. Vascular plants, lichens, and fungi are the primary organisms included in NTFPs.

old-growth forest—Old-growth forest is differentiated from younger forest by its structure and composition, and often by its function. Old-growth stands are typified by the presence of large older trees; variety in tree species, sizes, and spacing; multiple canopy layers; high amounts of standing and down dead wood; and broken, deformed, or rotting tops, trunks, and roots (Franklin et al. 1986).

other private lands—Lands in private ownership and not reported separately. These may include coal companies, land trusts, and other corporate private landowners (USDA Forest Service 2006).

overrun—Difference between the log scale of a shipment of timber and the volume of actual lumber obtained from it. http://forestry.about.com/library/glossary/blforglo htm. (21 March 2008).

overstory—That portion of the trees, in a forest of more than one story, forming the uppermost canopy layer (Helms 1998).

owner class—A variable that classifies land into categories of ownership. Current ownership classes are listed in the field manual (USDA Forest Service 2006).

owner group—A variable that combines owner classes into the following groups: Forest Service, other federal agency, state and local government, and private (USDA Forest Service 2006).

ownership—A legal entity having an ownership interest in land, regardless of the number of people involved. An ownership may be an individual; a combination of persons; a legal entity such as corporation, partnership, club, or trust; or a public agency. An ownership has control of a parcel or group of parcels of land (USDA Forest Service 2006).

ozone, tropospheric (O_3)—A regional, gaseous air pollutant produced primarily through sunlight-driven chemical reactions of nitrogen oxide (NO_2) and hydrocarbons in the troposphere (the lowest layer of the atmosphere). Ozone plays a significant role in greenhouse warming and urban smog and causes foliar injury to deciduous trees, conifers, shrubs, and herbaceous species (Air and Waste Management Association 1998).

pathogen—Parasitic organism directly capable of causing disease (Helms 1998).

phytotoxic—Poisonous to plants (Helms 1998).

prescribed burn—Deliberate burning of wildland fuels in either their natural or their modified state and under specified environmental conditions, usually to make the site less susceptible to severe wildfire. Synonym: controlled burn, prescribed fire (Adapted from Helms 1998).

private land—An ownership group that includes all family, individual, corporate, nonpublic conservation and natural resource organizations, unincorporated partnerships, associations, clubs, and Native American lands.

public land—An ownership group that includes all federal, state, county, and municipal lands (USDA Forest Service 2006).

pulpwood—Whole trees, tree chips, or wood residues used to produce wood pulp for the manufacture of paper products. Pulpwood is usually wood that is too small, of inferior quality, or the wrong species for the manufacture of lumber or plywood. http://nfdp.ccfm.org/compendium/products/terminology_e.php. (21 March 2008).

quadrat—The basic 3.28 square feet sampling unit for the Phase 3 Vegetation Indicator (USDA Forest Service 2006).

rangeland—Expansive, mostly unimproved lands on which a significant proportion of the natural vegetation is native grasses, grass-like plants, forbs, and shrubs. Rangelands include natural grasslands, savannas, shrublands, most deserts, tundra, alpine communities, coastal marshes, and wet meadows. http:/en.wikipedia.org/wiki/Rangeland. (21 March 2008).

regeneration (artificial and natural)—The established progeny from a parent plant, seedlings or saplings existing in a stand, or the act of renewing tree cover by establishing young trees naturally or artificially. May be artificial (direct seeding or planting) or natural (natural seeding, coppice, or root suckers) (Adapted from Helms 1998).

remote sensing—Capture of information about the Earth from a distant vantage point. The term is often associated with satellite imagery but also applies to aerial photography, airborne digital sensors, ground-based detectors, and other devices. http://www.nsc.org/ehc/glossar2 htm. (21 March 2008).

reserved forest land—Land permanently reserved from wood products utilization through statute or administrative designation. Examples include national forest wilderness areas and national parks and monuments (USDA Forest Service 2006).

richness—The number of different species in a given area, often referred to at the plot scale as alpha diversity and at the region scale as gamma diversity (USDA Natural Resources Conservation Service 2000).

riparian—Related to, living in, or associated with a wetland, such as the bank of a river or stream or the edge of a lake or tidewater. The riparian biotic community significantly influences and is influenced by the neighboring body of water (Helms 1998).

sampling error—Difference between a population value and a sample estimate that is attributable to the sample, as distinct from errors due to bias in estimation, errors in observation, etc. Sampling error is measured as the standard error of the sample estimate (Helms 1998).

sapling—A live tree 1.0 to 4.9 inches in diameter (USDA Forest Service 2006).

saw log—A log meeting minimum standards of diameter, length, and defect for manufacture into lumber or plywood. The definition includes logs, with a minimum diameter outside bark for softwoods of 7 inches (9 inches for hardwoods) (Adapted from Connor et al. 2004 and Azuma et al. 2004).

sawtimber trees—Live softwood trees of commercial species at least 9.0 inches in d.b.h. and live hardwood trees of commercial species at least 11.0 inches d.b.h. At least 25 percent of the board-foot volume in a sawtimber tree must be free from defect. Softwood trees must contain at least one 12-foot saw log with a top diameter of not less than 7 inches outside bark; hardwood trees must contain at least one 8-foot saw log with a top diameter of not less than 9 inches outside bark (Azuma et al. 2004).

seedlings—Live trees <1.0 inch d.b.h. and at least 6 inches in height (softwoods) or 12 inches in height (hardwoods) (USDA Forest Service 2006).

shrub—Perennial, multistemmed woody plant, usually less than 13 to 16 feet in height, although under certain environmental conditions shrubs may be single-stemmed or taller than 16 feet. Includes succulents (e.g., cacti) (USDA Forest Service 2007b).

shrubland—A shrub-dominated vegetation type that does not qualify as forest.

slope—Measure of change in surface value over distance, expressed in degrees or as a percentage (Helms 1998).

snag—Standing dead tree ≥5 inches d.b h. and ≥4.5 feet in length, with a lean of <45 degrees. Dead trees leaning more than 45 degrees are considered to be down woody material. Standing dead material shorter than 4.5 feet are considered stumps (USDA Forest Service 2007b).

softwood—Coniferous trees, usually evergreen having needles or scale-like leaves (Smith et al. 2004).

specific gravity constants—Ratio of the density (weight per unit volume) of an object (such as wood) to the density of water at 4 degrees C (39.2 degrees F) (Helms 1998).

stand age—Average age of the live dominant and codominant trees in the predominant stand size class (USDA Forest Service 2006).

state land—An ownership class of public lands owned by states or lands leased by states for more than 50 years (USDA Forest Service 2006).

stocked/nonstocked—In the FIA Program, a minimum stocking value of 10 percent live trees is required for accessible forest land (USDA Forest Service 2007b).

stocking—1. At the tree level, the density value assigned to a sampled tree (usually in terms of numbers of trees or basal area per acre), expressed as a percentage of the total tree density required to fully use the growth potential of the land. 2. At the stand level, the sum of the stocking values of all trees sampled (Bechtold and Patterson 2005).

stratification—A statistical tool used to reduce the variance of the attributes of interest by partitioning the population into homogenous strata (Bechtold and Patterson 2005).

succession—The gradual supplanting of one community of plants by another (Helms 1998).

surface fire—A fire that burns only surface fuels, such as litter, loose debris, and small vegetation (Helms 1998).

sustainability—The capacity of forests, ranging from stands to ecological regions, to maintain their health, productivity, diversity, and overall integrity in the long run, in the context of human activity and use (Helms 1998).

terrestrial—Of or relating to the Earth or its inhabitants; of or relating to land as distinct from air or water. http://www.merriam-webster.com/dictionary/terrestrial. (21 March 2008).

timberland—Forest land that is producing or capable of producing >20 cubic feet per year of wood at culmination of mean annual increment (MAI). Timberland excludes reserved forest lands (USDA Forest Service 2006).

transect—A narrow sample strip or a measured line laid out through vegetation chosen for study (Helms 1998).

tree—A woody perennial plant, typically large, with a single well-defined stem carrying a more or less definite crown; sometimes defined as attaining a minimum diameter of 3 inches and a minimum height of 15 feet at maturity. For FIA, any plant on the tree list in the current field manual is measured as a tree (USDA Forest Service 2006).

understory—All forest vegetation growing under an overstory (Helms 1998).

unreserved forest land—Forest land that is not withdrawn from harvest by statute or administrative regulation. Includes forest lands that are not capable of producing in excess of 20 cubic feet per acre per year of industrial wood in natural stands (Smith et al. 2004).

upland—Any area that does not qualify as a wetland because the associated hydrologic regime is not sufficiently wet to produce vegetation, soils, or hydrologic characteristics associated with wetlands. In flood plains, such areas are more appropriately termed non-wetlands. http://www.biology-online.org/dictionary/Upland. (21 March 2008).

veneer log—A high-quality log of a desirable species suitable for conversion to veneer. Veneer logs must be large, straight, of minimum taper, and free of defects. http://www.agnr.umd.edu/MCE/Publications/Publication.cfm?ID=78. (21 March 2008).

vascular plant—A plant possessing a well-developed system of conducting tissue to transport water, mineral salts, and sugars. http://www.biology-online.org/dictionary/Vascular_plant. (21 March 2008).

wilderness—1. According to the Wilderness Act of 1964, "a wilderness, in contrast with those areas where man and his works dominate the landscape, is hereby recognized as an area where the earth and its community of life are untrammeled by man, where man himself is a visitor who does not remain." 2. A roadless land legally classified as a component area of the National Wilderness Preservation System and managed to protect its qualities of naturalness, solitude, and opportunity for primitive recreation. Wilderness areas are usually of sufficient size to make maintenance in such a state feasible (Helms 1998).

wildfire—Any uncontained fire, other than prescribed fire, occurring on wildland. Synonym: wildland fire (Adapted from Helms 1998).

wildland—Land other than that dedicated for uses such as agricultural, urban, mining, or parks (Helms 1998).

wildland forest—A large continuous tract of forest with few or no developed structures on it. Delineated on aerial imagery for the purpose of detecting land use change. The FIA Program and the Oregon Department of Forestry jointly use a minimum of 640 acres with fewer than five developed structures to designate wildland forest.

wildland-urban interface (WUI)—A popular term used to describe an area where various structures (most notably private homes) and other human developments meet or are intermingled with forest and other vegetative fuel types. http://www.borealforest.org/nwgloss13.htm. (21 March 2008).

xeric—Pertaining to sites or habitats characterized by decidedly dry conditions (Helms 1998).

Common and Scientific Plant Names[1]

Common name	Scientific name
Trees:	
Alder	*Alnus* spp.
Ash	*Fraxinus* spp.
Aspen, quaking aspen	*Populus tremuloides* Michx.
Bigcone Douglas-fir	*Pseudotsuga macrocarpa* (Vasey) Mayr
Bigleaf maple	*Acer macrophyllum* Pursh
Birch	*Betula* spp.
Bishop pine	*Pinus muricata* D. Don
Bitter cherry	*Prunus emarginata* (Dougl. ex Hook.) D. Dietr.
Black cottonwood	*Populus balsamifera* L. ssp. *trichocarpa* (Torr. & A. Gray ex Hook.) Brayshaw
Blue oak	*Quercus douglasii* Hook. & Arn.
Boxelder	*Acer negundo* L.
Brewer spruce	*Picea breweriana* S. Wats.
Bristlecone pine	*Pinus aristata* Engelm.
California black oak	*Quercus kelloggii* Newberry
California Buckeye	*Aesculus californica* (Spach) Nutt.
California juniper	*Juniperus californica* Carr.
California nutmeg, California torreya	*Torreya californica* Torr.
California red fir	*Abies magnifica* A. Murr.
California sycamore	*Platanus racemosa* Nutt.
California white oak	*Quercus lobata* Née
California-laurel	*Umbellularia californica* (Hook. & Arn.) Nutt.
Canyon live oak	*Quercus chrysolepis* Liebm.
Cedar	*Thuja* spp.
Cherry and plum species	*Prunus* spp.
Coast live oak, California live oak	*Quercus agrifolia* Née

Common name	Scientific name
Cottonwood	*Populus* spp.
Coulter pine	*Pinus coulteri* D. Don
Curl-leaf mountain mahogany	*Cercocarpus ledifolius* Nutt.
Cypress	*Cupressus* spp.
Douglas-fir	*Pseudotsuga menziesii* (Mirbel) Franco
Elm	*Ulmus* spp.
Engelmann oak	*Quercus engelmannii* Greene
Engelmann spruce	*Picea engelmannii* Parry ex Engelm.
Foxtail pine	*Pinus balfouriana* Grev. & Balf.
Fremont cottonwood	*Populus fremontii* S. Wats.
Giant chinquapin, golden chinquapin	*Chrysolepis chrysophylla* (Dougl. ex Hook.) Hjelmqvist
Giant sequoia	*Sequoiadendron giganteum* (Lindl.) Buchh.
Grand fir	*Abies grandis* (Dougl. ex D. Don) Lindl.
Gray pine, ghost pine	*Pinus sabiniana* Dougl. ex Dougl.
Great Basin bristlecone pine	*Pinus longaeva* D.K. Bailey
Hawthorn	*Crataegus* spp.
Hemlock	*Tsuga* spp.
Incense-cedar	*Calocedrus decurrens* (Torr.) Florin
Interior live oak	*Quercus wislizeni* A. DC.
Jeffrey pine	*Pinus jeffreyi* Grev. & Balf.
Knobcone pine	*Pinus attenuata* Lemmon
Limber pine	*Pinus flexilis* James
Lodgepole pine	*Pinus contorta* Dougl. ex Loud.
Maple	*Acer* spp.
Mesquite	*Prosopis* spp.
Monterey cypress	*Cupressus macrocarpa* Hartw. ex Gord.
Monterey pine	*Pinus radiata* D. Don
Mountain hemlock	*Tsuga mertensiana* (Bong.) Carr.
Noble fir	*Abies procera* Rehd.
Oak	*Quercus* spp.
Oregon ash	*Fraxinus latifolia* Benth.
Oregon crabapple	*Malus fusca* (Raf.) Schneid.
Oregon white oak	*Quercus garryana* Dougl. ex Hook.
Pacific dogwood	*Cornus nuttallii* Audubon ex Torr. & Gray
Pacific madrone	*Arbutus menziesii* Pursh
Pacific silver fir	*Abies amabilis* (Dougl. ex Loud.) Dougl. ex Forbes
Pacific yew	*Taxus brevifolia* Nutt.
Pine, pinyon	*Pinus* spp.
Ponderosa pine	*Pinus ponderosa* P. & C. Lawson
Port-Orford-cedar	*Chamaecyparis lawsoniana* (A. Murr.) Parl.
Red alder	*Alnus rubra* Bong.
Redcedar, juniper	*Juniperus* spp.
Redwood, coast redwood	*Sequoia sempervirens* (Lamb. ex D. Don) Endl.
Sargent's cypress	*Cupressus sargentii* Jepson
Screwbean mesquite	*Prosopis pubescens* Benth.
Shasta red fir	*Abies magnifica* A. Murr. var. *shastensis* Lemmon
Singleleaf pinyon	*Pinus monophylla* Torr. & Frém.
Sitka spruce	*Picea sitchensis* (Bong.) Carr.
Spruce	*Picea* spp.
Subalpine fir	*Abies lasiocarpa* (Hook.) Nutt.
Sugar pine	*Pinus lambertiana* Dougl.
Tanoak	*Lithocarpus densiflorus* (Hook. & Arn.) Rehd.

Common name	Scientific name
Tasmanian bluegum	*Eucalyptus globulus* Labill.
True fir species	*Abies* spp.
Twoneedle pinyon, Colorado pinyon	*Pinus edulis* Engelm.
Utah juniper	*Juniperus osteosperma* (Torr.) Little
Washoe pine	*Pinus washoensis* Mason & Stockwell
Western hemlock	*Tsuga heterophylla* (Raf.) Sarg.
Western honey mesquite	*Prosopis glandulosa* Torr.
Western juniper	*Juniperus occidentalis* Hook.
Western larch	*Larix occidentalis* Nutt.
Western redcedar	*Thuja plicata* Donn ex D. Don
Western white pine	*Pinus monticola* Dougl. ex D. Don
White alder	*Alnus rhombifolia* Nutt.
White fir	*Abies concolor* (Gord. & Glend.) Lindl. ex Hildebr.
Whitebark pine	*Pinus albicaulis* Engelm.

Shrubs:

Blue elderberry	*Sambucus nigra* L. ssp. *cerulea* (Raf.) R. Bolli
California huckleberry	*Vaccinium ovatum* Pursh
California yerba santa	*Eriodictyon californicum* (Hook. & Arn.) Torr.
Chamise	*Adenostoma fasciculatum* Hook. & Arn.
Creeping barberry	*Mahonia repens* (Lindl.) G. Don
Currant spp.	*Ribes* spp.
Cutleaf blackberry	*Rubus laciniatus* Willd.
Dwarf mistletoe	*Arceuthobium* spp.
Dwarf Oregon grape	*Mahonia nervosa* (Pursh) Nutt.
English holly	*Ilex aquifolium* L.
English ivy	*Hedera helix* L.
European black elderberry	*Sambucus nigra* L.
Greanleaf manzanita	*Arctostaphylos patula* Greene
Hairy manzanita	*Arctostaphylos columbiana* Piper
Himalayan blackberry	*Rubus discolor* Weihe & Nees
Kinnikinnick	*Arctostaphylos uva-ursi* (L.) Spreng.
Manzanita	*Arctostaphylos* spp.
Oregon boxleaf	*Paxistima myrsinites* (Pursh) Raf.
Oregon grape	*Mahonia aquifolium* (Pursh) Nutt.
Pacific ninebark	*Physocarpus capitatus* (Pursh) Kuntze
Pinemat manzanita	*Arctostaphylos nevadensis* Gray
Pipsissewa	*Chimaphila umbellata* (L.) W. Bart.
Pursh's buckthorn	*Frangula purshiana* (DC.) Cooper
Red elderberry	*Sambucus racemosa* L.
Rose spp.	*Rosa* spp.
Salal	*Gaultheria shallon* Pursh
Scotch broom	*Cytisus scoparius* (L.) Link
Scouler's willow	*Salix scouleriana* Barratt ex Hook.
Skunkbush	*Rhus trilobata* Nutt.
Snowberry	*Symphoricarpos* spp.
Snowbrush ceanothus	*Ceanothus velutinus* Dougl. ex Hook.
Sticky whiteleaf manzanita	*Arctostaphylos viscida* Parry
Thinleaf huckleberry	*Vaccinium membranaceum* Dougl. ex Torr.
Vine maple	*Acer circinatum* Pursh
Willow	*Salix* spp.

Common name	Scientific name
Forbs:	
Brackenfern	*Pteridium aquilinum* (L.) Kuhn
British Columbia wildginger	*Asarum caudatum* Lindl.
Bull thistle	*Cirsium vulgare* (Savi) Ten.
Canada thistle	*Cirsium arvense* (L.) Scop.
Common beargrass	*Xerophyllum tenax* (Pursh) Nutt.
Common yarrow	*Achillea millefolium* L.
Hairy cat's ear	*Hypochaeris radicata* L.
Heartleaf arnica	*Arnica cordifolia* Hook.
Horsetail	*Equisetum* spp.
Mugwort	*Artemisia douglasiana* Bess.
Pacific trillium	*Trillium ovatum* Pursh
Purple foxglove	*Digitalis purpurea* L.
Spreading hedgeparsley	*Torilis arvensis* (Huds.) Link
St. John's wort	*Hypericum perforatum* L.
Stinging nettle	*Urtica dioica* L.
Swordfern	*Polystichum munitum* (Kaulfuss) K. Presl
Thistle spp.	*Cirsium* spp.
Western pearly everlasting	*Anaphalis margaritacea* (L.) Benth.
Western wormwood	*Artemisia ludoviciana* Nutt.
Yellow star-thistle	*Centaurea solstitialis* L.
Graminoids:	
Bristly dogstail grass	*Cynosurus echinatus* L.
Cheatgrass	*Bromus tectorum* L.
Common velvetgrass	*Holcus lanatus* L.
Compact brome	*Bromus madritensis* L.
False brome	*Brachypodium sylvaticum* (Huds.) Beauv.
Medusahead	*Taeniatherum caput-medusae* (L.) Nevski
Orchardgrass	*Dactylis glomerata* L.
Ripgut brome	*Bromus diandrus* Roth
Silver hairgrass	*Aira caryophyllea* L.
Slender oat	*Avena barbata* Pott ex Link
Soft brome	*Bromus hordeaceus* L.
Wild oat	*Avena fatua* L.
Lichens:	
Beard lichen	*Usnea hirta* (L.) F.H. Wigg.
Beard lichens	*Usnea* spp.
Brown-eyed sunshine lichen	*Vulpicida canadensis* (Rasanen) J. E. Mattsson & M.J. Lai
Crottle	*Parmelia saxatilis* (L.) Ach.
Lace lichen	*Ramalina menziesii* Taylor
Lungwort lichen	*Lobaria pulmonaria* (L.) Hoffm.
Old man's beard	*Bryoria fremontii* (Tuck.) Brodo & D. Hawksw.
Orange wall lichen	*Xanthoria polycarpa* (Hoffm.) Rieber
Rosette lichen	*Physcia adscendens* (Fr.) H. Olivier
Witch's hair lichen	*Alectoria sarmentosa* (Ach.) Ach.
Wolf lichen	*Letharia vulpina* (L.) Hue

[1] This table includes Latin and common names of plant species mentioned in this report and accompanying tables. A great many more species, particularly of life forms other than trees, are recorded in the inventory data but are absent from this table because they are not directly mentioned in this report.

Acknowledgments

First and foremost, we want to acknowledge the Pacific Northwest Research Station (PNW) Forest Inventory and Analysis (FIA) field crews and the National Forest System contracting companies for collecting the high-quality field data on which this report is based: Stacey Allen, Nicole Amato, Julie Andersen, Brett Anderson, Julie K Anderson, Brett Annegers, Laura M. Anzalone, James A. Arciniega, Dale Baer, Sheel Bansal, Richard E. Barich, Mary Jo Bartol, Jerry Bednarczyk, Kristen Bednarczyk, Gabriel Bellante, Amanda Benton, Joseph D. Berry, Andrew Black, Hana D. Blumenfeld, Mike P. Boldt, Brad L. Bolton, Tina Boucher, Matthew Brown, Chuck T. Brushwood, Will Bunten, Jon P. Burgbacher, Whitney G. Burgess, Johnny Carson, Melisa D. Casteel, John M. Chase, Kyle Christensen, Joel T. Clark, Daniel P. Coles, Cheryl R. Coon, Janelle Cossey, Brian Daum, Jessica M. Deans, Diane Decker, Paul T. Deignan, Sebastien A. Delion, Andrew L. Deutscher, Joseph L. Digranes, Erin Edwards, Ruth A. Epling, Mark Fain, Summer Farr, Joshua D. Feinberg, Matthew Ferrante, Roger Ferriel, Walter Foss, Rebecca S. Franklin, Cynthia Friedemann, Gerhard Gareis, Christian E. Gartmann, Jami H. Goldman, Jennifer M. Gomoll, Walter E. Grabowiecki, Colleen A. Grenz, Michael R. Griffin, Paul D. Guarnaccia, Christa Gullien, Nicholas S. Gunn, Michael J. Haldeman, Jamie Halperin, Sarah C. Hamilton, Jacob J. Hawkins, David Hernandez, Andrew M. Hoff, Jenifer L. Hutchinson, Jennifer Iaccarino, Chris Jansen, Hannah M. Johnson, Antti Kaartinen, John B. Kelley, Tristan P. Kelley, Esther Kim-Ambuehl, Nicci Lambert, Marc J. LaPine, Jesper Lesch, Brian S. Lewis, Pierre Luquet-Parisien, Eva S. Masin, Donald R. Matheson, Chris A. Moltzau, Eric Murphy, Paul J. Natiella, Yhtt Nighthawk, Brandon M. Nora, Sean Osborn, Art Osmin, Lynne M. Paschal, Andrew Peterson, Ben Phoal, Jessica F. Pijoan, Lisa M. Pinnick, Robert Poindexter, Camie Quilt, Peter D. Rahn, Jennifer Rankin, Scott Rash, Arielle J. Regier, Bob Rhoads, Erin Riggs, Danielle Robbins, Jenny Rogers, Amanda J. Rollwage, Tyler C. Ross, David C. Rutledge, Jason R. Sharp, Barry Skolout, Amy E. Snively, Samuel Solano, Jacob A. Somerset, Bruce N. Stevens, Eric Straley, Suzanne L. Stricker, Brent Stroud, John V. Syring, Zack R. Taylor, Jane Terzibashian, Jennifer Thompson, Steven T. Trimble, Cora J. Valentine, Missy Voigt, Marc H. Weber, James R. Weiser, Louis White, Jon Williams, Andrew M. Wood, Marcus A. Wood, Misha Yatskov, Vilius R. Zukauskas, East-West Forestry Association, and North State Resources.

In addition to the authors, many other individuals contributed significantly to this report. Our thanks to Dale Weyermann for GIS support; to Elaina Graham and John Chase for preparing the maps displayed in this report; to Brett Butler for providing National Woodland Owner Survey data; to Chuck Veneklase for field data recorder programming and support; to Ron Wanek and Kurt Campbell for compiling the data that are the foundation of this report; to Bruce Hiserote, Joel Thompson, Erica Hanson, and Adrianna Sutton for data correction work; to Khakie Jones for assistance with photographs; to Gail Wells and Carolyn Wilson for their writing and editorial assistance; and to Mike Arbaugh, Steve Brink, Steve Jones, Tim Robards, Mark Rosenberg, Bill Stewart, Todd Schroeder, and Tim Max for their thoughtful and helpful reviews of the draft manuscript. Finally, we want to acknowledge Sue Willits, our PNW FIA program manager, and the PNW FIA team leaders, George Breazeale and Bob Rhoads, for their unflagging support of this project.

Metric Equivalents

When you know:	Multiply by:	To find:
Inches	2.54	Centimeters
Feet	.3048	Meters
Miles	1.609	Kilometers
Acres	.405	Hectares
Board feet	.0024	Cubic meters
Cubic feet	.0283	Cubic meters
Cubic feet per acre	.06997	Cubic meters per hectare
Square feet	.0929	Square meters
Square feet per acre	.229	Square meters per hectare
Ounce	28349.5	Milligrams
Pounds	.453	Kilograms
Pounds per cubic foot	16.018	Kilograms per cubic meter
Tons per acre	2.24	Megagrams per hectare
Degrees Farenheit	.55 (°F − 32)	Degrees Celsius
Kilowatt hours	3,409	B.t.u. (mean)

Literature Cited

Air and Waste Management Association. 1998. Recognition of air pollution injury to vegetation: a pictorial atlas, 2nd ed. Sec. 2.0—Ozone. Pittsburgh, PA: Air and Waste Management Association. http://secure.awma.org/OnlineLibrary/ProductDetails.aspx?ProductID=226. (21 March 2008).

Animal and Plant Inspection Service [APHIS]. 2007. *Phytophthora ramorum*/sudden oak death. http://www.aphis.usda.gov/plant_health/plant_pest_info/phytopthora_ram/index.shtml. (28 February 2007).

Azuma, D.L.; Dunham, P.A.; Hiserote, B.A.; Veneklase, C.F. 2004. Timber resource statistics for eastern Oregon, 1999. Resour. Bull. PNW-RB-238. Portland, OR: U.S. Department of Agriculture, Forest Service, Pacific Northwest Research Station. 42 p.

Barbour, R.J.; Fried, J.S.; Daugherty, P.J.; Fight, R. 2008. Predicting the potential mix of wood products available from timbershed scale fire hazard reduction treatments. Forest Policy and Economics. 10: 400–407.

Beardsley, D.; Bolsinger, C.; Warbington, R. 1999. Old-growth forests in the Sierra Nevada: by type in 1945 and 1993 and ownership in 1993. Res. Pap. PNW-RP-516. Portland, OR: U.S. Department of Agriculture, Forest Service, Pacific Northwest Research Station. 46 p.

Beardsley, D.; Warbington, R. 1996. Old growth in northwestern California national forests. Res. Pap. PNW-RP-491. Portland, OR: U.S. Department of Agriculture, Forest Service, Pacific Northwest Research Station. 47 p.

Bechtold, W.A.; Patterson, P.L. 2005. The enhanced Forest Inventory and Analysis Program—national sampling design and estimation procedures. Gen. Tech. Rep. GTR-SRS-80. Asheville, NC: U.S. Department of Agriculture, Forest Service, Southern Research Station. 85 p.

Blackard, J.; Finco, M.; Helmer, E.; Holden, G.; Hoppus, M.; Jacobs, D.; Lister, A.; Moisen, G.; Nelson, M.; Riemann, R.; Ruefenacht, B.; Salajanu, D.; Weyermann, D.; Winterberger, K.; Brandeis, T.; Czaplewski, R.; McRoberts, R.; Patterson, P.; Tymcio, R. 2008. Mapping U.S. forest biomass using nationwide forest inventory data and moderate resolution information. [Biomass map with forest/nonforest mask, 250 m resolution]. Remote Sensing of the Environment. 112: 1658–1677.

Bolsinger, C.L. 1988. The hardwoods of California's timberlands, woodlands, and savannas. Resour. Bull. PNW-RB-148. Portland, OR: U.S. Department of Agriculture, Forest Service, Pacific Northwest Research Station. 148 p.

Bolsinger, C.L.; Waddell, K. 1993. Area of old-growth forests in California, Oregon, and Washington. Resour. Bull. PNW-RB-197. Portland, OR: U.S. Department of Agriculture, Forest Service, Pacific Northwest Research Station. 26 p.

Bolsinger, C.L. 1980. California forests: trends, problems, and opportunities. Resour. Bull. PNW-RB-89. Portland, OR: U.S. Department of Agriculture, Forest Service, Pacific Northwest Forest and Range Experiment Station. 138 p.

British Columbia Ministry of Forests. 2006. British Columbia's mountain pine beetle action plan, 2006-2011. http://www.for.gov.bc.ca/hfp/mountain_pine_beetle/actionplan/2006/Beetle_Action_Plan.pdf. (21 March 2008).

Butler, B.J.; Leatherberry, E.C.; Williams, M.S. 2005. Design, implementation, and analysis methods for the national woodland owner survey. Gen. Tech. Rep. NE-GTR-336. Newtown Square, PA: U.S. Department of Agriculture, Forest Service, Northeastern Research Station. 43 p.

California Department of Forestry and Fire Protection. 2003. The changing California: forest and range 2003 assessment. Sacramento, CA: Fire and Resource Assessment Program. 230 p.

California Fire Alliance. 2001. Characterizing the fire threat to wildland-urban interface. Sacramento, CA.

California Invasive Plant Council. 2005. Invasive plant inventory. http://www.cal-ipc.org/ip/inventory/index.php. (8 April 2008).

California Oak Mortality Task Force. 2006. Data created by the geospatial imaging and informatics facility at UC Berkeley, Berkeley, CA. http://kellylab.berkeley.edu/SODmonitoring/default.htm. (8 April 2008).

California Oak Mortality Task Force. 2007. Research page. http://nature.berkeley.edu/comtf/html/research_html. (8 April 2008).

California State Board of Equalization. 2006. Timber harvest statistics. http://www.boe.ca.gov/proptaxes/pdf/harvyr2.pdf. (10 January 2008)

Campbell, S.J.; Wanek, R.; Coulston, J.W. 2007. Ozone injury in west coast forests: results of 6 years of monitoring. Gen. Tech. Rep. PNW-GTR-722. Portland, OR: U.S. Department of Agriculture, Forest Service, Pacific Northwest Research Station. 53 p.

Cardille, J.A.; Ventura, S.J.; Turner, M.G. 2001. Environmental and social factors influencing wildfires in the Upper Midwest, United States. Ecological Applications. 11: 111–127.

Carroll, J.J.; Miller, P.R.; Pronos, J. 2003. Historical perspectives on ambient ozone and its effects on the Sierra Nevada. In: Bytnerowicz, A.; Arbaugh, M.J.; Alonso, R., eds. Ozone air pollution in the Sierra Nevada: distribution and effects on forests. Developments in environmental science. Oxford, England: Elsevier Sciences Ltd. 2: 111–155. Vol. 2.

Cleland, D.T.; Avers, P.E.; McNab, W.H.; Jensen, M.E.; Bailey, R.G.; King, T.; Russell, W.E. 1997. National hierarchical framework of ecological units. In: Boyce, M.S.; Haney, A., eds. Ecosystem management: applications for sustainable forest and wildlife resources. New Haven, CT: Yale University Press: 181–200.

Cleland, D.T.; Freeouf, J.A.; Keys, J.E., Jr. ; Nowacki, G.J.; Carpenter, C.A.; McNab, W.H. 2005. Ecological subregions: sections and subsections of the conterminous United States, 1:3,500,000 [CD-ROM]. Washington, DC: U.S. Department of Agriculture, Forest Service.

Cohen, J.D. 2000. Preventing disaster: home ignitability in the wildland-urban interface. Journal of Forestry. 98: 15–21.

Connor, R.C.; Adams, T.; Butler, B.J. 2004. The state of South Carolina's forests, 2001. Resour. Bull. SRS-RB-96. Asheville, NC: U.S. Department of Agriculture, Forest Service, Southern Research Station. 67 p.

Coulston, J.W.; Smith, G.C.; Smith, W.D. 2003. Regional assessment of ozone sensitive tree species using bioindicator plants. Environmental Monitoring and Assessment. 83: 113–127.

Cox, P.; Johnson, M.; Auyeung, J. 2006. California almanac of emissions and air quality, 2006 edition. http://www.arb.ca.gov/aqd/almanac/almanac06/pdf/toc06.pdf. (8 April 2008).

D'Antonio, C.M.; Vitousek, P.M. 1992. Biological invasions by exotic grasses, the grass/fire cycle, and global change. Annual Review of Ecology and Systematics. 23: 63–87.

Daugherty, P.J.; Fried, J.S. 2007. Jointly optimizing selection of fuel treatments and siting of biomass facilities for landscape-scale fire hazard reduction. INFOR: Information Systems and Operational Research. 45(1): 353–372.

Everett, Y. 1997. A guide to selected nontimber forest products of the Hayfork Adaptive Management Area, Shasta-Trinity and Six Rivers National Forests, California. Gen. Tech. Rep. PSW-GTR-162. Albany, CA: U.S. Department of Agriculture, Forest Service, Pacific Southwest Research Station. 64 p.

Fenn, M.E.; Poth, M.A.; Bytnerowicz, A.; Sickman, J.O.; Takemoto, B.K. 2003. Effects of ozone, nitrogen deposition, and other stressors on montane ecosystems in the Sierra Nevada. In: Bytnerowicz, A.; Arbaugh, M.J.; Alonso, R., eds. Ozone air pollution in the Sierra Nevada—distribution and effects on forests. Oxford, England: Elsevier Sciences Ltd.: 111–155.

Finney, M.A. 2001. Design of regular landscape fuel treatment patterns for modifying fire growth and behavior. Forest Science. 47(2): 219–228.

Franklin, J.F.; Cromack, K.; Denison, W.; McKee, A.; Maser, C.; Sedell, J.; Swanson, F.; Juday, G. 1981. Ecological characteristics of old-growth Douglas-fir forests. Gen. Tech. Rep. PNW-GTR-118. Portland, OR: U.S. Department of Agriculture, Forest Service, Pacific Northwest Forest and Range Experiment Station. 48 p.

Franklin, J.F.; Hall, F.; Laudenslayer, W. 1986. Interim definitions for old-growth Douglas-fir and mixed-conifer forests in the Pacific Northwest and California. Res. Note PNW-RN-447. Portland, OR: U.S. Department of Agriculture, Forest Service, Pacific Northwest Research Station. 15 p.

Fried, J.S. 2003. Evaluating landscape-scale fuel treatment policies with FIA data. Western Forester. 48(1): 6–7.

Fried, J.S. Barbour, J.; Fight, R. 2003. FIA BioSum: applying a multi-scale evaluation tool in Southwest Oregon. Journal of Forestry. 101(2): 8.

Fried, J.S.; Bolsinger, C.L.; Beardsley, D. 2004. Chaparral in southern and central coastal California in the mid-1990s: area, ownership, condition, and change. Resour. Bull. PNW-RB-240. Portland, OR: U.S. Department of Agriculture, Forest Service, Pacific Northwest Research Station. 86 p.

Fried, J.S.; Christensen, G. 2004. FIA BioSum: a tool to evaluate financial costs, opportunities, and effectiveness of fuel treatments. Western Forester. 49(5): 12–13.

Fried, J.S.; Christensen, G.; Weyermann, D.; Barbour, R.J.; Fight, R.; Hiserote, B.; Pinjuv, G. 2005. Modeling opportunities and feasibility of siting wood-fired electrical generating facilities to facilitate landscape-scale fuel treatment with FIA BioSum. In: Bevers, M.; Barrett, T.M., comps. Systems analysis in forest resources: proceedings of a 2003 symposium. Gen. Tech. Rep. PNW-GTR-656. Portland, OR: U.S. Department of Agriculture, Forest Service, Pacific Northwest Research Station: 195–204.

Goheen, E.M.; Willhite, E.A. 2006. Field guide to common diseases and insect pests of Oregon and Washington conifers. R6-NR-FID-PR-01-06. Portland, OR: U.S. Department of Agriculture, Forest Service, Pacific Northwest Region. 327 p.

Gray, A.N.; Azuma, D.L. 2005. Repeatability and implementation of a forest vegetation indicator. Ecological Indicators. 5: 57–71.

Hammer, R.B.; Radeloff, V.C.; Fried, J.S.; Stewart, S.I. 2007. Wildland-urban interface growth during the 1990s in California, Oregon, and Washington. International Journal of Wildland Fire. 16: 255–265.

Harmon, M.E.; Franklin, J.F.; Swanson, F.J.; Sollins, P.; Gregory, S.V.; Lattin, J.D.; Anderson, N.H.; Cline, S.P.; Aumen, N.G.; Sedell, J.R.; Lienkaemper, G.W.; Cromack, K., Jr. 1986. Ecology of coarse woody debris in temperate ecosystems. Advances in Ecological Research. 15: 302.

Haynes, R.W.; Adams, D.M.; Alig, R.J.; Ince, P.J.; Mills, J.R.; Zhou, X. 2007. The 2005 RPA timber assessment update. Gen. Tech. Rep. PNW-GTR-699. Portland, OR: U.S. Department of Agriculture, Forest Service, Pacific Northwest Research Station. 212 p.

Heinz Center (H. John Heinz III Center for Science, Economics, and the Environment). 2002. The state of the Nation's ecosystems: measuring the lands, waters, and living resources of the United States. New York: Cambridge University Press. 270 p.

Helms, J.A., ed. 1998. The dictionary of forestry. Bethesda, MD: The Society of American Foresters. 210 p.

Homer, C.C.; Huany, L.; Wylie, B.; Coan, M. 2004. Development of a 2001 national landcover database for the United States. Photogrammetric Engineering and Remote Sensing. 70(7): 829–840.

Houghton, R.A. 2005. Aboveground forest biomass and the global carbon balance. Global Change Biology. 11: 945-958.

Jenkins, J.C.; Birdsey, R.A.; Pan, Y. 2001. Biomass and net primary productivity estimation for the mid-Atlantic region using plot-level forest inventory data. Ecological Applications. 11(4): 1174–1193.

Jenny, H. 1941. Factors of soil formation; a system of quantitative pedology. New York: McGraw-Hill. 281 p.

Jones, E.T. 1999. Nontimber forest products Web site. http://www.ifcae.org/ntfp/. (8 April 2008).

Jovan, S. 2008. Lichen bioindication of biodiversity, air quality, and climate: baseline results from monitoring in Washington, Oregon, and California. Gen. Tech. Rep. PNW-GTR-737. Portland, OR: U.S. Department of Agriculture, Forest Service, Pacific Northwest Research Station. 115 p.

Jovan, S.; McCune, B. 2004. Regional variation in epiphytic macrolichen communities in northern and central California forests. The Bryologist. 107: 328–339.

Jovan, S.; McCune, B. 2005. Air-quality bioindication in the greater Central Valley of California, with epiphytic macrolichen communities. Ecological Applications. 15: 1712–1726.

Jovan, S.; McCune, B. 2006. Using epiphytic macrolichen communities for biomonitoring ammonia in forests of the greater Sierra Nevada, California. Water, Air and Soil Pollution. 170: 69–93.

Kliejunas, J.; Adams, D. 2003. White pine blister rust in California. Sacramento, CA: California Department of Forestry and Fire Protection Tree Notes Number 27. 4 p.

Laudenslayer, W.F., Jr.; Shea, P.J.; Valentine, B.E.; Weatherspoon, C.P.; Lisle, T.E. 2002. Proceedings of a symposium on the ecology and management of dead wood in western forests. Gen. Tech. Rep. PSW-GTR-181. Albany, CA: U.S. Department of Agriculture, Forest Service, Pacific Southwest Research Station. 949 p.

MacArthur, R.H.; MacArthur, J.W. 1961. On bird species diversity. Ecology. 42: 594–598.

McKinney, M.L. 2002. Urbanization, biodiversity, and conservation. BioScience. 52: 883–890.

McNab, W.H.; Cleland, D.T.; Freeouf, J.A.; Keys, J.E., Jr.; Nowacki, G.J.; Carpenter, C.A., comps. 2005. Description of ecological subregions: sections of the conterminous United States [CD-ROM]. Ecomap team, Washington, DC: U.S. Department of Agriculture, Forest Service. 80 p. http://www.na fs fed.us/sustainability/ecomap/section_descriptions.pdf. (8 April 2008).

Mengel, K.; Kirkby, E.A.; Kosegarten, H.; Appel, T. 2001. Principles of plant nutrition. 5th ed. Norwell, MA: Kluwer Academic Publishers. 864 p.

Mooney, H.A.; Hobbs, R.J.H. 2000. Invasive species in a changing world. Washington, DC: Island Press.

Moore, D.S.; McCabe, G.P. 1989. Introduction to the practice of statistics. New York: W.H. Freeman and Co. 790 p.

Morgan, T.A.; Keegan, C.E.; Dillon, T.; Chase, A.L.; Fried, J.S.; Weber, M.H. 2004. California's forest products industry: a descriptive analysis. Gen. Tech. Rep. PNW-GTR-615. Portland, OR: U.S. Department of Agriculture, Forest Service, Pacific Northwest Research Station. 55 p.

Morgan, T.A.; Spoelma, T.P. [In press]. California logging utilization, 2004. Western Journal of Applied Forestry. 7 p.

National Interagency Fire Center. 2007. Wildland fire statistics. http://www.nifc.gov. (13 March 2007).

National Research Council. 2000. Ecological indicators for the Nation. Washington, DC: Committee to Evaluate Indicators for Monitoring Aquatic and Terrestrial Environments. National Academy Press. 180 p.

Ohmann, J.L.; Waddell, K.L. 2002. Regional patterns of dead wood in forested habitats of Oregon and Washington. In: Laudenslayer, W.F., Jr.; Shea, P.J.; Valentine, B.E.; Weatherspoon, C.P.; Lisle, T.E., tech. coords. Proceedings of a symposium on the ecology and management of dead wood in western forests. Gen. Tech. Rep. PSW-GTR-181. Albany, CA: U.S. Department of Agriculture, Forest Service, Pacific Southwest Research Station. 949 p.

Old-Growth Definition Task Group. 1986. Interim definitions for old-growth Douglas-fir and mixed-conifer forests in the Pacific Northwest and California. Res. Note PNW-RN-447. Portland, OR: U.S. Department of Agriculture, Forest Service, Pacific Northwest Research Station. 7 p.

O'Neill, K.P.; Amacher, M.C.; Perry, C.H. 2005. Soils as an indicator of forest health: a guide to the collection, analysis, and interpretation of soil indicator data in the Forest Inventory and Analysis Program. Gen. Tech. Rep. NC-GTR-258. St. Paul, MN: U.S. Department of Agriculture, Forest Service, North Central Research Station. 53 p.

Pedersen, L. 2003. Premier's mountain pine beetle symposium. http://www.for.gov.bc.ca/hfp/mountain_pine_beetle/symposium/. (21 March 2008).

Perry, D.A. 1994. Forest ecosystems. Baltimore, MD: Johns Hopkins University Press.

Pimentel, D.; Zuniga, R.; Morrison, D. 2005. Update on the environmental and economic costs associated with alien-invasive species in the United States. Ecological Economics. 52: 273–288.

Radeloff, V.C.; Hammer, R.B.; Stewart, S.I.; Fried, J.S.; Holcomb, S.S.; McKeefry, J.F. 2005. The wildland-urban interface in the United States. Ecological Applications. 15(3): 799–805.

Randolph, K.C. 2006. Descriptive statistics of tree crown condition in the Southern United States and impacts on data analysis and interpretation. Gen. Tech. Rep. SRS-GTR-94. Asheville, NC: U.S. Department of Agriculture Forest Service, Southern Research Station. 17 p.

Reinhardt, E.; Crookston, N.L., tech. eds. 2003. The Fire and Fuels Extension to the Forest Vegetation Simulator. Gen. Tech. Rep. RMRS-GTR-116. Ogden, UT: U.S. Department of Agriculture, Forest Service, Rocky Mountain Research Station. 209 p.

Rose, C.L.; Marcot, B.G.; Mellen, T.K.; Ohmann, J.L.; Waddell, K.L.; Lindley, D.L.; Schreiber, B. 2001. Decaying wood in Pacific Northwest forests: concepts and tools for habitat management. In: Johnson, D.H.; O'Neil, T.A., manag. dirs. Wildlife-habitat relationships in Oregon and Washington. Corvallis, OR: Oregon State University Press: 580-612. Chapter 24.

Schmidt, K.M.; Menakis, J.P.; Hardy, C.C.; Hann, W.J.; Bunnell, D.L. 2002. Development of coarse-scale spatial data for wildland fire and fuel management. Gen. Tech. Rep. RMRS-GTR-87. Fort Collins, CO: U.S. Department of Agriculture, Forest Service, Rocky Mountain Research Station. 41 p. with CD-ROM.

Smith, W.B.; Miles, P.D.; Vissage, J.S.; Pugh, S.A. 2004. Forest resources of the United States, 2002. Gen. Tech. Rep. NC-GTR-241. St. Paul, MN: U.S. Department of Agriculture, Forest Service, North Central Research Station. 137 p.

Soulé, M.E. 1991. Land-use planning and wildlife maintenance: guidelines for conserving wildlife in an urban landscape. Journal of the American Planning Association. 57: 313–323.

Takemoto, B.; Bytnerowicz, A.; Fenn, M. 2001. Current and future effects of ozone and atmospheric nitrogen deposition on California's mixed-conifer forests. Forest Ecology and Management. 144: 159–173.

Theobald, D.M.; Miller, J.R.; Hobbs, N.T. 1997. Estimating the cumulative effects of development on wildlife habitat. Landscape and Urban Planning. 39: 25–36.

Tyler, C.M.; Kuhn, B.; Davis, F.W. 2006. Demography and recruitment limitations of three oak species in California. The Quarterly Review of Biology. 81: 2127–2152.

U.S. Department of Agriculture, Forest Service. 1932. Copeland Resolution Report, Senate Resolution 175. Washington, DC. 581 p.

U.S. Department of Agriculture, Forest Service. 1997. First approximation report for sustainable forest management: report of the United States on the criteria and indicators for sustainable management of temperate and boreal forests, June 1994. Washington, DC.

U.S. Department of Agriculture, Forest Service. 2005. California forest health highlights. http://www fs fed.us/r5/spf/publications/foresthealth/California2005.pdf

U.S. Department of Agriculture, Forest Service. 2006. Forest Inventory and Analysis glossary. http://socrates.lv-hrc.nevada.edu/fia/ab/issues/pending/glossary/Glossary_5_30_06.pdf. (9 April 2008).

U.S. Department of Agriculture, Forest Service. 2007a. Forest Vegetation Simulator. http://www fs fed.us/fmsc/fvs/index.php. (21 March 2008).

U.S. Department of Agriculture, Forest Service. 2007b. Forest Inventory and Analysis Program: field instructions for the annual inventory of Washington, Oregon, and California. Portland, OR: Pacific Northwest Research Station. 172 p.

U.S. Department of Agriculture, Forest Service. 2007c. Western core table reports. Pacific Southwest Region Remote Sensing Lab. http://www.fs fed.us/r5/rsl/publications/westcore/table01r/table01r-all073107 html. (9 April 2008).

U.S. Department of Agriculture, Natural Resources Conservation Service. 2000. The PLANTS database. Baton Rouge, LA: National Plant Data Center. http://plants.usda.gov. (21 March 2008).

U.S. Department of Agriculture and U.S. Department of the Interior [USDA and USDI]. 2001. Urban wildland interface communities within vicinity of federal lands that are at high risk from wildfire. Federal Register. 66: 751–777.

U.S. Environmental Protection Agency. 2006. Air quality criteria for ozone and related photochemical oxidants (final). EPA/600/R-05/004aF-cF. Washington, DC: Office of Research and Development. 821 p.

Vance, N.C.; Borsting, M.; Pilz, D.; Freed, J. 2001. Special forest products: species information guide for the Pacific Northwest. Gen. Tech. Rep. PNW-GTR-513. Portland, OR: U.S. Department of Agriculture, Forest Service, Pacific Northwest Research Station. 169 p.

Vance, N.; Gray, A.; Haberman, R. 2002. Assessment of western Oregon forest inventory for evaluating commercially important understory plants. In: Johnson, A.C.; Haynes, R.W.; Monserud, R.A., eds. Congruent management of multiple resources: proceedings from the Wood Compatibility Initiative workshop. Gen. Tech. Rep. PNW-GTR-563. Portland, OR: U.S. Department of Agriculture, Forest Service, Pacific Northwest Research Station: 183–190.

Vitousek, P.M.; D'Antonio, C.M.; Loope, L.L.; Westbrooks, R. 1996. Biological invasions as global environmental change. American Scientist. 84: 468–478.

Vogt, C.A.; Winter, G.; Fried, J.S. 2005. Predicting homeowners' approval of fuel management at the wildland-urban interface using the Theory of Reasoned Action. Society and Natural Resources. 18(4): 337–354.

Waddell, K.L.; Barrett, T.M. 2005. Oak woodlands and other hardwood forests of California, 1990s. Resour. Bull. PNW-RB-245. Portland, OR: U.S. Department of Agriculture, Forest Service, Pacific Northwest Research Station. 94 p.

Walker, R.; Rosenberg, M.; Warbington, R.; Schwind, B.; Beardsley, D.; Ramirez, C.; Fischer, L.; Frerichs, B. 2006. Inventory of tree mortality in southern California mountains (2001–2004) due to bark beetle impacts. Santa Rosa, CA: Fire and Resource Assessment Program, California Department of Forestry and Fire Protection. http://www.frap.cdf.ca.gov/projects/mast/reports/FULL_REPORT_6.14.06.pdf. (21 March 2008).

Warren, D.D. 1985–2000. Production, prices, employment and trade in Northwest forest industries. Resour. Bull. (various). Portland, OR: U.S. Department of Agriculture, Forest Service, Pacific Northwest Research Station.

Western Wood Products Association. 2006. 2005 statistical yearbook of the Western lumber industry. Portland, OR: Western Wood Products Association. 32 p.

Whittaker, R.H.; Likens, G.E. 1975. The biosphere and man. In: Leith, H.; Whittaker, R.H., eds. Primary productivity of the biosphere. Springer-Verlag: 305–328.

Winter, G.J.; Fried, J.S. 2001. Estimating contingent values for protection from wildland fire using a two-stage decision framework. Forest Science. 47: 349–360.

Winter, L.E.; Brubaker, L.B.; Franklin, J.F.; Miller, E.A.; DeWitt, D.Q. 2002. Canopy disturbances over the five-century lifetime of an old-growth Douglas-fir stand in the Pacific Northwest. Canadian Journal of Forest Research. 32: 1057–1070.

Appendix 1: Inventory Design and Methods

The Pacific Northwest Research Station's (PNW) Forest Inventory and Analysis (FIA) Program implemented the new annual inventory in California in 2001. The overall sampling design is a significant change from that of previous periodic inventories; the differences are discussed more fully below.

In the annual inventory system for the Pacific Northwest (coastal Alaska, Washington, Oregon, and California), the objective is to measure approximately 10 percent of the plots across an entire state each year. This annual subsample is referred to as a panel. The plots measured in a single panel are selected to ensure systematic coverage within each county, spanning both public and privately owned forests, and including lands reserved from industrial wood production such as national parks, wilderness areas, and natural areas.

Estimates of forest attributes can be derived from measurements of a single panel for areas as small as a survey unit or ecosection; however, such estimates are often imprecise because one panel represents only 10 percent of the full inventory sample. More-precise statistics are obtained by combining data from multiple panels. After at least 60 percent of plots have been sampled, change can be estimated through a comparison of average values across different sets of panels. Estimates from sampled plots in the five panels measured from 2001 to 2005 were combined to produce the statistics in this report. When all panels have been measured once (2010), each panel will be remeasured at 10-year intervals.

The FIA Program collects information in three phases. In phase 1, a sample of points is interpreted from remotely sensed imagery (either aerial photos or satellite data) and the landscape is stratified into meaningful groupings, such as forested and nonforested areas, ecologically similar regions, and forest types. In phase 2, field plots are measured for a variety of indicators that describe forest composition, structure, and the physical geography of the landscape. Phase 2 plots are spaced at approximate 3-mile intervals on a hexagonal grid throughout the forest. In phase 3, one of every 16 phase 2 field plots is visited and a variety of forest health measurements are taken.

Phase 1

The goal of phase 1 is to reduce the variance associated with estimates of forest land area and volume. Digital imagery collected by remote-sensing satellites is classed into a few similar strata (such as forest or nonforest) by means of standard techniques for image classification, and the total area of each of these strata is used to assign a representative acreage to each sample plot. Source data were derived from Landsat Thematic Mapper (98.4 feet resolution) imagery collected between 1990 and 1992. An image-filtering technique is used to classify individual plots through a summary of the 5- by 5-pixel region that surrounds the pixel containing a sample plot. The resulting 26 classes, or strata (ranging from entirely forested to entirely nonforested, for example), are combined with other geographic attributes likely to improve stratification effectiveness, such as owner class. The resulting strata are evaluated for each estimation unit (county, or combination of small counties), and collapsed as necessary to ensure that at least four plots are in each stratum. Stratified estimation is applied by assigning each plot to one of these collapsed strata and by calculating the area of each collapsed stratum in each estimation unit. The estimates of area and volume from stratified data are usually more precise than those from unstratified estimates.

Phase 2

The plot installed at each forested phase 2 location is a cluster of four subplots spaced 120 feet apart (fig. 89). Subplot 1 is in the center, with subplots 2 through 4 uniformly distributed radially around it. Each point serves as the center of a 1/24-acre circular subplot used to sample all trees at least 5.0 inches in diameter at breast height (d.b.h.). A 1/300-acre microplot, with its center located just east of each subplot center, is used to sample trees 1.0 to 4.9 inches d.b.h., as well as seedlings (trees less than 1.0 inch d.b.h.). On national forests in California, a hectare plot (a 185.1-foot fixed-radius plot centered on subplot 1) is also established to tally trees larger than 32 inches d.b.h. in the eastern part of the Northwest Forest Plan area and larger than 48 inches d.b.h. in the western part of the Northwest Forest Plan area.

All phase 2 plots identified by aerial photography as possibly being forested are established in the field without

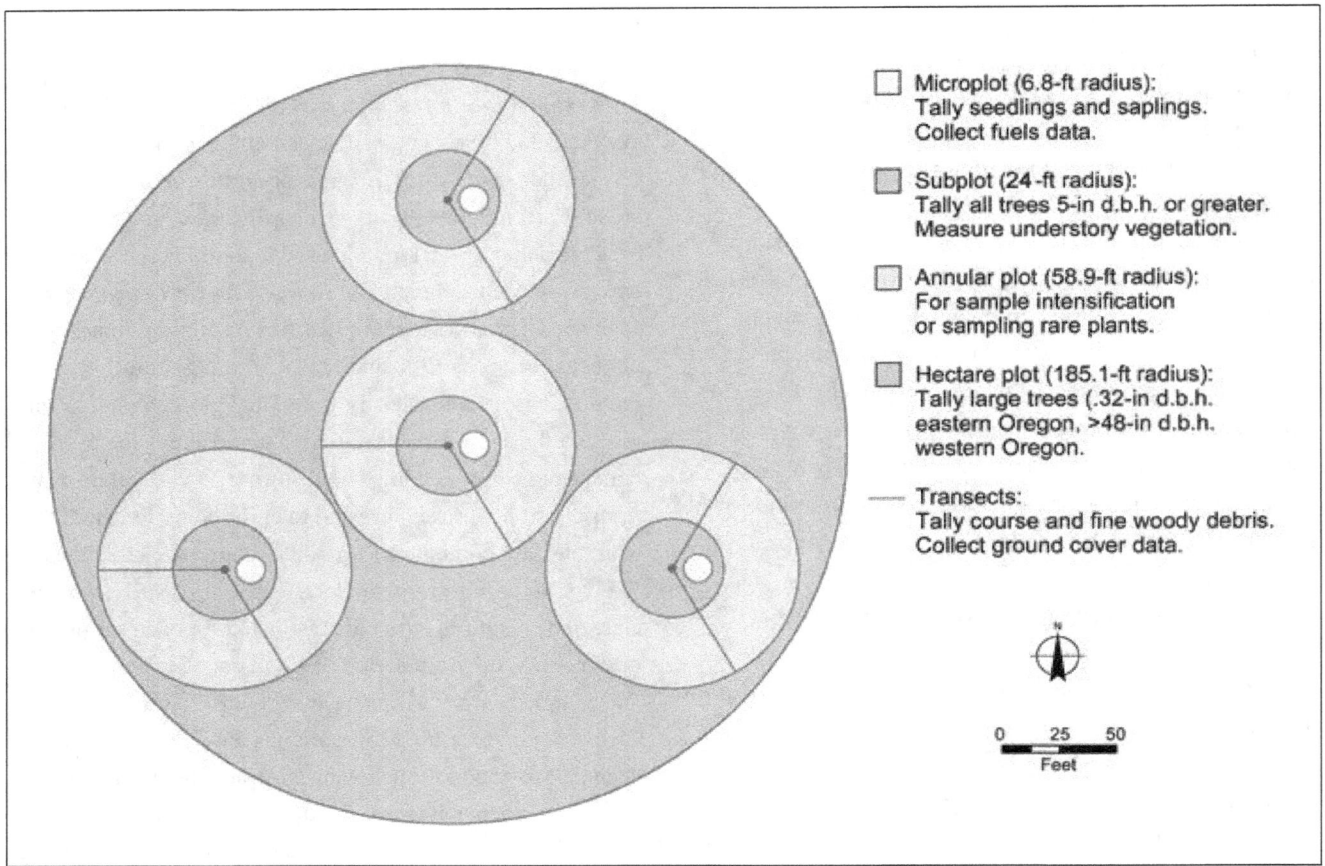

Figure 89—The Forest Inventory and Analysis plot design used in California, 2001–2005.

regard to land use or land cover. Field crews delineate areas that are comparatively less heterogeneous than the plot as a whole with regard to reserved status, owner group, forest type, stand size class, regeneration status, and tree density; these areas are described as condition classes. The process of delineating these condition classes on a fixed-radius plot is called mapping. All measured trees are assigned to the mapped condition class in which they are located.

On phase 2 plots, crews assess physical characteristics such as slope, aspect, and elevation; stand characteristics such as age, size class, forest type, disturbance, site productivity, and regeneration status; and tree characteristics such as tree species, diameter, height, damages, decay, and vertical crown dimensions. They also collect general descriptive information such as soil depth, proximity to water and roads, and the geographic position of the plot

in the larger landscape. In California, crews also assess height and cover of understory species, the structure of live and dead fuels, and the structure and composition of down wood as regional variables (see "Core, Core-Optional, and Regional Variables" section below).

The FIA Program sampled 3,542 forested phase 2 plots in California between 2001 and 2005. Estimates of timber volume and other forest attributes were derived from tree measurements and classifications made at each plot. Volumes for individual tally trees were computed with equations for each of the major species in California. Estimates of growth, removals, and mortality were determined from measurements taken at approximately 1,900 permanent sample plots established in the previous inventory and in conjunction with increment cores taken during the annual inventory.

Phase 3

More-extensive forest health measurements are collected in a 16-week period during the growing season (when most plants are in full leaf and many are flowering) on a subset (1/16) of phase 2 sample locations. At the phase 3 plots, measurements are taken on tree crowns, soils, lichens, downed woody material, and understory vegetation, in addition to the phase 2 variables. One forest health measurement, ozone injury, is conducted on a separate grid with all 65 ozone plots measured annually. The FIA Program sampled 351 forested phase 3 plots in California between 2001 and 2005. The relatively small number of phase 3 samples is intended to serve as a broad-scale detection monitoring system for forest health problems.

Core, Core-Optional, and Regional Variables

The majority of FIA variables collected in California are identical to those collected by FIA elsewhere in the United States—these are national "core" or "core optional" variables (as the name suggests, collection of core optional variables is optional but, if collected, they must be collected in the same way everywhere). A number of other variables are unique to PNW-FIA. These are "regional" variables and include such items as down woody material and understory vegetation on phase 2 plots (not to be confused with down woody and understory vegetation on phase 3 plots, which are measured using a slightly different protocol), as well as insect and disease damage, a record of previous disturbance on the plot, and measurements for special studies (such as nesting habitat assessment for the marbled murrelet (*Brachyramphus marmoratus*)).

Data Processing

The data used for this report are stored in the FIA National Information Management System (NIMS). It provides a means to input, edit, process, manage, and distribute FIA data. NIMS includes a process for data loading, a national set of edit checks to ensure data consistency, an error correction process, approved equations and algorithms, code to compile and compute calculated attributes, a table report generator, and routines to populate the presentation database. NIMS applies numerous algorithms and equa-

tions to calculate, for example, stocking, forest type, stand size, volume, and biomass. NIMS generates estimates and associated statistics based on county areas and stratum weights developed outside of NIMS. Additional FIA statistical design and estimation techniques are further reviewed in Bechtold and Patterson (2005).

Statistical Estimates

Throughout this report we have published standard errors (SE) for most of our estimates. These standard errors account for the fact that we measured only a small sample of the forest (thereby producing a sample-based estimate) and not the entire forest (which is the population parameter of interest). Because of small sample sizes or high variability within the population, some estimates can be very imprecise. The reader is encouraged to take the standard error into account when drawing any inference. One way to consider this type of uncertainty is to construct confidence intervals. Customarily, 66-percent or 95-percent confidence intervals are used. A 95-percent confidence interval means that one can be 95 percent confident that the interval contains the true population parameter of interest. For more details about confidence intervals, please consult Moore and McCabe (1989) or other statistical literature.

It is relatively easy to construct approximate 66-percent or 95-percent confidence intervals by multiplying the SE by 1.0 (for 66-percent confidence intervals) or 1.96 (for 95-percent confidence intervals) and subtracting and adding this to the estimate itself. For example, in table 2 of appendix 2, we estimated the total timberland in California to be 19,551 thousand acres, with a SE of 266. A 95-percent confidence interval for the total timberland area ranges from 19,030 to 20,072 thousand acres.

The reader may want to assess whether or not two estimates are significantly different from each other. The statistically correct way to address this is to estimate the SE of the difference of two estimates and either construct a confidence interval or use the equivalent z-test. However, this requires the original inventory data. It is often reasonable to assume that two estimates are nearly uncorrelated. For example, plots usually belong to one and only one owner. The correlation between estimates for different owners will be very small. If both estimates are assumed to be nearly uncorrelated, the standard error of the difference can be estimated by

$$SE_{Difference} = \sqrt{SE_{Estimate\ 1}^2 + SE_{Estimate\ 2}^2}$$

Using the SE of the difference, a confidence of the difference can be constructed with this method.

If two estimates are based on data that occur on the same plot at the same time, the above equation should not be used. For example, table 17 in appendix 2 contains estimates of tree volume by diameter class. If one wants to compare the volume of trees in the diameter class 9.0 to 10.9 d.b.h. (9,676 million board feet) with that of trees in the diameter class 21.0 to 22.9 d.b.h. (21,484 million board feet), the covariance between the estimates is not zero, and this equation should not be used.

There are two other approaches the reader could consider, but we do not recommend them. The first is to construct a confidence interval for **one** estimate and evaluate whether the other estimates falls within the interval. The problem is that unless both estimates are **highly positively** correlated, this approach will lead to a too-small confidence interval. The second approach is to construct confidence intervals for **both** estimates and determine whether or not they overlap. The problem here is that unless both estimates are highly negatively correlated, this approach will be very conservative. For more complex and indepth analysis, the reader may contact the PNW-FIA Program.

All estimates—means, totals and their associated SE—are based on the poststratification methods described in detail by Bechtold and Patterson (2005).

Access Denied, Hazardous, or Inaccessible Plots

Although every effort was made to visit all field plots that were entirely or partially forested, some were not sampled for a variety of reasons. Field crews may have been unable to obtain permission from the landowner to access the plot ("denied access"), and some plots were impossible for crews to safely reach or access ("hazardous/inaccessible"). Some

private landowners deny access to their land. Although permission to visit public lands is almost always granted, some public land lies in higher elevation areas with extreme topography that can be very difficult or impossible to reach.

This kind of missing data can introduce bias into the estimates if the nonsampled plots tend to be different from the entire population. Plots that are obviously nonforested (based on aerial photos) are rarely visited and therefore the proportion of denied-access, hazardous, or inaccessible plots is significantly smaller for them than it is for forested plots.

The poststratification approach outlined in Bechtold and Patterson (2005) removes nonsampled plots from the sample. Estimates are adjusted for plots that are partially nonsampled by increasing the estimates by the nonsampled proportion within each stratum. To reduce the possible bias introduced by nonsampled plots, we delineated five broad strata groups: census water, forested public land, nonforested public land, forested private land, and nonforested private land. Some of these five broad strata groups were further divided into smaller strata to reduce the variance. The tabulation below shows the percentage of denied-access and hazardous/inaccessible plots for each of the five broad strata groups in California, 2001–2005:

Strata group	Total plots	Denied access	Hazardous/ inaccessible
		Percent	
Census water	460	0	0
Private forest	1,869	12.54	0.54
Private nonforest	2,204	3.33	0.13
Public forest	4,881	0.51	2.18
Public nonforest	324	0.77	1.86
Total	9,738	3.44	1.29

Timber Products Output Survey

The timber products information presented in this report was based on a census of California's timber processors and out-of-state processors that use California timber. The census was conducted by the University of Montana's Bureau of Business and Economic Research in cooperation with PNW-FIA (Morgan et al. 2004). Through a written questionnaire or a phone interview, forest products manufacturers provided the following information for each of their facilities: plant production capacity and employment; volume of raw material received, by county and ownership; species of timber received; finished product volumes, types, sales value, and market locations; and utilization and marketing of manufacturing residue. This survey is designed to determine the size and composition of California's timber harvest and forest products industry, the industry's use of forest resources, and the generation and disposition of wood residues.

National Woodland Owner Survey

This survey of private forest owners is conducted annually by the FIA Program to increase our understanding of private woodland owners. Questionnaires are mailed to individuals and private groups owning woodlands in which FIA has established forest inventory plots. Nationally, 20 percent of these owners (about 50,000) are contacted each year, with more-detailed questionnaires sent to coincide with national census, inventory, and assessment programs. For California, 269 private noncorporate woodland owners were sent questionnaires, and the 124 that were returned provide the data that were summarized and presented in this report.

Periodic Versus Annual Inventories

The PNW-FIA Program began fieldwork for the fifth inventory of California in 2001. This was the first inventory that used the annual inventory system, in which 1/10 of all forested plots (referred to as one panel) were visited each year. The first statewide panel of field plots was completed in 2001. By 2006, half of all field plots in the state had been measured, prompting production of this congressionally mandated 5-year analysis of California's forest resources.

Data from new inventories are often compared with those from earlier inventories to determine trends in forest resources. However, for the comparisons to be valid, the procedures used in the two inventories should ideally be identical. Previous inventories of California's forest resources were completed in 1974, 1983, and 1994. These were periodic inventories in which all timberland plots in the state (outside of national forests and reserved areas

such as national parks) were visited within a 2- or 3-year window. The last periodic inventory on national forests was completed in 1999.

As a result of our ongoing efforts to improve the efficiency and reliability of the inventory and to conform to the national annual inventory design adopted by all FIA units, several changes in procedures and definitions have been made since the last California inventory in 1994. These changes included an increase in plot density of about 18 percent, a new plot footprint (changing from a five-subplot configuration, in which about 2.5 acres were sampled, to a four-subplot configuration in which less than 1 acre is sampled) (fig. 90), a new set of nationally consistent measurement protocols, a plot visitation schedule that calls for sampling of 10 percent of all forested plots in the state each year, and changes in timberland classification protocols. Although these changes will have little impact on statewide estimates of forest area, timber volume, and tree biomass, they have significantly affected estimates of timberland area (see below) and may affect plot classification variables such as forest type and stand size class, especially for estimates at the county level.

Explanation of disparities in timberland area from periodic and annual inventories

Estimates of timberland area from the annual inventory are noticeably larger than timberland estimates from periodic inventories in California. One reason for this is a significant change in the procedures used to classify forest land as either productive timberland or unproductive forest land. In the periodic inventory of the mid 1990s, forest land was often classified using aerial photos or stratified map layers, before plots were assessed in the field. Classifications were based on a number of factors such as species present, density/cover of trees, and geographic location. Timberland is defined as forests capable of producing at least 20 cubic feet/acre/year of continuous crops of commercial trees, where "commercieal" is defined in terms of size and quality of roundwood suitable for lumber or other manufactured products. All other forests (those not classified as timberland via aerial photos or field assessment) were assigned one the "unproductive" forest land labels (oak wooodland

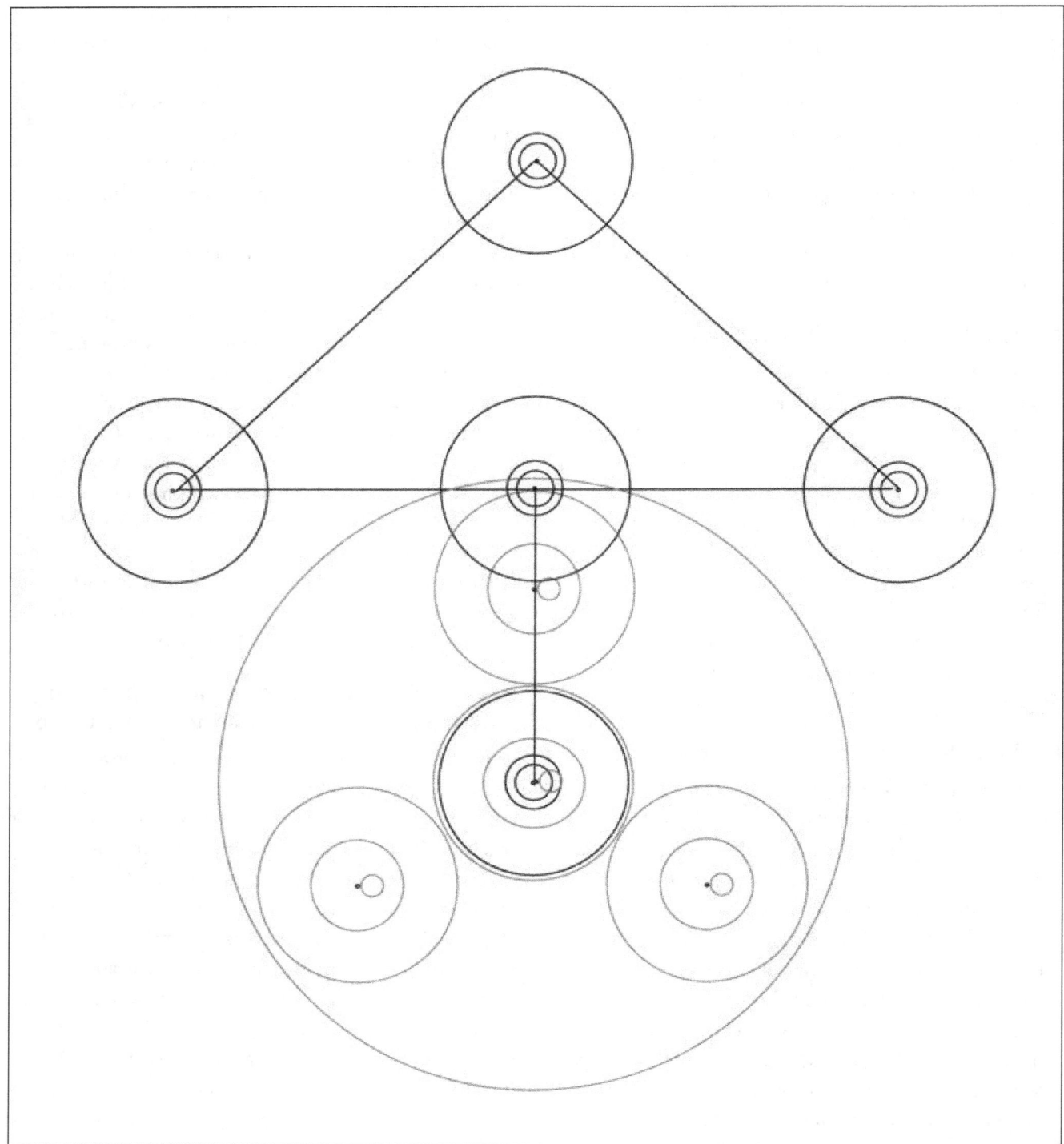

Figure 90—Relationship of periodic (upper, black figure) and annual (lower, red figure) inventory plot designs. Note that only one subplot center overlaps for both designs.

or pinyon-juniper, for example). Site trees were used to determine site index and the associated productivity index (mean annual increment, MAI) on all timberland plots. In some cases, the calculated MAI fell below the 20 cubic feet/acre/year threshold resulting in several plots being reclassified as unproductive forest.

With the intent of developing a more objective approach to classifying forest land, with the advent of annual inventory (which began implementation in California in 2001), FIA began collecting site trees on all forest land, including unproductive land. Instead of subjectively assigning forest land classes via visual inspection (of photos or plots on the ground) or based on the presence or absence of commercial species, site index equations areno used to estimate site index and calculate MAI to obtain an objective estimate of productivity. As before, MAI is the basis for assigning a site class to every forest condition on the plot, which, in turn, is used to determine whether forest land is timberland or unproductive forest. Because there are a limited number of site index equations available for each species, and there can be difficulty in located a representative site tree on some poor sites, the calculated MAI is sometimes unrepresentative of actual productivity. In some cases, conditions previously classified as unproductive forest are now classified as timberland under the new approach, even though it is unlikely that there was any real change in productivity. This has caused a substantial increase in the area of timberland reported in this 5-year summary of the California inventory from 2001 to 2005.

To learn the extent of the various factors that contribute to this issue, a timberland accounting was developed using plots that had been assessed in both the periodic and annual inventories. Using these "paired plots," the estimate of timberland area from annual inventory date is 2.7 million acres larger than the estimate from the periodic data. About 46 percent of this area was previously classified as oak woodland, 11 percent was pinyon-juniper, 26 percent was other types of forest land, and the rest was nonforets as represented in the periodic inventory data. Although some of these changes may be real and represent actual change, the majority are likely owing to changes in the approach to classifying forest land.

Estimates of growth, removals, and mortality (GRM) are particularly dependant on comparisons between inventories, and thus are most likely to be valid when based on remeasurements of the same plots and trees. Only half of the field plots (5 out of 10 panels) have been visited under the annual system to date, and the increase in plot density means about 18 percent of plots are new (they were not visited during a previous inventory). Unlike the five-subplot, variable-radius design used in the 1995 periodic inventory, the annual inventory uses fixed-radius sampling on four subplots, with only one subplot center coinciding with that of a periodic subplot. Thus, relatively few of the trees sampled at the periodic inventory were remeasured in the annual inventory. Estimates of GRM will eventually improve as the annual inventory becomes fully implemented, and several panels of plots are remeasured.

Appendix 2: Summary Data Tables

The following tables contain basic information about the forest resources of California as they relate to the discussions of current forest issues and basic resource information presented in this report. These tables aggregate data to a variety of levels, including county (fig. 5), ecosection (fig. 6), owner group (fig. 7), survey unit (fig. 8), and forest type, allowing Pacific Northwest Research Station Forest Inventory and Analysis (FIA) inventory results to be applied at various scales and used for various analyses. Many other tables could be generated from the California annual data, but space limits us to a few (60+) key ones. Data are also available for download in nonsummarized form at http://www.fia.fs fed.us.

The national FIA Web site (http://www.fia fs.fed.us/tools-data/data/) contains a tool for querying the California annual data and generating custom tables or maps. Some of the tables in this appendix contain summaries of regional variables; data for regional variables currently are not included in the national FIA database (FIADB). Additional information on regional variables can be requested from our office by e-mailing Karen Waddell (kwaddell@fs fed.us).

Please note that information in tables presented and in those generated from the FIADB may differ. As new data are added each year to FIADB, any tables generated from it will be based on the current full set of data in FIADB (e.g., 2001–2006, 2001–2007, etc.), whereas tables in this publication contain data from only 2001–2005. The user can take a snapshot of data from FIADB by selecting the desired years and generating tables that are similar, but probably not identical, to those presented here.

List of Tables

Table 17—Estimated net volume (Scribner rule) of saw-timber trees on timberland, by species group and diameter class, California, 2001–2005

Table 18—Estimated net volume (cubic feet) of sawtimber trees on timberland, by species group and ownership group, California, 2001–2005

Table 19—Estimated above-ground biomass of all live trees on forest land, by owner class and forest land status, California, 2001–2005

Table 20—Estimated above-ground biomass of all live trees on forest land, by diameter class and species group, California, 2001–2005

Table 21— Estimated biomass of live trees on forest land by softwood species group, for merchantable tree boles, tops, limbs, stumps, and small trees, California, 2001–2005

Table 22—Estimated mass of carbon of all live trees, by owner class and forest land status, California, 2001–2005

Table 23—Estimated biomass and carbon mass of live trees, snags, and down wood on forest land, by forest type group, California, 2001–2005

Table 24—Estimated average biomass and carbon mass of live trees, snags, and down wood on forest land, by forest type group, California, 2001–2005

Table 25—Estimated average biomass, volume, and density of down wood on forest land, by forest type group and diameter class, California, 2001–2005

Table 26—Estimated biomass and carbon mass of down wood on forest land, by forest type group and owner group, California, 2001–2005

Table 27—Estimated average biomass, volume, and density of snags on forest land, by forest type group and diameter class, California, 2001–2005

Table 28—Estimated biomass and carbon mass of snags on forest land, by forest type group and owner group, California, 2001–2005

Table 29—Mean cover of understory vegetation on forest land, by forest type group and lifeform, California, 2001–2005

Table 30—Mean cover of understory vegetation on forest land, by forest type class, age class, and life form, California, 2001–2005

Table 31—Estimated mean crown density and other statistics for live trees on forest land, by species group, California, 2001–2005

Table 32—Estimated mean foliage transparency and other statistics for live trees on forest land, by species group, California, 2001–2005

Table 33—Estimated mean crown dieback and other statistics for all live trees on forest land, by species group, California, 2001–2005

Table 34—Properties of the forest floor layer on forest land, by forest type, California, 2001, 2003–2005

Table 35—Properties of the mineral soil layer on forest land, by depth of layer and forest type, California, 2001, 2003–2005

Table 36—Chemical properties of mineral soil layers on forest land, by depth and forest type, California, 2001, 2003–2005

Table 37—Chemical properties (trace elements) of forest floor and mineral soils on forest land, by forest type, California, 2001, 2003–2005

Table 38—Compaction, bare soil, and slope properties of forest land, by forest type, California, 2001, 2003–2005

Table 39—Estimated number of live trees with damage on forest land, by species and type of damage, California, 2001–2005

Table 40—Estimated area of forest land with more than 25 percent of basal area damaged, by forest type and type of damage, California, 2001–2005

Table 41—Estimated gross volume of live trees with damage on forest land, by species and type of damage, California, 2001–2005

Table 42— Estimated number of live trees with damage, acres of forest land with greater than 25 percent of basal area damaged, and gross volume of live trees with damage, by survey unit and ownership group, California, 2001–2005

Table 1—Number of Forest Inventory and Analysis (FIA) plots measured from 2001 to 2005, by land class, sample status, and ownership group, California

Land class and sample status	National forest	Other public	Private	Total
		Thousands		
Forest land plots:				
Softwood types	1,582	224	437	2,212
Hardwood types	537	165	652	1,347
Nonstocked	76	8	19	103
Total	2,122	388	1,077	3,542
Nonforest land plots:	815	2,258	3,098	6,151
Unsampled plots:				
Denied access	1	1	330	363
Hazardous	166	43	25	206
Total	167	44	355	566
Total, all land plots	2,653	2,562	3,821	8,929

Table 2—Estimated area of forest land, by owner class and forest land status, California, 2001–2005

	Unreserved forests						Reserved forests						All forest land	
	Timberland[a]		Other forest[b]		Total		Productive[a]		Other forest[b]		Total			
Owner class	Total	SE	Total	SE	Total	SE	Total	SE	Total	SE	Total	SE	Total	SE
	Thousand acres													
USDA Forest Service:														
National forest	9,784	167	2,424	126	12,208	174	2,626	128	923	80	3,558	144	15,766	145
Total	9,784	167	2,424	126	12,208	174	2,626	128	923	80	3,558	144	15,766	145
Other federal government:														
National Park Service	—	—	—	—	—	—	886	85	396	64	1,282	97	1,282	97
Bureau of Land Management	471	74	923	102	1,393	120	43	23	214	51	256	56	1,650	130
U.S. Fish and Wildlife Service	—	—	—	—	—	—	12	12	6	6	18	14	18	14
Departments of Defense and Energy	31	20	55	24	86	31	—	—	—	—	—	—	86	31
Other federal	12	12	8	7	20	14	52	25	47	24	99	34	119	37
Total	514	106	986	133	1,499	165	993	145	663	145	1,655	201	3,155	309
State and local government:														
State	160	43	67	28	227	52	341	63	152	41	492	74	719	88
Local	97	33	144	39	242	51	40	23	51	23	91	32	333	60
Other public	1	1	—	—	1	1	—	—	12	12	12	12	13	12
Total	258	77	211	67	470	104	381	86	215	76	595	118	1,065	160
Corporate private:	4,402	182	338	61	4,740	189	—	—	—	—	—	—	4,740	189
Noncorporate private:														
Nongovernmental conservation or natural resource organizations	230	53	88	33	319	62	—	—	—	—	—	—	319	62
Unincorporated partnerships, associations, or clubs	52	26	27	16	79	30	—	—	—	—	—	—	79	30
Native American	142	41	60	28	202	49	—	—	—	—	—	—	202	49
Individual	4,169	190	3,732	181	7,912	237	—	—	—	—	—	—	7,912	237
Total	4,593	310	3,907	258	8,512	378	—	—	—	—	—	—	8,512	378
All owners	19,551	266	7,866	252	27,428	299	3,999	168	1,802	124	5,810	194	33,238	284

Note: Totals may be off because of rounding; data subject to sampling error; SE = standard error; — = less than 500 acres were estimated.

[a] Forest land that is capable of producing in excess of 20 cubic feet/acre/year of wood at culmination of mean annual increment.

[b] Forest land that is not capable of producing in excess of 20 cubic feet/acre/year of wood at culmination of mean annual increment

Table 3—Estimated area of forest land, by forest type group and productivity class, California, 2001–2005

Site productivity class[a] (cubic feet/acre/year) — *Thousand acres*

Forest type group	0–19 Total	0–19 SE	20–49 Total	20–49 SE	50–84 Total	50–84 SE	85–119 Total	85–119 SE	120–164 Total	120–164 SE	165–224 Total	165–224 SE	225+ Total	225+ SE	All productivity classes Total	All productivity classes SE
Softwoods:																
California mixed conifer	114	32	1,172	99	1,802	123	1,827	124	1,413	109	372	57	1,179	104	7,879	210
Douglas-fir			112	31	153	37	279	53	317	57	150	41	58	26	1,070	97
Fir/spruce/mountain hemlock	52	21	94	25	191	39	384	58	379	57	107	33	854	85	2,069	128
Western hemlock/Sitka spruce	—	—	—	—	—	—	—	—	—	—	15	13	2	2	17	13
Lodgepole pine	184	41	551	70	140	35	17	11	104	31	15	11	—	—	1,012	91
Other western softwoods	1,444	113	354	55	128	32	38	19	34	18	13	13	9	8	2,020	130
Pinyon/juniper	1,761	127	95	32	27	16	—	—	13	12	—	—	—	—	1,896	131
Ponderosa pine	91	29	846	84	673	75	286	51	276	50	76	24	59	22	2,307	134
Redwood	2	2	—	—	11	11	55	26	229	51	222	52	125	38	643	85
Western white pine	84	25	48	19	15	11	—	—	39	19	8	8	—	—	194	39
Total	3,731	177	3,271	161	3,141	158	2,886	156	2,804	156	979	99	2,287	141	19,106	280
Hardwoods:																
Alder/maple	16	10	3	3	44	21	45	18	86	30	29	17	44	21	268	50
Aspen/birch	17	10	10	6	22	13	—	—	27	16	2	2	2	2	80	24
Elm/ash/cottonwood	20	14	—	—	1	1	—	—	25	18	—	—	1	1	48	23
Exotic hardwoods	—	—	—	—	—	—	—	—	4	4	—	—	—	—	4	4
Other hardwoods	203	46	15	11	93	31	94	30	166	44	21	15	18	12	610	79
Tanoak/laurel	133	36	78	28	326	57	616	82	689	84	148	42	121	38	2,112	137
Western oak	5,100	206	893	90	1,674	130	962	100	933	98	64	25	128	37	9,768	266
Woodland hardwoods	301	57	138	33	16	11	3	3	—	—	—	—	34	18	492	69
Total	5,790	218	1,138	100	2,176	145	1,721	132	1,931	140	264	54	348	61	13,381	293
Nonstocked	147	36	240	47	155	34	94	27	41	19	34	19	40	16	751	79
All forest types	9,668	273	4,649	191	5,473	211	4,701	202	4,776	204	1,277	114	2,675	154	33,238	284

Note: Totals may be off because of rounding; data subject to sampling error; SE = standard error; — = less than 500 acres were estimated.
[a] Site productivity class refers to the potential productivity of forest land expressed as the mean annual increment (in cubic feet/acre/year) at culmination in fully stocked stands.

Table 4—Estimated area of forest land, by forest type group, ownership, and land status, California, 2001–2005

Thousand acres

Forest type group	USDA Forest Service Timberland[a] Total	SE	Other forest land Total	SE	Other federal Timberland[a] Total	SE	Other forest land Total	SE	State and local government Timberland[a] Total	SE	Other forest land Total	SE	Corporate private Timberland[a] Total	SE	Other forest land Total	SE	Noncorporate private Timberland[a] Total	SE	Other forest land Total	SE	All owners Total	SE
Softwoods:																						
California mixed conifer	4,092	141	1,105	87	67	28	289	57	14	12	70	29	1,608	120	16	14	617	81	1	1	7,879	210
Douglas-fir	324	45	63	22	12	12	36	21	38	22	12	12	22	16	—	—	281	55	—	—	1,070	97
Fir/spruce/mountain hemlock	1,077	86	446	57	—	—	184	45	12	12	22	16	244	53	—	—	84	31	—	—	2,069	128
Lodgepole pine	259	45	418	56	—	—	253	49	14	13	—	—	25	17	—	—	42	22	—	—	1,012	91
Other western softwoods	257	42	914	78	76	30	391	68	—	—	12	12	23	15	9	7	93	32	244	54	2,020	130
Pinyon/juniper	45	20	854	80	38	21	680	84	11	12	45	23	—	—	—	—	10	9	213	50	1,896	131
Ponderosa pine	1,240	88	206	40	18	13	62	27	5	5	10	9	390	64	13	13	362	62	1	1	2,307	134
Redwood	7	7	14	10	—	—	24	18	24	18	74	30	309	60	—	—	190	47	—	—	643	85
Western hemlock/Sitka spruce	—	—	—	—	—	—	2	2	—	—	—	—	14	13	—	—	1	1	—	—	17	13
Western white pine	46	19	134	32	—	—	—	—	—	—	—	—	14	13	—	—	—	—	—	—	194	39
Total	7,348	161	4,153	157	211	49	1,921	125	119	38	246	53	2,931	156	37	20	1,681	131	459	73	19,106	280
Hardwoods:																						
Alder/maple	53	19	21	11	8	8	20	15	3	3	12	12	90	32	—	—	48	22	12	9	268	50
Aspen/birch	35	17	31	14	—	—	3	3	—	—	2	2	—	—	—	—	8	8	—	—	80	24
Elm/ash/cottonwood	—	—	6	7	1	1	—	—	—	—	—	—	1	1	—	—	25	18	14	12	48	23
Exotic hardwoods	—	—	—	—	—	—	—	—	—	—	—	—	4	4	—	—	0	0	—	—	4	4
Other hardwoods	84	24	88	25	—	—	24	18	12	12	24	18	37	21	—	—	233	52	107	35	610	79
Tanoak/laurel	414	54	102	27	31	18	64	28	36	19	103	36	633	84	—	—	694	87	36	21	2,112	137
Western oak	1,361	95	1,255	89	217	50	471	71	88	32	419	67	668	89	301	57	1,804	138	3,183	167	9,768	266
Woodland hardwoods	149	34	148	35	—	—	102	35	—	—	—	—	—	—	—	—	18	13	74	30	492	69
Total	2,097	115	1,651	102	257	55	684	87	139	40	561	78	1,434	125	301	57	2,830	165	3,426	173	13,381	293
Nonstocked	339	49	177	37	46	23	37	21	—	—	—	—	37	19	—	—	93	32	22	14	751	79
All forest types	9,784	167	5,981	178	514	77	2,642	142	258	55	807	93	4,402	182	338	61	4,604	199	3,907	186	33,238	284

Note: Totals may be off because of rounding; data subject to sampling error; SE = standard error; — = less than 500 acres were estimated.

[a]Unreserved forest land that is capable of producing in excess of 20 cubic feet/acre/year of wood at culmination of mean annual increment.

Table 5—Estimated area of forest land, by forest type group and stand size class, California, 2001–2005

Forest type group	Large-diameter stands[a] Total	SE	Medium-diameter stands[b] Total	SE	Small-diameter stands[c] Total	SE	All size classes Total	SE
				Thousand acres				
Softwoods:								
California mixed conifer	7,277	204	219	44	383	60	7,879	210
Douglas-fir	914	89	77	30	79	28	1,070	97
Fir/spruce/mountain hemlock	1,952	125	6	3	111	29	2,069	128
Lodgepole pine	912	87	50	21	50	20	1,012	91
Other western softwoods	1,604	117	200	43	216	47	2,020	130
Pinyon/juniper	1,496	118	216	48	183	42	1,896	131
Ponderosa pine	1,964	125	205	40	138	34	2,307	134
Redwood	604	82	5	5	34	17	643	85
Western hemlock/Sitka spruce	17	13	—	—	—	—	17	13
Western white pine	132	31	9	8	52	22	194	39
Total	16,873	272	988	95	1,245	106	19,106	280
Hardwoods:								
Alder/maple	124	34	80	27	64	24	268	50
Aspen/birch	21	12	10	5	49	20	80	24
Elm/ash/cottonwood	32	20	2	1	14	12	48	23
Exotic hardwoods	4	4	—	—	—	—	4	4
Other hardwoods	224	48	146	40	240	49	610	79
Tanoak/laurel	1,339	113	456	70	317	55	2,112	137
Western oak	5,276	213	3,251	176	1,241	108	9,768	266
Woodland hardwoods	392	61	69	27	31	16	492	69
Total	7,412	244	4,013	194	1,956	134	13,381	293
Nonstocked	—	—	—	—	—	—	751	79
All forest types	24,285	304	5,001	213	3,201	167	33,238	284

Note: Totals may be off because of rounding; data subject to sampling error; SE = standard error; — = less than 500 acres were estimated.

[a] Stands with a majority of trees at least 11.0 inches diameter at breast height for hardwoods and 9.0 inches diameter at breast height for softwoods.

[b] Stands with a majority of trees at least 5.0 inches diameter at breast height but not as large as large-diameter trees.

[c] Stands with a majority of trees less than 5.0 inches diameter at breast height.

Table 6—Estimated area of forest land, by forest type group and stand age class, California, 2001–2005

Thousand acres

Forest type group	Stand age class (years)																										All forest land	
	1–20		21–40		41–60		61–80		81–100		101–120		121–140		141–160		161–180		181–200		201+		Unknown[a]			
	Total	SE	Total	SE	Total	SE	Total	SE	Total	SE	Total	SE	Total	SE	Total	SE	Total	SE	Total	SE	Total	SE	Total	SE	Total	SE
Softwoods:																										
California mixed conifer	250	46	271	50	788	88	1,667	121	1,619	116	748	80	431	62	404	56	282	49	410	59	1,009	87	—	—	7,879	210
Douglas-fir	59	24	259	54	246	52	151	39	102	29	34	20	—	—	52	23	35	18	40	18	90	25	—	—	1,070	97
Fir/spruce/mountain hemlock	41	19	42	17	196	41	341	57	413	59	169	36	152	36	221	43	97	28	212	44	175	38	9	8	2,069	128
Lodgepole pine	21	15	19	11	80	28	104	30	184	42	90	29	96	32	137	36	38	17	87	28	157	36	—	—	1,012	91
Other western softwoods	60	25	75	28	201	46	532	73	368	54	109	30	63	25	84	28	29	17	111	31	268	51	119	31	2,020	130
Pinyon/juniper	37	19	55	26	172	43	318	55	436	66	68	26	143	38	162	41	35	17	41	17	151	38	278	55	1,896	131
Ponderosa pine	211	40	237	43	212	45	574	72	642	74	147	34	53	20	90	27	8	8	66	25	56	22	11	12	2,307	134
Redwood	39	19	100	35	131	39	105	35	91	32	40	22	—	—	18	16	—	—	14	14	92	32	12	12	643	85
Western hemlock/Sitka spruce	—	—	16	13	—	—	—	—	—	—	1	1	—	—	—	—	—	—	—	—	—	—	—	—	17	13
Western white pine	14	13	—	—	17	11	17	11	8	8	8	8	8	8	8	8	18	12	23	14	74	23	—	—	194	39
Total	732	80	1,074	101	2,043	140	3,809	181	3,863	175	1,414	109	946	92	1,177	100	543	67	1,005	92	2,072	127	430	66	19,106	280
Hardwoods:																										
Alder/maple	44	17	85	31	65	27	17	10	28	17	9	9	—	—	6	7	—	—	6	6	—	—	7	5	268	50
Aspen/birch	8	5	5	6	7	5	10	8	8	8	6	6	—	—	—	—	8	8	7	7	8	8	13	13	80	24
Elm/ash/cottonwood	1	1	14	12	—	—	—	—	—	—	—	—	—	—	1	1	—	—	—	—	1	1	31	20	48	23
Exotic hardwoods	—	—	—	—	—	—	—	—	—	—	—	—	—	—	—	—	—	—	—	—	—	—	4	4	4	4
Other hardwoods	88	30	100	32	92	32	102	34	120	36	15	12	—	—	16	13	—	—	—	—	34	16	44	20	610	79
Tanoak/laurel	202	46	574	79	521	75	298	55	164	41	36	19	62	25	104	34	38	19	16	11	80	25	16	12	2,112	137
Western oak	524	67	571	74	1,746	133	2,197	149	1,891	137	419	66	263	49	335	57	96	30	62	25	115	33	1,550	124	9,768	266
Woodland hardwoods	—	—	26	15	74	25	153	37	88	31	36	20	8	8	9	9	—	—	19	14	17	10	62	25	492	69
Total	867	87	1,375	117	2,504	158	2,776	165	2,300	151	522	73	333	56	471	68	142	36	110	32	254	46	1,727	131	13,381	293
Nonstocked	—	—	—	—	—	—	—	—	—	—	—	—	—	—	—	—	—	—	—	—	—	—	—	—	751	79
All forest types	1,724	118	2,498	151	4,574	204	6,674	237	6,206	226	1,958	131	1,305	108	1,662	121	684	76	1,115	97	2,326	134	2,194	147	33,238	284

Note: Totals may be off because of rounding; data subject to sampling error; SE = standard error; — = less than 500 acres were estimated.

[a] The age of the stand is unknown on some plots because no trees were available for boring.

129

Table 7—Estimated area of timberland, by forest type group and stand size class, California, 2001–2005

Forest type group	Large-diameter stands[a]		Medium-diameter stands[b]		Small-diameter stands[c]		All size classes	
	Total	SE	Total	SE	Total	SE	Total	SE
	Thousand acres							
Softwoods:								
California mixed conifer	5,816	187	219	44	363	58	6,399	194
Douglas-fir	815	85	65	27	79	28	958	93
Fir/spruce/mountain hemlock	1,343	104	4	3	70	24	1,417	106
Lodgepole pine	279	49	29	16	32	15	340	54
Other western softwoods	339	53	30	16	81	30	450	63
Pinyon/juniper	104	33	—	—	—	—	104	33
Ponderosa pine	1,695	115	189	38	132	33	2,015	125
Redwood	493	74	5	5	34	17	531	77
Western hemlock/Sitka spruce	15	13	—	—	—	—	15	13
Western white pine	23	14	8	8	29	17	60	23
Total	10,922	234	548	68	819	86	12,290	244
Hardwoods:								
Alder/maple	108	32	48	21	47	22	203	44
Aspen/birch	15	11	6	5	22	15	44	19
Elm/ash/cottonwood	25	18	1	1	1	1	27	18
Exotic hardwoods	4	4	—	—	—	—	4	4
Other hardwoods	186	44	47	23	133	37	366	62
Tanoak/laurel	1,146	104	418	67	243	49	1,808	127
Western oak	2,445	153	1,216	111	465	64	4,127	193
Woodland hardwoods	132	34	17	10	18	10	168	37
Total	4,063	188	1,754	131	929	92	6,746	228
Nonstocked	—	—	—	—	—	—	515	66
All forest types	14,985	259	2,302	147	1,749	123	19,551	266

Note: Totals may be off because of rounding; data subject to sampling error; SE = standard error; — = less than 500 acres were estimated.

[a] Stands with a majority of trees at least 11.0 inches diameter at breast height for hardwoods and 9.0 inches diameter at breast height for softwoods.

[b] Stands with a majority of trees at least 5.0 inches diameter at breast height but not as large as large-diameter trees.

[c] Stands with a majority of trees less than 5.0 inches diameter at breast height.

Table 8—Estimated number of live trees on forest land, by species group and diameter class, California, 2001–2005

Species group	Diameter class (inches)															
	1.0–2.9		3.0–4.9		5.0–6.9		7.0–8.9		9.0–10.9		11.0–12.9		13.0–14.9		15.0–16.9	
	Total	SE	Total	SE	Total	SE	Total	SE	Total	SE	Total	SE	Total	SE	Total	SE
	Thousand acres															
Softwoods:																
Douglas-fir	540,741	41,419	230,294	18,759	144,833	7,057	98,972	4,910	71,985	3,791	49,616	2,785	37,398	2,100	30,772	1,936
Engelmann and other spruces	2,120	1,257	—	—	362	181	189	94	47	47	97	67	—	—	94	94
Incense-cedar	290,151	30,514	131,272	14,572	74,356	5,033	45,555	3,329	29,514	2,351	19,524	1,571	14,066	1,426	10,493	1,066
Lodgepole pine	95,775	18,495	51,999	10,818	33,162	4,605	19,434	2,370	16,949	2,343	12,543	1,550	11,594	1,487	7,642	1,095
Other western softwoods	159,226	21,919	62,785	9,480	49,776	4,012	36,481	2,790	24,565	1,867	18,397	1,474	12,364	1,107	9,749	930
Ponderosa and Jeffrey pines	248,740	25,472	135,225	12,753	113,551	6,525	88,115	5,231	68,639	4,023	47,640	2,865	35,475	2,074	26,957	1,799
Redwood	144,969	25,842	36,891	9,481	26,782	3,464	19,524	2,532	14,378	1,701	14,132	1,801	10,908	1,661	7,638	1,061
Sitka spruce	1,255	1,111	2,054	1,981	742	442	331	196	247	239	165	159	165	159	247	239
Sugar pine	50,882	8,534	20,426	4,960	12,897	1,418	10,719	1,099	7,109	910	5,412	647	2,913	440	3,934	578
True fir	589,989	49,556	257,329	20,679	164,640	7,953	119,343	5,651	83,851	4,163	61,437	3,213	47,872	2,511	34,917	2,014
Western hemlock	13,440	5,206	6,536	3,463	2,826	1,385	1,357	393	1,232	527	651	252	486	293	414	177
Western redcedar	—	—	—	—	73	75	220	225	46	47	—	—	147	150	—	—
Western white pine	23,813	5,849	8,673	2,894	6,596	1,020	4,418	667	3,084	514	1,914	364	1,657	335	1,335	306
Western woodland softwoods	53,143	20,971	33,124	5,969	21,255	2,433	16,123	1,793	15,563	1,725	12,660	1,483	11,012	1,399	8,378	1,007
Total	2,214,243	92,277	976,609	39,685	651,852	15,848	460,780	10,917	337,209	8,152	244,187	6,132	186,056	4,926	142,571	3,953
Hardwoods:																
Cottonwood and aspen	68,843	23,434	8,223	3,794	1,795	585	1,200	394	970	369	729	361	586	257	648	278
Oak	1,138,552	92,022	548,665	41,282	399,283	17,793	256,099	10,510	148,655	6,175	83,501	3,817	54,280	2,749	33,345	1,910
Other western hardwoods	1,157,168	83,263	383,113	31,809	233,351	12,369	133,945	7,398	79,595	4,894	53,049	3,653	31,354	2,435	20,583	1,850
Red alder	14,939	6,330	6,539	2,796	8,372	1,996	6,603	1,530	6,976	1,790	4,627	1,419	1,690	649	876	275
Western woodland hardwoods	48,278	12,436	29,339	10,222	22,834	3,025	16,694	2,552	10,693	1,725	6,817	1,107	4,878	826	2,561	573
Total	2,427,780	127,514	975,879	53,318	665,635	21,311	414,540	12,713	246,890	8,071	148,724	5,530	92,788	3,808	58,013	2,786
All species groups	4,642,023	158,831	1,952,488	66,578	1,317,487	25,923	875,320	16,163	584,099	11,012	392,911	8,087	278,844	6,116	200,584	4,707

Table 8—Estimated number of live trees on forest land, by species group and diameter class, California, 2001–2005 (continued)

| | Diameter class (inches) | | | | | | | | | | | | | | | |
| | 17.0–18.9 | | 19.0–20.9 | | 21.0–24.9 | | 25.0–28.9 | | 29.0–32.9 | | 33.0–36.9 | | 37+ | | All classes | |
Species group	Total	SE	Total	SE	Total	SE	Total	SE	Total	SE	Total	SE	Total	SE	Total	SE
Softwoods:																
Douglas-fir	20,516	1,341	12,995	1,010	18,981	1,343	11,597	611	8,123	455	5,947	368	13,083	810	1,295,852	64,428
Engelmann and other spruces	—	—	50	48	174	103	63	31	40	21	7	8	—	—	3,241	1,567
Incense-cedar	7,993	861	5,290	666	7,257	898	4,325	322	2,376	202	1,910	196	2,788	265	646,868	46,460
Lodgepole pine	7,728	1,056	5,122	755	7,518	1,005	3,940	452	2,219	291	957	169	704	116	277,288	34,965
Other western softwoods	8,048	903	6,683	773	7,626	910	3,544	372	2,314	265	1,329	186	1,914	283	404,801	32,504
Ponderosa and Jeffrey pines	19,064	1,324	15,090	1,127	16,662	1,160	10,338	535	6,588	408	3,928	278	5,091	358	841,105	43,079
Redwood	6,433	1,211	5,965	1,119	7,517	1,087	4,685	625	2,815	406	2,026	314	4,054	694	308,717	41,406
Sitka spruce	330	318	—	—	73	75	53	43	55	32	14	13	96	69	5,826	2,764
Sugar pine	2,774	435	3,288	516	4,658	532	2,763	220	2,005	209	1,339	136	2,624	229	133,742	13,843
True fir	27,252	1,691	19,514	1,293	27,026	1,640	16,574	904	10,430	622	6,554	455	10,689	810	1,477,418	77,970
Western hemlock	303	152	220	168	7	7	67	35	15	11	24	18	24	25	27,604	9,237
Western redcedar	—	—	—	—	—	—	37	37	57	50	69	63	71	53	720	634
Western white pine	973	303	543	183	1,120	268	813	126	668	106	466	83	1,076	146	57,150	9,199
Western woodland softwoods	5,372	681	3,460	580	3,147	537	1,312	184	457	85	298	68	267	65	185,571	26,333
Total	106,785	3,288	78,220	2,693	101,768	3,150	60,111	1,515	38,162	1,089	24,866	818	42,483	1,526	5,665,903	142,105
Hardwoods:																
Cottonwood and aspen	373	250	696	333	495	181	243	120	120	50	7	8	21	15	84,951	25,745
Oak	21,933	1,441	12,619	1,007	14,244	1,111	5,421	331	2,686	221	1,088	128	1,025	138	2,721,396	131,193
Other western hardwoods	13,981	1,414	7,695	893	10,056	1,091	3,148	315	1,358	173	689	117	596	129	2,129,681	115,777
Red alder	535	188	157	110	162	103	30	17	49	25	15	15	—	—	51,569	11,539
Western woodland hardwoods	1,545	327	816	259	1,153	311	209	62	55	29	12	12	24	18	145,908	24,886
Total	38,367	2,086	21,982	1,438	26,110	1,615	9,051	484	4,269	287	1,812	176	1,665	189	5,133,505	177,176

Note: Totals may be off because of rounding; data subject to sampling error; SE = standard error; — = less than 500 acres were estimated.

Table 9—Estimated number of growing-stock trees[a] on timberland, by species group and diameter class, California, 2001–2005

| | Diameter class (inches) | | | | | | | | | | | | | | | |
| | 1.0–2.9 | | 3.0–4.9 | | 5.0–6.9 | | 7.0–8.9 | | 9.0–10.9 | | 11.0–12.9 | | 13.0–14.9 | | 15.0–16.9 | |
Species group	Total	SE	Total	SE	Total	SE	Total	SE	Total	SE	Total	SE	Total	SE	Total	SE
							Thousand trees									
Softwoods:																
Douglas-fir	503,743	40,797	204,555	17,356	132,043	6,640	90,138	4,715	64,554	3,622	44,780	2,600	34,036	2,020	28,191	1,876
Engelmann and other spruces	915	935	—	—	73	75	—	—	—	—	—	—	—	—	—	—
Incense-cedar	265,068	29,742	119,284	13,996	65,281	4,737	40,637	3,151	26,334	2,242	17,208	1,495	12,500	1,366	9,534	1,033
Lodgepole pine	54,042	15,740	28,509	9,117	16,470	3,972	8,953	1,717	6,935	1,462	5,354	1,123	4,231	841	2,322	524
Other western softwoods	53,184	11,478	24,881	6,014	15,820	2,182	11,088	1,391	8,869	1,128	6,532	891	4,118	621	3,258	559
Ponderosa and Jeffrey pines	235,476	25,186	123,477	12,344	101,588	6,238	78,459	5,008	61,434	3,797	42,683	2,769	31,490	1,976	24,022	1,723
Redwood	138,894	25,398	35,976	9,436	25,533	3,411	18,569	2,497	13,300	1,643	12,909	1,642	10,200	1,615	7,315	1,049
Sitka spruce	1,255	1,111	2,054	1,981	330	194	166	114	247	239	165	159	165	159	247	239
Sugar pine	45,554	8,311	18,061	4,819	11,646	1,377	9,569	1,051	6,195	864	4,425	567	2,472	409	3,466	544
True fir	480,762	46,503	206,470	18,886	132,796	7,312	93,999	5,106	67,505	3,756	48,957	2,882	37,986	2,317	26,189	1,793
Western hemlock	11,503	5,002	5,954	3,412	2,432	1,358	875	311	1,085	505	610	248	413	283	294	153
Western redcedar	—	—	—	—	73	75	220	225	—	—	—	—	147	150	—	—
Western white pine	15,738	5,222	5,327	2,418	3,165	733	1,812	397	1,299	323	1,028	260	751	223	582	196
Total	1,806,134	84,839	774,548	36,342	507,251	14,733	354,483	10,148	257,759	7,431	184,652	5,499	138,507	4,374	105,422	3,538
Hardwoods:																
Cottonwood and aspen	36,399	18,347	915	935	1,188	531	867	348	652	293	187	108	416	179	477	250
Oak	619,800	60,632	277,164	28,533	209,006	12,195	133,304	7,563	75,355	4,350	43,728	2,945	26,991	1,948	17,339	1,373
Other western hardwoods	937,467	76,232	299,266	26,193	185,421	11,383	107,689	6,628	65,337	4,466	45,301	3,333	25,544	2,082	16,501	1,655
Red alder	11,363	5,012	6,539	2,796	6,834	1,812	4,683	1,150	5,014	1,432	2,966	978	984	436	646	242
Total	1,605,029	99,180	583,883	38,930	402,450	16,334	246,542	9,810	146,359	6,328	92,182	4,576	53,935	2,912	34,963	2,235
All species groups	3,411,164	134,493	1,358,432	54,094	909,701	22,203	601,025	14,142	404,117	9,669	276,833	7,135	192,442	5,271	140,384	4,117

Table 9—Estimated number of growing-stock trees[a] on timberland, by species group and diameter class, California, 2001–2005 (continued)

Species group	Diameter class (inches)														All classes	
	17.0–18.9		19.0–20.9		21.0–24.9		25.0–28.9		29.0–32.9		33.0–36.9		37+			
	Total	SE	Total	SE	Total	SE	Total	SE	Total	SE	Total	SE	Total	SE	Total	SE
	Thousand trees															
Softwoods:																
Douglas-fir	18,651	1,302	11,492	945	16,702	1,270	9,829	565	6,837	426	4,956	343	10,474	751	1,180,979	62,293
Engelmann and other spruces	—	—	—	—	101	89	—	—	8	8	—	—	—	—	1,098	1,014
Incense-cedar	7,262	824	4,468	617	5,812	802	3,688	298	1,970	184	1,503	174	2,050	226	582,600	44,920
Lodgepole pine	2,227	533	1,180	269	1,480	339	832	190	462	128	135	39	157	60	133,290	28,497
Other western softwoods	2,765	480	1,738	382	2,051	376	741	191	431	114	279	70	364	84	136,120	17,992
Ponderosa and Jeffrey pines	17,175	1,263	13,039	1,056	14,123	1,090	8,481	500	5,274	360	2,863	239	3,176	249	762,762	42,248
Redwood	6,057	1,200	5,568	1,100	6,655	1,010	3,985	554	2,423	381	1,611	265	2,379	480	291,374	40,613
Sitka spruce	330	318	—	—	—	—	53	43	27	19	—	—	82	67	5,121	2,697
Sugar pine	2,417	413	2,536	442	3,920	484	2,325	208	1,450	159	993	114	1,715	171	116,742	13,510
True fir	20,803	1,482	14,353	1,092	19,022	1,342	11,158	732	6,509	464	3,744	306	5,396	531	1,175,649	72,057
Western hemlock	82	80	—	—	—	—	55	33	8	8	—	—	—	—	23,311	9,006
Western redcedar	—	—	—	—	—	—	37	37	49	50	61	62	24	25	612	625
Western white pine	524	178	325	140	505	190	300	81	213	58	134	42	209	53	31,911	7,813
Total	78,292	2,913	54,700	2,297	70,370	2,601	41,483	1,306	25,662	909	16,281	670	26,026	1,188	4,441,569	132,953
Hardwoods:																
Cottonwood and aspen	—	—	386	237	286	142	180	112	101	47	7	8	—	—	42,062	19,105
Oak	10,214	905	5,707	633	7,694	821	2,864	227	1,552	157	519	85	490	98	1,431,729	91,610
Other western hardwoods	10,883	1,206	5,970	751	7,544	837	2,419	265	1,086	155	492	103	502	122	1,711,419	106,000
Red alder	492	183	82	80	162	103	30	17	42	23	—	—	—	—	39,837	10,063
Total	21,589	1,526	12,146	1,044	15,686	1,209	5,493	373	2,780	227	1,018	134	992	156	3,225,047	140,889
All species groups	99,880	3,276	66,847	2,518	86,056	2,864	46,976	1,370	28,442	942	17,299	692	27,018	1,209	7,666,616	198,381

Note: Totals may be off because of rounding; data subject to sampling error; SE = standard error; — = less than 500 trees were estimated.

[a] Growing-stock trees are live trees of commercial species that meet certain merchantability standards; excludes trees that are entirely cull (rough or rotten tree classes).

Table 10—Estimated net volume of all live trees, by owner class and forest land status, California, 2001–2005

	Unreserved forests						Reserved forests						All forest land	
	Timberland[a]		Other forest[b]		Total		Productive[a]		Other forest[b]		Total			
Owner class	Total	SE	Total	SE	Total	SE	Total	SE	Total	SE	Total	SE	Total	SE
	Million cubic feet													
USDA Forest Service:														
National forest	38,479	1,050	1,665	169	40,144	1,045	11,816	784	858	117	12,688	786	52,832	1,074
Other federal government:														
National Park Service	—	—	—	—	—	—	5,234	735	338	108	5,572	733	5,572	733
Bureau of Land Management	986	236	299	53	1,285	240	82	60	82	27	164	66	1,449	248
U.S. Fish and Wildlife Service	—	—	—	—	—	—	19	20	—	—	20	20	20	20
Departments of Defense and Energy	15	12	54	34	69	36	—	—	—	—	—	—	69	36
Other federal	43	43	4	3	47	44	352	199	105	71	457	210	504	215
Total	1,044	291	357	90	1,401	320	5,687	1,014	525	206	6,213	1,029	7,614	1,252
State and local government:														
State	854	296	61	37	916	298	3,111	1,191	191	58	3,302	1,191	4,217	1,222
Local	326	160	150	51	476	167	143	101	91	59	234	117	710	203
Other public	—	—	—	—	—	—	—	—	3	3	3	3	3	3
Total	1,180	456	211	88	1,392	465	3,254	1,292	285	120	3,539	1,311	4,930	1,428
Corporate private:	12,891	742	342	73	13,232	743	—	—	—	—	—	—	13,232	743
Noncorporate private:														
"Nongovernmental conservation or natural resource organizations"	734	191	36	21	770	192	—	—	—	—	—	—	770	192
"Unincorporated partnerships, associations, or clubs"	175	112	25	16	201	114	—	—	—	—	—	—	201	114
Native American	763	285	42	27	805	286	—	—	—	—	—	—	805	286
Individual	12,221	848	2,925	215	15,165	859	—	—	—	—	—	—	15,165	859
Total	13,893	1,436	3,028	279	16,941	1,451	—	—	—	—	—	—	16,941	1,451
All owners	67,488	1,495	5,603	293	73,109	1,488	20,757	1,599	1,667	194	22,438	1,597	95,547	2,006

Note: Totals may be off because of rounding; data subject to sampling error; SE = standard error;— = less than 500,000 cubic feet were estimated.

[a] Forest land that is capable of producing in excess of 20 cubic feet/acre/year of wood at culmination of mean annual increment.

[b] Forest land that is not capable of producing in excess of 20 cubic feet/acre/year of wood at culmination of mean annual increment

Table 11—Estimated net volume of all live trees on forest land, by forest type group and stand size class, California, 2001–2005

Forest type group	Large-diameter stands[a]		Medium-diameter stands[b]		Small-diameter stands[c]		All size classes	
	Total	SE	Total	SE	Total	SE	Total	SE
	Million cubic feet							
Softwoods:								
California mixed conifer	35,427	1,181	292	73	167	38	35,886	1,178
Douglas-fir	6,043	691	149	66	54	24	6,246	694
Fir/spruce/mountain hemlock	11,187	876	2	1	47	16	11,235	876
Lodgepole pine	3,431	395	77	46	5	3	3,512	397
Other western softwoods	1,258	146	55	22	17	6	1,330	148
Pinyon/juniper	648	76	18	6	10	3	676	76
Ponderosa pine	4,951	381	79	23	12	5	5,042	381
Redwood	6,427	1,416	9	8	14	8	6,449	1,416
Western hemlock/Sitka spruce	170	115	—	—	—	—	170	115
Western white pine	331	98	2	2	22	13	355	99
Total	69,872	2,000	683	113	347	51	70,901	1,995
Hardwoods:								
Alder/maple	657	206	228	85	38	22	924	224
Aspen/birch	60	37	7	4	9	5	76	38
Elm/ash/cottonwood	135	87	1	1	4	4	141	87
Exotic hardwoods	14	11	—	—	—	—	14	11
Other hardwoods	901	210	119	51	40	11	1,060	216
Tanoak/laurel	7,264	713	1,134	198	90	29	8,488	728
Western oak	10,088	541	3,281	231	265	34	13,634	571
Woodland hardwoods	223	40	21	10	3	2	248	41
Total	19,343	915	4,791	314	449	52	24,584	929
Nonstocked	—	—	—	—	—	—	62	13
All forest types	89,215	2,043	5,474	332	796	72	95,547	2,006

Note: Totals may be off because of rounding; data subject to sampling error; SE = standard error; — = less than 500,000 cubic feet were estimated.

[a] Stands with a majority of trees at least 11.0 inches diameter at breast height for hardwoods and 9.0 inches diameter at breast height for softwoods.

[b] Stands with a majority of trees at least 5.0 inches diameter at breast height but not as large as large-diameter trees.

[c] Stands with a majority of trees less than 5.0 inches diameter at breast height.

Table 12—Estimated net volume of all live trees on forest land, by species group and ownership group, California, 2001–2005

Species group	Forest Service Total	SE	Other federal Total	SE	State and local government Total	SE	Corporate private Total	SE	Noncorporate private Total	SE	All owners Total	SE
					Million cubic feet							
Scftwoods:												
Douglas-fir	13,071	635	923	245	628	182	3,282	312	3,585	422	21,489	852
Engelmann and other spruces	29	13	—	—	—	—	11	10	—	—	40	16
Incense-cedar	2,607	179	194	59	71	38	699	92	504	102	4,075	234
Lodgepole pine	2,256	231	1,011	230	26	24	142	73	96	59	3,531	339
Other western softwoods	1,593	170	456	109	88	33	86	26	525	62	2,748	215
Ponderosa and Jeffrey pines	8,763	380	740	146	175	82	1,662	186	1,643	210	12,983	494
Redwood	276	191	515	356	2,169	1,083	1,851	300	2,120	425	6,931	1,255
Sitka spruce	—	—	16	15	7	7	67	49	43	40	133	65
Sugar pine	2,694	184	269	98	52	27	533	73	166	53	3,714	228
True fir	14,867	732	2,207	431	270	112	1,893	236	572	106	19,809	892
Western hemlock	7	5	22	12	58	57	60	28	24	16	172	67
Western redcedar	54	41	—	—	—	—	—	—	—	—	54	41
Western white pine	790	92	75	28	7	6	21	11	11	7	904	97
Western woodland softwoods	319	37	220	45	17	9	—	—	34	9	591	60
Total	47,327	1,039	6,650	735	3,568	1,189	10,305	645	9,323	738	77,173	1,906
Hardwoods:												
Cottonwood and aspen	76	29	4	4	30	28	7	6	103	64	220	76
Oak	3,574	188	636	116	572	95	1,197	129	4,830	243	10,810	351
Other western hardwoods	1,704	164	224	66	711	175	1,472	205	2,633	256	6,743	392
Red alder	40	12	65	38	47	48	248	75	35	16	435	99
Western woodland hardwoods	111	18	34	12	1	2	3	2	17	9	167	23
Total	5,505	255	963	148	1,362	213	2,927	259	7,618	378	18,374	539
All species groups	52,832	1,074	7,613	776	4,930	1,238	13,232	743	16,941	917	95,547	2,006

Note: Totals may be off because of rounding; data subject to sampling error; SE = standard error; — = less than 500,000 cubic feet were estimated.

Table 13—Estimated net volume of all live trees on forest land, by species group and diameter class, California, 2001–2005

	Diameter class (inches)													
	5.0–6.9		7.0–8.9		9.0–10.9		11.0–12.9		13.0–14.9		15.0–16.9		17.0–18.9	
Species group	Total	SE	Total	SE	Total	SE	Total	SE	Total	SE	Total	SE	Total	SE
	Million cubic feet													
Softwoods:														
Douglas-fir	498	27	684	36	901	50	979	58	1,075	63	1,245	81	1,108	77
Engelmann and other spruces	—	—	—	—	—	—	1	1	—	—	3	3		
Incense-cedar	153	11	177	13	205	17	213	17	235	25	250	26	259	29
Lodgepole pine	74	11	95	13	159	23	188	25	264	36	256	37	349	51
Other western softwoods	66	7	107	10	137	12	168	15	178	18	187	20	225	30
Ponderosa and Jeffrey pines	203	12	326	19	510	31	605	37	743	45	842	59	847	62
Redwood	40	5	80	11	114	14	181	23	228	35	230	33	273	55
Sitka spruce	2	1	2	1	4	4	4	4	7	7	13	12	20	20
Sugar pine	25	3	41	4	57	8	70	9	60	9	122	18	126	20
True fir	355	18	543	27	729	39	899	49	1,064	57	1,110	68	1,238	81
Western hemlock	8	5	10	3	18	8	15	6	16	10	23	10	19	10
Western redcedar	—	—	1	2	1	1	—	—	3	3	—	—	—	—
Western white pine	10	2	14	2	19	3	21	4	30	6	34	9	36	11
Western woodland softwoods	28	4	35	4	58	8	69	11	88	16	92	18	61	8
Total	1,464	40	2,116	55	2,913	79	3,413	95	3,991	114	4,408	134	4,560	154
Hardwoods:														
Cottonwood and aspen	2	1	4	1	8	3	9	5	12	5	23	11	11	7
Oak	885	41	1,219	52	1,278	55	1,203	58	1,156	60	997	59	851	57
Other western hardwoods	503	28	642	38	727	47	797	56	729	59	654	61	616	66
Red alder	26	7	51	12	104	28	103	32	56	22	32	10	27	9
Western woodland hardwoods	14	2	21	4	23	4	22	4	24	4	16	4	13	3
Total	1,430	49	1,938	63	2,139	76	2,134	86	1,978	87	1,721	88	1,518	89
All species groups	2,895	63	4,054	84	5,052	109	5,547	130	5,969	144	6,129	158	6,078	177

	Diameter class (inches)													
	19.0–20.9		21.0–24.9		25.0–28.9		29.0–32.9		33.0–36.9		37.0+		All classes	
Species group	Total	SE	Total	SE	Total	SE	Total	SE	Total	SE	Total	SE	Total	SE
	Million cubic feet													
Softwoods:														
Douglas-fir	923	76	1,924	148	1,738	98	1,684	103	1,645	111	7,084	511	21,489	852
Engelmann and other spruces	1	1	17	11	8	4	6	3	2	2	—	—	40	16
Incense-cedar	227	29	430	55	400	31	300	26	325	35	900	95	4,075	234
Lodgepole pine	319	54	614	83	455	54	350	49	200	37	207	38	3,531	339
Other western softwoods	261	35	394	57	269	34	224	32	196	34	337	59	2,748	215
Ponderosa and Jeffrey pines	923	73	1,485	107	1,474	83	1,363	93	1,131	87	2,532	192	12,983	494
Redwood	327	63	589	87	590	84	490	76	466	74	3,323	1,139	6,931	1,255
Sitka spruce	—	—	7	7	8	7	12	7	4	4	50	37	133	65
Sugar pine	201	32	392	44	369	31	402	44	354	37	1,496	148	3,714	228
True fir	1,159	80	2,274	145	2,177	127	1,933	122	1,630	118	4,699	394	19,809	892
Western hemlock	27	23	1	1	10	5	4	3	5	4	15	15	172	67
Western redcedar	—	—	—	—	4	4	9	8	14	13	21	16	54	41
Western white pine	26	9	72	18	84	13	93	15	91	16	375	58	904	97
Western woodland softwoods	50	9	51	10	30	5	14	3	9	2	7	2	591	60
Total	4,445	167	8,249	275	7,616	212	6,881	218	6,071	217	21,045	1,396	77,173	1,906
Hardwoods:														
Cottonwood and aspen	45	22	47	19	33	17	17	7	1	1	7	5	220	76
Oak	640	54	1,025	84	584	38	411	36	202	27	359	57	10,810	351
Other western hardwoods	413	49	764	86	350	38	209	28	145	29	195	47	6,743	392
Red alder	11	8	11	8	3	2	8	4	3	3	—	—	435	99
Western woodland hardwoods	8	3	17	5	5	2	2	1	1	1	1	1	167	23
Total	1,116	78	1,863	123	975	57	648	47	352	40	562	74	18,374	539
All species groups	5,561	185	10,113	301	8,591	220	7,529	223	6,423	223	21,607	1,399	95,547	2,006

Note: Totals may be off because of rounding; data subject to sampling error; SE = standard error; — = less than 500,000 cubic feet

Table 14—Estimated net volume of growing-stock trees[a] on timberland, by species group and diameter class, California, 2001–2005

Species group	Diameter class (inches)																				All classes	
	5.0–6.9		7.0–8.9		9.0–10.9		11.0–12.9		13.0–14.9		15.0–16.9		17.0–18.9		19.0–20.9		21.0–28.9		29.0+		All classes	
	Total	SE	Total	SE	Total	SE	Total	SE	Total	SE	Total	SE	Total	SE	Total	SE	Total	SE	Total	SE	Total	SE
	Million cubic feet																					
Softwoods:																						
Douglas-fir	453	24	625	34	811	48	879	54	982	60	1,135	78	1,008	74	807	70	3,171	202	8,591	587	18,462	815
Engelmann and other spruces	0	0	—	—	—	—	—	—	—	—	—	—	—	—	—	—	11	10	1	1	13	10
Incense-cedar	135	10	159	12	184	16	188	16	211	24	227	25	235	27	195	28	700	70	1,190	112	3,423	215
Lodgepole pine	43	10	49	10	72	16	85	18	99	21	86	20	109	27	76	17	243	48	164	49	1,027	160
Other western softwoods	26	5	43	8	63	10	73	11	74	13	69	13	93	20	86	21	202	44	218	50	946	123
Ponderosa and Jeffrey pines	184	12	292	18	460	29	545	36	667	43	755	57	766	59	808	69	2,492	148	3,540	230	10,509	442
Redwood	39	5	77	11	106	14	169	23	211	34	221	33	256	55	308	62	1,028	143	1,966	319	4,380	526
Sitka spruce	1	1	1	1	4	4	4	4	7	7	13	12	20	20	—	—	8	7	51	41	111	63
Sugar pine	23	3	37	4	49	7	58	8	50	8	110	17	109	19	157	29	653	57	1,565	139	2,810	188
True fir	294	17	437	24	593	34	720	43	856	53	855	61	945	70	838	65	3,057	199	4,563	372	13,157	673
Western hemlock	8	5	6	2	16	8	15	6	14	10	16	8	4	4	—	—	8	5	1	1	88	33
Western redcedar	—	—	1	2	—	—	—	—	3	3	—	—	—	—	—	—	4	4	27	27	36	36
Western white pine	6	1	7	2	9	2	12	3	14	4	13	5	20	7	17	8	65	18	140	30	303	51
Total	1,210	38	1,735	52	2,367	74	2,748	87	3,187	104	3,499	124	3,566	140	3,293	143	11,643	373	22,017	894	55,265	1,355
Hardwoods:																						
Cottonwood and aspen	1	1	3	1	5	2	2	2	10	4	17	10	—	—	25	16	53	31	16	8	134	65
Oak	506	31	698	41	715	42	688	47	628	46	567	46	444	41	342	39	968	79	586	61	6,142	276
Other western hardwoods	405	26	528	34	616	43	690	51	608	51	532	56	483	57	335	43	869	86	448	80	5,512	346
Red alder	20	5	37	9	78	24	70	24	31	13	23	9	25	9	6	6	14	8	7	4	311	78
Total	933	40	1,266	52	1,414	64	1,450	74	1,276	71	1,139	75	951	71	710	62	1,904	125	1,056	101	12,100	461
All species groups	2,143	56	3,002	77	3,781	99	4,198	116	4,463	129	4,638	144	4,517	157	4,003	158	13,547	396	23,073	910	67,364	1,494

Note: Totals may be off because of rounding; data subject to sampling error; SE = standard error; — = less than 500,000 cubic feet were estimated.
[a] Growing-stock trees are trees of commercial species that meet certain merchantability standards; excludes trees that are entirely cull (rough or rotten tree classes).

Table 15—Estimated net volume of growing-stock trees[a] on timberland, by species group and ownership group, California, 2001–2005

Species group	Forest Service		Other federal		State and local government		Corporate private		Noncorporate private		All owners	
	Total	SE	Total	SE	Total	SE	Total	SE	Total	SE	Total	SE
	Million cubic feet											
Softwoods:												
Douglas-fir	10,892	616	487	161	257	135	3,276	312	3,550	421	18,462	815
Engelmann and other spruces	2	1	—	—	—	—	11	10	—	—	13	10
Incense-cedar	2,192	167	32	27	—	—	696	92	504	102	3,423	215
Lodgepole pine	763	129	—	—	26	24	142	73	96	59	1,027	160
Other western softwoods	540	104	36	15	47	30	56	21	267	53	946	123
Ponderosa and Jeffrey pines	7,109	348	101	39	43	22	1,630	186	1,626	210	10,509	442
Redwood	24	24	—	—	386	167	1,851	300	2,120	425	4,380	526
Sitka spruce	—	—	—	—	—	—	67	49	43	40	111	63
Sugar pine	2,109	166	10	6	6	6	519	73	166	53	2,810	188
True fir	10,595	619	12	7	95	80	1,884	236	570	106	13,157	673
Western hemlock	1	1	—	—	3	3	60	28	24	16	88	33
Western redcedar	36	36	—	—	—	—	—	—	—	—	36	36
Western white pine	265	49	—	—	7	6	21	11	11	7	303	51
Total	34,527	993	679	176	869	281	10,213	645	8,977	738	55,265	1,355
Hardwoods:												
Cottonwood and aspen	25	11	4	4	—	—	7	6	98	64	134	65
Oak	2,378	155	241	65	120	47	953	117	2,449	192	6,142	276
Other western hardwoods	1,429	154	104	49	186	73	1,464	204	2,329	246	5,512	346
Red alder	34	11	—	—	—	—	248	75	29	16	311	78
Total	3,867	226	349	90	306	91	2,671	252	4,906	338	12,100	461
All species groups	38,394	1,050	1,028	240	1,175	335	12,884	742	13,883	907	67,364	1,494

Note: Totals may be off because of rounding; data subject to sampling error; SE = standard error; — = less than 500,000 cubic feet were estimated.
[a] Growing-stock trees are trees of commercial species that meet certain merchantability standards; excludes trees that are entirely cull (rough or rotten tree classes).

Table 16—Estimated net volume (International 1/4-inch rule) of sawtimber trees[a] on timberland, by species group and diameter class, California, 2001–2005

| | Diameter class (inches) | | | | | | | | | | | | |
| Species group | 9.0–10.9 | | 11.0–12.9 | | 13.0–14.9 | | 15.0–16.9 | | 17.0–18.9 | | 19.0–20.9 | | 21.0–22.9 | |
	Total	SE	Total	SE	Total	SE	Total	SE	Total	SE	Total	SE	Total	SE
	Million board feet (International-1/4-inch rule)													
Softwoods:														
Douglas-fir	3,595	215	4,500	280	5,421	336	6,557	457	6,047	450	4,966	435	5,515	596
Engelmann and other spruces	—	—	—	—	—	—	—	—	—	—	—	—	—	—
Incense-cedar	679	60	810	70	1,003	115	1,143	127	1,236	146	1,070	153	1,083	183
Lodgepole pine	303	71	416	87	519	112	490	117	637	156	461	105	519	140
Other western softwoods	248	40	330	52	372	67	351	67	511	115	492	122	333	95
Ponderosa and Jeffrey pines	1,755	114	2,480	165	3,400	223	4,120	318	4,390	343	4,837	421	3,925	398
Redwood	410	54	775	107	1,072	173	1,195	181	1,446	316	1,801	364	1,914	351
Sitka spruce	20	19	25	24	41	39	78	75	126	121	—	—	—	—
Sugar pine	191	29	264	37	253	43	599	95	629	110	943	176	790	152
True fir	2,371	139	3,408	206	4,432	277	4,700	341	5,432	411	4,950	387	5,321	459
Western hemlock	71	36	78	33	80	54	99	52	25	24	—	—	—	—
Western larch	—	—	—	—	—	—	—	—	—	—	—	—	—	—
Western redcedar	—	—	—	—	16	17	—	—	—	—	—	—	—	—
Western white pine	34	10	56	15	71	22	66	23	109	38	98	43	66	32
Total	9,676	315	13,141	430	16,679	558	19,399	704	20,587	826	19,620	868	19,466	971
Hardwoods:														
Ash	—	—	—	—	—	—	—	—	—	—	—	—	—	—
Cottonwood and aspen	—	—	9	7	50	22	96	54	—	—	153	97	126	83
Oak	—	—	689	47	662	50	620	52	536	56	414	49	435	57
Other western hardwoods	—	—	2,219	184	2,000	192	1,738	210	1,602	213	1,335	186	1,458	255
Red alder	—	—	332	115	166	69	128	47	146	54	40	39	—	—
Total	—	—	3,250	219	2,878	211	2,582	230	2,284	226	1,942	219	2,018	274
All species groups	9,676	315	16,391	502	19,557	610	21,981	740	22,870	860	21,562	900	21,484	1,009

| | Diameter class (inches) | | | | | | | | | |
| Species group | 23.0–24.9 | | 25.0–26.9 | | 27.0–28.9 | | 29.0+ | | All classes | |
	Total	SE	Total	SE	Total	SE	Total	SE	Total	SE
	Million board feet (International 1/4-inch rule)									
Softwoods:										
Douglas-fir	5,252	497	5,122	347	4,692	357	60,277	4,196	111,942	5,435
Engelmann and other spruces	72	64	—	—	—	—	9	9	81	65
Incense-cedar	930	157	1,011	94	1,050	107	7,636	735	17,651	1,202
Lodgepole pine	338	105	363	99	320	81	1,098	334	5,464	905
Other western softwoods	364	88	237	77	278	92	1,422	337	4,939	742
Ponderosa and Jeffrey pines	3,944	370	4,139	286	3,905	301	24,656	1,629	61,551	2,771
Redwood	1,291	236	1,589	251	1,599	262	13,274	2,177	26,365	3,322
Sitka spruce	—	—	37	29	19	19	361	290	707	405
Sugar pine	1,284	180	979	102	1,051	132	10,959	990	17,943	1,259
True fir	4,457	411	4,850	349	4,577	372	31,224	2,589	75,724	4,182
Western hemlock	—	—	23	16	28	27	10	10	414	157
Western larch	—	—	—	—	—	—	—	—	—	—
Western redcedar	—	—	9	9	17	17	173	177	215	219
Western white pine	122	47	79	27	124	40	929	205	1,754	311
Total	18,055	834	18,438	666	17,660	701	152,028	6,302	324,750	8,781
Hardwoods:										
Ash	—	—	—	—	—	—	—	—	—	—
Cottonwood and aspen	56	25	51	31	108	74	98	47	749	404
Oak	428	61	268	27	237	27	1,012	124	5,301	289
Other western hardwoods	738	131	640	85	457	79	1,848	427	14,035	1,158
Red alder	66	50	12	9	8	7	47	26	944	235
Total	1,288	155	972	95	810	112	3,005	447	21,028	1,288
All species groups	19,343	857	19,410	677	18,470	712	155,034	6,363	345,779	9,095

Note: Totals may be off because of rounding; data subject to sampling error; SE = standard error; — = less than 500,000 board feet were estimated.

[a] Sawtimber trees have merchantability limits that differ for softwood and hardwood species as follows: ≥9 inches diameter at breast height for softwoods and ≥11 inches diameter at breast height for hardwoods.

Table 17—Estimated net volume (Scribner rule) of sawtimber trees[a] on timberland, by species group and diameter class, California, 2001–2005

					Diameter class (inches)								
	9.0–10.9		11.0–12.9		13.0–14.9		15.0–16.9		17.0–18.9		19.0–20.9		21.0–22.9	
Species group	Total	SE	Total	SE	Total	SE	Total	SE	Total	SE	Total	SE	Total	SE
					Million board feet (Scribner rule)								
Softwoods:														
Douglas-fir	2,698	162	3,562	222	4,440	277	5,499	386	5,170	387	4,307	380	4,860	529
Engelmann and other spruces	—	—	—	—	—	—	—	—	—	—	—	—	—	—
Incense-cedar	501	45	623	54	793	91	920	103	1,007	119	885	127	904	153
Lodgepole pine	226	53	326	68	420	91	408	98	539	133	397	91	453	122
Other western softwoods	185	30	257	41	299	55	285	55	424	98	415	104	282	81
Ponderosa and Jeffrey pines	1,301	84	1,923	128	2,728	180	3,394	263	3,690	290	4,145	363	3,410	348
Redwood	304	40	602	84	861	139	981	150	1,208	266	1,528	309	1,652	305
Sitka spruce	15	14	21	20	34	33	67	64	109	105	—	—	—	—
Sugar pine	141	21	205	29	202	34	493	78	528	93	809	151	680	131
True fir	1,760	103	2,659	161	3,570	224	3,878	283	4,570	348	4,219	331	4,595	399
Western hemlock	53	27	62	26	66	45	85	44	22	21	—	—	—	—
Western larch	—	—	—	—	—	—	—	—	—	—	—	—	—	—
Western redcedar	—	—	—	—	13	13	—	—	—	—	—	—	—	—
Western white pine	25	7	43	12	57	18	53	18	90	31	82	36	55	27
Total	7,210	235	10,283	339	13,482	453	16,062	587	17,356	702	16,788	748	16,891	851
Hardwoods:														
Ash	—	—	—	—	—	—	—	—	—	—	—	—	—	—
Cottonwood and aspen	—	—	8	6	42	18	81	46	—	—	134	85	113	75
Oak	—	—	601	41	537	40	494	41	425	46	325	39	342	45
Other western hardwoods	—	—	1,954	163	1,654	160	1,429	174	1,330	178	1,121	157	1,242	222
Red alder	—	—	298	103	141	59	108	40	125	46	35	34	—	—
Total	—	—	2,861	194	2,374	176	2,111	191	1,881	189	1,615	186	1,697	238
All species groups	7,210	235	13,144	408	15,856	498	18,173	618	19,237	730	18,403	775	18,587	884

					Diameter class (inches)				
	23.0-24.9		25.0-26.9		27.0-28.9		29.0+		All classes	
Species group	Total	SE	Total	SE	Total	SE	Total	SE	Total	SE
					Million board feet (Scribner rule)				
Softwoods:										
Douglas-fir	4,672	447	4,601	314	4,254	327	56,171	3,950	100,234	5,005
Engelmann and other spruces	64	57	—	—	—	—	8	8	72	57
Incense-cedar	780	133	856	80	899	92	6,697	652	14,866	1,027
Lodgepole pine	299	92	323	88	287	73	997	307	4,675	785
Other western softwoods	310	76	208	68	245	82	1,270	306	4,181	651
Ponderosa and Jeffrey pines	3,472	326	3,697	257	3,528	274	22,929	1,529	54,217	2,489
Redwood	1,118	206	1,396	223	1,419	234	12,011	1,980	23,081	2,950
Sitka spruce	—	—	34	27	18	17	338	271	633	361
Sugar pine	1,122	158	867	90	941	119	10,199	927	16,187	1,152
True fir	3,901	362	4,291	311	4,091	336	28,719	2,407	66,254	3,745
Western hemlock	—	—	20	14	25	25	9	9	341	130
Western larch	—	—	—	—	—	—	—	—	—	—
Western redcedar	—	—	8	8	14	15	153	156	189	192
Western white pine	104	40	69	23	108	35	840	187	1,526	274
Total	15,843	739	16,370	596	15,829	635	140,342	5,881	286,456	7,970
Hardwoods:										
Ash	—	—	—	—	—	—	—	—	—	—
Cottonwood and aspen	49	22	46	28	99	68	87	42	659	359
Oak	337	48	211	22	187	21	808	101	4,267	232
Other western hardwoods	629	114	550	74	400	70	1,653	393	11,962	1,003
Red alder	59	45	11	8	7	6	42	23	825	205
Total	1,075	134	818	82	692	100	2,591	408	17,714	1,115
All species groups	16,917	758	17,188	606	16,521	644	142,932	5,936	304,169	8,241

Note: Totals may be off because of rounding; data subject to sampling error; SE = standard error; — = less than 500,000 board feet were estimated.

[a] Sawtimber trees have merchantability limits that differ for softwood and hardwood species as follows: ≥9 inches diameter at breast height for softwoods and ≥11 inches diameter at breast height for hardwoods.

Table 18—Estimated net volume (cubic feet) of sawtimber trees[a] on timberland, by species group and ownership group, California, 2001–2005

Species group	Forest Service		Other federal		State and local government		Corporate private		Noncorporate private		All owners	
	Total	SE	Total	SE	Total	SE	Total	SE	Total	SE	Total	SE
	Million cubic feet											
Softwoods:												
Douglas-fir	10,275	600	457	154	242	131	2,844	287	3,230	405	17,048	788
Engelmann and other spruces	1	1	—	—	—	—	11	10	—	—	13	10
Incense-cedar	1,995	158	27	24	—	—	584	81	455	97	3,060	202
Lodgepole pine	674	120	—	—	24	23	128	65	83	53	908	147
Other western softwoods	487	101	30	13	46	29	46	18	245	50	854	119
Ponderosa and Jeffrey pines	6,701	337	94	36	41	21	1,477	176	1,521	200	9,834	426
Redwood	23	23	—	—	376	164	1,735	289	2,067	417	4,201	514
Sitka spruce	—	—	—	—	—	—	64	47	43	40	106	62
Sugar pine	2,052	164	9	6	6	6	493	71	158	52	2,717	185
True fir	9,930	596	10	6	89	75	1,659	219	484	92	12,172	645
Western hemlock	1	1	—	—	2	2	44	22	22	14	69	26
Western redcedar	34	35	—	—	—	—	—	—	—	—	34	35
Western white pine	250	48	—	—	7	6	20	11	10	7	286	50
Total	32,424	965	627	166	832	272	9,104	605	8,316	711	51,303	1,313
Hardwoods:												
Cottonwood and aspen	16	8	4	4	—	—	7	6	93	62	120	63
Oak	450	34	44	12	30	12	195	28	485	44	1,203	63
Other western hardwoods	602	78	40	24	93	40	652	104	1,112	149	2,499	196
Red alder	22	8	—	—	—	—	117	36	12	7	152	38
Total	1,091	88	88	30	123	42	970	116	1,702	172	3,973	220
All species groups	33,514	983	715	183	955	296	10,075	635	10,018	783	55,277	1,366

Note: Totals may be off because of rounding; data subject to sampling error; SE = standard error; — = less than 500,000 cubic feet were estimated.

[a] Sawtimber trees have merchantability limits that differ for softwood and hardwood species as follows: ≥9 inches diameter at breast height for softwoods and ≥11 inches diameter at breast height for hardwoods.

Table 19—Estimated above-ground biomass of all live trees on forest land, by owner class and forest land status, California, 2001–2005

Owner class	Unreserved forests						Reserved forests						All forest land	
	Timberland[a]		Other forest[b]		Total		Productive[a]		Other forest[b]		Total			
	Total	SE	Total	SE	Total	SE	Total	SE	Total	SE	Total	SE	Total	SE
	Million bone-dry tons													
USDA Forest Service:														
National forest	811.2	21.5	47.8	4.4	859.0	21.4	243.1	16.2	22.2	3.0	265.7	16.3	1,124.7	21.9
Other federal government:														
National Park Service	—	—	—	—	—	—	107.1	15.3	7.8	2.2	114.9	15.2	114.9	15.2
Bureau of Land Management	24.5	5.8	9.8	1.7	34.2	6.0	2.7	1.7	2.2	0.7	4.8	1.9	39.0	6.3
U.S. Fish and Wildlife Service	—	—	—	—	—	—	0.3	0.3	0.0	0.0	0.3	0.3	0.3	0.3
Departments of Defense and Energy	0.4	0.4	1.7	0.9	2.1	1.0	—	—	—	—	—	—	2.1	1.0
Other federal	1.1	1.2	0.1	0.1	1.3	1.2	7.1	4.1	2.0	1.3	9.1	4.3	10.4	4.5
Total	26.0	6.0	11.5	1.9	37.6	6.2	117.2	15.7	11.9	2.6	129.1	15.6	166.7	16.5
State and local government:														
State	21.3	7.1	2.6	1.5	23.9	7.2	68.6	23.5	5.5	1.8	74.1	23.5	98.0	24.4
Local	8.9	4.7	4.6	1.5	13.5	5.0	4.3	2.9	2.8	1.8	7.1	3.4	20.6	6.0
Other public	—	—	—	—	—	—	—	—	0.1	0.1	0.1	0.1	0.1	0.1
Total	30.2	8.5	7.2	2.1	37.5	8.7	72.9	23.6	8.4	2.5	81.3	23.7	118.8	25.1
Corporate private:	313.9	18.0	10.6	2.3	324.5	18.1	—	—	—	—	—	—	324.5	18.1
Noncorporate private:														
Nongovernmental conservation or natural resource organization	18.5	5.0	1.7	1.1	20.1	5.1	—	—	—	—	—	—	20.1	5.1
Unincorporated partnerships, associations, or clubs	4.3	2.7	0.9	0.6	5.2	2.8	—	—	—	—	—	—	5.2	2.8
Native American	17.2	6.2	1.4	0.9	18.6	6.3	—	—	—	—	—	—	18.6	6.3
Individual	308.8	20.5	96.8	7.0	406.1	21.1	—	—	—	—	—	—	406.1	21.1
Total	348.7	21.8	100.8	7.2	450.1	22.4	—	—	—	—	—	—	450.1	22.4
All owners	1,530.0	33.2	178.0	9.0	1,708.5	33.2	433.1	32.3	42.6	4.6	476.1	32.3	2,184.7	42.5

Note: Totals may be off because of rounding; data subject to sampling error; SE = standard error; — = less than 50,000 bone-dry tons were estimated; includes all live trees ≥1 inch diameter at breast height.

[a] Forest land that is capable of producing in excess of 20 cubic feet/acre/year of wood at culmination of mean annual increment.

[b] Forest land that is not capable of producing in excess of 20 cubic feet/acre/year of wood at culmination of mean annual increment.

Table 20—Estimated aboveground biomass of all live trees on forest land, by diameter class and species group, California, 2001–2005

Species group	Diameter class (inches)															
	1.0–2.9		3.0–4.9		5.0–6.9		7.0–8.9		9.0–10.9		11.0–12.9		13.0–14.9		15.0–16.9	
	Total	SE	Total	SE	Total	SE	Total	SE	Total	SE	Total	SE	Total	SE	Total	SE
	Million bone-dry tons															
Softwoods:																
Douglas-fir	2.84	0.23	5.5	0.48	10.69	0.56	14.26	0.74	17.74	0.97	18.76	1 11	20.57	1 18	23.44	1.52
Engelmann and other spruces	0.05	0.03	—	—	0.02	0.01	0.01	0.01	0.01	0.01	0.02	0.02	—	—	0.04	0.04
Incense-cedar	1.15	0 12	1.61	0 18	2.55	0 18	3	0.22	3.38	0.28	3.48	0.28	3.85	0.41	4 13	0.43
Lodgepole pine	1.44	0.28	1.3	0.27	1.65	0.24	1.76	0.23	2.65	0.38	3.01	0.39	4.09	0.55	3.9	0.56
Other western softwoods	1.44	0.25	1.32	0.26	2.06	0 17	2.88	0.23	3.29	0.26	3.82	0.32	3.92	0.37	4.11	0.41
Ponderosa and Jeffrey pines	0.92	0.1	2.12	0.21	4.92	0.29	7.48	0.45	10.53	0.64	11.65	0.71	13.66	0.83	14.97	1.05
Redwood	2.59	0.47	2.33	0.61	3.75	0.48	4.76	0.62	5.44	0.65	7.68	0.99	8.33	1.26	7.75	1.1
Sitka spruce	0.02	0.01	0.06	0.06	0.05	0.03	0.04	0.02	0.07	0.07	0.08	0.08	0.11	0.1	0.2	0.2
Sugar pine	0.18	0.03	0.25	0.07	0.44	0.05	0.73	0.07	0.94	0.12	1.18	0 15	1.01	0 16	2.05	0.3
True fir	8.32	0.69	6.9	0.59	9.82	0.49	13.43	0.65	16.26	0.83	19.13	1.02	22.32	1 18	23 12	1.38
Western hemlock	0.07	0.03	0.2	0.11	0.2	0.11	0.18	0.05	0.3	0 13	0.25	0.1	0.27	0 16	0.37	0 16
Western redcedar	—	—	—	—	—	—	0.02	0.02	0.01	0.01	—	—	0.05	0.05	—	—
Western white pine	0.33	0.08	0.2	0.07	0.24	0.04	0.29	0.04	0.34	0.06	0.34	0.07	0.47	0.1	0.52	0.13
Western woodland softwoods	0.83	0.17	1.06	0.24	0 98	0.12	1.01	0.12	1.46	0 19	1.66	0.24	2.02	0.34	2 1	0.39
Total	20.19	0.98	22.86	1.11	37.38	1.03	49.84	1.32	62.42	1.69	71.07	2.06	80.67	2.42	86.68	2.66
Hardwoods:																
Cottonwood and aspen	0.33	0.11	0.13	0.06	0.06	0.02	0.09	0.03	0.14	0.05	0.17	0.08	0.21	0.09	0.39	0 18
Oaks	5.7	0.48	15.8	1.25	32.51	1.5	42.57	1.84	43.26	1.89	38.94	1.89	37.07	1.96	31.58	1.85
Other western hardwoods	4.56	0.35	9.69	0.91	17.75	1.02	20.75	1.23	21.96	1.44	23.08	1.65	20.13	1.62	17.7	1.65
Red alder	0.05	0.02	0.14	0.07	0.61	0 15	0 98	0.23	1.89	0.5	1.88	0.58	1.03	0.39	0.6	0 19
Western woodland hardwoods	0.09	0.02	0.12	0.04	0.27	0.04	0.4	0.07	0.44	0.07	0.42	0.07	0.44	0.08	0.31	0.07
Total	10.72	0.61	25.88	1.56	51.21	1.77	64.79	2 15	67.69	2.38	64.49	2.56	58.88	2.58	50.58	2.54
All species groups	30 92	1 15	48.73	1.93	88.59	2.04	114.63	2.49	130.11	2.85	135.56	3.27	139.55	3.52	137.26	3.6

Species group	Diameter class (inches)															
	17.0-18.9		19.0-20.9		21.0-24.9		25.0-28.9		29.0-32.9		33.0-36.9		37.0+		All classes	
	Total	SE	Total	SE	Total	SE	Total	SE	Total	SE	Total	SE	Total	SE	Total	SE
	Million bone-dry tons															
Softwoods:																
Douglas-fir	21.01	1.42	17.4	1.41	36.15	2.72	32.88	1.83	32.5	1.96	32.08	2.12	142 1	10.2	427.91	16.69
Engelmann and other spruces	—	—	0.05	0.05	0.24	0 15	0.12	0.06	0 1	0.05	0.02	0.03	—	—	0.68	0.26
Incense-cedar	4.32	0.48	3.85	0.5	7.37	0.93	6.84	0.52	5.26	0.46	5.75	0.63	16.7	1.75	73.24	4.12
Lodgepole pine	5.3	0.75	4.78	0.8	9.15	1.25	6 98	0.83	5.37	0.73	3.02	0.56	3.22	0.58	57.63	5.38
Other western softwoods	4.72	0.6	5.21	0.66	8.03	1.1	5.42	0.64	4.77	0.62	4.01	0.67	7.71	1.29	62.71	4.41
Ponderosa and Jeffrey pines	14.76	1.08	15.75	1.24	24.6	1.78	23.91	1.34	21.71	1.47	17.84	1.35	39.28	2.97	224 1	8.27
Redwood	8.51	1.65	9.73	1.85	16.72	2.43	15.21	2 11	12.23	1.84	11.34	1.78	72.56	22.37	188.94	26.96
Sitka spruce	0.32	0.31	—	—	0 1	0 11	0.13	0 11	0.2	0 11	0.06	0.06	0.81	0.6	2.25	1.07
Sugar pine	2.12	0.34	3.46	0.55	7.04	0.78	6.77	0.55	7.54	0.8	6.95	0.71	33.76	3.39	74.45	4.67
True fir	25.28	1.61	23.64	1.59	46.55	2.89	44.71	2.53	40.14	2.45	34.35	2.42	103.77	8.42	437.73	18.74
Western hemlock	0.34	0.17	0.41	0.34	0.01	0.01	0.16	0.08	0.06	0.04	0.08	0.06	0.23	0.23	3.11	1.08
Western redcedar	—	—	—	—	—	—	0.06	0.07	0.14	0.12	0.25	0.21	0.4	0.31	0.93	0.69
Western white pine	0.54	0 16	0.39	0 13	1.09	0.27	1.27	0.2	1.43	0.23	1.38	0.25	6 1	0.96	14.93	1.57
Western woodland softwoods	1.4	0 18	1.13	0 19	1.29	0.22	0.79	0.12	0.35	0.07	0.31	0.07	0.36	0.09	16.76	1.51
Total	88.61	3 12	85.81	3.31	158.36	5.35	145.23	4 17	131.81	4 19	117.44	4.25	427	27.52	1,585.38	38.71
Hardwoods:																
Cottonwood and aspen	0.22	0 13	0.73	0.36	0.78	0.3	0.57	0.3	0.3	0 13	0.02	0.02	0.12	0.09	4.26	1.31
Oak	27.54	1.84	20.53	1.68	31.74	2.53	18.32	1.2	12.71	1 11	6.75	0.79	11.64	1.74	376.66	11.97
Other western hardwoods	16.14	1.71	10.96	1.28	20.46	2.22	9.16	0.95	5.39	0.68	3.76	0.69	4 93	1 14	206.42	11.37
Red alder	0.51	0 18	0.2	0 14	0.3	0.2	0.07	0.04	0.17	0.09	0.07	0.07	—	—	8.5	1.85
Western woodland hardwoods	0.25	0.05	0.2	0.07	0.3	0.08	0.11	0.04	0.05	0.04	0.02	0.02	0.03	0.02	3.45	0.47
Total	44.65	2.55	32.62	2.2	53.58	3.43	28.22	1.59	18.62	1.31	10.62	1.07	16.72	2.07	599.29	16.62
All species groups	133.25	3.99	118.44	3.96	211 95	6.33	173.46	4.48	150.43	4.39	128.07	4.43	443.72	27.63	2,184.67	42.46

Note: Totals may be off because of rounding; data subject to sampling error; SE = standard error; — = less than 5,000 bone-dry tons were estimated; includes all live trees ≥1 inch diameter at breast height.

Table 21—Estimated biomass of live trees on forest land by softwood species group, for merchantable tree boles, tops, limbs, stumps, and small trees, California, 2001–2005

| Softwood species group | Trees ≥ 8 in d.b h. | | | | Trees < 8 in d.b.h. | | | |
| | Merchantable tree boles | | Tops, limbs, and stumps | | Whole tree | | Total above-ground biomass | |
	Total	SE	Total	SE	Total	SE	Total	SE
				Million dry tons				
Douglas-fir	308.2	12.7	94.0	3.6	25.7	1.3	427.9	16.7
Engelmann and other spruces	0.5	0.2	0.1	0.1	0.1	0.0	0.7	0.3
Incense-cedar	43.7	2.6	22.8	1.4	6.7	0.5	73.2	4.1
Lodgepole pine	42.1	4.1	10.4	1.0	5.2	0.8	57.6	5.4
Other western softwoods	38.6	3.0	17.9	1.4	6.1	0.6	62.7	4.4
Ponderosa and Jeffrey pines	152.1	5.8	60.7	2.3	11.4	0.7	224.1	8.3
Redwood	75.7	13.7	102.4	13.2	10.9	1.6	188.9	27.0
Sitka spruce	1.5	0.8	0.6	0.3	0.1	0.1	2.3	1.1
Sugar pine	40.1	2.5	33.1	2.2	1.3	0.1	74.4	4.7
True firs	224.3	10.2	182.0	8.0	31.4	1.7	437.7	18.7
Western hemlock	2.1	0.8	0.4	0.1	0.6	0.2	3.1	1.1
Western redcedar	0.6	0.4	0.4	0.3	0.0	0.0	0.9	0.7
Western white pine	10.4	1.1	3.7	0.4	0.9	0.2	14.9	1.6
Western woodland softwoods	9.0	0.9	4.4	0.4	3.3	0.4	16.8	1.5
Total	948.8	22.9	532.9	16.2	103.7	3.0	1,585.4	38.7

Note: Totals may be off because of rounding; data subject to sampling error; SE = standard error; — = less than 50,000 bone-dry tons were estimated; includes all live trees ≥1 inch diameter at breast height; the merchantable bole is from a 1-foot stump to a 4-inch top.

Table 22—Estimated mass of carbon of all live trees, by owner class and forest land status, California, 2001–2005

| Owner class | Unreserved forests | | | | | | Reserved forests | | | | | | All forest land | |
| | Timberland[a] | | Other forest[b] | | Total | | Productive[a] | | Other forest[b] | | Total | | | |
	Total	SE	Total	SE	Total	SE	Total	SE	Total	SE	Total	SE	Total	SE
						Million bone-dry tons								
USDA Forest Service:														
National forest	418.9	11.1	24.2	2.2	443.1	11.1	126.0	8.4	11.3	1.5	137.5	8.4	580.5	11.3
Other federal:														
National Park Service	—	—	—	—	—	—	55.5	7.9	4.0	1.1	59.5	7.9	59.5	7.9
Bureau of Land Management	12.4	3.0	5.0	0.8	17.4	3.0	1.3	0.9	1.1	0.4	2.5	0.9	19.8	3.2
U.S. Fish and Wildlife Service	—	—	—	—	—	—	0.2	0.2	—	—	0.2	0.2	0.2	0.2
Departments of Defense and Energy	0.2	0.2	0.8	0.5	1.0	0.5	—	—	—	—	—	—	1.0	0.5
Other federal	0.6	0.6	0.1	0.0	0.6	0.6	3.7	2.1	1.0	0.7	4.7	2.2	5.3	2.3
Total	13.2	3.0	5.8	1.0	19.0	3.1	60.6	8.1	6.2	1.3	66.8	8.1	85.8	8.5
State and local government:														
State	10.9	3.6	1.3	0.8	12.2	3.7	35.3	12.2	2.7	0.9	38.0	12.2	50.2	12.7
Local	4.6	2.4	2.3	0.7	6.8	2.5	2.2	1.5	1.4	0.9	3.6	1.7	10.4	3.0
Other public	—	—	—	—	—	—	—	—	0.1	0.1	0.1	0.1	0.1	0.1
Total	15.5	4.4	3.6	1.0	19.0	4.5	37.4	12.3	4.2	1.2	41.6	12.3	60.7	13.0
Corporate private:	161.0	9.2	5.3	1.1	166.2	9.3	—	—	—	—	—	—	166.2	9.3
Noncorporate private:														
"Nongovernmental conservation or natural resource organization"	9.4	2.6	0.8	0.5	10.3	2.6	—	—	—	—	—	—	10.3	2.6
"Unincorporated partnerships, associations, or clubs"	2.2	1.4	0.5	0.3	2.6	1.4	—	—	—	—	—	—	2.6	1.4
Native American	8.7	3.2	0.7	0.5	9.4	3.2	—	—	—	—	—	—	9.4	3.2
Individual	156.7	10.5	47.8	3.5	204.7	10.8	—	—	—	—	—	—	204.7	10.8
Total	177.0	11.1	49.7	3.5	227.0	11.4	—	—	—	—	—	—	227.0	11.4
All owners	785.5	17.1	88.6	4.4	874.4	17.1	224.0	16.7	21.7	2.4	245.9	16.7	1,120.2	21.9

Note: Totals may be off because of rounding; data subject to sampling error; SE = standard error; — = less than 50,000 bone-dry tons were estimated; includes all live trees ≥1 inch diameter at breast height.

[a] Forest land that is capable of producing in excess of 20 cubic feet/acre/year of wood at culmination of mean annual increment.

[b] Forest land that is not capable of producing in excess of 20 cubic feet/acre/year of wood at culmination of mean annual increment.

Table 23—Estimated biomass and carbon mass of live trees, snags, and down wood on forest land, by forest type group, California, 2001–2005

| | Biomass | | | | | | Carbon | | | | | | |
| | Live trees (≥1 in d.b.h.) | | Snags (≥5 in d.b.h.) | | Down wood[a] (≥3 in l.e.d.) | | | Live trees (≥1 in d.b.h.) | | Snags (≥5 in d.b.h.) | | Down wood[a] (≥3 in l.e.d.) | | |
Forest type group	Total	SE	Total	SE	Total	SE	TOTAL	Total	SE	Total	SE	Total	SE	TOTAL
						Million bone-dry tons								
Softwoods:														
California mixed conifer	724 1	23.3	72.1	3.9	82.8	3.9	879.0	375.6	12.1	37.4	2.0	42.8	2.0	455.8
Douglas-fir	140.0	15.3	10.0	1.6	14.2	2.4	164.2	72.3	7.9	5.2	0.8	7.3	1.2	84.7
Fir/spruce/mountain hemlock	240.7	18.2	34.7	3.6	22.8	2.1	298.2	125.4	9.5	18 1	1.9	11.8	1.1	155.3
Lodgepole pine	61.2	6.8	6.4	1.1	8.9	1.3	76.4	31.9	3.5	3.3	0.6	4.7	0.7	39.9
Other western softwoods	31.7	3.1	2.4	0.4	4.9	0.7	39.0	16.5	1.6	1.3	0.2	2.5	0.4	20.2
Pinyon/juniper	18.7	1.9	1.7	0.4	2.2	0.3	22.6	9.7	1.0	0.9	0.2	1.2	0.2	11.8
Ponderosa pine	92 1	6.9	3.5	0.5	9.3	0.9	104.8	47.8	3.6	1.8	0.3	4.8	0.5	54.4
Redwood	160.9	30.1	11.1	2.8	16.5	4.2	188.5	83.5	15.7	5.8	1.4	8.5	2.2	97.8
Western hemlock/Sitka spruce[b]	3.5	2.5	1.5	1.4	0.3	0.3	5.3	1.8	1.3	0.8	0.7	0.2	0.1	2.8
Western white pine	6.6	1.8	0.9	0.3	0.8	0.3	8.3	3.4	0.9	0.5	0.2	0.4	0.1	4.3
Total	1,479.4	41.2	144.2	6.1	162.7	6.3	1,786.3	767.8	21.4	74.9	3.2	84.2	3.3	927.0
Hardwoods:														
Alder/maple	20.9	5.0	2.7	0.9	4.9	1.5	28.5	10.6	2.5	1.4	0.5	2.6	0.8	14.6
Aspen/birch	1.7	0.7	0.6	0.5	0.2	0.1	2.5	0.8	0.4	0.3	0.3	0 1	0.1	1.3
Elm/ash/cottonwood	2.7	1.6	—	—	—	—	2.7	1.3	0.8	—	—	—	—	1.3
Exotic hardwoods[b]	0.4	0.3	—	—	—	—	0.4	0.2	0.2	—	—	—	—	0.2
Other hardwoods	27.8	5.5	1.9	0.6	2.2	0.5	31.9	13.9	2.8	1.0	0.3	1 1	0.3	16.0
Tanoak/laurel	230.9	18.8	10.5	1.4	25.6	2.8	267.0	116.2	9.5	5.3	0.7	13.2	1.5	134.7
Western oak	414 1	16.3	20.8	1.7	27.1	2.1	462.0	205.9	8.1	10.5	0.9	13.8	1.1	230.2
Woodland hardwoods	5.6	1.0	0.7	0.2	1.1	0.3	7.4	2.8	0.5	0.3	0.1	0.5	0.1	3.7
Total	704.0	24.5	37.3	2.5	61.1	3.8	802.4	351.7	12.3	18.9	1.3	31.3	2.0	401.9
Nonstocked	1.3	0.3	6.3	2.0	2.0	0.4	9.6	0.7	0.1	3.3	1.0	1 1	0.2	5.1
All forest types	2,184.7	42.5	187.8	6.6	225.8	7.0	2,598.3	1,120.2	21.9	97 1	3.4	116.6	3.6	1,333.9

Note: Totals may be off because of rounding; data subject to sampling error; SE = standard error; — = less than 50,000 bone-dry tons were estimated; d.b.h. = diameter at breast height; l.e.d. = large-end diameter of the log.

[a] Down wood in this table includes coarse woody material (CWM) only; an additional 123 million tons of biomass and 62 million tons of carbon were estimated for fine woody material (FWM).

[b] These forest type groups are represented by <5 plots.

Table 24—Estimated average biomass and carbon mass of live trees, snags, and down wood on forest land, by forest type group, California, 2001–2005

	Biomass							Carbon						
	Live trees (≥1 in d.b.h.)		Snags (≥5 in d.b.h.)		Down wood[a] (≥3 in l.e.d.)			Live trees (≥1 in d.b.h.)		Snags (≥5 in d.b.h.)		Down wood[a] (≥3 in l.e.d.)		
Forest type group	Mean	SE	Mean	SE	Mean	SE	TOTAL	Mean	SE	Mean	SE	Mean	SE	TOTAL
	Bone-dry tons per acre													
Softwoods:														
California mixed conifer	91.9	2.0	9.2	0.5	10.5	0.4	111.6	47.7	1.0	4.7	0.2	5.4	0.2	57.8
Douglas-fir	130.9	8.6	9.3	1.3	13.2	1.7	153.4	67.6	4.5	4.8	0.7	6.8	0.9	79.2
Fir/spruce/mountain hemlock	116.4	5.2	16.8	1.4	11.0	0.8	144.2	60.6	2.7	8.7	0.7	5.7	0.4	75.0
Lodgepole pine	60.5	4.0	6.3	0.9	8.8	1.0	75.6	31.5	2 1	3.3	0.5	4.6	0.5	39.4
Other western softwoods	15.7	1 1	1.2	0.2	2.4	0.3	19.3	8.2	0.6	0.6	0 1	1.3	0.2	10.1
Pinyon/juniper	9.9	0.7	0.9	0.2	1.2	0.2	12.0	5.1	0.4	0.5	0 1	0.6	0 1	6.2
Ponderosa pine	39.9	1.9	1.5	0.2	4.0	0.3	45.4	20.7	1.0	0.8	0 1	2.1	0.2	23.6
Redwood	250.3	33 1	17.3	3.7	25.7	5.4	293.3	129.9	17.2	9.0	1.9	13.3	2.8	152.2
Western hemlock/Sitka spruce[b]	198.4	25.7	87.5	17 1	16.5	4.2	302.4	102.7	13.5	45.5	8.9	8.6	2.2	156.8
Western white pine	33.8	6.5	4.9	1.4	4.2	1 1	42.9	17.6	3.4	2.5	0.7	2.2	0.5	22.3
Total	77.4	1.9	7.5	0.3	8.5	0.3	93.4	40.2	1.0	3.9	0.2	4.4	0.2	48.5
Hardwoods:														
Alder/maple	78.1	10.6	10.1	2.8	18.4	4.2	106.6	39.6	5.4	5.2	1.5	9.5	2.2	54.3
Aspen/birch	20.7	6.8	7.5	6.0	2.3	1.4	30.5	10.4	3.4	3.9	3 1	1.1	0.7	15.4
Elm/ash/cottonwood	55.8	16 1	1.0	0.7	1.1	0.4	57 9	27.4	7.9	0.5	0.3	0.5	0.2	28.4
Exotic hardwoods[b]	82.0	19 1	—	—	2.7	0 1	84.7	40.3	9.4	—	—	1.3	0 1	41.6
Other hardwoods	45.6	6.8	3.1	0.8	3.5	0.7	52.2	22.8	3.4	1.6	0.4	1.8	0.3	26.2
Tanoak/laurel	109.3	5.4	5.0	0.6	12.2	1 1	126.5	55.0	2.7	2.5	0.3	6.2	0.5	63.7
Western oak	42.4	1.2	2.1	0.2	2.8	0.2	47.3	21.1	0.6	1.1	0 1	1.4	0 1	23.6
Woodland hardwoods	11.4	1.2	1.4	0.3	2.1	0.4	14.9	5.8	0.6	0.7	0.2	1.1	0.2	7.6
Total	52.6	1.5	2.8	0.2	4.6	0.3	60.0	26.3	0.7	1.4	0 1	2.3	0 1	30.0
Nonstocked	1.8	0.3	8.3	2.5	2.6	0.5	12.7	0.9	0.2	4.3	1.3	1.4	0.3	6.6
All forest types	65.7	1.2	5.6	0.2	6.8	0.2	78.1	33.7	0.6	2.9	0 1	3.5	0 1	40.1

Note: Means are calculated using a ratio of means formula across plots within forest type groups; data subject to sampling error; SE = standard error; — = less than 0.05 bone-dry tons per acre were estimated; d.b.h. = diameter at breast height; l.e.d. = large-end diameter of the log.

[a] Down wood in this table includes coarse woody material only.

[b] These forest type groups are represented by <5 plots.

Table 25—Estimated average biomass, volume, and density of down wood on forest land, by forest type group and diameter class, California, 2001–2005

Forest type group	Biomass FWM <3 in Mean	SE	Biomass CWM 3 to 19 in Mean	SE	Biomass CWM ≥20 in Mean	SE	Biomass CWM Total Mean	SE	Volume FWM <3 in Mean	SE	Volume CWM 3 to 19 in Mean	SE	Volume CWM ≥20 in Mean	SE	Volume CWM Total Mean	SE	Density CWM 3 to 19 in Mean	SE	Density CWM ≥20 in Mean	SE	Density CWM Total Mean	SE
	Bone-dry tons per acre								*Cubic feet per acre*								*Logs per acre*					
Softwoods:																						
California mixed conifer	4.9	0.3	4.6	0.2	5.9	0.3	15.4	0.8	391.9	19.5	548.4	21.8	786.6	41.0	1,726.9	81.4	225.5	7.0	9.5	0.5	235.0	7.2
Douglas-fir	6.6	0.7	4.4	0.4	8.8	1.6	19.8	2.0	478.0	56.0	526.1	41.6	1,164.2	229.0	2,168.3	265.9	191.8	13.9	16.5	2.8	208.3	14.7
Fir/spruce/mountain hemlock	5.0	0.3	4.7	0.3	6.3	0.7	16.0	0.9	434.4	22.6	600.8	34.8	872.3	91.0	1,907.5	115.2	224.6	12.5	11.5	1.1	236.1	12.7
Lodgepole pine	1.8	0.2	3.3	0.5	5.5	0.7	10.6	1.1	150.5	16.8	420.3	57.3	740.3	90.6	1,311.1	142.4	109.8	12.1	9.1	1.2	118.9	12.6
Other western softwoods	1.2	0.1	1.1	0.1	1.3	0.2	3.6	0.4	83.3	7.8	123.4	14.5	179.0	35.1	385.7	56.7	49.1	4.8	3.0	0.6	52.1	5.0
Pinyon/juniper	1.3	0.1	0.9	0.1	0.3	0.1	2.5	0.2	101.4	8.7	101.1	12.4	28.7	8.6	231.2	21.1	55.0	6.3	0.7	0.2	55.7	6.4
Ponderosa pine	2.1	0.1	2.0	0.1	2.0	0.2	6.1	0.8	178.2	12.0	236.9	15.3	286.4	33.1	701.5	94.5	121.8	7.4	4.4	0.6	126.2	7.6
Redwood	6.2	1.0	7.8	0.8	18.0	5.2	32.0	5.3	63.0	87.1	952.9	93.6	2,466.9	696.3	3,482.8	703.5	307.1	35.3	27.1	4.3	334.2	35.6
Western hemlock/Sitka spruce	5.2	1.7	4.5	1.0	12.0	3.1	21.7	3.0	5.3	147.4	706.7	158.6	1,746.9	458.9	2,458.9	498.4	226.8	25.3	36.8	9.7	263.6	27.6
Western white pine	1.3	0.2	1.6	0.4	2.7	0.9	5.6	1.0	8.3	19.8	199.0	51.2	307.1	100.5	514.4	117.8	96.6	17.0	5.8	2.7	102.4	17.7
Total	4.0	0.1	3.5	0.1	5.0	0.3	12.5	0.4	326.6	10.1	429.3	12.3	667.3	35.5	1,423.2	50.6	170.8	4.1	8.5	0.4	179.3	4.2
Hardwoods:																						
Alder/maple	6.5	1.0	4.2	0.6	14.2	3.8	24.9	4.2	509.8	74.8	569.6	82.1	1,865.5	514.7	2,944.9	573.8	183.2	23.6	23.7	5.5	206.9	27.0
Aspen/birch	2.4	0.6	1.1	0.4	1.2	1.1	4.7	1.4	196.1	45.9	153.5	58.7	197.5	190.3	547.1	236.3	106.4	32.0	1.5	1.5	107.9	32.7
Elm/ash/cottonwood	4.5	0.8	1.1	0.4	—		5.6	0.5	330.1	32.9	156.6	53.7	—		486.7	81.4	78.9	27.9	—		78.9	27.9
Other hardwoods	4.9	1.0	2.5	0.5	1.1	0.4	8.5	1.3	314.4	71.6	188.5	36.7	128.7	40.8	631.6	112.7	95.8	23.2	2.6	1.1	98.4	23.4
Tanoak/laurel	6.1	0.4	4.9	0.3	7.3	1.0	18.3	1.3	395.3	26.3	531.1	32.0	840.1	102.8	1,766.5	124.2	202.4	12.2	12.2	1.4	214.6	12.5
Western oak	3.1	0.1	1.7	0.1	1.1	0.2	5.9	0.3	169.3	6.0	167.9	8.2	128.9	24.3	466.1	28.7	83.9	3.5	1.6	0.2	85.5	3.6
Woodland hardwoods	3.1	0.5	1.5	0.3	0.6	0.2	5.2	0.7	197.6	26.2	134.2	29.9	74.0	31.0	405.8	53.4	89.3	18.3	1.7	1.0	91.0	18.2
Total	3.7	0.1	2.3	0.1	2.3	0.2	8.3	0.3	220.2	7.8	235.2	9.0	273.7	28.1	729.1	35.1	107.2	3.7	3.8	0.3	111.0	3.8
Nonstocked	1.7	0.2	2.1	0.4	0.5	0.2	4.3	0.7	133.7	16.1	247.2	52.4	62.1	19.8	443.0	72.7	76.4	13.7	1.1	0.4	77.5	13.8
All forest types	3.8	0.1	3.0	0.1	3.8	0.2	10.6	0.3	276.5	6.6	347.0	8.1	495.2	23.5	1,118.7	32.6	143.0	2.8	6.4	0.2	149.4	2.9

Note: Means are calculated using a ratio of means formula across plots within forest type groups; data subject to sampling error; SE = standard error; — = less than 0.05 bone-dry tons per acre, 0.05 cubic feet per acre, and 0.05 logs per acre were estimated; CWM = coarse woody material; FWM = fine woody material.

a The diameter at the large end is used to classify CWM with decay classes of 1–4; diameter at the point of intersection with the transect is used for heavily decomposed CWM (decay class 5) and for all FWM.

b An estimate of pieces per acre is not possible for FWM.

Table 26—Estimated biomass and carbon mass of down wood[a] on forest land, by forest type group and owner group, California, 2001–2005

Forest type group	USDA Forest Service Biomass	USDA Forest Service Carbon	Other federal Biomass	Other federal Carbon	State and local governments Biomass	State and local governments Carbon	Corporate private Biomass	Corporate private Carbon	Noncorporate private Biomass	Noncorporate private Carbon	All owners Biomass	All owners Carbon
						Million bone-dry tons						
Softwoods:												
California mixed conifer	55.8	28.9	5.1	2.6	0.8	0.4	15.4	8	5.7	2.9	82.8	42.8
Douglas-fir	4.5	2.3	0.7	0.4	0.5	0.2	6	3.1	2.5	1.3	14.2	7.3
Fir/spruce/mountain hemlock	15.5	8	2.9	1.5	0.5	0.2	3	1.6	0.9	0.5	22.8	11.8
Lodgepole pine	5.2	2.7	3	1.6	0.1	0	0.1	0.1	0.5	0.3	8.9	4.7
Other western softwoods	3.3	1.7	0.7	0.4	—	—	0.2	0.1	0.7	0.3	4.9	2.5
Pinyon/juniper	1.5	0.8	0.6	0.3	—	—	—	—	0.1	0.1	2.2	1.2
Ponderosa pine	6.4	3.3	0.2	0.1	—	—	1.5	0.8	1.2	0.6	9.3	4.8
Redwood	0.5	0.3	3.9	2	1.8	0.9	7	3.6	3.4	1.7	16.5	8.5
Western hemlock/Sitka spruce	—	—	—	—	—	—	0.3	0.2	—	—	0.3	0.2
Western white pine	0.8	0.4	—	—	—	—	—	—	—	—	0.8	0.4
Total	93.5	48.4	17.1	8.9	3.7	1.7	33.5	17.5	15	7.7	162.7	84.2
Hardwoods:												
Alder/maple	0.9	0.5	0.1	0.1	0.2	0.1	3.2	1.6	0.6	0.3	4.9	2.6
Aspen/birch	0.2	0.1	—	—	—	—	—	—	—	—	0.2	0.1
Other hardwoods	0.9	0.5	—	—	—	—	0.4	0.2	0.9	0.4	2.2	1.1
Tanoak/laurel	6	3.1	0.6	0.3	0.8	0.4	8.9	4.6	9.3	4.8	25.6	13.2
Western oak	11.2	5.7	1.5	0.8	0.8	0.4	4.5	2.3	9.1	4.6	27.1	13.8
Woodland hardwoods	0.8	0.4	0.1	—	—	—	—	—	0.2	0.1	1.1	0.5
Total	20	10.3	2.3	1.2	1.7	0.9	17	8.7	20.1	10.2	61.1	31.3
Nonstocked	1.7	0.9	0.2	0.1	—	—	0.1	0.1	—	—	2	1.1
All forest types	115.2	59.6	19.6	10.2	5.4	2.6	50.6	26.3	35.1	17.9	225.8	116.6

Note: Totals may be off because of rounding; data subject to sampling error; — = less than 50,000 bone-dry tons were estimated.
[a] In this table, down wood includes logs ≥3 inches diameter at the large end (coarse woody material). An additional 123 million tons of biomass and 62 million tons of carbon were estimated for fine woody material in the state.

Table 27—Estimated average biomass, volume, and density of snags on forest land, by forest type group and diameter class, California, 2001–2005

Forest type group	Biomass — Diameter class (inches at large end) — Bone-dry tons per acre								Volume — Diameter class (inches at large end) — Cubic feet per acre								Density — Diameter class (inches at large end) — Trees per acre							
	5 to 19		20 to 39		≥40		Total		5 to 19		20 to 39		≥40		Total		5 to 19		20 to 39		≥40		Total	
	Mean	SE	Mean	SE	Mean	SE	Mean	SE	Mean	SE	Mean	SE	Mean	SE	Mean	SE	Mean	SE	Mean	SE	Mean	SE	Mean	SE
Softwoods:																								
California mixed conifer	2.7	0.2	3.6	0.2	2.9	0.3	9.2	0.5	114.7	7	160.5	10.2	117.3	10.8	392.5	19.4	15.6	0.8	2.2	0.1	0.4	0.4	18.1	0.9
Douglas-fir	2.2	0.3	2.8	0.5	4.3	1.1	9.3	1.3	78.5	11.8	110.0	21	126.3	28.9	314.8	41.8	16.0	2.6	1.9	0.4	0.6	0.1	18.5	2.7
Fir/spruce/mountain hemlock	3.9	0.4	7.3	0.7	5.6	0.8	16.8	1.4	149.1	17.8	259.1	27.5	153.4	24.7	561.6	49.7	19.4	1.9	4.1	0.4	0.7	0.1	24.2	2
Lodgepole pine	2.0	0.3	3.1	0.5	1.2	0.4	6.3	0.9	114.5	18.6	173.3	28.7	54.5	20.4	342.3	50.3	9.6	1.5	2.1	0.3	0.2	0.1	12.0	1.6
Other western softwoods	0.6	0.1	0.5	0.1	0.1	0.1	1.2	0.2	29.7	6.8	29.9	5.8	7.3	3	67.0	11.1	5.7	1.1	0.6	0.1	—	—	6.2	1.2
Pinyon/juniper	0.7	0.1	0.2	0.2	—	—	0.9	0.2	27.8	6.4	11.1	2.5	0.2	0.2	39.0	7.7	7.2	1.6	0.6	0.1	—	—	7.7	1.7
Ponderosa pine	0.7	0.1	0.7	0.1	0.2	0.1	1.5	0.2	32.5	5.8	38.1	7.2	8.4	3.4	79.0	11.5	5.5	0.7	0.5	0.1	0.1	0.1	6.1	0.8
Redwood	2.5	0.7	4.9	1.6	9.9	2.4	17.3	3.7	42.7	12.7	116.5	58.6	166.6	44.3	325.8	94.2	9.0	1.7	2.8	0.7	1.6	0.3	13.4	2.2
Western hemlock/Sitka spruce	4.3	11	7.6	5.8	75.6	19.3	87.5	17.1	149.8	38.2	349.0	386.8	975.9	249.3	1,474.7	271	42.5	10.9	7.1	6.2	7.8	2	57.5	9.7
Western white pine	1.0	0.3	2.7	1.1	1.2	0.6	4.9	1.4	58.0	20.8	127.8	52.4	39.7	179	225.5	68.2	6.8	2.3	1.7	0.7	0.3	0.1	8.8	2.5
Total	2.0	0.1	3.0	0.1	2.5	0.2	7.6	0.3	85.9	3.9	124.0	61	83.7	59	293.5	11.2	12.3	0.5	1.9	0.1	0.3	0.3	14.5	0.5
Hardwoods:																								
Alder/maple	2.3	0.6	1.2	0.4	6.7	2.7	10.1	2.8	104.4	28.4	42.1	18	160.0	73.8	306.4	83.1	17.8	4.4	0.7	0.3	0.9	0.3	19.4	4.4
Aspen/birch	3.2	2.4	2.8	2.3	1.4	1.4	7.5	6.0	144.9	104.3	127 1	99.1	73.3	69.3	345.2	271.5	22.6	11.3	2.0	1.6	0.2	0.2	24.8	13
Elm/ash/cottonwood	0.9	0.6	0.1	0.1	—	—	1.0	0.7	30.0	18.2	2.5	2.6	—	—	32.4	19.2	6.1	4.6	0.1	0.2	—	—	6.2	4.8
Other hardwoods	2.3	0.7	0.3	0.2	0.5	0.3	3.1	0.8	85.2	26.4	11.7	6	25.8	14.8	122.7	33.8	12.0	2.6	0.3	0.1	0.1	0.1	12.3	2.7
Tanoak/laurel	1.8	0.3	1.3	0.3	1.9	0.3	5.0	0.6	61.0	10.7	46.4	10.7	60.2	12.4	167.7	21.1	11.1	1.1	0.9	0.1	0.3	0.1	12.3	11
Western oak	1.2	0.1	0.7	0.1	0.2	0.1	2.1	0.2	41.4	3.7	33.1	3.5	10.2	2.4	84.8	7	7.8	0.6	0.5	0.1	—	—	8.3	0.6
Woodland hardwoods	0.9	0.2	0.4	0.2	0.1	0.1	1.4	0.3	40.7	9.5	19.8	7.8	2.7	2.7	63.2	13.9	17.1	3.2	0.6	0.2	—	—	17.7	3.3
Total	1.4	0.1	0.8	0.1	0.6	0.1	2.8	0.2	48.3	3.6	34.4	3.2	21.9	3.2	104.6	6.8	9.2	0.5	0.6	0.6	0.1	0.1	9.8	0.5
Nonstocked	3.5	1.0	3.6	1.4	1.2	0.6	8.3	2.5	148.9	42.1	175.2	70	68.3	35.2	392.3	122	26.3	7	1.9	0.6	0.2	0.1	28.3	7.3
All forest types	1.8	0.1	2.1	0.1	1.7	0.1	5.7	0.2	72.2	2.8	89.1	4	58.4	3.7	219.7	7.5	11.3	0.4	1.3	0.1	0.2	0.2	12.9	0.4

Note: Means are calculated using a ratio of means formula across plots within forest type groups; data subject to sampling error; SE = standard error; — = less than 0.05 bone-dry tons per acre, 0.05 cubic feet per acre, and 0.05 trees per acre were estimated; includes snags ≥5 inches diameter at breast height.

Table 28—Estimated biomass and carbon mass of snags on forest land, by forest type group and owner group, California, 2001–2005

Million bone-dry tons

Forest type group	USDA Forest Service Biomass Total	SE	Carbon Total	SE	Other federal Biomass Total	SE	Carbon Total	SE	State and local governments Biomass Total	SE	Carbon Total	SE	Corporate private Biomass Total	SE	Carbon Total	SE	Noncorporate private Biomass Total	SE	Carbon Total	SE	All owners Biomass Total	SE	Carbon Total	SE
Softwoods:																								
California mixed conifer	57.2	3.4	28.6	1.7	5.2	1.5	2.6	0.8	1.0	0.6	0.5	0.3	6.3	0.9	3.2	0.5	2.4	0.7	1.2	0.3	72.1	3.9	36.1	2.0
Douglas-fir	4.9	0.9	2.5	0.5	0.2	0.1	0.1	0.0	0.2	0.1	0.1	0.1	2.6	1.1	1.3	0.5	2.0	0.7	1.0	0.3	10.0	1.6	5.0	0.8
Fir/spruce/mountain hemlock	26.1	2.9	13.0	1.5	5.5	1.8	2.7	0.9	0.9	0.7	0.5	0.3	1.2	0.4	0.6	0.2	1.0	0.7	0.5	0.4	34.7	3.6	17.3	1.8
Lodgepole pine	3.2	0.5	1.6	0.3	2.0	0.8	1.0	0.4	—	—	—	—	0.4	0.3	0.2	0.1	0.7	0.5	0.4	0.3	6.3	1.1	3.2	0.5
Other western softwoods	1.9	0.4	0.9	0.2	0.3	0.1	0.2	0.1	—	—	—	—	—	—	—	—	0.2	0.1	0.1	0.0	2.4	0.4	1.2	0.2
Pinyon/juniper	0.7	0.2	0.4	0.1	0.8	0.3	0.4	0.1	—	—	—	—	—	—	—	—	0.2	0.1	0.1	0.1	1.7	0.3	0.9	0.2
Ponderosa pine	2.6	0.5	1.3	0.2	0.2	0.1	0.1	0.0	—	—	—	—	0.5	0.2	0.2	0.1	0.2	0.1	0.1	0.0	3.4	0.5	1.7	0.3
Redwood	0.4	0.4	0.2	0.2	0.5	0.5	0.3	0.2	1.6	0.8	0.8	0.4	3.0	1.0	1.5	0.5	5.6	2.4	2.8	1.2	11.1	2.8	5.5	1.4
Western hemlock/Sitka spruce	—	—	—	—	—	—	—	—	—	—	—	—	1.4	1.4	0.7	0.7	0.1	0.1	—	—	1.5	1.4	0.8	0.7
Western white pine	0.9	0.3	0.5	0.2	—	—	—	—	—	—	—	—	—	—	—	—	—	—	—	—	0.9	0.3	0.5	0.2
Total	97.9	4.3	49.0	2.1	14.7	2.3	7.3	1.2	3.7	1.2	1.8	0.6	15.5	2.3	7.7	1.1	12.4	2.7	6.2	1.4	144.2	6.1	72.1	3.0
Hardwoods:																								
Alder/maple	1.1	0.5	0.5	0.3	0.2	0.2	0.1	0.1	0.7	0.7	0.3	0.3	0.6	0.3	0.3	0.2	0.2	0.1	0.1	0.1	2.7	0.9	1.4	0.5
Aspen/birch	0.6	0.5	0.3	0.3	—	—	—	—	—	—	—	—	—	—	—	—	—	—	—	—	0.6	0.5	0.3	0.3
Elm/ash/cottonwood	—	—	—	—	—	—	—	—	—	—	—	—	—	—	—	—	—	—	—	—	—	—	—	—
Other hardwoods	0.9	0.4	0.5	0.2	—	—	—	—	—	—	—	—	0.1	0.11	—	—	0.9	0.4	0.4	0.2	1.9	0.6	1.0	0.3
Tanoak/laurel	3.4	0.7	1.7	0.3	0.3	0.2	0.2	0.1	1.4	0.7	0.7	0.3	3.3	0.8	1.7	0.4	2.1	0.5	1.0	0.3	10.5	1.4	5.3	0.7
Western oak	10.8	1.1	5.4	0.6	1.4	0.5	0.7	0.3	0.5	0.2	0.2	0.1	2.0	0.5	1.0	0.2	6.3	1.1	3.2	0.5	20.8	1.7	10.4	0.9
Woodland hardwoods	0.5	0.2	0.3	0.1	0.1	0.1	0.1	0.1	—	—	—	—	—	—	—	—	0.1	0.0	—	—	0.7	0.2	0.3	0.1
Total	17.3	1.6	8.6	0.8	2.0	0.6	1.0	0.3	2.6	1.0	1.3	0.5	5.9	1.0	3.0	0.5	9.5	1.2	4.8	0.6	37.3	2.5	18.6	1.2
Nonstocked	6.0	2.0	3.0	1.0	0.2	0.2	0.1	0.1	—	—	—	—	—	—	—	—	—	—	—	—	6.3	2.0	3.1	1.0
All forest types	121.2	4.7	60.6	2.4	16.9	2.4	8.5	1.2	6.2	1.5	3.1	0.8	21.4	2.4	10.7	1.2	22.0	3.0	11.0	1.5	187.8	6.6	93.9	3.3

Note: Totals may be off because of rounding; data subject to sampling error; — = less than 50,000 bone-dry tons were estimated; includes snags ≥ 5 inches in diameter at breast height.

Table 29—Mean cover of understory vegetation on forest land, by forest type group and life form, California, 2001–2005

Forest type group	Seedlings and saplings Mean	SE	Shrubs Mean	SE	Forbs Mean	SE	Graminoids Mean	SE	All understory plants Mean	SE	Bare soil Mean	SE
					Percent							
Softwoods:												
California mixed conifer	6.3	0.2	17.6	0.6	5.2	0.2	3.6	0.2	31.0	0.7	4.7	0.2
Douglas-fir	7.7	0.8	24.4	2.0	8.9	1.1	4.8	0.9	43.4	2.4	3.5	0.6
Fir/spruce/mountain hemlock	3.5	0.3	17.2	1.3	5.8	0.5	2.9	0.3	28.0	1.4	5.6	0.5
Lodgepole pine	3.7	0.5	10.9	1.3	8.9	0.9	11.0	1.4	31.6	2.1	5.9	0.8
Other western softwoods	1.7	0.2	14.9	1.0	7.6	0.6	14.1	0.9	35.9	1.4	14.1	0.9
Pinyon/juniper	1.0	0.2	17.6	0.9	4.9	0.4	6.9	0.6	29.4	1.3	16.5	1.2
Ponderosa pine	3.0	0.3	23.3	1.2	6.0	0.4	8.5	0.7	39.0	1.3	6.0	0.5
Redwood	7.9	0.9	21.7	2.4	12.5	1.7	3.5	0.7	43.3	2.8	3.4	0.8
Western hemlock/Sitka spruce	0.7	0.3	24.6	16.5	23.4	7.4	2.5	2.8	44.0	14.3	0.2	0.1
Western white pine	10.0	3.8	18.0	4.4	8.9	2.2	5.4	1.1	39.1	6.0	12.5	3.7
Total	4.6	0.1	18.1	0.4	6.3	0.2	6.0	0.2	33.2	0.5	7.2	0.2
Hardwoods:												
Alder/maple	7.5	1.7	35.4	4.6	18.1	2.8	3.6	1.2	58.7	4.4	1.8	0.8
Aspen/birch	14.9	3.1	26.6	5.6	12.6	3.3	8.7	1.7	57.1	6.7	5.1	2.2
Elm/ash/cottonwood	2.2	1.6	51.5	8.7	2.7	1.2	25.7	10.8	69.5	9.8	1.4	0.7
Exotic hardwoods	10.0	0.0	0.0	0.0	0.0	0.0	0.0	0.0	10.0	0.0	0.0	0.0
Other western hardwoods	5.5	0.8	20.7	1.8	7.8	0.8	15.8	2.0	47.3	2.5	9.0	1.5
Tanoak/laurel	12.1	0.8	16.7	1.3	7.2	0.7	4.0	0.8	38.2	1.7	3.0	0.4
Western oak	4.0	0.2	18.2	0.7	11.7	0.5	28.7	0.9	57.5	0.9	4.0	0.2
Total	5.5	0.2	18.7	0.6	10.8	0.4	23.1	0.8	53.7	0.8	4.2	0.2
Nonstocked	1.6	0.6	28.9	2.8	10.7	1.4	16.0	2.3	53.9	2.9	16.0	2.1
All forest types	4.9	0.1	18.6	0.3	8.2	0.2	13.1	0.3	41.9	0.4	6.2	0.2
Chaparral on national forest	0.7	0.2	61.5	1.3	5.9	0.5	6.0	0.5	72.0	1.1	9.0	0.5

Note: Data subject to sampling error; SE = standard error.

Table 30—Mean cover of understory vegetation on forest land, by forest type class, age class, and life form, California, 2001–2005

Forest type class[a] and age class	Seedlings and saplings		Shrubs		Forbs		Graminoids		All understory plants		Bare soil	
	Mean	SE	Mean	SE	Mean	SE	Mean	SE	Mean	SE	Mean	SE
					Percent							
Dry conifer:												
0–19	2.6	0.4	25.0	2.2	8.5	1.0	12.9	1.6	47.3	2.5	16.5	1.8
20–39	4.3	0.7	30.0	2.6	6.6	1.1	11.0	1.8	46.9	2.7	7.5	1.1
40–79	4.6	0.3	19.7	0.9	6.3	0.4	7.2	0.5	35.9	1.0	7.6	0.5
80–159	4.5	0.2	16.1	0.6	6.0	0.3	6.8	0.4	31.6	0.7	7.4	0.4
160+	3.9	0.3	16.7	0.8	5.5	0.4	5.2	0.5	29.8	1.0	8.3	0.6
All ages	4.3	0.2	18.2	0.4	6.1	0.2	7.1	0.3	33.8	0.5	8.2	0.3
Wet conifer:												
0–19	6.3	1.4	35.2	5.9	10.5	2.7	6.9	1.9	54.8	7.9	10.6	2.3
20–39	5.5	0.8	34.2	3.4	10.8	1.5	3.8	1.7	51.7	3.3	6.0	1.9
40–79	5.2	0.5	23.5	1.9	7.5	0.9	3.8	0.6	37.9	2.1	3.8	0.5
80–159	5.0	0.5	13.7	1.2	7.4	0.9	3.2	0.4	27.9	1.7	5.1	0.5
160+	6.4	0.8	18.5	2.3	7.5	1.0	3.2	0.6	33.9	2.4	3.8	0.7
All ages	5.4	0.3	20.0	1.0	7.9	0.5	3.5	0.3	35.0	1.2	4.6	0.3
Dry hardwood:												
0–19	13.1	1.3	32.9	3.0	10.1	1.3	14.3	2.4	65.4	2.6	9.2	1.4
20–39	10.0	1.1	24.5	2.0	7.4	0.9	8.6	1.7	47.2	2.3	3.0	0.6
40–79	4.8	0.3	18.4	0.9	9.9	0.6	21.6	1.2	50.6	1.3	3.6	0.3
80–159	4.8	0.4	16.3	1.0	10.5	0.6	25.4	1.3	52.7	1.4	4.4	0.4
160+	3.5	0.5	14.0	1.2	14.3	1.1	33.9	2.2	60.4	2.0	4.1	0.7
All ages	5.4	0.2	18.2	0.6	10.7	0.4	23.6	0.8	53.5	0.8	4.2	0.2
Wet hardwood:												
0–19	11.5	2.9	24.3	9.7	11.0	4.1	8.9	4.2	52.1	10.0	1.5	0.7
20–39	9.8	3.2	45.9	7.5	20.5	4.1	3.0	2.0	68.4	6.2	0.6	0.2
40–79	7.2	2.8	36.9	6.0	15.3	3.7	4.5	1.4	59.9	6.3	1.0	0.3
80–159	7.0	2.2	29.2	7.6	16.7	6.7	4.8	2.6	54.6	8.8	4.6	3.3
160+	8.0	3.7	27.1	7.6	7.4	3.3	18.4	7.0	52.8	9.2	5.7	3.0
All ages	8.4	1.4	35.4	3.5	15.2	2.1	7.2	1.7	59.6	3.4	2.4	0.8
All forest type classes:												
0–19	7.2	0.6	28.7	1.7	9.3	0.7	13.1	1.3	55.1	1.8	13.0	1.2
20–39	7.4	0.6	29.1	1.5	8.5	0.7	8.2	1.0	49.1	1.5	4.8	0.6
40–79	4.8	0.2	19.7	0.6	8.2	0.3	13.6	0.6	43.4	0.8	5.2	0.3
80–159	4.7	0.2	16.0	0.5	7.8	0.3	12.8	0.5	38.5	0.7	6.1	0.3
160+	4.1	0.3	16.2	0.7	8.7	0.5	14.7	0.9	40.8	1.0	6.3	0.4
All ages	4.9	0.1	18.6	0.3	8.2	0.2	13.1	0.3	41.9	1.1	6.2	0.5

Note: Data subject to sampling error; SE = standard error.

[a] Dry conifer includes the pinyon/juniper; ponderosa, western white, and lodgepole pines; other softwoods; mixed conifer; and nonstocked forest types. Wet conifer includes the Douglas-fir, fir/spruce/mountain hemlock, hemlock/Sitka spruce, and redwood forest types. Dry hardwood includes the western oak, tanoak/laurel, other hardwoods, and exotic forest types. Wet hardwood includes the elm/ash/cottonwood, aspen/birch, and alder/maple forest types.

Table 31—Estimated mean crown density and other statistics[a] for live trees on forest land, by species group, California, 2001–2005

| Species group | Plots | Trees | Crown density | | | | |
			Mean	SE	Minimum	Median	Maximum
	- - *Number* - -		- - - - - - - - - - - - - - - - *Percent* - - - - - - - - - - - - - -				
Softwoods:							
Douglas-fir	86	685	39.4	0.9	0	40	85
Incense-cedar	53	340	39.5	1.2	10	40	75
Lodgepole pine	20	262	38.4	2.2	5	40	85
Other western softwoods	63	292	41.8	1.3	0	40	80
Ponderosa and Jeffrey pines	103	781	40	1.1	5	40	95
Redwood	11	153	33.8	2.3	0	35	65
Sugar pine	42	150	41.9	1.8	0	40	80
True fir	97	1,159	43.9	0.9	0	40	99
Western white pine	15	68	36.5	1.7	15	35	55
Western woodland softwoods	16	77	47.9	4.8	10	45	90
Total	303	5,454	44.2	0.9	0	40	99
Hardwoods:							
Cottonwood and aspen	5	49	26.7	2.8	0	25	60
Oak	147	1,904	33.6	0.6	0	35	85
Other western hardwoods	66	906	34.6	1.2	0	35	85
Red alder	6	59	43	2.8	15	40	70
Western woodland hardwoods	19	181	38.1	2.8	5	35	85
Total	194	3,099	34.2	0.6	0	35	85
All species groups	327	7,077	38	0.5	0	35	99

Note: Data subject to sampling error; SE = standard error; includes live trees >4.9 inches diameter at breast height.

[a] The mean, SE, and median calculations consider the clustering of trees on plots.

Table 32—Estimated mean foliage transparency and other statistics[a] for live trees on forest land, by species group, California, 2001–2005

Species group	Plots	Trees	Foliage transparency				
			Mean	SE	Minimum	Median	Maximum
	- - Number - -		*- - - - - - - - - - - - - - - - - Percent - - - - - - - - - - - - - -*				
Softwoods:							
Douglas-fir	86	685	18.9	0.4	0	20	40
Incense-cedar	53	340	18.7	0.5	5	20	35
Lodgepole pine	20	262	17.2	0.8	10	15	40
Other western softwoods	63	292	18.7	0.9	5	15	40
Ponderosa and Jeffrey pines	103	781	20.3	0.5	5	20	65
Redwood	11	153	19.2	1.4	0	20	99
Sugar pine	42	150	19.3	0.5	10	20	65
True fir	97	1,159	16.8	0.4	0	15	99
Western white pine	15	68	18.2	1.4	15	15	30
Western woodland softwoods	16	77	17.7	1.3	5	20	30
Total	266	3,978	18.4	0.2	0	20	99
Hardwoods:							
Cottonwood and aspen	5	49	25.4	2.9	15	25	99
Oak	147	1,904	22.3	0.5	0	20	99
Other western hardwoods	66	906	21.2	0.9	5	20	99
Red alder	6	59	20.6	0.5	15	20	25
Western woodland hardwoods	19	181	26.1	2.0	15	25	60
Total	194	3,099	22.2	0.4	0	20	99
All species groups	327	7,077	20.1	0.3	0	20	99

Note: Data subject to sampling error; SE = standard error; includes live trees >4.9 inches diameter at breast height.

[a] The mean, SE, and median calculations consider the clustering of trees on plots.

Table 33—Estimated mean crown dieback and other statistics[a] for all live trees on forest land, by species group, California, 2001–2005

Species group	Plots	Trees	Crown density				
			Mean	SE	Minimum	Median	Maximum
	- - *Number* - -		- - - - - - - - - - - - - - - - *Percent* - - - - - - - - - - - - - - -				
Softwoods:							
Douglas-fir	86	686	0.8	0.2	0	0	90
Incense-cedar	53	340	2.0	0.4	0	0	90
Lodgepole pine	20	262	1.3	0.4	0	0	25
Other western softwoods	63	293	2.0	0.4	0	0	75
Ponderosa and Jeffrey pines	103	781	1.1	0.3	0	0	80
Redwood	11	153	2.5	1.9	0	0	99
Sugar pine	42	150	1.1	0.5	0	0	50
True fir	97	1,159	2.0	0.5	0	0	99
Western white pine	15	69	2.2	1.1	0	0	40
Western woodland softwoods	16	77	4.9	1.3	0	0	30
Total	266	3,981	1.6	0.2	0	0	99
Hardwoods:							
Cottonwood and aspen	5	49	6.0	4.5	0	0	99
Oak	148	1,924	4.6	0.6	0	0	99
Other western hardwoods	66	917	2.6	0.7	0	0	99
Red alder	6	59	3.7	1.4	0	5	15
Western woodland hardwoods	19	181	8.0	2.6	0	5	80
Total	195	3,130	4.2	0.5	0	0	99
All species groups	327	7,111	2.8	0.2	0	0	99

Note: Data subject to sampling error; SE = standard error; includes live trees >4.9 inches diameter at breast height.
[a] The mean, SE, and median calculations consider the clustering of trees on plots.

Table 34—Properties of the forest floor layer on forest land, by forest type, California, 2001, 2003–2005

Forest type	Samples	Moisture content (oven-dry basis)	Organic carbon	Total nitrogen
	Number	*Percent*	*- - - - - - - Percent - - - - - - -*	
Bigleaf maple	1	6.35	19.33	0.56
Blue oak	20	8.42	24.80	0.90
California black oak	10	32.34	29.01	0.77
California mixed conifer	61	21.41	33.81	0.73
California white oak (valley oak)	2	10.91	28.21	0.74
Canyon live oak	22	18.57	26.94	0.65
Coast live oak	9	26.68	30.23	0.93
Cottonwood	1	9.92	32.27	0.86
Cottonwood/willow	1	15.12	26.00	0.84
Douglas-fir	5	64.51	27.17	0.84
Gray pine	7	15.67	28.30	0.79
Interior live oak	10	9.56	29.77	0.82
Jeffrey pine	7	11.07	37.71	0.83
Juniper woodland	5	14.36	24.91	0.54
Knobcone pine	1	9.39	28.57	0.66
Lodgepole pine	11	15.32	33.51	0.79
Miscellaneous western softwoods	2	12.37	41.84	0.62
Mountain brush woodland	4	5.52	30.48	1.11
Nonstocked	6	8.49	32.67	0.69
Oregon white oak	4	16.92	35.66	0.94
Other hardwoods	1	22.10	33.03	1.17
Pacific madrone	3	16.27	40.15	0.87
Pinyon/juniper woodland	5	13.27	31.42	0.71
Ponderosa pine	11	27.38	36.74	0.80
Port-Orford-cedar	1	20.68	41.06	1.21
Red alder	1	46.61	31.33	0.83
Red fir	6	18.76	29.47	0.64
Redwood	2	15.67	33.98	0.38
Tanoak	16	48.24	30.27	0.70
Western juniper	9	22.00	32.31	0.71
Western white pine	2	10.37	26.44	0.67
White fir	14	44.52	32.42	0.93
Whitebark pine	1	7.74	37.32	1.22

Note: Data subject to sampling error.

Table 35—Properties of the mineral soil layer on forest land, by depth of layer and forest type, California, 2001, 2003–2005

Depth of layer and forest type	Samples	Texture	Moisture content (oven-dry basis)	Coarse fragments	Bulk density
			Soil properties		
	Number	*Most common*	- - - - - - - - - -Percent- - - - - - - - - - -		*g/cm³*
Mineral layer 1 (0–10 cm):					
Bigleaf maple	1	Clayey	8.19	19.72	1.23
Blue oak	18	Loamy	5.46	31.90	1.28
California black oak	9	Loamy	59.37	40.12	0.96
California mixed conifer	52	Loamy	11.36	38.41	1.00
California white oak (valley oak)	2	Sandy	5.79	36.31	1.63
Canyon live oak	18	Loamy	11.09	43.73	1 12
Coast live oak	7	Clayey	10.88	46.25	1 15
Cottonwood	1	Loamy	33.57	65.29	1.23
Cottonwood/willow	1	Sandy	6.04	8.00	0.77
Douglas-fir	3	Loamy	21.26	53.11	0.84
Gray pine	7	Clayey	7.02	28.37	1.43
Interior live oak	8	Loamy	6.20	25.22	1 15
Jeffrey pine	6	Loamy	6.04	24.05	1 19
Juniper woodland	4	Sandy	2.00	19.88	1.57
Knobcone pine	1	Clayey	5.25	35.50	1.52
Lodgepole pine	10	Loamy	5.64	24.36	1.05
Misc. western softwoods	1	Loamy	29.04	18.54	—
Mountain brush woodland	2	Loamy	7.42	13.98	1 10
Nonstocked	5	Loamy	11.70	26.04	1.05
Oregon white oak	2	Clayey	9.79	38.00	0.99
Pacific madrone	3	Loamy	8.77	34.44	1.06
Pinyon/juniper woodland	4	Sandy	1.42	21.76	1.65
Ponderosa pine	6	Loamy	11.53	16.72	1.04
Red alder	1	Loamy	19.14	44.96	0.90
Red fir	5	Loamy	10.76	32.18	0.83
Redwood	1	Loamy	7.88	40.31	0.87
Tanoak	13	Loamy	17.28	42.49	0.95
Western juniper	7	Loamy	8.25	20.68	1.05
Western white pine	1	Loamy	5.52	43.59	—
White fir	13	Loamy	17.02	39.48	0.85
Mineral layer 2 (10–20 cm):					
Bigleaf maple	1	Clayey	9.92	19.03	1.37
Blue oak	17	Loamy	5.88	27.56	1.40
California black oak	7	Loamy	13.13	40.89	1.01
California mixed conifer	47	Loamy	12.01	37.39	1.20
California white oak (valley oak)	2	Sandy	7.38	43.95	1.77
Canyon live oak	14	Loamy	14.64	39.33	1.22
Coast live oak	5	Clayey	9.70	42.18	1.30
Cottonwood	1	Loamy	13.53	54.02	1.37
Cottonwood/willow	1	Sandy	11.51	19.85	1 13
Douglas-fir	3	Loamy	21.21	42.27	1.08
Gray pine	6	Clayey	8.32	37.38	1.47
Interior live oak	7	Loamy	6.87	28.40	1.33
Jeffrey pine	6	Loamy	7.18	27.23	1.22
Juniper woodland	2	Sandy	2.54	29.65	1.93
Knobcone pine	1	Clayey	6.28	34.31	1.08
Lodgepole pine	10	Loamy	6.70	26.28	1.28
Misc. western softwoods	1	Loamy	28.00	27.28	—
Mountain brush woodland	2	Loamy	9.91	40.16	1.54
Nonstocked	5	Loamy	11.59	30.36	1.27
Oregon white oak	2	Clayey	11.59	49.17	1.26
Pacific madrone	3	Loamy	11.31	20.55	1 19
Pinyon/juniper woodland	3	Sandy	2.05	28.04	1.58
Ponderosa pine	6	Loamy	11.69	26.42	1.39
Red alder	1	Clayey	16.17	53.25	0.67
Red fir	4	Loamy	12.59	34.74	0.96
Redwood	1	Loamy	9.44	69.92	1.01
Tanoak	13	Clayey	19.35	39.98	1.08
Western juniper	6	Clayey	11.24	34.43	1.02
Western white pine	1	Loamy	6.31	13.34	—
White fir	12	Loamy	17.91	38.47	0.89

Note: Data subject to sampling error; — = No data available for this sample.

Table 36—Chemical properties of mineral soil layers on forest land, by depth and forest type, California, 2001, 2003–2005

Depth of layer and forest type	Samples	pH		Organic carbon	Inorganic carbon	Total nitrogen	Extractable phosphorus	Exchangeable cations						Extractable sulfur
		H₂O	CaCl₂					Na	K	Mg	Ca	Al	ECEC[a]	
	Number			----- Percent -----			mg/kg	----- mg/kg -----					cmolc/kg	mg/kg
Mineral layer 1 (0–10 cm):														
Bigleaf maple	1	5.95	5.20	3.82	0.22	0.19	15.29	22.64	357.80	594.50	2360.03	1.86	17.70	0
Blue oak	18	6.36	5.83	2.41	0.20	0.20	20.56	9.60	259.36	463.05	2125.87	3.07	15.16	7.18
California black oak	9	6.02	5.25	7.83	0.19	0.40	41.16	10.19	226.40	239.70	2377.54	20.77	14.69	4.07
California mixed conifer	52	5.88	5.24	4.27	0.17	0.17	57.49	14.78	247.81	255.03	1557.13	27.97	10.88	5.85
California white oak (valley oak)	2	6.33	5.74	1.73	0.16	0.12	27.82	0	169.86	123.24	1462.40	0	8.75	17.19
Canyon live oak	18	6.07	5.42	4.54	0.22	0.23	61.23	13.47	222.02	182.40	2061.75	26.04	12.70	5.08
Coast live oak	7	6.23	5.76	3.83	0.27	0.27	18.26	9.43	270.01	605.10	2268.31	2.09	17.05	7.94
Cottonwood	1	7.51	7.36	1.71	0.67	0.15	4.68	539.9	386.00	839.90	5881.00	0.76	39.60	956.30
Cottonwood/willow	1	7.05	6.65	0.78	0.18	0.07	16.66	0	157.70	600.50	3016.00	0	20.39	0.93
Douglas-fir	3	5.67	5.01	5.78	0.15	0.29	66.91	16.25	233.33	221.97	2030.98	44.01	13.12	5.48
Gray pine	7	6.42	5.72	1.89	0.20	0.12	15.32	16.04	228.65	596.60	1978.33	2.07	15.46	4.87
Interior live oak	8	6.06	5.44	2.92	0.20	0.17	28.37	13.51	188.67	198.39	1444.81	17.8	9.58	2.94
Jeffrey pine	6	6.18	5.34	2.63	0.18	0.18	105.67	17.35	208.46	75.72	1319.39	17.27	8.01	3.12
Juniper woodland	4	6.56	5.90	0.80	0.13	0.08	19.62	6.94	158.53	253.23	1486.24	0	9.93	0.37
Knobcone pine	1	5.95	5.24	1.43	0.23	0.09	12.20	0.10	160.50	145.30	670.00	3.92	4.99	0
Lodgepole pine	10	5.21	4.47	2.86	0.12	0.12	90.51	3.26	90.65	46.62	450.04	73.68	3.69	2.03
Misc. western softwoods	1	6.49	5.95	7.80	0.33	0.46	2.57	44.45	113.88	3925.00	174.60	0	33.63	4.72
Mountain brush woodland	2	6.36	5.81	3.30	0.20	0.29	35.83	11.00	537.78	274.70	3310.50	1.06	20.21	5.94
Nonstocked	5	6.27	5.73	3.26	0.31	0.19	16.33	5.67	263.39	238.54	2563.38	70.43	16.23	8.66
Oregon white oak	2	6.69	6.10	3.00	0.25	0.14	48.95	26.73	392.45	439.10	2424.00	0	16.83	9.61
Pacific madrone	3	5.54	4.90	3.07	0.18	0.15	100.71	0.64	198.68	146.51	1037.95	18.71	7.10	18.11
Pinyon/juniper woodland	4	6.80	6.22	0.59	0.19	0.04	26.39	3.59	95.67	69.95	1176.25	0.08	6.71	1.61
Ponderosa pine	6	6.08	5.36	3.92	0.28	0.20	32.39	11.40	449.95	265.89	2688.83	1.55	16.82	5.48
Red alder	1	5.40	4.68	4.86	0.12	0.26	86.82	17.66	273.90	153.70	1117.93	45.84	8.13	5.74
Red fir	4	5.41	4.67	4.98	0.13	0.17	77.84	14.35	109.42	25.49	467.58	93.77	3.93	2.65
Redwood	4	12.80	0.31	0.43	68.20	21.66	462.57	725.20	5454.00	3.17	34.49	5.48		
Tanoak	13	5.02	4.33	3.80	0.19	0.14	18.15	14.88	220.90	204.32	880.33	212.06	9.06	6.11
Western juniper	7	6.41	5.78	4.66	0.21	0.37	15.24	12.67	235.10	406.62	2222.44	16.67	15.28	3.76
Western white pine	1	4.91	4.30	4.73	0.20	0.09	40.70	0	54.23	38.03	588.90	81.46	4.30	3.75
White fir	13	5.94	5.34	6.81	0.22	0.32	37.86	17.13	255.54	149.49	2124.62	30.85	12.90	7.94

Table 36—Chemical properties of mineral soil layers on forest land, by depth and forest type, California, 2001, 2003–2005 (continued)

Depth of layer and forest type	Samples	pH H₂O	pH CaCl₂	Organic carbon	Inorganic carbon	Total nitrogen	Extractable phosphorus	Na	K	Mg	Ca	Al	ECEC[a]	Extractable sulfur
	Number			Percent	Percent	Percent	mg/kg	mg/kg					cmolc/kg	mg/kg
Mineral layer 2 (10–20 cm):														
Bigleaf maple	1	6.18	4.98	1.14	0.20	0.12	8.30	0	173.6	530.7	1683	10.49	13.32	1.11
Blue oak	17	6.35	5.73	1.57	0.18	0.14	19.44	9.41	254.27	449.26	2066.02	6.06	14.76	3.29
California black oak	7	5.78	5.08	4.04	0.17	0.21	30.37	10.37	216.37	144.07	1375.31	44.49	9.14	10.03
California mixed conifer	47	5.90	5.19	2.56	0.13	0.10	29.91	8.32	225.73	208.45	1141.47	31.69	8.38	6.18
California white oak (valley oak)	2	6.06	5.18	1.21	0.14	0.09	57.44	3.95	153.95	118.28	1115.75	2.43	6.98	7.48
Canyon live oak	14	6.16	5.49	2.89	0.15	0.15	46.92	10.38	209.46	164.60	1838.23	20.83	11.34	6.32
Coast live oak	5	5.66	4.90	1.95	0.20	0.15	11.02	11.45	164.09	645.86	1197.04	37.98	12.18	3.49
Cottonwood	1	7.54	7.33	0.40	0.34	0.03	2.52	134.70	268.60	345.40	3549	0	21.82	442.10
Cottonwood/willow	1	7.12	6.66	1.67	0.21	0.11	13.98	1.13	170.30	630.20	3173	0	21.46	0.12
Douglas-fir	3	5.63	4.99	4.25	0.16	0.19	77.74	14.22	212.37	143.40	1286.40	27.55	8.51	1.76
Gray pine	6	6.34	5.49	0.93	0.14	0.08	11.06	12.10	210.22	805.02	1920.36	4.14	16.84	1.18
Interior live oak	7	6.08	5.21	1.17	0.17	0.12	38.24	13.51	172.13	151.57	1098.60	45.52	7.73	3.09
Jeffrey pine	6	5.99	5.39	2.07	0.14	0.10	67.85	10.01	162.11	55.79	1011.27	20.71	6.19	2.16
Juniper woodland	2	6.72	5.95	0.66	0.18	0.10	16.91	4.57	74.73	122.15	1624.5	1.10	9.33	0.41
Knobcone pine	1	5.58	4.90	1.58	0.20	0.07	9.57	0	126.50	122.40	558.30	7.53	4.20	0
Lodgepole pine	10	5.48	4.62	1.66	0.14	0.08	73.62	9.68	94.87	47.17	401.26	62.41	3.37	2.77
Misc. western softwoods	1	6.47	6.01	9.16	0.26	0.48	1.46	31.45	136.46	3741	195.70	0	32.23	14.63
Mountain brush woodland	2	6.71	6.02	1.22	0.11	0.11	5.39	19.5	226.31	177.15	2174.55	0.72	12.98	3.61
Nonstocked	5	6.56	5.96	1.26	0.37	0.08	8.65	8.34	191.16	227.21	2149.88	50.77	13.69	58.11
Oregon white oak	2	6.48	5.79	1.77	0.12	0.10	40.34	21.10	217.70	530.40	1975	0	14.87	4.13
Pacific madrone	3	5.62	4.93	2.60	0.17	0.14	65.12	3	166.94	102.68	749.57	23.16	5.28	3.74
Pinyon/juniper woodland	3	7.22	6.49	0.45	0.17	0.03	4.95	16.41	117.17	78.08	1537.73	0.70	8.69	18.85
Ponderosa pine	6	6.22	5.41	3.38	0.14	0.16	24.13	4.27	379.51	190.87	1687.60	4.33	11.03	3.12
Red alder	1	5.62	4.82	4.61	0.21	0.24	108.91	10.11	150.60	103.80	1242	23.52	7.74	5.61
Red fir	3	5.46	4.70	2.79	0.16	0.08	51.01	18.86	126.13	15.20	310.43	68.25	2.84	8.46
Redwood	1	6.02	5.38	4.99	0.20	0.17	59.60	0	393.81	425.90	3066	2.32	19.83	5.72
Tanoak	13	5.23	4.60	2.70	0.17	0.12	17.50	13.77	175.21	189.05	851.42	190.83	8.43	4.58
Western juniper	6	6.34	5.68	2.72	0.15	0.15	9.80	10.49	207.70	454.36	1982.75	28.66	14.53	3.05
Western white pine	1	5	4.39	2.01	0.20	0.05	253	0	54.36	5.49	151.70	84.19	1.88	0
White fir	12	6.07	5.35	4.17	0.17	0.24	27.51	7.04	230.58	109.92	1805.57	13.29	10.68	2.88

Note: Data subject to sampling error; — = less than 0.005 cmolc/kg were estimated; H₂O = water, CaCl₂ = calcium chloride, Na = sodium, K = potassium, Mg = magnesium, Ca = calcium, and Al = aluminum.

[a] ECEC = effective cation exchange capacity.

Table 37—Chemical properties (trace elements) of forest floor and mineral soils on forest land, by forest type, California, 2001, 2003–2005

Depth of layer and forest type	Samples	Extractable						
		Manganese	Iron	Nickel	Copper	Zinc	Cadmium	Lead
	Number	- *mg/kg* -						
Mineral layer 1 (0–10 cm):								
Bigleaf maple	1	19.11	—	—	—	0.35	0.11	—
Blue oak	18	10.83	0.12	0.35	—	0.23	0.06	0.06
California black oak	9	30.26	0.07	0.39	—	0.10	0.06	0.18
California mixed conifer	52	35.40	0.95	0.80	0.01	0.26	0.05	0.07
California white oak (valley oak)	2	8.63	0.19	—	—	—	0.07	—
Canyon live oak	18	21.88	0.60	0.10	—	0.40	0.05	0.43
Coast live oak	7	30.19	0.10	0.26	0.03	0.34	0.05	0.09
Cottonwood	1	3.69	0.54	—	—	—	0.07	0.13
Cottonwood / willow	1	9.99	—	—	—	—	0.01	—
Douglas-fir	3	53.51	0.02	0.24	0.32	0.36	0.07	0.09
Gray pine	7	17.70	0.15	0.39	—	—	0.05	0.10
Interior live oak	8	8.05	1.26	0.10	0.02	0.21	0.05	0.02
Jeffrey pine	6	14.58	0.08	—	0.34	0.46	0.13	0.15
Juniper woodland	4	6.73	0.02	0.05	—	0.04	0.05	—
Knobcone pine	1	14.67	—	—	—	—	0.02	0.03
Lodgepole pine	10	25.89	0.01	0.12	—	0.55	0.03	0.15
Misc. western softwoods	1	8.83	—	10.74	—	—	0.06	1.18
Mountain brush woodland	2	16.26	0.35	0.12	—	—	0.01	—
Nonstocked	5	6.58	2.74	0.26	—	0.11	0.02	—
Oregon white oak	2	10.48	0.54	0.10	—	0.13	0.02	0.18
Pacific madrone	3	26.84	0.30	0.10	—	0.01	0.07	0.04
Pinyon/juniper woodland	4	5.93	—	0.02	—	0.04	0.05	—
Ponderosa pine	6	16.32	1.07	0.06	—	0.22	—	0.11
Red alder	1	36.22	—	0.49	—	0.61	0.04	—
Red fir	4	23.33	5.70	0.07	—	0.68	0.04	0.21
Redwood	1	28.42	—	—	—	0.03	0.06	—
Tanoak	13	39.40	5.76	0.65	—	0.46	0.04	0.17
Western juniper	7	17.32	0.74	0.10	—	0.11	0.02	0.02
Western white pine	1	102.70	3.56	0.05	—	1.80	0.05	0.07
White fir	13	37.57	1.58	0.30	0.06	0.53	0.03	0.03
Mineral layer 2 (10–20 cm):								
Bigleaf maple	1	7.20	—	0.25	—	0.10	0.05	—
Blue oak	17	9.40	0.06	0.35	0.01	0.01	0.04	0.10
California black oak	7	33.50	0.08	0.56	0.01	0.11	0.02	0.03
California mixed conifer	47	17.24	1.13	0.34	0.03	0.18	0.03	0.25
California white oak (valley oak)	2	6.69	0.22	0.01	—	—	0.05	0.07
Canyon live oak	14	12.81	0.13	0.03	0.02	0.09	0.02	0.17
Coast live oak	5	19.96	—	1.18	0.01	1.10	0.02	0.37
Cottonwood	1	3.65	—	0.01	—	—	0.06	—
Cottonwood / willow	1	6.87	—	—	—	—	0.01	—
Douglas-fir	3	25.16	0.01	0.15	—	0.31	0.03	0.60
Gray pine	6	6.75	0.23	0.67	—	0.10	0.01	0.28
Interior live oak	7	4.04	2.87	0.13	0.04	0.26	0.03	0.27
Jeffrey pine	6	8.40	0.51	0.04	0.09	0.31	0.10	0.16
Juniper woodland	2	6.18	—	—	—	0.04	0.02	0.41
Knobcone pine	1	20.35	0.27	0.06	—	—	0.04	0.13
Lodgepole pine	10	19.17	0.10	0.14	0.04	0.31	0.01	0.6
Misc. western softwoods	1	8.56	—	—	—	0.11	—	0.71
Mountain brush woodland	2	6.59	—	0.11	—	—	0.02	—
Nonstocked	5	3.11	0.28	0.15	0.04	0.05	0.01	0.21
Oregon white oak	2	8.23	—	0.11	0.19	0.01	0.02	0.07
Pacific madrone	3	21.24	—	—	—	0.03	0.01	0.07
Pinyon/juniper woodland	3	2.97	—	—	—	0.30	0.01	0.13
Ponderosa pine	6	11.57	—	—	—	0.08	0.01	0.17
Red alder	1	38.77	—	0.54	—	0.70	0.12	1.15
Red fir	3	8.17	3.65	—	—	—	0.01	0.01
Redwood	1	15.65	—	—	—	—	0.04	—
Tanoak	13	23.85	2.33	0.24	0.03	0.13	0.02	0.25
Western juniper	6	14.81	0.79	0.14	0.02	0.14	0.02	0.19
Western white pine	1	53.11	—	—	—	0.69	0.01	—
White fir	12	10.97	0.37	0.64	—	0.17	0.02	0.03

Note: Data subject to sampling error; — = less than 0.005 mg/kg were estimated.

Table 38—Compaction, bare soil, and slope properties of forest land, by forest type, California, 2001, 2003–2005

Forest type	Plots sampled	Plots reporting compaction	Compacted area per plot	Bare soil cover	Slope
	Number	- - - - - - - - - - - - - - - - - - *Percent* - - - - - - - - - - - - - - - - - -			
Bigleaf maple	1	0	0	2.33	65
Blue oak	22	14	24.99	6.85	21.86
California black oak	9	5	3.30	3.08	42.44
California mixed conifer	62	26	5.42	5.31	30.90
California white oak (valley oak)	2	0	0	3	27.50
Canyon live oak	21	7	2.23	6.06	54.38
Coast live oak	9	1	0.33	4.28	37.56
Cottonwood	1	1	6.25	17.5	0
Cottonwood / willow	2	2	18.25	1.50	7
Douglas-fir	3	0	0	1	36
Gray pine	7	4	1.89	5.07	14.17
Interior live oak	11	2	0.89	3.77	26.78
Jeffrey pine	7	1	0.36	5.60	23.71
Juniper woodland	5	2	2.75	28	30.8
Knobcone pine	1	1	2.50	12.75	28
Lodgepole pine	11	3	0.89	15.06	13.09
Misc. western softwoods	2	0	0	5.50	45
Mountain brush woodland	5	0	0	6.07	24.8
Nonstocked	6	0	0	4.07	19.83
Oregon white oak	4	0	0	2.17	28.33
Other hardwoods	1	0	0	0.75	63
Pacific madrone	2	0	0	2.13	47
Pinyon/juniper woodland	6	0	0	17.29	35
Ponderosa pine	11	3	3.07	10.41	17.82
Port-Orford-cedar	1	0	0	1	25
Red alder	1	1	25	5	37
Red fir	6	2	2.71	8.92	30.83
Redwood	3	0	0	3	44.67
Tanoak	17	9	4.42	4.75	39.63
Western juniper	9	4	1.83	9.68	15.63
Western white pine	2	0	0	1.50	30.50
White fir	12	6	9.06	7.15	22.50
Whitebark pine	1	0	0	5.50	38

Note: Data subject to sampling error.

Table 39—Estimated number of live trees[a] with damage on forest land, by species and type of damage, California, 2001–2005

Species	Total number of live trees — Total	Total number of live trees — SE	Number of live trees with damage[b] — Total	Number of live trees with damage[b] — SE	Animal	Bark beetles	Cankers	Defoliators	Dwarf mistletoe	Leafy mistletoe	Foliage diseases	Stem decay	Other insects	Physical damage or defect	Root disease	Weather
								Thousand trees								
Softwoods:																
Bigcone Douglas-fir	1,064	443	312	131	—	—	—	—	—	—	—	54	—	266	—	—
Bishop pine	1,979	1,314	413	328	—	—	8	—	82	—	—	—	—	331	—	—
Brewer spruce	2,991	1,558	919	747	—	—	55	—	—	—	—	8	—	174	—	736
Bristlecone pine	3,096	1,676	1,866	1,005	8	—	—	—	—	—	—	559	—	1,095	—	795
California juniper	44,081	21,500	4,962	1,443	64	8	—	—	2,180	—	8	—	3,175	—	82	—
California red fir	330,563	38,590	124,434	22,711	415	1,766	10,266	17	49,797	—	5,530	1,353	59	52,967	1,457	30,072
California torreya	15,283	5,429	1,260	626	—	—	—	—	23	—	—	297	—	1,094	13	—
Coulter pine	3,309	988	793	295	—	8	—	—	—	—	—	—	—	749	—	—
Cypress	608	523	47	47	—	—	—	—	—	—	—	8	—	47	—	—
Douglas-fir	1,295,852	64,428	139,100	9,707	4,709	412	23,182	748	5,793	—	1,117	15,109	294	95,713	1,345	684
Engelmann spruce	250	170	100	97	—	—	—	—	100	—	—	—	—	50	—	—
Foxtail pine	3,118	1,314	1,635	685	—	—	26	—	—	—	—	74	—	1,544	—	222
Giant sequoia	1,844	1,869	82	—	—	—	—	—	—	—	—	—	—	—	—	—
Grand fir	6,492	3,274	82	80	—	—	—	—	—	—	—	—	—	82	—	—
Gray pine	46,120	7,510	13,699	2,820	134	861	1,626	—	5,866	—	170	546	—	6,097	—	47
Incense-cedar	646,868	46,460	66,645	7,181	293	186	475	158	12,422	5,168	7,608	1,989	6	51,354	1,792	1,954
Jeffrey pine	237,458	21,331	50,045	5,835	1,027	1,685	1,897	53	2,425	—	905	727	188	31,877	1,591	2,424
Knobcone pine	44,600	15,343	8,095	2,671	156	297	1,768	—	—	—	582	140	—	4,808	47	—
Limber pine	4,316	1,806	1,630	649	8	—	—	—	—	55	—	1,404	—	328	—	—
Lodgepole pine	277,288	34,965	94,066	12,464	693	1,250	11,291	—	12,573	—	2,400	1,755	54	60,136	2,103	13,494
Monterey cypress	2,165	2,210	294	300	—	—	—	—	147	—	—	73	—	220	—	—
Monterey pine	124	96	96	81	—	—	—	—	—	—	—	82	—	96	—	—
Mountain hemlock	57,325	14,647	21,858	10,201	50	7	408	—	2,008	—	850	334	—	12,968	—	11,303
Noble fir	584	307	103	73	—	—	—	—	—	—	—	—	—	7	—	94
Pacific silver fir	7	8	7	8	—	—	—	—	—	—	—	—	—	—	—	—
Pacific yew	23,114	8,913	680	247	93	—	—	—	—	—	—	91	—	546	—	—
Ponderosa pine	603,647	38,572	105,753	9,229	800	3,679	9,299	503	18,031	—	1,095	1,620	1,145	67,482	9,063	511
Port-Orford-cedar	7,605	3,190	708	339	17	—	—	—	—	—	—	240	8	535	—	50
Redwood	308,717	41,406	37,854	5,780	3,197	—	2,386	—	102	—	143	2,568	—	32,046	31	215
Sargent's cypress	8,449	7,774	—	—	—	—	—	—	—	—	—	—	—	—	—	—
Shasta red fir	29,492	12,553	9,913	6,893	622	1,187	—	—	3,924	—	634	257	8	4,805	—	3,971
Singleleaf pinyon	135,682	14,649	32,699	4,787	109	—	665	—	8,224	—	47	895	—	22,919	—	1,397
Sitka spruce	5,826	2,764	2,397	2,067	1,109	—	—	—	55	—	—	14	—	1,233	—	—
Subalpine fir	101	102	—	—	—	—	—	—	—	—	—	—	—	—	—	—
Sugar pine	133,742	13,843	24,693	3,473	171	386	6,529	39	1,174	—	247	698	—	18,255	394	1,200
Utah juniper	5,809	2,059	3,652	1,867	36	—	—	—	—	370	—	12	—	3,422	—	—
Washoe pine	3,614	3,760	1,183	1,230	—	101	73	—	—	—	—	—	—	88	—	1,095
Western hemlock	27,604	9,237	2,028	945	376	—	—	—	1,103	—	—	73	—	1,041	—	—
Western juniper	111,496	11,374	23,704	3,664	641	—	—	—	151	7,510	3,405	2,403	337	10,834	41	372
Western redcedar	720	634	262	219	—	106	—	7	—	—	—	39	—	254	—	—
Western white pine	57,150	9,199	20,053	4,909	168	—	5,298	—	420	—	273	357	—	13,635	39	2,655
White fir	1,110,177	61,449	217,543	21,749	1,382	5,917	21,570	2,658	42,755	7,144	767	3,881	219	114,401	33,555	11,884
Whitebark pine	65,574	15,106	25,188	7,016	153	—	—	—	—	—	—	759	—	21,138	—	5,938
Total	5,665,903	142,105	1,040,770	49,029	16,423	17,849	96,838	4,183	167,176	22,373	25,775	37,077	2,317	638,897	51,471	91,521

Table 39—Estimated number of live trees^a with damage on forest land, by species and type of damage, California, 2001–2005 (continued)

Species	Total number of live trees		Number of live trees with damage^b		Type of damage											
	Total	SE	Total	SE	Animal	Bark beetles	Cankers	Defoliators	Dwarf mistletoe	Leafy mistletoe	Foliage diseases	Stem decay	Other insects	Other damage or defect	Physical Root disease	Weather
					Thousand trees											
Hardwoods:																
Ash spp.	6,848	6,619	6,594	6,615	—	—	—	—	—	—	—	—	—	6,594	—	—
Bigleaf maple	126,583	18,861	18,869	3,465	—	—	—	—	—	—	—	3,268	—	16,389	—	—
Bitter cherry	16,329	8,591	—	—	—	—	—	—	—	—	—	—	—	—	—	—
Black cottonwood	9,378	6,679	744	486	—	—	—	—	—	—	—	197	—	633	—	—
Blue oak	266,209	27,283	73,801	6,713	308	—	817	4,698	—	7,583	93	9,560	326	59,971	—	82
Boxelder	1,857	1,393	1,046	750	—	—	—	—	—	—	—	799	—	551	—	—
Buckeye spp.	1,981	1,768	582	584	—	—	—	—	—	—	—	—	—	582	—	—
California black oak	456,356	38,774	107,309	9,729	127	14	3,534	10,418	—	5,828	857	16,294	1,119	82,654	250	178
California buckeye	90,582	21,484	25,140	6,382	—	—	—	—	—	—	—	3,483	—	23,480	—	93
California live oak	120,265	14,458	54,186	7,356	258	—	709	1,148	—	426	163	11,865	—	48,282	—	154
California sycamore	1,529	727	419	194	—	—	—	—	—	—	—	221	—	419	—	—
California white oak	22,062	5,694	6,837	2,012	167	—	97	—	—	796	—	383	—	5,863	—	—
California-laurel	350,245	50,953	31,565	5,524	82	—	165	—	—	—	—	7,898	—	26,850	—	237
Canyon live oak	1,203,727	95,051	217,773	19,985	1,093	—	5,653	5,095	—	6,430	1,199	33,815	2,375	178,079	—	2,584
Cherry and plum spp.	2,736	1,878	1,072	793	—	—	555	—	—	—	—	—	517	—	—	—
Curl-leaf mountain mahogany	143,258	24,838	51,078	8,401	1,044	73	—	12	—	—	2,562	1,664	50	47,410	147	220
Engelmann oak	367	253	89	74	—	—	—	—	—	—	—	22	—	68	—	—
Eucalyptus spp.	813	824	222	225	—	—	—	—	—	—	—	—	—	222	—	—
Fremont cottonwood	1,137	836	1,062	780	—	—	177	—	—	—	25	354	—	658	—	—
Golden chinquapin	39,306	14,964	3,831	1,584	—	—	—	—	—	—	324	—	3,605	—	—	—
Interior live oak	501,735	66,790	97,443	13,674	280	—	2,109	781	—	8,149	162	20,742	1,027	76,354	—	—
Mesquite	1,261	1,255	306	305	—	—	—	—	—	—	—	—	—	306	—	—
Oregon ash	19,920	13,502	5,596	2,627	—	—	—	—	—	—	—	1,151	152	5,355	—	—
Oregon white oak	150,674	25,891	36,204	6,726	78	—	975	293	—	5,066	261	3,190	484	28,190	—	—
Pacific dogwood	82,450	16,657	3,300	1,505	—	—	—	—	—	—	120	722	—	2,719	—	—
Pacific madrone	220,502	29,665	40,672	4,520	127	—	253	—	—	—	—	11,531	14	32,558	89	98
Quaking aspen	74,436	24,881	15,847	10,253	208	—	203	50	—	—	—	2,030	—	5,248	—	9,300
Red alder	51,569	11,539	5,404	2,041	753	—	257	—	—	—	—	645	—	4,183	102	—
Tanoak	1,117,293	85,352	110,132	10,332	1,718	—	605	2,356	—	—	203	21,973	—	87,698	885	1,248
Tasmanian bluegum	949	933	—	—	—	—	—	—	—	—	—	—	—	—	—	—
Walnut spp.	73	75	73	75	—	—	—	—	—	—	—	—	—	73	—	—
Western honey mesquite	1,390	883	1,014	760	—	—	—	—	—	—	—	—	—	1,014	—	—
White alder	29,145	12,747	4,073	1,497	259	—	14	—	—	—	—	156	—	3,729	—	228
Willow spp.	20,539	19,811	—	—	—	—	—	—	—	—	—	—	—	—	—	—
Total	5,133,505	177,176	922,284	35,973	6,501	88	15,567	25,405	—	34,278	5,646	152,285	5,547	750,255	1,473	14,423
All species	10,799,408	224,623	1,963,054	59,500	22,923	17,936	112,404	29,588	167,176	56,651	31,421	189,363	7,864	1,389,151	52,945	105,944

Note: Data subject to sampling error; SE = Standard error; — = less than 500 trees were estimated.
^a Includes live trees ≥1 inch diameter at breast height.
^b Number of live trees ≥1 inch diameter at breast height with one or more types of damage recorded.

Table 40—Estimated area of forest land with more than 25 percent of basal area damaged, by forest type and type of damage, California, 2001–2005

Species	Total forest land		Forest land with damage[a]		Type of damage (Thousand acres)											
	Total	SE	Total	SE	Animal	Bark beetles	Cankers	Defoliators	Dwarf mistletoe	Leafy mistletoe	Foliage diseases	Stem decay	Other insects	Physical damage or defect	Root disease	Weather
Softwoods:																
Bigcone Douglas-fir	7	7	7	7	—	—	—	—	—	—	—	—	—	7	—	—
Bishop pine	21	15	7	7	—	—	—	—	—	—	—	—	—	—	—	—
California mixed conifer	7,879	210	4,307	176	7	38	80	—	449	105	92	137	—	2,649	133	36
Coulter pine	31	15	4	4	—	—	—	—	—	—	—	—	—	4	—	—
Douglas-fir	1,024	96	420	65	26	—	2	—	—	2	—	61	—	228	—	—
Foxtail/bristlecone pine	99	31	99	31	—	—	—	—	—	—	—	15	—	99	—	21
Giant sequoia	7	7	—	—	—	—	—	—	—	—	—	—	—	—	—	—
Jeffrey pine	927	87	403	59	13	15	8	—	39	—	—	—	—	296	27	—
Juniper woodland	452	72	97	32	—	—	—	—	—	35	—	—	—	62	—	—
Knobcone pine	60	26	20	15	—	—	—	—	—	—	—	—	—	6	—	—
Limber pine	55	23	55	23	—	—	2	—	—	—	—	8	—	35	—	13
Lodgepole pine	1,012	91	828	84	7	13	57	—	81	—	27	1	—	660	7	56
Misc. western softwoods	49	22	12	12	—	—	—	—	—	—	—	—	—	—	—	—
Mountain hemlock	149	35	122	32	—	—	—	—	22	—	18	7	—	103	—	7
Pinyon/juniper woodland	1,444	113	728	82	12	—	20	—	134	29	—	34	—	554	—	26
Ponderosa pine	1,349	105	531	70	6	23	—	—	85	3	—	2	—	300	40	—
Port-Orford-cedar	39	17	32	16	—	—	—	—	—	—	—	8	—	24	—	7
Red fir	695	75	489	64	—	6	21	—	200	—	24	8	—	263	14	—
Redwood	636	84	272	56	—	—	11	—	—	—	—	12	—	206	—	—
Sitka spruce	17	13	4	3	—	—	—	—	1	—	—	—	—	2	—	—
Subalpine fir	2	2	—	—	—	—	—	—	—	—	—	—	—	—	—	—
Western juniper	1,514	112	747	84	8	6	—	—	7	161	51	106	8	481	—	20
Western white pine	194	39	131	31	—	—	8	—	9	—	—	—	—	114	—	—
White fir	1,223	101	707	78	—	26	28	12	118	30	14	20	—	507	31	—
Whitebark pine	222	42	172	38	—	—	—	—	—	—	—	—	—	132	—	35
Total	19,106	280	10,194	251	79	127	237	12	1,145	366	227	418	8	6,732	252	221

Table 40—Estimated area of forest land with more than 25 percent of basal area damaged, by forest type and type of damage, California, 2001–2005 (continued)

Species	Total forest land Total	Total forest land SE	Forest land with damage[a] Total	Forest land with damage[a] SE	Animal	Bark beetles	Cankers	Defoliators	Dwarf mistletoe	Leafy mistletoe	Foliage diseases	Stem decay	Other insects	Physical damage or defect	Root disease	Weather
											Thousand acres					
Hardwoods:																
Aspen	80	24	32	17	17	—	—	—	—	—	—	10	—	22	—	13
Bigleaf maple	82	25	19	9	—	—	—	—	—	—	—	15	—	7	—	—
Blue oak	2,419	146	1,566	124	10	25	34	54	43	236	—	264	—	1,108	—	—
California black oak	1,513	120	838	92	—	—	38	—	12	55	3	141	—	554	—	—
California laurel	381	62	143	38	—	—	—	—	—	—	—	14	—	74	—	—
California white oak	278	54	161	43	—	—	—	—	3	25	—	24	—	114	—	—
Canyon live oak	2,450	148	1,416	116	8	—	8	20	17	64	6	336	—	964	—	14
Coast live oak	971	91	693	76	—	—	9	24	—	12	3	221	—	628	—	—
Cottonwood	32	20	31	20	—	—	—	—	—	—	—	25	—	31	—	—
Cottonwood/willow	2	1	—	—	—	—	—	—	—	—	—	—	—	—	—	—
Eucalyptus	4	4	—	—	—	—	—	—	—	—	—	—	—	—	—	—
Evergreen oak woodland	14	12	11	12	—	—	—	—	—	—	—	—	—	11	—	—
Giant chinquapin	44	18	3	3	—	—	—	—	—	—	—	—	—	3	—	—
Gray pine	520	73	362	62	7	14	—	—	96	—	—	39	—	212	—	—
Interior live oak	1,004	103	666	85	—	—	6	—	7	53	—	148	—	452	—	—
Mesquite woodland	56	25	31	18	—	—	—	—	—	—	—	—	—	31	—	—
Mountain brush woodland	422	63	287	52	5	9	—	—	—	6	8	7	—	269	—	—
Oregon ash	14	12	—	—	—	—	—	—	—	—	—	—	—	—	—	—
Oregon white oak	613	77	379	62	—	—	3	—	—	27	—	81	14	280	—	—
Other hardwoods	293	54	194	46	—	—	7	—	—	11	11	30	—	153	—	11
Pacific madrone	317	58	214	48	—	—	—	—	11	—	—	28	—	171	—	—
Red alder	186	43	89	32	27	—	—	—	—	—	—	—	—	77	—	—
Tanoak	1,687	125	781	90	—	—	—	—	—	—	—	122	—	460	—	—
Total	13,381	293	7,916	253	74	48	105	98	189	489	31	1,504	14	5,621	—	38
Nonstocked	751	79	183	42	7	—	—	—	6	25	—	14	17	128	—	—
All forest types	33,238	284	18,293	325	160	175	342	110	1,341	881	258	1,936	38	12,480	252	259

Note: Data subject to sampling error; SE = standard error; — = less than 500 acres were estimated.

[a] Acres of forest land with >25 percent of tree basal area with one or more type of recorded damage.

Table 41—Estimated gross volume of live trees[a] with damage on forest land, by species and type of damage, California, 2001–2005

Thousand acres

Species	Total gross volume of live trees[a]		Gross volume of trees with damage[b]		Type of damage											
	Total	SE	Total	SE	Animal	Bark beetles	Cankers	Defoliators	Dwarf mistletoe	Leafy mistletoe	Foliage diseases	Stem decay	Other insects	Physical damage or defect	Root disease	Weather
Softwoods:																
Bigcone Douglas-fir	54,432	19,166	23,411	8,926	—	—	473	—	—	—	—	7,581	—	16,939	—	—
Bishop pine	45,343	35,836	8,817	6,778	—	—	—	1,041	—	—	—	—	7,776	—	—	—
Brewer spruce	31,314	14,329	15,971	8,425	—	—	4,139	—	—	—	—	1,408	—	11,000	—	3,515
Bristlecone pine	76,296	38,320	60,976	32,046	810	—	—	—	—	—	—	23,028	—	41,701	—	21,138
California juniper	152,400	37,414	36,171	10,825	311	—	240	—	—	15,560	—	240	—	23,698	—	449
California nutmeg	14,162	6,187	5,590	2,822	—	—	—	—	—	—	—	4,311	—	3,822	—	—
California red fir	6,660,989	621,844	3,083,261	331,155	5,344	83,067	250,656	2,178	1,129,692	—	257,292	122,704	12,606	1,882,633	84,103	57,122
Coulter pine	117,876	34,463	45,859	17,039	—	3,428	—	—	3,776	—	—	743	—	30,027	11,313	—
Cypress	9,319	7,274	1,060	1,064	—	—	—	—	—	—	—	—	—	1,060	—	—
Douglas-fir	22,294,535	898,634	5,574,662	336,442	84,260	23,728	283,160	8,232	326,300	—	72,063	1,698,788	7,712	3,483,425	36,925	27,176
Engelmann spruce	12,242	10,029	908	883	—	—	—	—	908	—	—	—	—	83	—	—
Foxtail pine	196,897	76,074	119,219	48,196	—	—	3,759	—	—	—	—	8,024	—	113,093	—	17,347
Giant sequoia	3,586	3,580	—	—	—	—	—	—	—	—	—	—	—	—	—	—
Grand fir	70,836	27,730	5,792	5,587	—	—	—	—	—	—	—	—	—	5,792	—	—
Gray pine	657,617	68,311	280,859	44,132	12,451	40,708	5,148	—	85,498	—	11,759	32,162	700	132,231	—	347
Incense-cedar	4,237,392	241,895	1,518,218	115,719	13,545	3,350	10,697	366	—	257,455	115,487	180,869	—	1,159,563	21,569	12,241
Jeffrey pine	4,597,608	291,638	1,626,917	117,292	25,952	71,526	12,146	2,968	255,064	—	93,426	83,747	2,084	1,241,477	57,981	44,018
Knobcone pine	138,001	32,057	57,128	18,014	1,114	7,170	9,156	—	10,667	—	—	2,358	—	30,632	1,260	—
Limber pine	101,516	37,693	57,842	21,177	—	—	779	—	—	—	—	2,113	—	54,665	—	6,370
Lodgepole pine	3,669,155	350,158	1,601,808	180,994	22,163	50,832	148,820	—	101,767	—	92,713	119,889	258	1,266,116	5,959	36,125
Monterey cypress	3,130	3,196	960	980	—	—	—	—	476	—	—	128	—	718	—	—
Monterey pine	16,946	11,698	9,279	6,321	—	—	—	—	—	—	—	4,720	—	9,279	—	—
Mountain hemlock	656,077	163,383	267,868	80,215	3,666	983	17,660	—	28,058	—	53,955	15,718	—	175,010	—	7,890
Noble fir	31,525	22,846	3,775	3,614	—	—	—	—	—	—	—	—	—	1,107	—	2,668
Pacific silver fir	2,071	2,155	2,071	2,155	—	—	—	—	—	—	—	—	—	2,071	—	—
Pacific yew	9,211	2,733	1,743	680	390	—	—	—	—	—	—	371	—	1,230	—	—
Ponderosa pine	8,577,267	430,669	2,345,070	164,256	33,019	138,103	54,950	3,477	402,556	—	45,005	126,704	3,636	1,680,765	99,440	16,720
Port-Orford-cedar	178,268	81,039	81,294	38,883	4,614	—	—	—	—	—	—	31,065	872	72,170	2,906	18
Redwood	7,210,577	1,296,103	2,547,631	664,250	118,081	—	46,313	—	23,517	—	7,450	322,081	—	2,295,273	—	11,823
Sargent's cypress	968	890	—	—	—	—	—	—	—	—	—	—	—	—	—	—
Shasta red fir	690,488	214,524	168,292	64,781	—	—	—	—	14,835	—	20,155	43,973	2,573	108,498	—	314
Singleleaf pinyon	455,929	48,253	160,461	23,505	319	5,058	3,535	—	33,586	—	68	8,380	—	123,161	—	1,694
Sitka spruce	134,418	66,101	50,415	30,832	129	—	—	—	29,377	—	—	3,599	—	20,909	—	—
Subalpine fir	2,566	2,574	—	—	—	—	—	—	—	—	—	—	—	—	—	—
Sugar pine	3,826,002	234,219	1,254,084	109,568	2,537	14,998	175,783	3,085	78,300	—	23,642	125,089	—	951,016	9,182	33,003
Utah juniper	35,264	9,447	20,047	7,500	1,037	—	—	—	—	3,525	—	394	—	16,894	—	—
Washoe pine	3,801	3,954	353	368	—	—	—	—	—	—	—	—	—	353	—	—
Western hemlock	174,651	67,051	53,276	21,705	6,068	4,223	5,476	—	17,180	—	—	6,839	—	37,256	—	—
Western juniper	563,502	47,720	213,306	24,316	8,295	—	—	—	1,790	49,053	18,011	30,237	2,407	125,689	—	5,689
Western redcedar	58,371	43,291	47,014	34,551	—	—	—	—	—	—	—	14,981	—	44,112	95	—
Western white pine	964,865	104,761	415,897	52,925	4,609	7,987	33,851	877	10,627	—	11,211	75,821	—	320,541	207	10,623
White fir	12,781,608	632,054	4,155,289	266,590	15,773	151,089	207,570	81,331	800,878	154,900	27,173	276,849	3,311	2,779,879	351,696	68,718
Whitebark pine	117,304	26,696	50,012	12,594	3,977	—	—	—	—	—	—	6,006	—	42,162	—	5,878
Total	79,636,327	1,965,533	25,972,608	932,317	368,466	606,250	1,274,310	102,515	3,355,892	480,493	849,411	3,380,922	36,157	18,313,827	682,635	390,885

Table 41—Estimated gross volume of live trees[a] with damage on forest land, by species and type of damage, California, 2001–2005 (continued)

Species	Total gross volume of live trees[a]		Gross volume of trees with damage[b]		Type of damage											
	Total	SE	Total	SE	Animal	Bark beetles	Cankers	Defoliators	Dwarf mistletoe	Leafy mistletoe	Foliage diseases	Stem decay	Other insects	Physical damage or defect	Root disease	Weather
					Thousand acres											
Hardwoods:																
Ash spp.	2,505	2,160	444	445	—	—	—	—	—	—	—	—	—	444	—	—
Bigleaf maple	465,395	61,895	150,229	26,108	—	—	—	—	—	—	—	64,037	—	104,759	—	—
Bitter cherry	236	241	—	—	—	—	—	—	—	—	—	—	—	—	—	—
Black cottonwood	73,630	34,516	33,245	15,156	—	—	—	—	—	—	—	4,779	2,757	29,260	—	—
Blue oak	1,599,438	112,636	722,761	62,355	6,695	—	11,438	35,626	—	104,686	2,393	207,167	—	498,045	—	2,525
Boxelder	32,382	28,804	16,557	14,244	—	—	—	—	—	—	—	14,394	—	4,021	—	—
Buckeye spp.	250	251	—	—	—	—	—	—	—	—	—	—	—	—	—	—
California black oak	3,595,773	202,214	1,467,227	98,494	10,595	2,126	45,399	27,867	—	186,735	6,037	515,962	2,991	936,510	12,885	3,585
California buckeye	78,127	13,832	58,558	11,485	—	—	—	—	—	—	—	14,323	—	52,462	—	315
California live oak	1,433,726	148,142	784,586	93,154	2,735	—	10,659	8,582	—	23,036	3,773	273,142	—	639,408	—	4,932
California sycamore	68,145	25,978	25,976	10,027	—	—	—	—	—	—	—	20,769	—	25,976	—	—
California white oak	365,511	70,288	120,362	29,911	5,818	—	103	—	—	22,441	—	21,255	—	80,786	—	—
California-laurel	751,740	98,594	238,386	50,851	499	—	847	—	—	—	—	123,520	—	183,102	—	2,456
Canyon live oak	3,442,586	217,938	1,374,558	109,664	10,439	—	26,912	8,062	—	56,310	3,229	488,157	9,650	935,318	—	10,398
Curl-leaf mountain mahogany	163,575	23,166	114,097	19,661	5,162	368	—	556	—	—	7,322	3,671	236	103,823	58	296
Engelmann oak	15,778	10,042	10,091	6,399	—	—	—	—	—	—	—	5,892	—	4,198	—	—
Eucalyptus spp.	10,869	11,014	2,010	2,037	—	—	—	—	—	—	5,592	—	—	2,010	—	—
Fremont cottonwood	89,914	66,071	78,581	57,743	—	—	11,153	—	—	—	—	29,272	—	39,834	—	—
Golden chinquapin	140,615	50,759	48,506	16,764	—	—	—	—	—	—	—	11,179	—	39,137	—	—
Interior live oak	747,510	91,772	350,543	43,343	1,167	—	1,823	384	—	23,729	3,736	139,887	—	239,541	—	—
Oregon ash	34,111	20,475	16,550	9,183	—	—	—	—	—	—	—	6,085	991	13,461	—	—
Oregon white oak	591,830	72,969	213,507	37,564	444	—	3,837	1,155	—	53,482	2,154	60,855	3,744	147,438	—	—
Pacific dogwood	9,145	3,969	3,760	2,159	—	—	—	—	—	—	158	706	—	3,760	—	—
Pacific madrone	1,867,729	162,072	899,310	94,988	1,752	—	6,665	—	—	—	—	383,863	7,949	607,672	821	4,225
Quaking aspen	63,743	25,017	23,078	8,377	4,085	—	285	508	—	—	—	5,493	—	16,228	—	320
Red alder	448,688	100,667	72,766	20,113	13,032	—	1,967	—	—	—	—	12,967	—	41,244	11,735	—
Screwbean mesquite	615	612	615	612	—	—	—	—	—	—	—	—	—	615	—	—
Tanoak	3,614,293	292,515	1,105,090	108,840	7,677	—	9,579	2,309	—	—	704	475,540	—	717,361	11,026	3,719
Tasmanian bluegum	4,159	3,011	—	—	—	—	—	—	—	—	—	—	—	—	—	—
Walnut spp.	306	313	306	313	—	—	—	—	—	—	—	—	—	306	—	—
Western honey mesquite	8,681	5,946	7,180	5,538	—	—	—	—	—	—	—	—	—	7,180	—	—
White alder	121,735	31,461	35,847	13,725	3,639	—	2,319	—	—	—	—	4,057	—	28,434	—	612
Total	19,842,740	575,606	7,974,727	279,832	73,742	2,493	132,986	85,048	—	470,420	35,098	2,886,973	28,316	5,502,332	36,525	33,383
All species	99,479,067	2,076,190	33,947,336	979,226	442,208	608,743	1,407,296	187,563	3,355,892	950,912	884,508	6,267,895	64,473	23,816,159	719,160	424,268

Note: Data subject to sampling error; SE = Standard error; — = less than 500 cubic feet were estimated.
[a] Includes the gross volume of live trees ≥5 inches diameter at breast height.
[b] Includes the gross volume of live trees ≥5 inches diameter at breast height with one or more types of damage recorded.

Table 42—Estimated number of live trees with damage, acres of forest land with greater than 25 percent of basal area damaged, and gross volume of live trees with damage, by survey unit and ownership group, California, 2001–2005

Survey unit and ownership group	Number of live trees with damage[a]		Acres of forest land with damage[b]		Gross volume of live trees with damage[c]	
	Total	SE	Total	SE	Total	SE
	Thousand trees		*Thousand acres*		*Thousand cubic feet*	
North Coast:						
Public	79,484	9,645	592	68	2,846,484	649,651
Private	215,107	15,308	1,598	116	3,430,270	277,886
Total	294,591	17,995	2,190	133	6,276,754	703,661
North Interior:						
Public	354,980	28,372	3,354	130	7,147,368	312,224
Private	185,249	17,157	1,577	116	1,767,519	142,744
Total	540,230	33,151	4,930	174	8,914,887	343,079
Sacramento:						
Public	257,945	21,483	1,929	102	5,025,768	276,211
Private	210,952	29,801	1,580	114	2,003,438	152,050
Total	468,897	36,690	3,509	151	7,029,206	314,956
Central Coast:						
Public	71,005	11,416	774	83	1,169,987	275,628
Private	74,842	9,869	827	87	1,201,676	219,181
Total	145,847	14,890	1,600	117	2,371,663	350,626
San Joaquin:						
Public	328,674	21,988	3,716	143	7,567,997	406,760
Private	94,678	11,252	1,397	114	1,132,089	131,527
Total	423,353	24,648	5,113	182	8,700,086	427,041
Southern:						
Public	66,658	10,383	819	82	575,917	93,181
Private	23,479	10,633	131	38	78,823	29,684
Total	90,137	14,860	951	91	654,740	97,785
Total, California:						
Public	1,158,748	44,289	11,184	236	24,333,521	895,930
Private	804,307	40,424	7,108	233	9,613,815	411,912
Total	1,963,054	59,500	18,293	325	33,947,336	979,226

Note: Data subject to sampling error; SE = standard error.
[a] Number of live trees ≥1 inch diameter at breast height.
[b] Number of forest land acres with more than 25 percent of basal area damaged.
[c] Gross volume of live trees ≥5 inches diameter at breast height.

Table 43—Estimated area of forest land covered by selected nonnative vascular plant species, by life form and species, California, 2001–2005

Plant life form		Area covered	
Scientific name	Common name	Total	SE
		Acres	
Shrubs:			
Cytisus scoparius	Scotch broom	3,000	1,400
Hedera helix	English ivy	300	300
Ilex aquifolium	English holly	200	200
Rubus discolor	Himalayan blackberry	34,400	9,100
Rubus laciniatus	cutleaf blackberry	1,400	1,000
Forbs:			
Centaurea solstitialis	yellow star-thistle	32,300	8,100
Cirsium	thistle spp.	21,800	3,600
Cirsium arvense	Canada thistle	1,000	800
Cirsium vulgare	bull thistle	2,000	800
Digitalis purpurea	purple foxglove	100	100
Hypericum perforatum	common St. John's wort	1,800	800
Hypochaeris radicata	hairy cat's ear	500	200
Torilis arvensis	spreading hedgeparsley	23,800	6,300
Grasses:			
Aira caryophyllea	silver hairgrass	14,200	4,000
Avena barbata	slender oat	27,300	9,700
Avena fatua	wild oat	50,000	12,500
Bromus diandrus	ripgut brome	47,100	11,600
Bromus hordeaceus	soft brome	78,800	18,300
Bromus madritensis	compact brome	13,400	6,100
Bromus tectorum	cheatgrass	144,400	17,400
Cynosurus echinatus	bristly dogstail grass	96,000	21,200
Dactylis glomerata	orchardgrass	1,800	1,300
Holcus lanatus	common velvetgrass	100	100
Taeniatherum caput-medusae	medusahead	63,800	14,700

Note: Estimates are likely low for most grasses and some forbs because of short flowering seasons and difficulty of species identification. Data subject to sampling error; SE = standard error.

Table 44—Summary of lichen community indicator species richness on forest land, by location, California, 1998–2001, 2003

Parameter	Location			
	California	Greater Central Valley	Greater Sierra Nevada	Northwest Coast[a]
Number of plots[b]	288	76	133	68
Number of plots by lichen species richness category:				
0–6 species	61	7	43	3
7–15 species	141	41	67	31
16–25 species	62	19	18	24
>25 species	24	9	5	10
Median	12	13	9	16
Range of species richness per plot (low-high)	0–39	2–31	0–34	1–39
Average lichen species richness per plot (alpha diversity)	12.59	14.38	9.87	17.21
Standard deviation of lichen species richness per plot	7.97	6.82	7.06	8.05
Species turnover rate (beta diversity)[c]	16.52	9.11	16.92	9.36
Total number of species per area (gamma diversity)	208	131	167	161

[a] Coastal area bordering the greater Central Valley and covering northwestern California.
[b] Plot totals do not include quality assurance surveys.
[c] Beta diversity is calculated as gamma diversity divided by alpha diversity.

Table 45—Summary of air quality on forest land in the greater Central Valley as indicated by the Lichen Community Indicator, California, 1998–2001, 2003

Parameter	Greater Central Valley	On-frame[a]	Off-frame[b]
Number of plots surveyed[c]	108	76	32
Number of plots by air quality index category:[d]			
1 (Worst) : -0.99 to 0.13	45	19	26
2: 0.13 to 0.55	23	19	4
3: 0.55 to 0.85	22	20	2
4 (Best): 0.85 to 1.58	18	18	0
Air quality index extremes	-0.99 to 1.58	-0.86 to 1.58	-0.99 to 0.70
Average score	0.28	0.52	-0.27
Standard deviation	0.61	0.50	0.46

[a] On-frame plots are on the Forest Inventory and Analysis sampling grid.
[b] Off-frame plots were located in cities, agricultural areas, and/or near air quality monitors.
[c] Plot totals do not include quality assurance surveys or plots without lichens present.
[d] Categories are based on the data quartiles for on-frame data.

Table 46—Summary of air quality on forest land in the greater Sierra Nevada as indicated by the Lichen Community Indicator, California, 1998–2001, 2003

Parameter	Greater Sierra Nevada	On-frame[a]	Off-frame[b]
Number of plots surveyed[c]	146	122	24
Number of plots by air quality index category:[d]			
1 (Best): -43.36 to -15.88	35	31	4
2: -15.88 to -8.22	31	30	1
3: -8.22 to 4.35	33	30	3
4 (Worst): 4.35 to 66.49	47	31	16
Air quality index extremes	-43.36 to 66.49	-43.36 to 66.49	-32.38 to 41.61
Average score	-2.77	-5.13	10.27
Standard deviation	19.28	18.32	19.60

[a] On-frame plots are on the Forest Inventory and Analysis sampling grid.

[b] Off-frame plots were located in cities, agricultural areas, and/or near air quality monitors.

[c] Plot totals do not include quality assurance surveys or plots without lichens present.

[d] Categories are based on the data quartiles for on-frame data.

Table 47—Summary of climate on forest land as indicated by the Lichen Community Indicator, derived from the temperature gradient of Jovan and McCune's (2004) model, California, 1998–2001, 2003

Parameter	Total	Greater Central Valley[a]	Greater Sierra Nevada[a]	Northwest Coast[b]
Number of plots surveyed[c]	264	76	121	67
Number of plots by climate index category:[d]				
Warmest (-2.59 to -1.04)	67	44	6	17
Warm (-1.04 to 0.01)	65	25	15	25
Cool (0.01 to 0.87)	66	5	43	18
Coolest (0.87 to 2.14)	66	2	57	7
Climate index extremes	-2.59 to 2.14	-2.59 to 2.10	-2.07 to 2.14	-2.46 to 1.27
Average score	-0.02	-0.96	0.73	-0.32
Standard deviation	1.13	0.79	0.88	0.92

[a] The greater Central Valley (GCV) and greater Sierra Nevada are mapped in Volume 1, figures 57 and 58.

[b] The Northwest Coast borders the GCV and covers northwestern California.

[c] Plot totals do not include quality assurance surveys or plots without lichens present.

[d] Categories are based on data quartiles.

Table 48—Summary of climate on forest land as indicated by the Lichen Community Indicator, derived from the moisture gradient of Jovan and McCune's (2004) model, California, 1998–2001, 2003

Parameter	Total	Greater Central Valley[a]	Greater Sierra Nevada[a]	Northwest Coast[b]
Number of plots surveyed[c]	264	76	121	67
Number of plots by climate index category:[d]				
Wettest (-2.28 to -0.71)	66	5	16	45
Wet (-0.71 to 0.13)	66	11	39	16
Dry (0.13 to 0.89)	68	25	40	3
Driest (0.89 to 2.22)	64	35	26	3
Climate index extremes	-2.28 to 2.22	-1.17 to 2.22	-2.20 to 2.13	-2.28 to 1.57
Average score	0.08	0.77	0.21	-0.92
Standard deviation	1.04	0.83	0.82	0.83

[a] The greater Central Valley (GCV) and greater Sierra Nevada are mapped in Volume 1, figures 57 and 58.

[b] The Northwest Coast borders the GCV and covers northwestern California.

[c] Plot totals do not include quality assurance surveys or plots without lichens present.

[d] Categories are based on data quartiles.

Table 49—Ozone injury summary information from ozone biomonitoring plots, by year, California, 2000–2005

Ozone biomonitoring plots	Year of monitoring						All years
	2000	2001	2002	2003	2004	2005	
Number of plots	22	29	61	65	65	65	307
Number of plots with injury	6	11	20	16	22	24	99
Number of plots by biosite index category[a] (percentage of plots):							
0 to 4.9 (least injured)	18 (81.8)	24 (82.8)	52 (85.2)	56 (86.2)	57 (87.7)	48 (73.8)	255 (83.1)
5.0 to 14.9	1 (4.5)	2 (6.9)	7 (11.5)	7 (10.8)	3 (4.6)	2 (3.1)	22 (7.2)
15 to 24.9	0 (0)	1 (3.4)	1 (1.6)	1 (1.5)	3 (4.6)	5 (7.7)	11 (3.6)
>25 (most injured)	3 (13.6)	2 (6.9)	1 (1.6)	1 (1.5)	2 (3.1)	10 (15.4)	19 (6.2)
Average biosite index score	6.7	3.4	2.2	2.1	2.5	9.3	4.4
Average number of species per plot	1.8	2.1	2.2	2.3	2.3	2.4	2.1
Number of plants evaluated	1,078	1,492	3,865	4,295	4,370	4,177	19,277
Number of plants injured	98	114	207	119	165	254	957
Number of plants evaluated by species:							
Blue elderberry	100	133	452	499	407	304	1,895
California black oak	43	13	0	0	0	0	56
Jeffrey pine	161	330	410	480	566	563	2,510
Mugwort	120	187	599	600	632	684	2,822
Pacific ninebark	0	0	30	30	22	30	112
Ponderosa pine	325	434	984	1,016	1,112	1,075	4,946
Quaking aspen	159	166	237	288	322	313	1,485
Red alder	0	0	112	120	120	90	442
Red elderberry	0	0	30	30	47	30	137
Scouler's willow	0	25	100	96	60	90	371
Skunkbush	0	0	254	270	328	262	1,114
Snowberry	170	204	627	776	724	706	3,207
Western wormwood	0	0	30	90	30	30	180
Percentage of forest land by biosite index category[b]							
0 to 4.9 (least injured)	—	—	—	—	—	—	75.7
5.0 to 14.9	—	—	—	—	—	—	22.1
15 to 24.9	—	—	—	—	—	—	2
>25 (most injured)	—	—	—	—	—	—	0.2

Note: — = no value calculated.

[a] The biosite index is based on the average injury score (amount × severity) for each species averaged across all species on the plot. Biosite categories represent a relative measure of tree-level response to ambient ozone exposure.

[b] Percentage of forest land is estimated after interpolating the biosite values (2000–2005) to generate a biological response surface across the landscape.

Table 50—Total acres of forest land with a forest fire incident, by year and ecosection group, California, 1995–2004

Year	Total		Northern Interior		West/ Central		Sierra		North Coast		Southern California	
	Total	SE	Total	SE	Total	SE	Total	SE	Total	SE	Total	SE
	Acres											
1995	212,069	44,344	72,832	26,426	7,807	7,807	110,023	31,667	12,604	12,604	8,803	7,036
1996	116,046	29,746	51,710	20,496	1,741	1,741	48,224	18,978	—	—	14,371	10,198
1997	105,732	30,625	19,998	14,476	32,181	16,674	49,688	20,893	—	—	3,866	3,866
1998	116,317	30,225	55,764	21,909	22,675	12,193	22,264	12,884	—	—	15,614	11,039
1999	278,900	48,628	103,211	27,987	26,013	14,150	107,678	31,894	12,604	12,604	29,394	14,741
2000	264,432	50,648	86,780	30,082	22,462	13,110	101,327	29,975	—	—	53,862	24,408
2001	263,680	53,974	131,070	37,058	—	—	122,123	37,926	—	—	10,487	10,487
2002	344,993	75,600	15,669	15,669	—	—	254,604	63,940	—	—	74,720	37,288
2003	284,307	91,618	125,234	62,614	—	—	80,452	47,138	31,916	31,916	46,705	35,174
2004	143,439	101,407	—	—	—	—	143,439	101,407	—	—	—	—
Average	212,992	19,010	66,227	9,473	11,288	2,934	103,982	14,732	5,712	3,655	25,782	6,192

Note: Data subject to sampling error; SE = standard error; — = less than 0.5 acre was estimated.

Table 51—Estimated gross growth, net change, removals, and mortality of growing stock for softwood species on timberland, by species group and owner, California, 2001–2005

Thousand cubic feet

	All owners						National forest					
	Current gross annual growth		Average annual net change		Average annual removal and mortality		Current gross annual growth		Average annual net change		Average annual removal and mortality	
Species group	Total	SE	Total	SE	Total	SE	Total	SE	Total	SE	Total	SE
Softwoods:												
Douglas-fir	410,507	34,656	322,719	97,031	87,787	92,083	192,351	19,966	197,764	77,366	-5,413	73,788
Incense-cedar	73,232	10,548	51,136	36,487	22,096	36,652	41,183	5,591	62,069	33,819	-20,886	34,152
Lodgepole pine	15,488	5,258	-25,690	27,879	41,177	26,498	11,098	4,186	-28,536	27,725	39,634	26,435
Other western softwoods	24,039	5,417	-6,374	22,521	30,413	23,355	6,742	2,393	-28,027	21,049	34,769	22,588
Ponderosa and Jeffrey pines	240,960	20,521	-39,834	90,770	280,794	91,405	140,881	13,920	-15,825	84,800	156,706	85,872
Redwood	207,415	55,206	19,545	47,202	187,870	66,176	—	—	—	—	—	—
Sugar pine	51,211	7,132	-52,219	41,406	103,430	41,905	37,605	6,171	-23,253	38,237	60,858	38,676
True fir	350,663	30,996	-116,643	110,361	467,306	108,317	270,873	27,774	-82,232	106,643	353,106	104,248
Western hemlock	8,504	5,600	684	4,144	7,820	3,861	—	—	—	—	—	—
Western white pine	8,445	5,303	36,470	17,512	-28,025	16,652	7,727	5,260	35,081	17,464	-27,354	16,640
Total	1,390,463	79,408	189,794	194,246	1,200,669	197,737	708,462	39,023	117,042	168,537	591,420	166,787

Thousand cubic feet

	State and local government						Corporate private					
	Current gross annual growth		Average annual net change		Average annual removal and mortality		Current gross annual growth		Average annual net change		Average annual removal and mortality	
Species group	Total	SE	Total	SE	Total	SE	Total	SE	Total	SE	Total	SE
Softwoods:												
Douglas-fir	3,883	1,745	7,905	5,132	-4,022	3,986	120,540	24,780	24,514	32,300	96,026	31,035
Incense-cedar	—	—	-5,076	4,856	5,076	4,856	25,093	8,630	2,197	9,348	22,897	9,158
Lodgepole pine	—	—	—	—	—	—	4,186	3,180	3,619	2,505	568	1,054
Other western softwoods	3,598	2,454	5,714	4,245	-2,116	2,348	1,661	1,373	-313	529	1,975	1,842
Ponderosa and Jeffrey pines	1,950	1,168	-13,389	15,159	15,339	15,570	45,245	9,811	-27,332	22,548	72,577	22,029
Redwood	30,804	17,096	4,110	8,562	26,694	12,931	81,717	24,126	24,281	36,259	57,436	32,398
Sugar pine	—	—	—	—	—	—	9,300	3,046	-16,451	10,755	25,751	10,289
True fir	3,078	2,249	-3,311	4,751	6,389	4,305	56,681	11,698	-20,074	24,719	76,755	25,719
Western hemlock	713	679	-2,769	2,262	3,482	2,473	5,304	5,046	3,632	3,456	1,672	1,590
Western white pine	701	670	1,358	1,299	-657	628	—	—	—	—	—	—
Total	44,728	19,567	-5,458	23,093	50,187	26,663	349,728	43,747	-5,929	65,842	355,657	63,774

Table 51—Estimated gross growth, net change, removals, and mortality of growing stock for softwood species on timberland, by species group and owner, California, 2001–2005 (continued)

Species group	Noncorporate private					
	Current gross annual growth		Average annual net change		Average annual removal and mortality	
	Total	SE	Total	SE	Total	SE
	Thousand cubic feet					
Softwoods:						
Douglas-fir	93,732	15,275	92,536	48,713	1,195	45,222
Incense-cedar	6,956	2,389	-8,054	8,767	15,009	8,421
Lodgepole pine	203	130	-772	1,500	976	1,480
Other western softwoods	12,037	3,968	16,253	6,771	-4,215	5,130
Ponderosa and Jeffrey pines	52,884	11,651	16,713	17,639	36,171	16,195
Redwood	94,894	47,118	-8,845	28,974	103,740	56,558
Sugar pine	4,306	1,887	-12,516	11,701	16,822	12,439
True fir	20,030	7,142	-11,026	13,211	31,056	13,883
Western hemlock	2,486	2,366	-179	171	2,666	2,536
Western white pine	17	16	31	29	-14	13
Total	287,545	52,562	84,140	67,023	203,405	81,492

Note: Data subject to sampling error; SE = standard error; — = less than 500 cubic feet were estimated.

Table 52—Total roundwood output by product, species group, and source of material, California, 2000

Product and species group	Growing-stock trees		Other sources	All sources
	Sawtimber	Poletimber	Other sources	All sources
	Thousand cubic feet			
Saw logs:				
Softwoods	364,162	1,350	21,331	386,843
Hardwoods	2	—	—	2
Total	364,164	1,350	21,331	386,845
Veneer logs:				
Softwoods	29,433	109	2,065	31,608
Hardwoods	377	1	4	382
Total	29,810	111	2,069	31,990
Pulpwood:				
Softwoods	—	—	—	—
Hardwoods	2,367	9	24	2,400
Total	2,367	9	24	2,400
Poles and posts:				
Softwoods	401	—	4	405
Hardwoods	0	—	—	—
Total	401	—	4	405
Other miscellaneous:				
Softwoods	123	—	1	124
Hardwoods	0	—	—	—
Total	123	—	1	124
Total industrial products:				
Softwoods	394,118	1,460	23,402	418,980
Hardwoods	2,746	10	28	2,784
Total	396,864	1,470	23,430	421,764
Fuelwood:				
Softwoods	45,953	170	115,086	161,209
Hardwoods	0	10	44,848	44,858
Total	45,953	180	159,934	206,067
All products:				
Softwoods	440,071	1,630	138,488	580,189
Hardwoods	2,746	20	44,877	47,643
Total	442,817	1,650	183,365	627,831

Note: Data subject to sampling error; excludes removals from precommercial thinnings; — = less than 500 cubic feet found.

Table 53—Volume of timber removals by type of removal, source of material, and species group, California, 2000

Removal type	Growing stock			Other sources			All sources		
	Softwoods	Hardwoods	Total	Softwoods	Hardwoods	Total	Softwoods	Hardwoods	Total
	Thousand cubic feet								
Roundwood products:									
Saw logs	365,512	2	365,514	21,331	—	21,331	386,843	2	386,845
Veneer logs	29,542	379	29,921	2,065	4	2,069	31,608	382	31,900
Pulpwood	—	2,376	2,376	—	24	24	—	2,400	2,400
Fuelwood	46,123	10	46,133	115,086	44,848	159,935	161,209	44,858	206,067
Posts, poles, and pilings	401	—	401	4	—	4	405	—	405
Miscellaneous products	123	—	123	1	—	1	124	—	124
Total	441,701	2,766	444,467	138,488	44,877	183,365	580,189	47,643	627,831
Logging residues	24,592	171	24,764	118,297	778	119,074	142,889	949	143,838
All removals	466,293	2,937	469,231	256,785	45,654	302,439	723,078	48,591	771,670

Note: Data subject to sampling error; excludes removals from precommercial thinnings; — = less than 500 cubic feet found.

Table 54—Estimated area of forest land covered by vascular plant nontimber forest products, by plant group and species, California, 2001–2005

Plant group and scientific name	Common name	Total	SE
		Acres	
Tree seedlings and saplings:			
Abies magnifica	California red fir	46,700	4,600
Abies procera	noble fir	100	100
Calocedrus decurrens	incense-cedar	99,100	5,900
Crataegus spp.	hawthorn species	1,000	1,000
Juniperus occidentalis	western juniper	16,900	2,000
Pseudotsuga menziesii	Douglas-fir	128,100	6,500
Taxus brevifolia	Pacific yew	2,800	1,000
Thuja plicata	western redcedar	600	400
Shrubs:			
Acer circinatum	vine maple	19,200	5,900
Arctostaphylos columbiana	hairy manzanita	7,000	3,000
Arctostaphylos nevadensis	pinemat manzanita	118,100	15,900
Arctostaphylos patula	greenleaf manzanita	387,500	27,900
Arctostaphylos spp.	manzanita species	87,900	15,500
Arctostaphylos uva-ursi	kinnikinnick	7,000	3,200
Arctostaphylos viscida	sticky whiteleaf manzanita	226,800	31,100
Ceanothus velutinus	snowbrush ceanothus	116,300	18,600
Chimaphila umbellata	pipsissewa	30,500	3,700
Cytisus scoparius	Scotch broom	3,000	1,400
Eriodictyon californicum	California yerba santa	5,100	1,700
Frangula purshiana	Pursh's buckthorn	5,700	2,100
Gaultheria shallon	salal	83,600	12,400
Mahonia aquifolium	Oregon grape	6,700	2,200
Mahonia nervosa	dwarf Oregon grape	41,300	7,500
Mahonia repens	creeping barberry	500	300
Paxistima myrsinites	Oregon boxleaf	7,900	2,500
Ribes spp.	currant spp.	131,300	10,300
Rosa spp.	rose spp.	39,800	3,800
Sambucus nigra	European black elderberry	2,100	800
Sambucus racemosa	red elderberry	6,100	3,000
Vaccinium membranaceum	thinleaf huckleberry	3,200	1,800
Vaccinium ovatum	California huckleberry	265,000	31,800
Herbs:			
Achillea millefolium	common yarrow	19,100	2,400
Anaphalis margaritacea	western pearly everlasting	1,700	500
Arnica cordifolia	heartleaf arnica	1,300	700
Asarum caudatum	British Columbia wildginger	1,600	500
Equisetum spp.	horsetail spp.	10,300	3,000
Hypericum perforatum	common St. John's wort	1,800	800
Polystichum munitum	western swordfern	176,200	21,700
Pteridium aquilinum	western brackenfern	141,600	14,000
Trillium ovatum	Pacific trillium	400	100
Urtica dioica	stinging nettle	4,000	1,800
Xerophyllum tenax	common beargrass	18,600	5,700

Note: Data subject to sampling error; SE = standard error.

Table 55—Percentage of forested plots with selected lichen nontimber forest products present, by species, California, 2001–2005

Scientific name	Common name	Percent
Alectoria sarmentosa	Witch's hair lichen	13.5
Bryoria fremontii	Old man's beard	13.1
Letharia vulpina	Wolf lichen	53.8
Lobaria pulmonaria	Lungwort	6.9
Parmelia saxatilis	Crottle	1.5
Ramalina menziesii	Lace lichen	2.9
Usnea	Beard lichens	38.2
Usnea hirta	Beard lichen	1.1
Vulpicida canadensis	Brown-eyed sunshine lichen	8.4

Note: Data subject to sampling error; 275 forested plots were sampled.

www.ingramcontent.com/pod-product-compliance
Lightning Source LLC
Chambersburg PA
CBHW081428310526

45790CB00020B/1738